ISBN: 9781314452143

Published by:
HardPress Publishing
8345 NW 66TH ST #2561
MIAMI FL 33166-2626

Email: info@hardpress.net
Web: http://www.hardpress.net

UNIVERSITATIS · CALIFORNIENSIS

SIGILLVM

FIAT LVX

MDCCCLXVIII

EX LIBRIS

SOCIETY IN THE COUNTRY HOUSE

Demy 8vo, cloth, **15/-** *net.*

Studies in Biography. By Sir SPENCER
WALPOLE, K.C.B., Author of " History of England
from 1815," " Life of Lord John Russell," etc., etc.

CONTENTS.

SIR ROBERT PEEL—GIBBON—RICHARD COBDEN—
PRINCE BISMARCK—BENJAMIN DISRAELI—NAPO-
LEON III.—LORD DUFFERIN—DECISIVE MAR-
RIAGES IN ENGLISH HISTORY.

LONDON: T. FISHER UNWIN.

BY

AUTHOR OF "KING EDWARD AND HIS COURT," "SOCIAL TRANSFORMATIONS
OF THE VICTORIAN AGE," ETC., ETC.

LONDON

ADELPHI TERRACE
MCMVII

DEDICATORY PREFACE

TO

MAJOR H. P. MOLINEUX,

OF ISFIELD, SUSSEX, AND MORNINGTON, EASTBOURNE.

MY DEAR SIR,—Of those who have been good enough to interest themselves in the writing of this book and to enable me to verify personal and local details, you are the only friend with whom to-day I find myself in touch; while, in all that relates to the South of England, I have found your assistance of the most practical value. To you, therefore, do I venture to inscribe this work, merely adding that, whenever it has been chronologically possible, the country houses mentioned are confined to those with which I am personally acquainted. Describing, therefore, chiefly, so far as was possible, persons and places actually visited by me, as a native of the South-west of England, I have naturally dwelt most on ground familiar from its earliest associations. This book only concerns itself with the social characteristics or story of representative or interesting houses. It was, therefore, unnecessary to dwell on architectural details, famous interiors, or their contents, accurately and minutely catalogued by guide-books already universally familiar or accessible.

With all respect and regard, obliged and truly yours,

T. H. S. ESCOTT.

HOVE,
  BRIGHTON,
    August, 1906.

CONTENTS

Contents

Contents

Contents

Contents

CHAPTER IX

CHAPTER X

Contents

Contents

CHAPTER XII

Halswell—The Tyntes—The Bridgwater elections—
" The Man in the Moon "—Baron Tripp, the introducer of
the waltz and his colleagues—Bulwer Lytton's presence of
mind—Brymore, the home of John Pym—Its connection
with Francis Bacon—Pym's mother, Lady Rous, and wife,
Anna Hooker—Lady Rous's funeral sermon preached by
Charles Fitz-Geoffrey—Wentworth (Strafford) at Brymore
—Pym and Hampden—Brymore's later owners—Guests
at Brymore during Pym's life, Sir John Popham, Thomas
Coryate—Cricket-St. Thomas, the house of Sir Amias
Preston—Ralph, Lord Hopton—Ralph Cudworth—Dr.
Joseph Wolff at Ile-Brewers Rectory—Archdeacon
Denison at East Brent Rectory—Freeman at Sommerleaze—Sir William Pynsent of Burton-Pynsent—His
legacies to Chatham—William Pitt's childhood at Burton-
Pynsent—Ralph Allen's Prior Park, standing in the same
relation to Bath as Stanmer to Brighton—Allen, the
original of Squire Alworthy in " Tom Jones "—Prior Park
an open house—Its guests—Warburton—Literary Visitors
—Dean Swift—Bowood—First Marquis of Lansdowne,
his descent from the Pettys and the Fitzmaurices—His
grandparents, the Earl and Countess of Kerry—Bowood
parties—Bentham, Dumont, Priestly—Lansdowne's household accounts—The third Marquis—Thomas Moore and
other visitors—Bowood in the present day—The poet
Bowles at Bremhill—Barley Wood, the home of Hannah
More—Raikes, the founder of the Sunday School and his
Cotswold guests—Blaise Castle, the home of Wilberforce's
friend, Harford.

CHAPTER XIII

Mr. Percy Wyndham at Clouds—The Clouds house-parties
and modern politics—East Knoyle House—The Seymours
— Breamore — Fonthill — William Beckford — Samuel
Rogers as his guest—Beckford's eccentricities—His Lans-
downe tower at Bath—Beckford compared by Rogers with
E. A. Poe—Ford Abbey—Jeremy Bentham and the Mills—
Life at Ford Abbey—Jean Nicolas Grou, the French
divine, at Lulworth—Bryanston and the Portmans—

Contents

Hambledon House and the Pitt ladies—The Grange—
Lord and Lady Ashburton and their guests—Carlyle—
His snub to John Forster—Mrs. Carlyle—Highclere—The
cedars—Highclere owners, the Pembroke and Carnarvon
Herberts—The fourth Earl of Carnarvon—Political parties
at Highclere—Boer guests—Hurstbourne—Count Munster
—Lord and Lady Granville—Memorials of Isaac Newton
J. C. Jeaffreson—Tedworth—Thomas Assheton Smith,
the celebrated sportsman—At Eton—As a Parliamentary
candidate—His fight with the coal-heaver—Smith as a
Hampshire squire—His opinion of Canning—Hursley—
Sir William Heathcote and Keble—F. Rogers (Lord
Blachford)—Hursley to-day—Strathfieldsaye—Anecdotes
of the great Duke of Wellington—The second Duke—
The Rev. G. R. Gleig—"Copenhagen's" grave—The
Duke of Malakhoff's shooting performance—Henry Irving
and other guests at Strathfieldsaye.

CHAPTER XIV

Heron Court—The second and third Earls Malmesbury
—Heron Court anecdotes—The duel between O'Connell
and Alvanley—The American lady in Italy—Heron Court
guests—Sir Henry Drummond Wolff at Boscombe Tower
—Henry Reeve's Foxholes—The Longmans at Farn-
borough Hill—Sclater-Booth (Lord Basing) and Disraeli—
Farnborough Hill as the home of the Empress Eugénie—
Her household—Hazeley, the home of Mrs. Singleton
(Lady Currie)—Lady Strangford, her only rival in con-
versational qualities—Matthew Arnold as the guest of
Lord and Lady Greville—John Evelyn's house at Wotton
Mr. F. Leveson-Gower's Epsom parties at Holmbury—
"Mr. Simpson" at the Rookery—Mrs. George Grote and
her eccentricities—Henry Reeve and Mrs. Grote—Mrs.
Craven—Her admiration for General Gordon—Her
imitations of public men—Her comment on Palmerston
—"Conversation" Sharpe at Fridley Farm—The Fridley
portraits—Sir James Mackintosh—Marden Park—William
Wilberforce and the French *emigré*—"The Gallic tem-
perament"—Marden's associations of Pitt—Robert Lowe
—Nelson's farewell at Merton—Henry Hope's home, the
Deepdene—Hope's influence on Disraeli's novels—"Young
Englandism"—The Duke of York's guests at Oatlands

Contents-

15

Contents

CHAPTER I

THE EVOLUTION OF THE COUNTRY HOST

Introduction—The arrangement of the book in its chronological and geographical relations explained—The country house unknown till Chaucer's day—Why—The franklin—Baronial despotism—How the country house grew.

"It snowëd in his house of meat and drink,
Of all the dainties whereon one could think."

CHAUCER'S portrait of the fourteenth century franklin is a sketch from life of the mediæval country gentleman who was the first representative and lineal progenitor of the hosts that are to figure prominently in the following pages. The rural home of the English gentleman appears as a centre of social or political life and interest during the period covered by the "Canterbury Tales." I shall briefly sketch the conditions under which the country-house system became possible. I shall next pass to the most typical and interesting instances of its complete organisation in Tudor times, showing how it then discharged many of the functions fulfilled to-day by the newspaper, by the circulating library, or by more exclusive methods of information ; how, at the same time, it began to occupy a recognised place in the organisation of party politics; and how, from the seventeenth century to the present hour, in all the great movements of English life, the opportunities of the country house have proved the necessary and the eventful supplements to the agencies of parliament and platform. The same houses have supplied the scene for events equally interesting, but belonging to widely separated periods. To each house one visit must suffice. The unities of time must therefore be sacrificed to the unities of place. Geography will supply the only practicable principle of grouping. The series of country-house visits that the reader is now invited to pay will conveniently commence with the south-east corner of England. The route will then proceed through the southern and western counties. The line taken through the Midlands will bring us fairly into East Anglia. Thence progress will be made in a northern direction. At all points there will be the opportunity of illustrating differences between the new and the old *régime* in country-house life.

Nor will the connection of the country house with other national interests and occupations, often of a mutually opposite character, be ignored. Anglicanism, evangelicalism, the social and spiritual awakening which resulted in the reform of the prison, of the poor-law system, and in the abolition of the slave trade, are as rich in country-house associations as the chase, the turf, the stage.

Before attempting to work up into a consistent picture the available details of country-house society during the franklin period, it may be as well to summarise the obvious reasons why the country house could only have begun to exist between the thirteenth and the fifteenth centuries. The fusion of Norman and Anglo-Saxon gentry had not, at an earlier date, come within measurable distance of completeness. The very idea of middle-class traders being socially incorporated into the aristocratic or squirearchical order would have been unintelligible. The condition of England was, as will presently be seen, one, not merely of social disorganisation, but of chronic and dangerous disturbance. Agricultural depression, long lasting and intensified by a continuance of bad seasons, had rendered quite impossible anything like regular hospitalities on the part of landlords, small or great. In Chaucer's day, prosperity in foreign commerce had given timely relief to hosts of all degrees. In every part of the country were well-kept houses, belonging to representative owners, of the commercial class, but of aristocratic associations and prejudices. Chaucer's Shipman in the "Canterbury Tales" may have hailed from Dartmouth. That western seaport, in the opulence of its suburban residents, as well as in its collective contributions to the State navy at times of national peril, was characteristic of the nation and the times. It was the age in which a London Lord Mayor, John Philipot, by successful ventures like those of Chaucer's "Shipman," had amassed a fortune; he had manned a squadron, ready, as occasion might arise, for incorporation into the royal navy. Nor was this the only way in which, like other great citizens, he

The Evolution of the Country Host

served the State. His business skill brought him into requisition with the Court for arranging the subsidies in the French wars. His influence must at least have been as great on land as on sea. The "Shipman" of the "Canterbury Tales," possibly something of a pirate as well as a trader, seems to have come from the banks of the Devonshire Dart. John Philipot, to his estate near Dartford in his native county of Kent, added houses and lands in other parts of the country. He was, in fact, one of those large and hospitable proprietors whose *clientèle* included a number of vavasors or smaller owners who saw their natural patrons in their many-acred and wealthier neighbours. To Philipot and others in his position belonged the house where—

"His table dormant in the hall alway,
Stood ready covered all the longë day."

These rural homes of mediæval England were much more than mere centres of hospitality. The trade routes to the Baltic, the Mediterranean, the Levant, and to remoter parts were also those followed by the chivalry, the diplomacy, and the literature of England in their communication with the world beyond seas. Among the guests of the Chaucerian Franklin or of the historic Philipot, were business men who had seen the practical working of the commercial policy pursued by Edward III.; its alleged injuries to native manufactures and trade; the increasing severity of Flemish and German competition with British fishermen and weavers; above all, the dangerously growing monopoly by

20

foreign companies of the world's banking business. Such were the conversational topics discussed by experts at these mediæval week-end parties. In the way already described, Philipot and others of his class had given practical proofs of their patriotism. Their social comments on the imperial policy of the Court in its relation with national industry and trade often reached the ears of the king and his ministers. In this way, therefore, something of the work allotted to chambers of commerce to-day was performed by the hospitalities of provincial mansions in the Middle Ages. The entertainments given at the castles of the great aristocracy, a Percy or a Nevill, were for princes and nobles. Of such places nothing was known by common folk except the largess of food to all comers. Such was the English version of the sportula of imperial Rome. Colossal structures like those of Alnwick and Raby were not in those early days popularly associated with good cheer any more than they were with the promotion of national interests in Church or State, in council chamber or mart. With the true founders of the English country house, the franklins or squires, there was talk as well as food to suit all tastes. The men had their politics. The ladies learned what were the latest novelties and vagaries in dress. Comparing notes of impressions among themselves, they soon reproduced the originals which they knew from travellers' tales, in such a way as to set the fashion for a village, a neighbourhood, a town, or an entire county. Other personages of the famous Prologue mingled with the franklin and his guests. The

The Evolution of the Country Host

whole of social England at that time, it must be remembered, was suggestive rather of a family party than of a complex, diversified, and heterogeneous nationality. The four great pestilences between 1348 and 1376 had, on the accession of Richard II., reduced the whole population of the realm to two millions and a half. Classes in the community were separated from each other by none of the modern gulfs. All persons of liberal calling or education were at least mutually as well known among themselves as the average members of a modern club. The Churchmen, the man of law, and the physician who met at the Southwark Tabard, before starting for Thomas à Beckett's shrine, found themselves habitually guests beneath the same country roof. The doctor seems to have been more in consideration as the franklin's guest than among his brother pilgrims on the Old Kent Road. An unwritten law, if not a formal statute, limited the ecclesiastic's visit to three days, lest he should be tempted to stay away too long from his spiritual cure. The professor of the healing art was exempt from any such restriction, and, if he did not outwear his welcome, was apt to presume on the elasticity of its limits. Still, his purple overcoat and professional hood of blue with white fur were undoubtedly in social demand, during this insanitary period. The greater the distance from a large town, the more desirous were the rural hosts of securing the presence of the faculty at their week-end parties. What the physician was in Chaucer's day he practically remained to the end of the Middle Ages. Most departments of human knowledge have been doomed to go through a preliminary state, in which the true science has been so obscured by vagueness of doctrine, or so stretched beyond its limits by pretenders, as to excite against it the prejudice of the world. Astronomy began in astrology. Chemistry was the child of alchemy. Geology had once been cosmogony. History grew out of a mere confusion of legends, genealogies, and superstitions. Medicine had been witchcraft; its professors, throughout the whole of the franklin's epoch, retained many signs of its unscientific origin. That fact, however, made the doctor of the day more, rather than less, acceptable as a guest. The ladies of the families he visited were interested, as well as impressed, by his conversational knowledge of professional mysteries.

Receiving with pious gratitude the remedial drugs produced from the recesses of his ample cloak, they listened with reverent credulity to the array of authorities which his memory or his invention enabled him to quote in support of any medicine that his ingenuity prescribed. He began his dinner with citations from Galen, Hippocrates, at a classical house from the Podalirius and Machaon of the Iliad, or, at a religious house, from the beloved physician, St. Luke. By the time the table was being cleared and, for the better repose of the company, servants were bringing fresh rushes into the hall, the prophet of the healing art was treating his hearers to a little anticipation of Hahnemann's leading doctrines and, with instances well known to his hearers, was illustrating the homœopathic cure for inflammation by a course of gazing at red draperies.

The Evolution of the Country Host

The great householder, the St. Julian [1] in his own country, so fond of all good living as much for his friends as for himself, valued his ease and dignity too highly to become a shire knight like Chaucer, or a borough member like Bailly the host of the Tabard Inn. Thus he lived all the year round on his own estate, kept open house at every season, asked nothing more of his visitors than that they should bring him the latest information from those parts of the world of which they knew something, and bring perhaps also, as gifts for his womenkind, specimens of the latest vogue in headdresses and gowns. As the name indicates, he was first a freeman, then a freeholder. A country gentleman, whose estate consisted in free land and was not subject to feudal service or payment,[2] he anticipated the most intelligent, profuse, and modish of twentieth century St. Julians.

As a national institution, his life was too merry not to be short. In the next century to Chaucer, indeed, Fortescue speaks of the franklin as the head of a family, enriched with great possessions.[3] According to the New English Dictionary, the franklin in the fourteenth and fifteenth centuries was a landowner of free, but not noble, birth, ranked next below the gentry. Later the designation so depreciated in value as to mean little more than a well-to-do farmer. So much at least may be inferred from the position given

[1] The patron saint of hospitality also expressed the idea of the perfect host.

[2] Warton's " History of Poetry," vol. ii. p. 202, edition 1841.

[3] " Paterfamilias magnis ditatus possessionibus."

24

to the franklin by Shakespeare. Thus (Cymbeline, 3. ii. 79) Imogen asks to be provided with "a riding suit no costlier than would fit a franklin's housewife." Again (Winter's Tale, 5. ii. 173) boors and franklins classed together, under the title of common people, are contrasted with gentlemen. Its social connotation went through further depressions till, in the seventeenth century, the term seems quite to have gone out of use.

But in the early part of the mediæval period not only did the lord of the manor, so often absent and hampered by mortgages, yield in importance to the franklin; he was often of less social consideration than the well-to-do miller. The franklin's residence always bore without, as well as within, the marks of comfort and wealth. The mediæval manor-house was habitually distinguished from the labourers' cottages, rather by standing at some distance from them than by superiority of accommodation. The franklin's house was often called a hall. Sometimes fresh rooms were added on the basement floor; the house became a castle. As in the village economy the parson represented the principle of the Church, so for about a hundred years the State impersonated itself in the franklin. Those were the days when constituencies prayed for relief from the obligation of returning members to Parliament. The franklin's public duties were limited to local politics and manor courts. His hospitalities made him a power in the land. He was far too wise a man to let them exceed his means. From the first he had supplemented his income by well-judged investments in the wardship of neighbouring properties;

The Evolution of the Country Host

these placed in his pocket the profits of the land during the ward's minority. His fortunes expanded with those of his age and nation. His Chaucerian friend the " Shipman," the forerunner of the Elizabethan adventurers, gave him early notice of any particularly good business there might be on. The country gentleman therefore of the Middle Ages, in his commercial and territorial character, is to be regarded as the lineal ancestor of those whose hospitalities—the Buckinghamshire Rothschilds, the Tranby Croft Wilsons—have been thought the twentieth century's exclusive products.

Sportsmen and courtiers, politicians, leaders of society as well as pillars of commerce, celebrities of all kinds, well-introduced travellers from every part, were, during his palmy period, the franklin's habitual guests. Was his residence passed by any one primed with the latest gossip about the quarrel between John of Gaunt and Speaker de la Mare, or concerning the former's social or political intrigues generally, that wayfarer took his place at our franklin's dinner table. There he found himself sitting next to a king's messenger, full of Court small-talk from London or travellers' tales from Europe.

The franklin's establishment thus became a local centre, whence radiated throughout the district the latest news of Yorkish intrigue with the Court of Burgundy, of changes in the crusaders' plan of campaign or the quarrels of the chiefs, Coeur de Lion, Barbarossa, and Philip of France, who had each vowed to be the first in wresting the Holy Sepulchre from the infidel.

Decline of the Peers

Above the franklin, as the representative of the untitled gentry, in political power but not in social importance, still less as country hosts, came the larger landlords and nobles. The latter of these, after the Battle of Bosworth, had deteriorated in physique as well as diminished in numbers and power. From being cast in the magnificent mould of Warwick the Kingmaker, their persons were now, for the most part, small and weak. And visitors, high or humble, expected to find the master of a stately mansion built of something like the same scale as the structure which he owned. Usually possessing town houses at York or some other provincial capital, these peers owed their decline in influence less to lack of money for supporting their traditional state than to the fact that they compared disadvantageously, in point of ability and attainments, with the prosperous country gentlemen of the time. Their estates, indeed, were for the most part heavily mortgaged. Court ceremonials and costly dresses often drained them of their ready money. Comparative poverty would not, however, have proved fatal to their national influence, had it been compensated by great qualities like those of Warwick, or fearless sympathy with the higher interests of life and the nobler aspirations of the age, such as, before Warwick, had animated Stephen Langton's colleague, Pembroke. Thus early did the titular aristocracy of the realm justify their description in " Lothair " as living in the open air, never reading, and speaking no language but their own. They had fought shy of the renaissance. They had held aloof from each subsequent stage in the revival of letters. Failing to represent the best life of the nation, they had not so much forfeited public respect as disqualified themselves for being its object. They may even be said in many cases to have sacrificed their own identity. Impoverished by pecuniary mismanagement, they often broke up their own establishments and took their place among the retainers of the wealthier and more powerful members of their order. Thus, at the end of the fifteenth century, several nobles, once of great position, had accepted a voluntary degradation by entering the households of men who often proved as formidable rivals to the Crown as Richard Nevill himself. Of that select class at the time just mentioned, the wealthiest member seems to have been Edward, Duke of Buckingham, descended from Thomas Plantagenet, Duke of Gloucester, the Earl of Northumberland's brother-in-law and father-in-law of the Duke of Norfolk. The Venetian ambassador Giustinian, reputed an adept in such calculations, estimated his income at 30,000 ducats, about £180,000 of English money. In the great hall of Thorbury, the daily average of guests at breakfast and dinner was two hundred. The pages who waited on them were often noblemen's sons. Buckingham may have surpassed all his peers in opulence. Northumberland had no superior in power. The state kept at Alnwick was only less than that of the royal Court at Windsor. Wherever these uncrowned kings happened to be, they lived upon the same magnificent scale. If travelling, they were accompanied by retainers whose numbers and equipment made them a warrior host.

Rightly Called "Pulle"

The whole country had not yet got out of the disturbed condition which was the social ground-swell following the tempest of civil wars. The turbulent oligarchy of nobles which misgoverned it may have fed their retainers, but did not diffuse an influence favourable to an interchange of rural hospitalities between their neighbours or themselves. Six oxen were slaughtered daily to furnish Northumberland's followers with breakfast on the journey to London. But these supplies of beef were requisitioned, not bought and paid for. From the Stanleys in the North to the Courtenays in the West, the lawless patricians owned the soil and bullied the countryside. The Earl of Devon, finding no cash in his chest, proceeded to rob Exeter Cathedral of its plate, just as he might have seized some local Jew's strong box. With a force of 800 cavalry and 4,000 foot soldiers, he held the country gentlemen to ransom. Elsewhere, abduction was not less the noble vogue than sacrilege. Sir John Botler's widow, of Beausey, Cheshire, vainly sought deliverance from, or redress against, an amorous territorialist named Pulle who, having removed her to Bidstone, dragged her by brute force to the altar.

Yet there is Hallam's authority for believing that, in comparison with continental Europe, England enjoyed domestic tranquillity. The tumultuary epoch of baronial despots was not without its socially harmonising aspect. The provincial mansions of these men were not, indeed, so much private homes as national caravanserais. The hospitality dispensed may often have been seasoned with contempt; it

29

recognised many invidious distinctions among the
guests. Still, beneath those feudal roofs, all classes
met and began to know each other. In the retinues
of the nobles, whose normal condition seemed one
of civil war, might be found all the materials for
organising the *generosi*. Here were the men of gentle
birth who derived their lineage from ancestors who
wore coat armour. These comprised the knight,
whether banneret or bachelor, and the squire. These
were they who from the first had made their ancestral
homes agencies of domestic civilisation. That was
the class which, at all periods, has formed a link of
union between the great lords of the land on one
hand and its cultivators, whether yeomen or tenant
farmers, on the other. With the men just described
there mingled, in a constantly increasing degree, the
born representatives of the trading class who had
used commercial success as a means of incorporation
into that order which was above their own, only
by the accident of origin and the conventions of social
precedence. The old House of Lords was the true
parent of the modern House of Commons. The
country gentlemen who created the country-house
system were the neighbours, sometimes the kinsmen,
of the baronial "creatures of flood and field," to whom
sufficed "the good old rule, the simple plan,"

> "That they should take who have the power,
> And they should keep who can."

How the lawless greed, the unbridled and despotic
self-indulgence of these men proved in their social

The Country Host Evolved

results unfavourable for the interchange of friendly visits between country neighbours has been already shown at sufficient length. At the same time, even amidst the feudal autocracy and the baronial tyranny of that wild age, there were growing up habits of social intercourse and ideas of a mutual inter-dependence of classes which really served as a pre-paration for the country-house developments of a later day. On the lines already indicated and at first following the course of the sun, we begin with the Sussex dukeries. These will be visited in the next chapter.

CHAPTER II

THE SUSSEX DUKERIES AND NON-DUKERIES

"IT is a nothing on a fine hill. The site is fine. There are some good tombs of the Fitzalans at the church. Of the castle little remains. In its room is a modern brick house. In the late duke's time the ghost of a giant, Oliver Cromwell *incog.*, walked there. The present Duke has laid it in the Red Sea of claret." Such in the eighteenth century seemed to Horace Walpole the chief features of the Sussex stronghold that, according to the route already explained, forms the natural starting-point of the present country-house expeditions. What chiefly impresses one about Arundel Castle, to-day, is that it dominates the south coast landscape not less conspicuously than Windsor fills the prospect of Thames

32

An Apocryphal Arundel Tooth

valley or St. Peter's and its dome enter into every view, near or distant, of the city on the Tiber. This, not because the Duke of Norfolk's pile competes at any point in height with the loftiest parts of the English palace, still less with the Italian cathedral. The apparent ubiquity of Arundel in the panorama arises less from the height of its towers than from the vastness of the whole structure and the commanding aspect of the elevation on which it is set. As a building, Arundel Castle existed in the tenth century and was mentioned by King Alfred in his will. The Norman Conqueror's followers and councillors included one of his relatives, Roger de Montgomery. Commanding at the Battle of Hastings the archers, one of whose arrows pierced Harold's eye, he received for a reward an earldom and the manor of Arundel to support the title. In the twelfth century, reverting to the crown, the estate fell to Henry I.'s second wife. She, in her widowhood, married a foreign knight who had come over with the Duke of Normandy and who belonged to the Albini family; he was best known as " William of the strong hand." A tooth, said to have come from the mouth of the king of beasts, discovered in comparatively recent times among the Arundel treasures,[1] supplied the explanation of the name. Cast, as the story runs, into a lion's den for refusing to marry the Queen of France, Albini put his hand into the animal's mouth and tore out its heart. As Lord of Buckenham, Albini, with his wife,

[1] The best refutation of this local legend comes from the Duke of Norfolk himself: "I have never heard of this tooth, and I think I might have done so had it really ever been found."

The Sussex Dukeries and Non-Dukeries

kept almost royal state at the castle, made Arundel the great baronial centre of the south and entertained claimants, as well as possessors, of crowns. The most memorable among the earliest royal visits to Arundel took place in the twelfth century. Albini's guest then was Henry I.'s daughter, the Empress Maud, the true heiress to the throne violently filled by Stephen. The usurper laid prompt siege to Arundel. Albini not only beat off the beleaguering force ; he caused the siege to be permanently abandoned. He thus enabled the royal lady safely to reach Bristol and take ship for the Continent. This service to his mother was rewarded by Henry II. with the gift of the earldom of Sussex to the owner of the castle, already Earl of Arundel and Chichester. The marriage of an Albini to a Fitzalan, on the Albini family's extinction, gave the castle to the Fitzalans. In the reign of Elizabeth, it formed the marriage dowry of Mary Fitzalan who married Thomas, Duke of Norfolk.

The Arundel of Horace Walpole's day belonged to the ninth and tenth of its ducal owners. The more modern recreator of the place is the eleventh duke. This peer, familiarly known as the " Jockey," began, with his hospitalities, the social history of the place. A shrewd, tolerably read, voluble man, with a smatter-ing of literature and science that passed, in a duke, for learning, he said some clever things, about Ireland in particular, but more that were merely coarse, on all subjects in general. His habitual table-talk was a choice selection of conversational flowers that come to maturity in the stable-yard or in the smoking-room,

"The Jockey" and "Barny"

towards the small hours. Belonging to that section
of the party which shared Fox's detestation of Shelburne, he stood foremost among those Whigs to whom
the leadership of Lord Grenville seemed not less
intolerable than the Tory ascendancy of the younger
Pitt. Such were the men who, wearied of the traditional style, were now ready to adopt the radical
faith and name. Of these the "Jockey" posed as
the patron, and made his Sussex home their holiday
ground.

> "Half froth, half venom, spits himself abroad.
> In puns, or politics, or tales, or lies,
> Or spite, or smut, or rhymes, or blasphemies."

Pope's familiar lines alone perhaps can do justice
to the eleventh Duke of Norfolk as a talker. With
those themes others mingled. On the morning after
a particularly wet night, his grace, renovated by
sleep, showed himself indifferently ready to discuss
the Deity's foreknowledge or his own henchman's
claims to a share in the Tory plunder. His tamest
parasites were forced to confess that their Arundel
visits wanted one Christian-like person to enjoy them
with and a few comforts such as towels, soap, and
water to make the thing complete.

The Arundel house parties had, as has been seen,
first acquired notoriety under the "Jockey," Duke
Charles. They were continued by the twelfth duke
(Bernard Howard) who, like his predecessor, had
many intimates below his own station. With these
he answered to the diminutive of "Barny." During
the earlier part of his reign the socio-political re-

35

sources of Arundel conspicuously contributed to the collapse of the bill against Queen Caroline. What the Duke called "a jollification" followed. The country round was ablaze with bonfires. The castle keep and the adjoining streets ran red with burgund and port. A decade later, during the period of the Grey Reform Bill, from this scene of carnival the place transformed itself into a political auction mart. No ducal dealer in seats at St. Stephen's drove harder bargains for rotten boroughs than was done both by the "Jockey" and "Barny" with the agents of the Grey cabinet at Arundel. While the principals were negotiating in the grand drawing-room or library, other apartments, pleasantly called by the master of the mansion "the indoor kennels," swarmed with the parliamentary creatures of the great house. They whimpered and fawned on the author of their political being like frightened spaniels. Surely they were not to be sent adrift without some provision for their future by the magnate for whom they had faithfully fetched and carried. They might have served for the originals of Taper and Tadpole in "Coningsby," who, between the schedules of the bill and the shifting relations of their patrons with the premier, found their parliamentary lives not worth a day's purchase. Among these threatened and abased suppliants was a gentleman of mature age, whose exuberance of snowy frilled shirt-front and caressing blandness of manner at first seemed to identify him with the family physician. He was, however, the Duke's Irish henchman, the diarist Thomas Creevey, whom his patron had just elbowed

36

out of Thetford, for which he had sat as the Arundel deputy. To the Duke's mother-in-law, then supreme at Arundel, "Old Mother Stafford, always as sulky as be d——d" (the Duchess of Sutherland), Creevey thought he owed his dismissal.

Arundel uniquely combines radicalism and ecclesiasticism in the past with recognition of social democracy in the present. The priors of Pynham, near Arundel, divided with the Arundel burgesses the privilege of pasturing cattle in the castle fields and of felling timber in the castle woods. After the dissolution of the monasteries under the Tudors, these rights belonged exclusively to the Arundel citizens. The civic interest in the ducal demesne is symbolised to this day by the Mayor of Arundel being also, in succession to the monastic holders of the office, bridge-warden of the castle. The highest order of the peerage occasionally furnishes first magistrates to provincial municipalities. His eighth grace of Devonshire has been mayor of Eastbourne. The fifteenth Duke of Norfolk may not have served similarly elsewhere than in the Yorkshire capital of cutlery. His popular affinities, however, show themselves really more at Arundel than at Sheffield. The chief characteristic, indeed, of the place is the dramatic meeting of picturesquely ancient traditions and prosaically modern associations. In the fourteenth century, the parish church of St. Nicholas was the chapel of a college, consisting of a master and twelve canons ; its stately dimensions have submitted to no contraction ; the Gothic monuments and the splendid tombs of Fitzalans and Howards are only in a less

The Sussex Dukeries and Non-Dukeries

perfect state of preservation than when they were
visited by Horace Walpole. The oldest, the collegiate
portion of this church, containing the family sepul-
chres, is walled off from that part of the building
where the Protestant parishioners still worship.
" The Church," as Disraeli in his " Lothair " makes
the cardinal say, "glories in being the friend of invention and science." Appropriately enough, therefore,
the Catholic cathedral, dwarfing the older temple
into insignificance, had for its architect, in 1873,
Joseph Aloysius Hansom, who, thirty-nine years
earlier, had made his family name a household word
by the cab called after it.

Under its twentieth-century possessor, Arundel
has become the most impartially enlightened, the
most representatively comprehensive and the most
demonstratively sympathetic with the modern spirit
among the Sussex dukeries. In 1879 Pope Leo
XIII., by way of showing his own enlarged sense of
spiritual and intellectual merit and of confirming the
moderates in their allegiance, sent for John Henry
Newman at the Birmingham oratory to place the hat
of the sacred college on his head. Returning from
Rome, the newly made cardinal consented to become
the lion of the London season, In addition to the
state dinner parties at Norfolk House, St. James's
Square, there were garden fêtes at Arundel. The guest
of all these occasions filled the place of honour, in his
character, not so much of a great ecclesiastic, as of
a fellow citizen in whom all Englishmen took pride.
Manning, if I remember rightly, was abroad at the
time. Disraeli and Gladstone may both have been at

Sussex Houses Characterized

the London dinner. Neither of them seems to have been at the historic Sussex garden party. Here the guests, both Papal and Protestant, had been purposely taken from the masses rather than the classes. Not a great Catholic house of business, metropolitan or provincial, whose heads of departments, over and above their own invitations, had not been asked to mention members of their staffs whom it would be proper to ask also. At the neighbouring Petworth smartness is a speciality ; the thing is unavoidably recognised at Goodwood also. There is nothing of the sort at Arundel. That baronial stronghold of mediæval history, the political emporium or the convivial rendezvous of a later age, so far as concerns the habitual composition of its guests, has become, to its own great credit, a popular institution. Of other Sussex homes on the grand scale—Goodwood for comfort, Petworth for rank and splendour—some may have been in earlier years disposed to add for iciness of social temperature ! Before the house at Petworth is entered there may as well be some introduction to its owners. The Leconfield title is Yorkshire. The family name, Wyndham, a contraction of Wymondham, suggests that the descendants of the pure Saxon stock who bear it were originally settled in Norfolk. Thence, in the sixteenth century, a migration to Somersetshire, and the consolidation of the Wyndham estate in the Quantock country, to be reverted to hereafter. Now for the house. The ground on which it stands, like the whole family property, in Sussex and elsewhere, first belonged to the Percies. From them by marriage, by royal grant or by purchase in the

The Sussex Dukeries and Non-Dukeries

market, these territories passed to the Wyndhams.
As a country house Petworth may claim an earlier
pedigree even than this. Belonging to her brother,
Jocelyn de Louvaine, it often received the widow
of Henry I. She, while mistress of Arundel, as
wife of William Albini, organised and, to the minutest
detail, superintended the Petworth house-parties of
the twelfth century. By a coincidence worth notice
in passing, Albini of Arundel himself, brother-in-law
of the first owner of Petworth, found a grave in
that East Anglian Wymondham whence, as has
been seen, the Petworth Wyndhams derive their
patronymic. The desolation of magnificence, an
infinite vista of chambers, passages, and halls opening
out of each other, apparently peopled only by human
forms carved in marble. Such, on entering the
house, was the general effect produced on the visitor
of a bygone day. The severity of its splendour has
since been mitigated by the introduction of graces and
comforts unknown when, in 1825, Lord Sefton and
his companion Creevey, having passed into the grand
hall, found their eyes and senses for some moments
dazzled and dizzied by the glories of an apparently
uninhabited palace. Gradually recovering themselves,
they were received by their host, Lord Egremont.
"The best pictures that I consider here," he at once
began, "are those which pleased Horace Walpole,
Sir Joshua's Prince Boothby and his mistress." The
male original, it may be added, was a rather second-
rate dandy of the period whose Christian name had
been given, as to Mr. Turvydrop's son, from the
Regent. The shrewd, eccentric peer, who, with

40

these words, began his duties as cicerone, affected as nearly as a man with £100,000 a year alone can afford to do, the dress and bearing of a day labourer. On he shambled through the rooms of his palace, delivering all the time an entertaining commentary on their contents, till at last he brought the new guest to his bachelor's bedroom, some thirty feet long by twenty broad, high in proportion, with a bed large enough to hold six people without the slightest inconvenience to each other.

With the nineteenth century began the building of Goodwood by the third Duke of Richmond. Dying in 1806, he lived long enough to finish the house but not to furnish it. That was taken in hand by later dukes, who gradually completed the work at the rate of a room a year. The perfected work was pronounced as faultless as its progress had been gradual. "Defies improvement" formed, in 1827, the universal verdict of the guests. These included the then ubiquitous Creevey and Greville, both chaperoned by the Lord Sefton of the day, who kindly undertook the task of towing favourite commoners through the palaces of his own order. Only a few of the Holland House luminaries had then begun to blaze. But to Goodwood followed Samuel Rogers in the condescending Sefton's train. "I am obliged," said the banker-poet, "to say sharp things about people, because, my voice being weak, no one would trouble to hear me if I spoke more charitably. Creevey's disgust knew no bounds when, entering the new drawing-room, sixty feet long, just furnished with the brightest yellow satin, the first person he saw was Rogers ; "what a snarling beast this Rogers is; such a fellow for talking about the grandees he lives with and his 'bonnes fortunes.' Sefton and I think him a d——d bore." Sharp and clever talk abounded in this latest addition to the Sussex dukeries. In the apartment just described, the ladies of the family founded the conversational tradition which their successors have often illustrated. Hence perhaps came the inspiration of a Duchess of Richmond's remark to her daughter in 1842. On going rather late to the Chapel Royal they could find no places. "Come away, Louisa ; at any rate we have done the civil thing." Even before the existing house was entirely finished, the race meetings in the Park and the house-parties had begun. In 1845 the place had become the greatest of the Conservative sporting and political houses in the south. In 1846 it was used by Lord George Bentinck, with Benjamin Disraeli for right-hand man, to rally the Tory malcontents against the free traders, Peelite and Whig. It had also become the cradle of the imperialism, then in its infancy, whose later development was postponed for the next century. In 1819 a Duke of Richmond had died from the bite of a fox during his term of office as Governor-General of Canada. There had gone out with him as secretary one of the most frequent and esteemed of the Goodwood guests. This was General Ready, Lord Milner's grandfather, who afterwards accompanied his chief to Ireland in the same capacity as to North America, and who himself ended as Governor of the Isle of Man. He had married the daughter of one of George Canning's

"The Lady's Last-Stake"

strongest local supporters, the great Liverpool ship-owner, Sir John Tobin. Tobin was brought more than once by his son-in-law to Goodwood. He communicated to the most phlegmatic among his Tory fellow-guests at the place something of that enthusiastic faith in the greatness of England's future beyond the seas, which he had derived from the statesman who boasted of having called a new world into existence to redress the balance of the old. The exact spot in the Goodwood grounds where these exalting subjects were discussed seems to have been beneath the magnificent cedars, bodily transplanted from Lebanon. Here too is commanded that superb view of the racecourse with the strange ravine dividing its two extremities. The pictures then chiefly admired in the Goodwood galleries were, first of course, the Vandyke and other portraits; then Sir Joshua's incomparable "Third Duchess." There were, however, two canvases, both absolutely unique, neither of them so well-known that they need be unmentioned here. These were respectively the "Cenotaph of Lord Darnley," and Hogarth's most curious work, "The Lady's Last Stake."

During the sixties or seventies of the nineteenth century, the next of the Sussex dukeries now to be visited was the scene of a *rencontre* worth, perhaps, a passing mention. A middle-aged man, indistinguishable from an ordinary tourist, with the student's stoop in his figure, and the air of one looking for something, was wandering through the grounds of Battle Abbey. To him, a man whose dress proclaimed the gardener: "Allow me to show you the

The Sussex Dukeries and Non-Dukeries

spot you are looking for." "My good fellow," came the reply, "don't bother me. I have a letter from the Duke of Cleveland permitting me to wander by myself where I want." "But," returned the other, " I am the Duke of Cleveland." The stranger was the historian of the Norman Conquest, E. A. Freeman.

"The best situation of the sort in England" was Horace Walpole's remark on the Sussex building, which successively belonged to the Brownes and Websters, before it passed to the Vanes. The local title found by the scientific historian for the Norman victory still survives, not in the Abbey grounds but in that portion of Battle town or village, east of the church, known as Sanguelac or Senlac. Science, however, has still to decide whether the sanguinary association of the name is due to the fight in which Harold fell, or from the ruddy waters of some local chalybeate springs. Built as a thankoffering for his success in the field by William, the Abbey, as a monastic foundation, whatever may have been the deserts of other like institutions, abundantly merited its destruction by Henry VIII. and Thomas Cromwell. From 1067 to 1539, a monastery; from the latter date to the present time, a country house. Such in brief are the two periods in Battle Abbey's history. Sir Anthony Browne was not only Master-of-Horse to Cromwell's sovereign; he had been the king's proxy in the formalities preceding the marriage with Anne of Cleeves. Cromwell, as a return for his part in that marriage, lost his head; Browne obtained a grant of the Battle estate. "What charming things we should

44

Barn, Church, or Dining-room ?

have done," exclaims Walpole, "if Battel Abbey had
been to be sold at Mrs. Chevenix's as Strawberry
was!" The repairers of the Norman Abbey, or
the defacers and despoilers as they were in Walpole's
eyes, were not its first owners, the Brownes, but
those who followed them, the Websters; it was a
miss of that family who clothed a fragment of the
old monastic portico with cockle-shells. This portico,
part of the ancient cloister, is incorporated into the
front of the existing house. The later buildings
were begun and carried some way by Sir Anthony
Browne after he became the first Lord Montacute.
Montacute religiously respected all remnants or
suggestions of antiquity; even the vandalism of the
sacrilegious Websters did not prevent Horace
Walpole, in his minute examination of the place,
from making a discovery for which he took special
credit to himself; hitherto an outlying building,
which had become a barn, had passed by an un-
questioned tradition for the old refectory. Walpole,
on his visit to Battle in 1752, returned from an
archæological morning in the park with an unusually
radiant air; had he not lighted on reasonably conclusive evidence that the modern barn had never
been used of old for eating purposes, that, in fact,
it was the original church? How many of the rural
homes of England are there that, like Battle, built
on the morrow of the Conquest, 838 years ago, still
retain, visible and almost intact, so much of their
earliest masonry? In addition to the structure
specially investigated by Walpole, be it refectory or
church, there are still in good preservation the

45

The Sussex Dukeries and Non-Dukeries

Conqueror's cloisters, as well as the great gateway and outer wall, built between 1327 and 1377. The conversion of the place from a monastery into a country house, was not only begun but practically completed by its first private owner, Sir Anthony Browne. He certainly built the banqueting hall that has since disappeared; he may have begun the great feature of the house, the arched drawing-room with its Purbeck marble columns. Then came the Webster additions, as to Horace Walpole they seemed defacements. The Websters had purchased the property from that member of the Browne clan, who became the fourth Lord Montacute. After his family had held it for about a century and a half, Sir Godfrey Webster, in 1857 sold it to Lord Harry Vane, the future Duke of Cleveland. Of late the Websters had wanted the money for the proper maintenance of the place. Its nineteenth-century purchaser repaired the disastrous dilapidations, extensively renovated and added to the fabric. Amongst his creations was the fine library, to-day the chief reception-room. It may be well here to review the steps in the peerage which gave Battle a place in the Sussex dukeries. The viscountcy of Bernard and the earldom of Darlington had been created in 1754. William Harry Vane (1766–1842), succeeded his father as third Earl of Darlington. Most of his time he spent as a sportsman, rather than as a great noble or a politician, at his Durham castle of Raby, to be visited in a later chapter. One of the revolution Whigs, he united keen partizanship with courageous conviction; he showed himself one of the Whig stalwarts amid the intestine

Raby Keeps Battle

agitation and intrigue against the Grey Reform Bill. Under him, therefore, Battle became, in the south of England, what Raby had already proved in the north —a social agency for counter-working the political disaffection, long growing against the Prime Minister. Among the noble borough-mongers of the time none was more heavily threatened in influence and purse by the Whig disfranchising proposals than this master of Battle. He not only pocketed the loss, he expended all the resources of his station and wealth in urging on "the Bill, the whole Bill, and nothing but the Bill." Already, in 1827, he had been created Marquis of Cleveland. The day of Whig triumph decorated Battle Abbey with the strawberry-leaf. The new title was worn successively by its first bearer's three sons; none of them left an heir to inherit it. The youngest was the Duke of Cleveland of our own day. His wife was that Duchess of Cleveland who, born Lady Wilhelmina Stanhope, had become, by her first marriage with Lord Dalmeny, Lord Rosebery's mother.

With her begins the latter-day visitors' book of Battle Abbey. The place, already, as has been seen, a headquarters of Whiggism, now became the most interesting as well as distinguished of Sussex country houses. The taste and judgment of the Duchess made the Battle gardens what visitors see them to-day. Battle owes much to the sister estate of its dukes, Raby, in Durham. The Sussex revenues would have been unequal to its progressive beautification without the colliery income from the district whence its owners took their title. The

The Sussex Dukeries and Non-Dukeries

first Duke of Cleveland died in 1842, worth £110,000 a year, and with nearly £1,000,000 in hard cash at his bankers'. His eldest son, though inheriting only the entailed property, had an assured annual income of £70,000. The two other sons were left equally well off. The Duke of Cleveland of our day owed his reputation to other causes than the wealth whose inheritance rendered his hospitalities possible. In 1836, before coming into his title, he added to the prestige of his rank at home the distinction of being the most polished and agreeable Briton abroad; he was a great figure in the Comtesse de Mailly's salon. "My handsome Duke," said the hostess, pointing to the destined lord of Raby and Battle, "is the only Englishman who was ever perfectly at home in the best French society, and therefore as popular in Paris as in London." Nothing in later years more delighted him who had known the Faubourg St. Germain as well as he knew St. James's Street, than to gather round him, at his Sussex house-parties, citizens of the world, as varied in their antecedents or vocations as in their nationalities, who had brought introductions to him in London, or whom he had first known in Paris, at Geneva, at other capitals, at Spa, then the smart watering-place. The vivacity of the Duchess, her unobtrusive but unfailing attention to her guests of all degrees, had won her an European fame that lasted throughout her life. Some among the brightest and most representative of these Battle gatherings took place in 1876. Here in the drawing-room is the host talking to his particular old friend, Henry Reeve, editor of the *Edinburgh*. The Duke is Gladstonian up to a point, but believes the Bulgarian atrocities agitation, then going on, to be mischievously over-done. "Why not," he says to the editor, "protest in your next number?" The hint is taken; "the old buff-and-blue" comes out with an article which the fifteenth Lord Derby called "the first thing that turned the tide." "That," said the Duke of Cleveland at his next Battle party, "is only the beginning. Another month or two and the people will be as loud for attacking the Russians as they have been for coercing the Turks." The other visitors on this occasion contained the Mrs. Stanley of those days, some of the Lincolnshire Banks-Stanhopes, the Duchess's kinsfolk, Lord Raglan Somerset, the Mercer Hendersons and the two very popular Charles Newtons. Each of these Newtons was a contrast to the other—the one, the Marlborough Street magistrate, the other, his exact namesake, the expert in Hellenic art. "A brazen mask talking his own novels." That was the description of Lord Beaconsfield's conversation given by Mr. Arthur Balfour, the Prime Minister of 1905, at a Battle house-party (1881). Exception was at once taken to the caricature by another of the guests, the Duchess's kinsman, Mr Edward Stanhope. But he, of course, had known Disraeli intimately, whereas Mr. Balfour, only entering the House in 1874, had been but two years in it before the great chief was improved into Lord Beaconsfield, and indeed only touched the great man's surface at one or two chance meetings in society. At an earlier time the great Lord Brougham might have been described as one of the Battle and Raby "tame cats." His twentieth-century successor, who had not then come into his title, was also of the Battle company in the last century. So were his friends Sir Richard and Lady Musgrave, the latter of whom became Mrs. Brougham in the course of the next year. Tennyson, then Laureate but not Lord, seems to have been expected, but did not appear. The future commander-in-chief, General Roberts, made on this occasion his first great country house success, was to have stayed throughout the week, but had the earliest of his pressing engagements in the Transvaal. Later in this year the Duke of Cleveland entertained, at almost a *tête-à-tête* visit, a life-long friend and a north-country neighbour, the sixth Duke of Northumberland. Their two graces were about the same age, were not really unlike in appearance, and had each of them the same little wheezy, auriferous cough, which I have heard described as peculiar to territorial magnates who are also overburdened with wealth. "These," remarked a business gentleman who appeared at lunch one day, "are the persons who make the fortunes of the great private West End banks ; they take a pride in keeping a standing balance for which they never receive sixpence, but whose interest would make a hole in the National Debt." Presently the two noble plutocrats fell to talking about the business details of land-purchase. "When," asked one, "this sort of business involves your paying out thousands or millions, how do you manage?" "Simplest thing in the world!" rejoined the other : "cheque on Coutts." The last Duke of Cleveland died in 1891, leaving Battle to his widow for her life. After her death the place went to his grand-nephew, Captain Francis Forester. The Webster connection with Battle would not have been thus broken but for an inconveniently noticeable incident in the family fortunes. When the place was bought by the Duke of Cleveland, five dowager Lady Websters were all simultaneously drawing their jointures. These were the good Lady Webster, Grace, Lady Webster, the great Lady Webster, and two others undistinguished by any special epithet. Each of these lived chiefly at Hastings, and each seems in her day, however brief, to have reigned like a queen at Battle. A property impoverished by this remarkable coincidence of claims could only be recuperated by wealth beyond that of the Cleveland heir. Captain Forester's necessity was to prove the Webster opportunity, and to bring Battle back to a descendant of its earlier owners. Its purchaser from Captain Forester was Sir Augustus Frederick Walpole Edward Webster, the grandson of the possessor from whom Lord Harry Vane had bought it. He having been fortunate enough to marry the daughter and heiress of a Halifax capitalist, Miss Crossley, found himself in a position, not only to buy his family estate, but to keep it up. As a fact, however, he has never lived there, and has let Battle on lease to Mr. Michael Paul Grace, the well-known American banker, already a brevet territorialist in the old country, as the owner or tenant of a fine Hertfordshire property, one of whose daughters is married to Lord Donoughmore, the (1905) Under-Secretary for War. The gardens and park remain to-day what the last Duchess of Cleveland left them. The interior, however, has been much improved by the present tenant. The vandalism of which Horace Walpole accused the Websters is not at least chargeable against the Graces. The comfort and health of the place have been increased by the modern improvements. The drainage, within and without, has been thoroughly overhauled; there are bathrooms on every floor; the electric light penetrates every corner. With these exceptions, no extensive modernisation has been attempted; every fitting or piece of furniture, made to suit the antiquity of the place, remains. Thus, the only gilded decorations in the whole Abbey are those left by the Duchess of Cleveland, and belong to the pictures in the drawing-room, chiefly portraits of the Webster family or of Cabinet ministers, modern as well as antique.

The last of the Sussex dukeries, architecturally and historically, is not to be compared with Arundel, Goodwood, or Battle. Its recent associations have made it a real centre of social or political gravity. Dukedoms have a way of connecting themselves with watering-places as well as with collieries. Tynemouth, where the German Ocean receives the river that washes the Northumbrian coal capital, is an annex of Alnwick. On the south coast, the spot that mimics Brighton, in a greater degree than the inland spa of the Derbyshire Buxton, owes its existence to the Cavendishes. The amalgamation of four fishing hamlets constitutes the Eastbourne that we know; the name is taken from the largest of the four villages now fused into one town. Something of international significance clinging to the neighbourhood in the

A Compton Place-Celebrity

eighteenth century presaged the cosmopolitan characteristics that to-day mark the spot generally, and
especially its ducal patron's house Compton Place.
The younger Pitt's martello towers, lining this portion
of the Sussex littoral, provided Sheridan with several
jokes much appreciated by the smart Whig society
of his time. The Cavendishes, whether in their
Piccadilly mansion, at Chatsworth, or at their Eastbourne *pied de terre*, have divested themselves of
some of their Whiggism ; they have found compensation for the loss in taking on a smartness that their
ancestors of a hundred years ago might not have
understood. Eastbourne itself, if the Brighton of a
younger growth, presents aspects which are entirely
its own. The collective power of British matronhood
carried to the *n*th, would convey an imperfect idea of
the intensity of decorum pervading every pleasure
ground and promenade in the town resting under the
shadow of Beachy Head. The austere orthodoxy
of the Mrs. Tanquerays with a past may sometimes be mistaken for the unsophisticated innocence of the debutante. To whichever of these
classes Eastbourne may belong, no earthly spot
could perhaps be so virtuous as Eastbourne looks.
It has, however, its secular and cosmopolitan
side as well. Rolling out from the Compton Place
grounds, might, at the last century's end, be seen a
citizen of the world, for whose malady, " *une certaine
protuberance abdominale*," his Paris physician had that
year prescribed the Sussex shore instead of his usual
" *etretat*." This lumbering man-mountain of mind
and matter was, of course, none other than the most

53

cosmopolitan guest entertained by a Cavendish, the famous *Times* correspondent, the Chevalier de Blowitz himself. Talking of Eastbourne, he conveys his idea of it to his host by comparing it less to a professional *religieuse* than to a once frisky matron now leading a secluded or devout life, but who has not quite died to the after-dinner thirst for a cigarette and a small glass of green châtreuse with the black coffee. Near the Chevalier and about this period one used to meet Musurus Pasha the First, his chief European friend then Algernon Borthwick, now Lord Glenesk, upon one memorable occasion Lord Beaconsfield himself between the two, somewhere hovering near them Sir Ellis Ashmead Bartlett and Mr. Herman Merivale, dramatist and poultry farmer. But now for the Duke of Devonshire's marine villa and its visitors' book. Compton Place, as regards the *personnel* of its habitual guests, is as universal as becomes the pretty town whose social citadel it constitutes. When the head of the Cavendishes is not entertaining his sovereign at Chatsworth or being entertained by him at Windsor, King Edward VII. has perhaps arrived or is expected at the seaside château of his " right trusty and well-beloved cousin." The other guests symbolise in their names and persons the various foreign *ententes* which, as the greatest diplomatist of his time, his Majesty periodically promotes. Prince Kinsky, in the intervals of steeplechasing, finds time to be of the company ; the dinner table would lack its centrepieces with the Grand-duke Michael and his wife, the Countess Torby. Not that from these gatherings are excluded the national representatives of statesmanship, fashion, or sport. Lord Abergavenny doubles the parts of Sussex squire and tutelary genius of the British constitution ; genial, natty, and knowing Sir Walter Gilbey, though the first Hertfordshire squire of his line, had, even in youth, perfectly acquired the expression and manner which are, as a rule, the outward and visible sign of ancestral conversance with horsiness and its attendant spirits. The collateral descendant of the kingmaker, Warwick, and the father of the wine trade *à la mode* respectively personify feudalism and commerce. Compton Place was also the scene in the last quarter of the nineteenth century of another visit, so significant and, in its results, so far reaching as to be historical. The relations between the Cavendishes and the Churchills had not for some time been remarkable for cordiality ; over personal as well as political issues the former leader of the " fourth party " and the Lord Hartington of old had often crossed swords. Then Mr. Gladstone's possible conversion to Parnellism began to be whispered. Of late Lord Hartington and Lord Randolph had been observed to avoid each other less pointedly at the Turf Club. By and by one heard that Mr. and Mrs. Henry Oppenheim had arranged a little dinner in their pretty Bruton Street house, already in a way ennobled by its associations with the second Lord Granville and the fourth Lord Carnarvon. At the Oppenheim banquets the chief guests were to be the two men between whom a common interest in the turf had long been exercising a mediatorial influence. In those days Churchill had a Brighton *pied de terre* at the Orleans Club. Why should he not run across to Eastbourne, inspect some improvements in the Compton House stables, and see taken out for their exercise some drafts lately made into the Eastbourne foxhounds. The visit was paid. Its fruits were seen in Lord Randolph Churchill's Manchester speech (March 3, 1886), announcing the formation of the Union Party. Among country houses, therefore, Compton Place is historical, if for no other reason than that it shares with Waddesdon Manor, Baron Ferdinand de Rothschild's Buckingham- shire seat, hereafter to be visited, the distinction of having cradled the political combination that ruled the country from 1886 to 1905.

North-west Sussex abounds in monuments of a country-house regime, represented to-day only by memories and names. Cowdray, Hurstmonceux, and Stanstead are mentioned all together by Horace Walpole because they were each visited by him during his Sussex progress in 1778. The first Earl of Egmont accumulated great wealth out of his official salaries. As President of the Court of Admiralty he bought, from his annual savings, Nork House in Surrey, and about the same time Cowdray Park in Sussex. After the Cowdray fire in 1793, the chief ornaments of the place were transferred to the contiguous Woolbeding. Amongst these was the fountain designed by Benvenuto Cellini. Of that, writing in 1827, Creevey had heard enough from Horace Walpole to make him say, "This Italian, they tell me, was a famous man ; look him up in the diction- ary, that I may not expose my ignorance." Wool- beding, socially speaking a branch of the Oxfordshire Blenheim, was the most interesting and instructive

Won at Play

of Sussex houses in the eighteenth century. Its then grave, venerable owner had bought it about 1792, with his winnings at "faro," the game which proved so fatal to Charles Fox. The lucky gamester was Lord Robert Spencer, the third Duke of Marlborough's third son. "This is indeed exquisite," was Sheridan's exclamation, as the owner of Woolbeding pointed out his beautifully arranged plantations and the surprising variety of unexpected views that they disclosed. The associations of the place were as diversified as the prospects of the grounds. In the next village, the fifteenth-century lord of the manor had been the Lord Camoys who commanded the left wing of the English at Agincourt; his wife, depicted in brass effigy by her husband's side in Trotton Church, had been Hotspur's widow, daughter of Edmund Mortimer, Earl of March. To the author of "The School for Scandal," Woolbeding would have recalled the fact that the dramatist Otway had been born in the parish. The archæological Barré delighted in the Agincourt relics, gifts from the Trotton neighbours. The quality admitted by all to be its distinctive charm, was the cosmopolitan diversity of its guests and table-talk. All its most regular *habitués* were citizens of the world, who had been everywhere, done everything, known everybody, and who could be variously reminiscent without lapsing into boredom. Charles James Fox had a standing invitation from the host to bring with him any friends he chose. Those selected were his particular disciples, social as well as political. Their personal appearance attested at once fidelity to their chief and the characteristic influence exercised by him upon the costume, as well as ideas, of the period. Till the middle of the eighteenth century the fashionable country-house dress for men was that which a few years later restricted itself to the levee or the drawing-room. The Whig leader struck out a new line of his own, and made its adoption a sign of smartness ; he had already brought a certain affectation of indifference about externals into fashion at the clubs (where, a little earlier, Fox and his friend Lord Carlisle had flattered the revolutionary dandyism of France by wearing the red shoes, which were to that day what the ruby necktie, set off by the white hat, has been to ours). A costume blending that of the artizan and the gamekeeper displayed Charles Fox as the Jacobin *à la mode* in 1793. In that year, thus habited, he electrified his Woolbeding friends as he entered the drawing-room with cropped hair, no hair powder, neither ruffles to his sleeves nor buckles to his shoes, but as a substitute for the latter positively nothing less vulgar than strings. " My dear Charles," said Lord Robert Spencer, with a twinkle in his eye, as he looked at his visitor, " I protest, to make the thing complete, you must give us your friend Jean de Lille's Marseillaise hymn." Women of fashion piqued themselves on quickly catching the inspiration of "dear Charles." Hitherto a lock of hair like that stolen from Miss Arabella Fermor by Lord Petre, immortalised by Pope, had been the universal vogue. Suddenly these tresses disappeared ; ladies of all ages and of all ranks exhibited heads, rounded *à*

la victime and *à la guillotine*, as if ready for the stroke
of the axe. At the same time the more Conservative
of the rural dames in the Woolbeding drawing-room
could scarcely stifle an expression of surprise when
their London cousins appeared in draperies, classic,
elegant, luxuriant and picturesque, but more suited
to the climate of Greece or Italy than to the keen
south-down air, with grass whitened by the first
autumnal frost.

Among Woolbeding's eighteenth-century guests
were many others as important as and, from society's
point of view, more interesting than those already
mentioned. The best *raconteur* of his period, Sir
Thomas Wroughton, never seemed in greater force
than at the Woolbeding dinner-table. In his youth
he had been the handsomest member of the European
corps diplomatique. Even after he had crossed the
threshold of middle age, the polished animation of his
manner and the easy flow of anecdote remained.
With years he put on a little too much flesh. So, for
that matter, had another of the Woolbeding guests,
Lord Alvanley himself. Neither years nor corpulence
prevented him, any more than they prevented Alvanley,
from being a good shot, a bold, well-judging rider, the
brightest, the wittiest, and the most informatory of
country-house talkers. Wroughton went in the diplomatic service to St. Petersburg when little more than
twenty. He brought back to England nothing less
than conversational omniscience about the inner life,
not only of the Russian Court, but of every palace in
central or eastern Europe. No Englishman had
lived so intimately with the two Czarinas, Elizabeth

The Sussex Dukeries and Non-Dukeries

and Catharine. Wroughton had heard her physicians tell Elizabeth that her life depended in moderation in drinking. She gave no heed to the caution ; persisting in her excesses, she actually died with a glass of cherry-brandy at her lips. Catharine's favour had given Wroughton more than one step in professional pro-motion. The Empress may have admired his imposing figure in the flower of his handsome youth. " It is," he was careful to add to his country-house listeners, " a pure lie to say that this great and sage sovereign ever gave me the slightest encouragement of a gentler kind. If you must know, Count Poniatowski was her lover ; I was only her humble friend and servant." The Platonic character of the friendship did not prevent the Empress's husband from being desperately jealous of the debonair Briton. The best houses of those days as in England, so abroad, were famous for the strength of their construction. That did not keep off a dry rot. " I was," said Wroughton, "one of a dinner party in the Russian palace near San Souci when, as the dessert was being placed on the table, a large piece of ceiling fell down, covering the company with confusion and dust. A few years later, as the guest of the Duke of Buckingham at Stowe, I witnessed a similar casualty. The next day I heard of exactly the same mishap disturbing a banquet at Lansdowne House, Berkeley Square." As a *raconteur*, Wroughton had his match in another of the Woolbeding and Stanstead guests, Sir William Hamilton, the ambassa-dor at Naples, the husband of Nelson's Emma, and the son of Lord Archibald Hamilton, whose wife had attracted the favour of Frederick Prince of Wales.

60

A Fond Husband

Among the distinguished strangers entertained by Sir William Hamilton at Naples was the Grand-duke Paul of Russia, accompanied by the Grand-duchess. "On the first drive," said Hamilton, "that I took them, unconscious apparently of my being in the carriage, my visitor threw his arms round the Grand-duchess and began kissing her with all the warmth of a newly made bridegroom. I tried not to see; I affected abstraction in surrounding objects. It was no good. Turning to me the Grand-duke said, 'You see, Monsieur le chevalier, that I love my wife very much.' After this the embraces were resumed. The ceremony, with the comment '*j'aime ma femme beaucoup*,' was repeated through the successive stages of our drive." The story was made the droller by the unemotional and smileless solemnity with which it was told. Hamilton's and Wroughton's stories sometimes wore a more sombre hue. Lady Hamilton had discovered a good deal about the extensive use in high society of the Italian poison "*aqua tufana*," so called after the Greek woman who first employed it, bringing large stores of it with her to Italy. As early as 1717 the British ministers at Naples and Genoa had told Addison, when Secretary of State, of what was going on; he peremptorily warned the Commissioners of Customs in England to be on their guard against the introduction of the deadly drug. Lady Hamilton, said Sir William, personally knew a Sicilian lady of the highest rank, who was in close confinement for a series of secret assassinations by poison. On calling, as she had been requested, Lady Hamilton found the murderess a gentle creature, under twenty-five,

61

The Sussex Dukeries and Non-Dukeries

with the softest manner and the most intensely feminine presence one can conceive. It was the *beauté de diable* of the Poppaea Sabina type. About the same time an acquaintance of Hamilton and Wroughton, a young Irish doctor, practising at Rome, named Ogilvy, was driven off in a stranger's carriage to attend, as he was told, a critical case some little way out of town. "Your patient," said the messenger, "is a lady of ancient family, whose name and address are to be a profound secret. Before entering the house your eyes must be bandaged for a few minutes." After a narrow staircase had been ascended, the use of his eyes was restored to him. It had become necessary, he then heard, to deprive of life a lady who had dishonoured her family. A refusal to perform the office could only, Ogilvy was assured, cause his immediate death without averting that of the lady. Eventually the doctor took out his lancet, opened her veins. Having thus bled her to death with all the celerity of science, he was offered a bag of gold as his fee. According to his own account he refused it. To regain freedom in the light of day was the only payment he wanted. And so after another drive he found himself again at his own door. Many other experiences of the same kind, though none from Italy, had reached Sir William Hamilton's ears. On the banks of the Danube, when a guest of the Prince of Tour and Texas, near Ratisbon, he had seen at least two castles, inside whose walls similar terrors had been enacted. Sir Horace Mann, Walpole's friend, British minister at the Court of Tuscany, was another of the Sussex country house guests, full of

A Prince of the Empire

curious or interesting reminiscences. "The last of the Medici Grand-dukes," he said, "John Gaston, was quite the most accomplished man of his nation I ever knew. The want of an heir threatened his line with extinction. He had, however, in the prime of manhood a clerical, therefore an unmarried uncle, Cardinal Francesco Maria. Surely, to save the Medici duchy from incorporation in some European monarchy, the holy father would absolve a prince of the Church from his celibacy vows. The dispensation was given; the ecclesiastic took a princess for his wife. Even thus, no heir appeared. The combined energies of Church and State could not prevent the grand-ducal line ending with John Gaston." Tuscany, however, was yet to have a better ruler than any of the Medicis in the Grand-duke Leopold; under his sway Florence first grew into English favour and fame. At a house which, like Woolbeding, was socially the creation of the Spencer-Churchills, it seemed appropriate to hear how the Grand-duke Leopold had secured for an Englishman, Earl Cowper, the only princedom of the German Empire bestowed on a British subject since the great Duke of Marlborough. Leopold himself had asked the future Lady Cowper to be his wife. She gave him so winningly sweet a refusal that the rejected lover could not be less magnanimous than to secure for the lady's husband the title of prince. The Woolbeding of to-day retains its gardens and grounds in the same beauty that delighted Hamilton, Wroughton, Burke, Fox, and Sheridan, and is still approached through the loveliest of Sussex lanes. The house itself has of course shed those distinctive features

63

The Sussex Dukeries and Non-Dukeries

which its eighteenth-century visitors admired and loved. An avenue of magnificent Scotch firs leads up to the gorgeous flower-beds ; these are looked down upon by the high roof and dormer windows of the famous house. Any modernisations that have taken place are due to Lord Lanerton. Lady Lanerton continued to entertain at Woolbeding till 1892 ; during that period, Arundel Castle supplied Woolbeding with some of its most interesting guests ; among these was Cardinal Howard. Of him till then little had been seen by his fashionable friends of old days since he was the smartest of young guardsmen. "Observe," remarked one of these, Mr. Augustus Hare, "the air of stately self-satisfaction with which he marches along the garden walks, holding back his robes on one side as a lady does her dress." "*E troppo soldato*," murmured an Italian priest who happened to be of the company. The rheumatism which confined Lady Lanerton to her wheeled chair, did not impair the gravely gentle urbanity with which she received her guests, or mar the beautiful expression of grateful patience and humble hope as of one awaiting the last summons. Woolbeding's twentieth-century associations have not severed its traditional connection with the best varieties of Whiggism. Its owner is Colonel Henry Arthur Lascelles, the son of a well-known Whig privy councillor, who used periodically to reappear in the earlier part of the Victorian age. He also is a grandson of the sixth Earl of Carlisle, a descendant of Charles Fox's chief crony, who frequently entered the Woolbeding drawing-room in the red shoes already spoken of, before Jacobinism had discarded those and other vanities of the toilette.

Near Woolbeding, a few miles closer to the Hampshire border, is a house whose predecessors, mostly destroyed by fire on the same spot, supplied Sussex with a famous, as well as to a large extent politically, neutral mansion, remarkable for the human curiosities often to be found within its walls. Before mingling with the guests, let us learn something about the place. An earlier edifice had suffered severely from Sir William Waller's attack during the Civil War. In 1687 it was replaced by Lord Scarborough, with a mansion, most of which still remains, after designs by Wyatt and Bonomi, who made it their business to extend the earlier work of William Talman. The exterior was cased with white brick; for the removal of the old wings compensation came in the addition of two porticoes of the Doric order; these also connected a new wing with the main structure. An entirely fresh feature in the eighteenth-century dwelling was the ingenious hydraulic arrangement for ensuring a good water supply. The castellated building in the park, now a ruin, was the work of another occupant, Lord Halifax. Among the *habitués* of the place stands forth the diplomatist, the stately and polished Sir John Stepney; he, indeed, was to the Stanstead of Georgian days what Hamilton and Wroughton were to Woolbeding. The chief social interest of Stanstead lay in its being a place of picturesquely strange and unexpected meetings, set

The Sussex Dukeries and Non-Dukeries

in the beech-wooded park (formerly called " the forest ") which, on his progress to the sea at Shoreham, after Worcester, sheltered Charles II.

Issuing from a recess in these same beech woods, was espied from the windows, by one of the eighteenth-century Stanstead guests, evidently bound for the house, a gentleman in a green coat, with tally-ho buttons. "Charles Turner, by all that is amazing!" murmured the observer, Lord North, as he beheld the most violent and eccentric of his St. Stephen's assailants walk up to the door. Turner, a Yorkshire member of immense wealth, dressed the part of Squire Western to the life. His character, however, was rather that of Allworthy. Rockingham had just made him a baronet. This was how the two Stanstead guests entered into conversation :— North : "You have often accused me of falsehood, but never was I guilty of any lie so gross as that which I have just read in the *Gazette* : ' The King has been *pleased* to appoint Lord Rockingham, Mr. Fox,' &c." It was only a week or so earlier that Turner had raised roars of laughter in the House against North, whose supporters had called the Opposition "a rope of sand." "The noble lord in the blue ribbon and his companions," came the retort, "are a rope of onions, for they stink in the nation's nostrils." "How is it, Wilkes," asked a fellow-guest of the demagogue at Stanstead, "that you sat silent through all the French Revolution debates?" "The fact is," came the reply, "I am a burnt-out volcano." The rejoinder, of course, suggests Disraeli's "exhausted volcanoes" at Manchester, 1872. It **was**

French Politicians at Stanstead

however, no case of plagiarism, only an undesigned coincidence. The present writer, mentioning the words of Wilkes to Lord Beaconsfield, was told, "Thanks, it looks like a crib, but it is the first time I knew Wilkes ever said anything worth repeating and fit for publication." Thanks chiefly to Sir John Stepney, even into the nineteenth century, Stanstead, like so many other country houses, abounded in French Revolutionary stories. At the first sitting of the Directory, irritated by something Carnot had said, Barras exclaimed : "Your remark is, within your own knowledge, a lie." The lie was given back, with the added words : "In proof of what I say, I lift up my hand to heaven." "Pray do nothing of the kind," rejoined Barras, "or drops of blood will run down upon the table." Throughout its existence as a social centre, Stanstead never wanted the international cachet. Nowhere else were the French Orleanists more at home in England. Here the Duc de Broglie and Guizot first made their début in an English drawing-room—de Broglie the picture of a French nobleman ; Guizot, of the intellectual face, but with something of the school usher in his presence. The rooms that were the scene of these cosmopolitan meetings, in point of historic interest and picturesque charm do not yield to the exterior or to the park that surrounds it. The ornamental carving and woodwork are to-day what they were when Grinling Gibbons had finished his work. The Arras tapestry has neither received alteration nor needed repair since being placed in its present position by Lord Scarborough. Several

The Sussex Dukeries and Non-Dukeries

family lines of successive owners have, in different ways, left their mark at Stanstead. The spot must have been included in one of King John's southern progresses, since in the January of 1215 that sovereign dated a writ from Stanstead. Between three and four centuries later, in the autumn of 1591, Queen Elizabeth slept at the Stanstead mansion of that date. Its less remote story opens, as has been already seen, with the eighteenth century. George I. was received there in 1722, six years after his son, as Prince of Wales, had been Lord Scarborough's guest. From the Scarborough family Stanstead passed to the Ways; one of these, a clergyman, the Rev. Lewis Way, made, in 1800, the most conspicuous of the modern additions to the old structure. This was the private chapel, with its strikingly beautiful stained-glass window at the east end, representing "the Holy of Holies." Beneath is a family vault, where rest the purchaser of Stanstead from the Way trustees, Charles Dixon, and those owners who have passed away since him. The Dixons have been followed by the present Wilders.

CHAPTER III

THE FASHIONABLE SOUTH DOWNS

FROM Stanstead we go to the next of Horace
Walpole's favourite Sussex houses, Hurstmonceux. Its earlier story is darkened by the gloom of
melodrama and disasters recalling those of Greek
tragedy. Its later interest is that of a social centre,
much affected by the aristocratic and cultured
Anglicanism of the day. The old castle's stern and

weird exterior was in keeping with the sombre incidents that took place within its walls. About 1720 it had come by inheritance to Miss Grace Naylor, the most attractive and desirable heiress of her day. A few years later, when little more than twenty, the new owner perished mysteriously within its walls, starved to death, as was locally believed, by her former governess. The property then went to the family with which, above all others, the modern Hurstmonceux is identified. This was that of the many-friended and extensively cousined Hares. Miss Naylor's successor in the property, Francis Hare, had for his father that chaplain of the Duke of Marlborough who had ridden by the great captain's side at Blenheim, at Ramillies, and who afterwards, thanks to the Pelhams and Walpoles, became the richest pluralist of his age : he held simultaneously the deanery of St. Paul's, the bishoprics of Chichester, and of St. Asaph ; he thought himself hardly used because he had missed being Archbishop of Canterbury. This ecclesiastic's son, dying childless, left the Sussex estate to his half-brother, a godson of Sir Robert Walpole. "Let the boy," said the godfather, "go into the Church, that I may make him a canon of Winchester." Parson Robert Hare married successively two wealthy women. The second of these, Henrietta Henckel, jealous to madness of the first wife's sons, made her husband pull down the old building and erect in its place a huge and hideous castle, to be settled, with the lands, upon her own children by a former marriage. Nemesis, as in a Greek play, was near. The new structure had

The Two Beautiful Georgianas

scarcely been finished when it was discovered to stand upon entailed ground. It thus passed to a certain Francis Hare-Naylor; the ill-starred building itself became known as Hurstmonceux Place. Mrs. Henckel Hare, in a remorseful dotage, bewailed her destructive work; wandering round the ruins night and day, " Who," she idiotically exclaimed, "could have been so wicked as to pull down this beautiful old place ? " The Hurstmonceux estates were only saved from sharing the ruin of the edifice by a miracle of romance. At the darkest moment of his money difficulties, the good looks of Mrs. Henckel Hare's eldest stepson were noticed by Georgiana, the beautiful Duchess of Devonshire. She introduced him to her cousin, her rival or even superior in loveliness, another Georgiana, the Bishop of St. Asaph's daughter, Lord Peterborough's great-niece. The father strongly disapproved the acquaintance. Her Grace of Devonshire, however, arrayed the country-house influences and opportunities on the side of the lovers. In 1785 the young couple eloped, dividing their time, for some years, between Carlsruhe and Rome, on £200 a year allowed them by the Duchess. A little later Mrs. Francis Hare was brought back to England by the death of her father-in-law, Sir Robert Walpole's canon of Winchester. She settled in the new building already mentioned, known as Hurstmonceux Place. Her chief friends and visitors belonged to her own family. The most regular among the Hurstmonceux Place guests were the hostess' sister, Lady Jones, and her husband, the famous Orientalist; the latter, after Harrow and Oxford, became private

71

tutor at Althorp and was helped by Earl Spencer, his pupil's father, into the public service. Hurstmonceux Place, which thus replaced the castle as the Hares' country house, forms a massive square with projecting circular bows at the corner. Its comforts inside have received the addition of beauty in the staircase, floors, and doors, as well as in the old panelled hall, with its stags'-horns hangings brought bodily from the old castle and ancient deer park. Long after the castle had been shorn of feudal dignity and the latter day representatives of its historic lords were sufficiently depressed in the county scale, Hurstmonceux Place witnessed many pleasant house-parties. The Hares, who were its inhabitants from the close of the eighteenth century to the middle of the nineteenth, had brought back with them from their long continental stay foreign habits ; their very dress was un-English. The châtelaine of the place could be recollected by many of her humbler neighbours, till lately living, as riding daily on a white ass to the mineral springs in the park, and as accompanied everywhere by a white doe which, at church, stood waiting for its mistress, during the service, at the pew door. This was the lady who, after her husband's death, sustained her reputation for intellectual interests by a correspondence with learned men abroad, who themselves had been deterred from visiting Hurstmonceux, lest its master should insist upon reading to them the dull plays he wrote and on their studying themselves his duller histories. The Hurstmonceux tent of the bewilderingly complicated Hare family was pitched at different points in the locality, now at a little

Churchmen and Writers at Hurstmonceux

house called Lime, now at the Rectory. The latter of these abodes in Archdeacon Hare's day became famous and powerful throughout Europe. The south of England possessed no other centre of Anglican learning and breeding whose influences saturated so much of the nation's best social life. The Oxford movement of 1833 needed for the permanent diffusion of its influences the social organisation of the Hares and Hurstmonceux as well as the spiritual energies of Newman aud Pusey at Oxford. Conversational vivacity, a quality of affectionateness, the best associations of English village life and of clerical life in its aristocratic aspects ;—these were the things which their contemporaries associated with the Hares, particularly with the archdeacon ; at his vicarage open house was habitually kept. Hither came, on almost weekly visits, Bunsen, the Mozleys, and all that was highly educated, tolerant, polished in the thought, literature, or churchmanship of the time. Lay thought was equally represented at the Archdeacon's house-parties. The imposing person and imperious manner of Walter Savage Landor occasionally imparted to these gatherings the bustling animation diffused around him by Harold Boythorn in " Bleak House." In his Hurstmonceux library Julius Hare wrote his " Mission of the Comforter," but compromised himself with the Evangelicals by writing also the affectionate memoir of Sterling and by infusing into the "Guesses at Truth," in which he collaborated with his brother Augustus, the undenominational religion of Thomas Arnold, Bunsen, Coleridge, and F. D. Maurice. The younger Sterling, the *Times* " Thunderer's " son, as

Hare's former curate, knew this library well, and had hoped that if anything about him ever were written it might be by his old rector, whose memoirs, already mentioned, did indeed set Carlyle on his better known biography of the man.

In purely secular letters the neighbouring or not remote Parham is not less distinguished than the semi-ecclesiastical Hurstmonceux. From the sixteenth to the nineteenth centuries this Elizabethan roof has periodically covered the most famous representatives of European intellect and art. When occupied by its early owner, Sir Thomas Palmer, it was among Queen Elizabeth's halting places on her journey to Cowdray. From the Palmers it passed to the Bisshopps; a representative of that family, the Lord De la Zouche, wrote at Parham a book much talked of in its day, " The Monasteries of the Levant." An ancestor of that peer brought home with him, from a long stay in Italy, the ambition of making his Sussex seat a museum and a Tusculum. His predecessors had left him the nucleus for a priceless collection of antique gems, metal-work, and the earliest specimens extant of the printing art. The most precious treasures belonging to the last category were the first editions of Homer and Virgil. There were pictures with a history, as well as epitomes of epochs in the shape of jewels. Such was Angelica Kauffman's portrait of Lady De la Zouche. This had been hung, at Sir Joshua's special instance, in the first Royal Academy exhibition at Somerset House. It is the painting particularly mentioned by Miss Thackeray in her story based on the artist's strange fortunes. The most

Fashion, Art, and Letters at Parham

magnificent among the eighteenth-century visitors at Parham was the chief ornament of the Court, that Lord Hertford who held the white wand of Chamberlain during half a generation, the master-mind in every palace ceremonial. The most amusing of the visitors was George Selwyn. It was in the Parham drawing-room that Selwyn related his Paris experiences on a trip he had just made, for seeing Damiens or Ravaillac broken on the wheel. " A colleague, sir ? " asked the executioner, on seeing the Englishman intent upon gaining a good place, " Alas ! sir, no—I am but an amateur ! " Of Voltaire's alleged visit to Parham during his stay in England, if it ever occurred, no record seems to exist. From Parham, however, undoubtedly, English men of letters first heard of the new light on Milton, thrown by Voltaire's researches. The poet, travelling as a youth in Italy, witnessed a representation, at the Milan theatre, of Andreino's comedy, " Adam, or the Original Sin." Dedicated to the French queen, Marie de Medicis, the play, abounding in absurdities, if not impieties, flashed upon the English spectator the grand possibilities of the theme. Discarding the frivolities of the Italian original, Milton began with preserving Andreino's dramatic form. As the work went on, he soon saw it to be better adapted to the epic treatment of Homer or Virgil.

Beneath any roof frequently visited by Selwyn, by Sir Joshua, and by Topham Beauclerk, Samuel Johnson was sure occasionally to find himself. It was Johnson's idea, first expressed at Parham, of going into the House to support Lord North, that set the *quid nuncs* on speculating whether, if his idea were fulfilled, he would be a failure, a silent member like Addison and Gibbon, or achieve a boisterous notoriety like a minor litterateur, Onslow, member for Guildford, spoken of at Parham, as everywhere, by his nickname, " Cocking George." At Parham, too, did another guest, Horace Walpole, call Gibbon's historical masterpiece "a tiresome compilation," the first volumes of which he had scarcely patience to read.

If Byron never visited Parham, he has associated himself with it by one of his best known little poems. It was Mrs. Wilmot Horton whose beauty and whose dress, white spangles on black, suggested the lines beginning " She walks in beauty." In the Parham dining-room, attached to Gainsborough's portrait of the lady, are the lines in the poet's handwriting. Politics at Parham were only looked at incidentally from the fashionable literary or artistic standpoint. " So Sir Joshua Reynolds," said the Parham ladies, with a scornful titter, " is going to stand for Plympton." " He is not," put in George Selwyn, " to be despised. I know no abler man on a canvass." " So, my dear George," remarked the Whig magnate, Lord Carlisle, "your seat is to be attacked by a timber merchant. What, I should like to know, can be meant by a man without an idea, apart from a square foot of Norway deal, desiring to be in Parliament? " Edmund Burke had been the brains of Administrations but had always been kept out of the Cabinet. He was known to resent the exclusion. " What a pity," exclaimed the Parham drawing-room, " that so clever a man should

not know his place.   The Cabinet, indeed, for him ! "
" My idea," said Selwyn, "is that our grandchildren
will see colliers privy councillors and day labourers
Cabinet ministers."   Surely this was said with a prophetic eye to the promotion in 1906 of Mr. John
Burns and Mr. Thomas Burt !   Parham itself was to
supply, a little later, an object lesson in the democratic
tendency which had so disgusted the fine guests of
the house.   Disraeli's novels contain no more amusing
episode than that of the civil and obliging club servant
in " Sibyl," whom one of the members takes out to
India as his valet, who before the voyage is over is
advanced to private secretary, who, returning to
England a rich man, goes into Parliament and dies
a peer.   The original of this story was Sir Thomas
Rumbold.   From being a waiter at White's, he became
Governor of Madras ; in February, 1812, he died
member for Yarmouth, Isle of Wight, always visiting
Parham en route to his constituency.   On like journeys
to his Lymington electors, Edward Gibbon revelled
in the patrician and learned atmosphere of Lord De
la Zouche's Sussex home.   Gibbon, when he appeared
at Parham, had come over from his chief Sussex
headquarters, Sheffield Place, to-day best known in
connection with cricket and military manœuvres.   In
Gibbon's day it was not only the haunt of London
wits, but an asylum for French refugees during the
storms of revolution, and thus socially of kin with an
East Anglian and a Buckinghamshire country house,
hereafter to be visited.

" People tell me I want to abandon our colonies ;
the truth is I want to retain them by their affections."

The Fashionable South Downs

So said Richard Cobden at Manchester, January, 1849.
The policy expressed by the words had begun to
shape itself in his mind twenty years earlier. When
revisiting the Sussex district where later he lived, he
meditated the programme of the Colonisation Society,
founded by his political friends in 1829. Born beneath
the farm roof known as Dunford, owned, with the
adjoining land, by his father, the future Free Trader
had seen it pass to strangers. This uprooting of his
family from their old soil inspired him with a resolution like that of Warren Hastings in connection·with
the paternal Dalesford. Young Cobden determined to
buy back the old home from the hands to which it
might have gone. He did so in 1850, replacing the
farm building by the Dunford House, where, except
during his periodical Parliamentary absences in
London, he lived for the most part till his death in
1865. His Dunford guests numbered among them John
Bright, J. E. Thorold Rogers, his neighbour Lady
Dorothy Nevill, then living six miles off at Dangstein,
C. P. Villiers and T. Bayley Potter. Among the
Dunford visitors also were habitually the courtliest
as well as the most scientific of officials and economists,
Sir Lewis Mallet, Mr. and Mrs. Milner Gibson, and,
at least once, the first Lord Westbury. Of these, as
of many other visitors, Lady Dorothy Nevill is (1906)
the sole survivor. Charles Villiers, who, till late in
the nineteenth century, periodically reappeared in his
old Sussex haunts, was one of Cobden's most essential
allies. Newman has spoken of Pusey as bringing
to the Oxford movement of 1833 the social influence,
the impetus of aristocracy's learning, without which

78

it would not have become a national force. Something like that was the service rendered by Villiers to the policy of freeing the ports. Thorold Rogers began by recommending the cause to intellectual Oxford ; he illustrated and enforced its principles by a rare combination of genius and research. After the death of his friend and master, he co-operated with T. Bayley Potter in founding the Cobden Club. Mr. T. B. Potter not only for twenty-five years represented his friend's opinions in the House of Commons, but presided over the association formed as a bulwark against attack on Cobden's principles. On retiring from St. Stephen's, he settled in Cobden's native district. On the Dunford estate, now belonging to Cobden's two daughters, is a house formerly known as Hurst. Here T. B. Potter pitched his tent, and here, in 1898, he died. Since that date there has been a change of name ; what was Hurst has became Oatscroft. Its hospitable traditions are perpetuated by those of Richard Cobden's family whose country home it is. Dying in London lodgings, 23, Suffolk Street, Pall Mall, the destroyer of the Corn Laws was buried in West Lavington churchyard, close to Dunford. Samuel Wilberforce, in his Oxford diocesan days the episcopal lord of Lavington Manor, was a neighbour whom Cobden at Dunford frequently visited. At Lavington, in the August of 1855, he met among other guests Sir Roundell Palmer and the ex-Premier of the Crimean epoch, Lord Aberdeen. " Believe me, Mr. Cobden," said the latter, " I shall never cease to lament having suffered myself to be drawn into the Russian War. I ought to have resigned." How the sense of something like blood-guiltiness haunted the old statesman to the last may be judged from the fact that he refused to rebuild the old church, now a ruin, near Haddo House. " I must not," he said, "do it myself ; my hands are bathed in blood ; let it be done by him who shall come after me." By the side of his son, in the churchyard already mentioned, Richard Cobden was laid to rest in 1865. Here, on the Sunday following the funeral, his friend Thorold Rogers, then in Anglican orders, preached the commemorative sermon. In West Lavington Church, too, the future Cardinal Manning preached his last sermon as an Anglican clergyman (1850). Manning, indeed, was not only Rector of Lavington, but the builder of West Lavington Church, to supplement the older Lavington Church. In Lavington (proper) churchyard, Manning's wife and his brother-in-law, Bishop Wilberforce, rest. Bishop Samuel Wilberforce's marriage with the Rev. John Sargent's daughter, the future Cardinal Manning's sister-in-law, made him, like his wife's father, a Sussex squarson. With woods both for background and foreground, Lavington House is close to the churchyard. Hither, on a certain July day, 1873, had come from far and near laymen and clerics of all persuasions and schools of thought. " Bishop of the diocese ; rector of the parish," rang out the clear voice of Samuel Wilberforce's son, now Bishop of Chichester. Thus hailed by names or titles, which did or did not belong to all of us, we entered the churchyard to say farewell to the coffin inscribed with the words, " Samuel Wilberforce, Bishop of the Church of God." Lavington had been, in his father-in-law's

" A Confirmed Old Papist "

time, a country house, whose most welcome guests scarcely belonged to the High Church school. Mrs. Sargent, the mistress of the place, was decidedly Evangelical, thinking Keble, of "The Christian Year," and his curate, Wilson, went a little too far. She never forgave Wilberforce for speaking disrespectfully of the Reformation. John Henry Newman, the oracle of sect, was roundly stigmatised by the lady of the house as "a confirmed old Papist." In the same district as Lavington is a house which has always belonged to a line of Sussex squires, each of them from father to son a *beau ideal* of his order. Since a time to the contrary of which memory runneth not, Stopham has been the home of Sussex knights of the shire of the Barttelot name. It was a favourite haunt of Disraeli in Sir Walter Barttelot's day. That chivalrous Tory gentleman thought he had done Mr. Bradlaugh an injustice. He made the amend by inviting the member for Northampton to visit him at the family place near Pulborough. "You ought," said Lord Beaconsfield, with his grim smile, " to have asked also Mrs. Besant, Henry Labouchere, and Gladstone. 'The Fruits of Philosophy,' 'My old Friend Homer' and 'Truthful Tommy' might have made a mixture that would almost have blown the Stopham roof off." We are now in that part of the county abounding in Shelley associations. The poet's collateral ancestors invested his natal house, Field Place, with no literary or refining connections of any kind. From father to son these Shelleys belonged to the fastest set of men about town, and contributed more than one ornament to the Regent's household

81   F

The Fashionable South Downs

at the Brighton Pavilion. Field Place had come to
the poet's grandfather, Sir Bysshe Shelley, through
his marriage with the heiress of the Michell family,
to which it had immemorially belonged. The Shelley
owners of the property were famous for their week-
end gatherings of fine or fast London visitors and for
the racey stories told or the good things said by the
company. All were the personal intimates of Charles
James Fox. All, too, wished him to marry a rich wife,
and so end the periodical necessity of frequently
sending round the hat. Miss Pulteney, to whom
Pitt afterwards gave a peerage, was the greatest
heiress of the day and had, it was hoped, a liking
for "dear Charles." The lady's complexion was
light, that of Fox, of course, very dark. Speculating
on the possible issue of such a marriage, General
Fitzpatrick or Hare put the Field Place table in a
roar by suggesting that the offspring would be duns
with black manes and tails. Fox's marriage with Mrs.
Armstead, it should be said, was not acknowledged
till 1794. Field Place in the last quarter of the
eighteenth century was richer in Fox stories and
in good sayings about the Fox and North coalition
than any other country house in England. No one
took Pitt's rival seriously. "Charles, first Lord of
the Treasury!" exclaimed his great friend Fitzpatrick,
at the Field Place dining-table; "one can as easily
imagine the second Charles Stuart Archbishop of
Canterbury!" Hearty were the laughs at Field Place
over Lord North's humorous vindication of his
union with Fox. The two men, who were not on
speaking terms, in the Eddystone Lighthouse, risked

the destruction of the English Navy rather than break silence to each other. "Animated by more enlarged sentiments we considered the safety of the vessel of State our primary duty, and at all events agreed that the fire in the lighthouse should not be extinguished." The most noticeable of the Field Place hospitalities in the late years of the eighteenth century or the first quarter of the nineteenth, had included among the guests the two diarists of the period, "Punch" Greville, the Clerk of the Council, and Thomas Creevey. P. B. Shelley passed some time there after leaving Eton in 1809, writing partly in the house itself, more often in his boat on Warnham Pond, a sheet of water covering one hundred acres, "Queen Mab" and "The Wandering Jew." Chesworth, the next country house to Denne Park in this neighbourhood, illustrates, in its vicissitudes, one aspect of country house history. The stately home of perhaps the most ancient and powerful Sussex family, the Braoses, Chesworth was the rallying ground of Stuart supporters till the eve of the Restoration. It then passed to strangers. To-day, like many other manorial mansions with a famous past, it is a farm house. Warnham Court, directly behind Field Place, has experienced changes of ownership different from those known by Chesworth, but still equally typical in the chequered narrative of country house evolution. Under the trees of Warnham Court, Nicholas of Horsham, the leading Sussex physician of the fifteenth century, meditated new methods of medical treatment, which afterwards saved the life of Warnham Court's then owner.

The Fashionable South Downs

Nearly three hundred years later the publisher, Bernard Lintot, also a native of the same Horsham, read, before sending them to his printer, Gay's "Trivia" and Pope's "Illiad," and "Odyssey." Early in the eighteenth century the place was rebuilt by the Sussex squire, to whom it had come, Sir Henry Treadcroft. A generation or two later, when inhabited by Sir H. Pelly, it was in high favour with a little company of Christchurch "tufts," who were frequently its then owner's guests in the 1860's. This company included the Duke of Hamilton of that day, better known by his sobriquet, "ruddier than the cherry," than by his title. That salutation, by way of serenade, had often been heard outside his grace's rooms in Canterbury quad. The Duke was pleasantly reminded of it by his fellow-guests at Warnham, including as these did the present Lord Rosebery, Lord Tweedmouth, and the late Lord Randolph Churchill. Since then this delightful possession, a real microcosm of the county's most characteristic charms, has passed into the family of Lucas. Such a line of descent, conspicuously illustrated in the rural homes of England, does but bring the country-house system into closer touch with the tendency of national progress and the spirit of the time. The men who have attained to wealth and station by success in scientific or commercial enterprise, assimilate, as landlords or hosts, the best attributes of their forerunners who, noble or knightly, owed position and title to achievements in the council-chamber or battle-field.

Like several interesting houses in the district, the

Stanmer as the Parent of Brighton

Sussex home of the Pelhams rises from a basin of trees. A quiet country house cannot often boast of a noisy watering-place as its offspring. Stanmer, however, as will presently be seen, is the undoubted parent of Brighton. The chance excursion of a royal visitor at Stanmer to the adjacent fishing-village had, for its direct consequence, the raising of the palace by the sea, known as the Pavilion, and the consequent conversion of Brighthelmstone into Brighton. Of the Pelham habitations in Sussex, Plumpton Place, Laughton, Bishopstone Manor, and Halland were famous long before Stanmer. Henry Pelham, the earlier of the two Prime Minister brothers, lived at Esher, the Duke at Halland, at Bishopstone, and at Pelham House, Lewes. At Halland especially, Holles, Duke of Newcastle, Thomas Pelham, resided in great luxury and extravagance. A beautiful building picturesquely situated, it has, like the ancient Braose seat, near Horsham, become a farm; the decorative design of the Pelham Buckle, still visible on the walls, proclaims its original ownership and character. Bishopstone is also a farm; of the original structure only the huge cellars remain. The local account represents Walpole's personal friends, political disciples, and ministerial successors, Henry Pelham first, Thomas Pelham, Duke of Newcastle, afterwards, as domiciled at Stanmer. This fiction has naturally grown out of a confusion of names. Between 1744 and 1754 a certain Thomas Pelham undoubtedly lived at Stanmer; he was the Duke of Newcastle's cousin as well as namesake. The Duke, therefore, may have visited the place. The legend of his

85

The Fashionable South Downs

having been accompanied by his preceptor and predecessor in office is easily explained. Sir Robert Walpole, at Houghton, cared only less for forestry and tree-planting than for his dogs or his game preserves. "You should see," said the ducal Pelham, "how they manage these things at Stanmer." The fifth Lady Chichester obligingly went through the family papers for some evidence of this visit having been actually made by Sir Robert Walpole. It does not, however, seem to have advanced beyond the stage of intention. If not, like Stanstead and Wool-beding, the resort of eighteenth-century statesmen, Stanmer was the frequent guest-house of sovereigns or their kin. These visits and their results form an entirely unique chapter in country-house history. Its later record has associated Stanmer with the encouragement of, and the active participation in, various philanthropic or useful enterprises, both in the interests of the whole country side and especially those connected with the town already described as socially a child of Stanmer, in its turn to become the parent of the smart rural hospitalities of a later date, the neighbouring Brighton. This is how Stanmer stands to Brighton in the parental relation already claimed for it. In the August of 1782, the Princess Amelia, the Prince of Wales's aunt, stayed with the then Lord and Lady Pelham at Stanmer. A chance excursion was planned to the adjoining Bright-helmstone. The repetition of the visit next year endowed Sussex with the most popular and fashionable of watering-places. Stanmer, the royal visiting-house first, the centre of friendship and patronage

86

The Genesis of Rural Smartness

of all that is good and beneficent afterwards; then the Brighton Pavilion, combining the freedom of club life with a sort of family existence, and thus, however indecorously, providing the earliest pattern for the respectable smartness of twentieth century country-house life; these seem the links in the present social chain. Of that presently. Meanwhile let us pause at two more houses in rural Sussex, which a popular writer has made his own. In the first half of the nineteenth century the novelist, Harrison Ainsworth, was editing *Bentley's Magazine* and other periodicals, with Charles Dickens among his contributors. The two men made many excursions through different parts of England together, including in their rambles much of the South Down country. The Sergison manor house, Cuckfield, with its labyrinth of secret chambers within, its diversified and far-spreading park without, seems to have given Ainsworth some ideas for the scenery of the novel, "Rookwood," which first secured his fame. Several seats in this part of Sussex connect themselves with the wandering and escapes of the second Charles, after Worcester. They may, therefore, as was done by Ainsworth, suitably be peopled with Stuart partisans and followers. Whatever may have been the facts as to this novelist's personal acquaintance with Cuckfield, he knew every stone, within and without, of Ovingdean Grange before composing his story of that name. Evelyn in his diary mentions a present of richly embroidered purple velvet and most noble plate as given to the then newly built St. James's Church, Piccadilly, by Sir R. Geere. This, at the period of Charles's stay, was the head of the family which supplied the royal fugitive with his host. The Geeres were succeeded at Ovingdean by a family whose name is given in Ainsworth's novel. The Beard of the book was the parish clergyman; his historical namesake's descendant became the possessor of the Grange. A man of hospitable instincts and educated tastes, he invited Harrison Ainsworth to one of his literary parties. The invitation in due course bore its fruit in the novel; its author perpetuates the historic name of the Stuart host, though not in the historic context. The " Martin " Geere is mentioned as a dependant of the household instead of its head.

The eighteenth century had yet eighteen more years to run when his Stanmer hosts, under the circumstances already explained, planned an excursion for the future George IV. to Brighthelmstone. In the next year, 1783, came the Prince's formal introduction to the place of which, as yet, he had merely caught a glimpse. The Duke and Duchess of Cumberland, in the second of the years just mentioned, 1783, had established themselves at Grove House, Brighthelmstone, for sea-bathing. On Sunday, September 7th, the heir-apparent was to pay his uncle and aunt a visit; at midday he was received not only by his relatives but, with great ceremony on their part, by the chief people of the place as well as of the neighbourhood, including the Stanmer Pelhams. After dinner in the evening, the Duke of Cumberland took his visitor for a walk on the Steine. No Sabbatical prejudices interfered with an elaborate show of fireworks at night, in the then open space now covered

Prince George at Brighton

by the Pavilion Parade and Prince's Street. From the Grove House windows the Prince viewed the fireworks and the illuminations. On Monday came more junketing by day, and at night the most splendid ball ever known in the " Castle," then the first, if not the only considerable hotel in the place. The festivities were prolonged throughout the next week, till, indeed, the 19th of the month. Delighted equally by his reception and its surroundings, the departing Prince left behind him the promise of soon returning for a longer stay. The Brighton Pavilion still contains some departments known as " Wellsher's rooms." That is a corruption of Weltjie, the Prince's German factotum. This man first introduced his enormously stout body and ludicrously short legs to the admiring Brighthelmstonians in the July of 1784 ; he had come to engage for his employer a house belonging to Thomas Kemp. In this way was the germ of the Pavilion formed. The physicians had recommended the Prince to follow his uncle Cumberland's example of sea-bathing. The royal visitor would therefore become a frequent resident on the shore to which he had been introduced by his Stanmer hosts. About daybreak, July 23, 1784, the august creator of the modern Brighton took possession of the tenement, which in three years and at a cost of, not the millions mentioned by Byron, but several tens of thousands, were expanded into the Georgian palace by the sea. Mr. Kemp's roof, destined to so glorious an enlargement, was spoken of by the banker-poet Rogers as a " respectable farm-house." Brighthelmstone's accessibility to continental Europe had given it a certain cosmopolitan vogue even in the days of its aboriginal simplicity. When, in 1784, the future ruler of Great Britain may have dreamed of the Pavilion's coming glories, he was saluted on the Old Steine by the Duc de Chartres, better known as Philippe Egalité, King Louis Philippe's father and one of the royal victims, after Louis XVI., claimed by the guillotine. Other foreigners of equal distinction soon flocked to the Sussex Court. The fishing-village had been changed by a stroke into the world's place of pleasure. A few weeks later (August 10th) the English and French royalties with their hangers-on went in state to the Brighton races. Untold wealth and unbridled debauchery had not improved the personal appearance of the heir-apparent's chief guest. The Duc de Chartres's complexion had deepened to the colour of burnished copper relieved by dark studs of carbuncles. From the Brighton meeting of the princes of two nations, followed the introduction to France of English dress and customs, the method of English riding, Yorkshire jockeys and English racers for the foreign turf. The patron whom Brighton owed to the Pelhams at Stanmer at once began to " make things hum." The opening years of the twentieth century enlivened the London and Brighton road with the pedestrian competitions of Stock Exchange athletes, waitresses and serving-men. It was all merely a revival of a Georgian fashion. More than one hundred years earlier the Regent gave the word and set the pace for riding matches between the Old Steine and his London palace. He himself rode the double journey in ten hours. By and by that feat was surpassed by

Le Roi S'Amuse on the Sussex Coast

an officer of the Light Dragoons, who rode from Brighton to Westminster on the same horse in three hours and twenty minutes, stopping only at Reigate to take a glass of wine, pouring the rest of the bottle down his horse's throat. Such were only a few of the items in the royal programme. The Prince was as much at home with his gun as in the saddle ; he could bring down pigeons with rifle-bullets on the Steine. If he occasionally missed his bird, he did great execution among his neighbour's chimney-pots. Some years later, one of the royal suite, Colonel Hanger, planned a foot-race on the Old Steine between his black servant and the Horsham carrier. Hanger's great success as Master of the Revels was a series of races between women for a new smock and a hat, and between twenty geese and twenty turkeys over a ten mile course for £500. Whether the debauch which inspired this great idea took place at the embryonic Pavilion or at Carlton House, it was on the Brighton beach that Hanger troubled his patron to settle a bet of several hundred or thousand pounds which he had lost over the contest. When staying at Stanmer, the Prince played at cricket in the park. "When you visit me at Brighton," he said to his host, "you will find the luxuries of a London club and country freedom combined beneath the same roof." Piquing himself on his skill with the bat and ball, he started a cricket ground on the Lewes Road, where now stands Park Crescent. He kept the Duke of York, the athletic Lord Egremont, the corpulent Lord Alvanley, and one of the Shelleys from Field Place alternately fielding and feasting for seven whole days. All this was healthy and decorous enough. On the slopes towards the Downs the entertainment was less refined. The ground covered to-day by Clifton Terrace, witnessed "Jingling" races, run by blackguards covered with bells, a favourite sport. Two oxen having been baited to death and roasted whole, were cut up and distributed to the crowd by the two chief butchers of the place, Measor and Russel, both in high favour at the Pavilion. Then there were cheeses to roll down-hill as a prize for whoever stopped them, tobacco doles to be grinned for, good hats to be cudgelled for, a pig to go to whoever could catch him by the tail. A little below the social level of the butchers whom royalty delighted to honour were the ex-groom, Sir John Lade, and his wife, her ladyship, whose accomplishments can be judged from the fact that "to swear like Letty Lade" passed into a proverb. "Hellgate," "Newgate," and "Cripplegate" were the names familiarised by the three Barrymore brothers. Their sister must have been a good second to Lady Lade, rejoicing as she did in the sobriquet of "Billingsgate." There were state processions, almost daily, from the Pavilion to the race-ground during the summer season. First in order came the royal barouche, or "German wagon" as it was then called, driven by Sir John Lade, with six bay horses. In it were Beau Brummel, the Duke of Bedford, Lord Jersey, Richard Brinsley Sheridan, frequently, and, less often, Charles James Fox. The gang included also more disreputable, if less notorious *roués*—the Duke of Rutland, Colonel St. Leger, Lord Headfort, Bradshaw, Sir William Curtis, the Lombard Street banker, the clever, good-looking Irish card-sharper, O'Byrne, who, at a single sitting at the Cocoa-tree Club, having won from Admiral Hervey £100,000, thought it well to lose back to his antagonist £90,000, that he might accept £10,000 in full payment of all demands. Mrs. Fitzherbert limited her duties at the Pavilion to doing its domestic honours, and seldom left its grounds. The Prince himself was conspicuous, in green jacket, white hat, tight nankeen pantaloons, and shoes. It was well that the high-bred manner and handsome presence of the "first gentleman in Europe" secured for these efforts to amuse his future subjects, the social and moral support of the pillars of the peerage. The Regent heard of his Chancellor, Lord Thurlow, being at Brighton ; he graciously announced his intention of calling on the keeper of the royal conscience. " Say to His Royal Highness," answered Thurlow, " I shall be honoured by his visit, and when he comes I hope he will leave his scum behind him." The most critical and consummate gourmet of the age, the Marquis de Sillery, also read his host of the Pavilion a little lecture of another kind. The Regent's hope that his guest had liked his repast elicited the remark, " No, sire, you have yet to learn how to dine ; I will try to teach you." The practical lesson learned by the Regent from accepting this offer was that the hours of eating, between three and nine, were better employed when there were never more than two dishes on the table at once. There was another great country-house figure of the period who gave as wide a berth to the Pavilion as Lord Thurlow. His person, manners, and conversation made Sir John Irwine the most universally coveted guest of his day. His native grace and dignity, set off by perfect dress with his ribbon and star, realised St. Simon's description of Louis the Fourteenth's most stately field-marshal. A brave general, he was also a heavy drinker and not ashamed. "They tell me, Sir John," said George III. to him, "that you love a glass of wine." Bowing deeply, Irwine answered, "Those, sir, who have so reported of me, have done me great injustice. They should have said a bottle." His friends, Lord Lake, who first broke the Mahratta power in India, and Admiral Payne, the ancestor of the turfite of the Victorian age, George Payne, both Pavilion *habitués*, were in vain commissioned by the Prince to secure Irwine as his guest.

The county in which we are still lingering, in perhaps unique abundance has produced, at different times, every kind of the English rural seat, amongst others that particular variety which, combining all that is most sumptuous and ornamental in Babylon with whatever is fragrantly decorative and characteristically costly in Arcadia, constitutes the smart country house of our own day. Without Stanmer, as has been seen, there might have been no Brighton. An undiscovered Brighton would have meant an unbuilt Pavilion. "Smartness" was cradled in the second Charles Stuart's Court. Without the Regent's Villa on the Sussex coast there would have been no eighteenth or early nineteenth century type of "smartness" out of town. Stanmer, therefore, has been remarkably prolific in its social offspring. Brighton and the Pavilion were both its

94

children. From these there later descended Bayham Abbey, Lamberhurst, and West Dean. Of these places the two former bring us to the Kent and Sussex frontier. Bayham, like Battle in the pre-Webster period, belonged to the Elizabethan Brownes. It became a fashionable centre when it passed to the ennobled branch of the Pratt family, the Camdens. The other mansion distinguishing Lamberhurst village, Wadhurst Hall, now belonging to Mr. Julius Drew, was in the last century a typical country house of the new order. The family and the name of Murietta figured prominently for many years in the chronicle of fashion. The brothers Murietta became synonyms for brilliancy of achievement on the polo-field and in every form of sport which cements together the various social or political sections constituting the polity of *ton*. In 1894 came the Baring crash. The Muriettas were submerged by it. Before that, however, the brothers of this family just referred to had converted their South of England home into a residential club for non-paying guests. One left the Orleans Club on the King's Road, Brighton, to find oneself, after a picturesque journey, in another club, better fitted up and located beneath a private roof. Wadhurst Hall, under the Murietta dispensation, formed the earliest instance of an English country home whose arrangements were modelled upon those of a fashionable restaurant or a Pall Mall club. To begin with, breakfast was served at any hour liked by the individual guest. As a fact, we most of us had it between eleven and twelve in an apartment which daily, till noon, looked like the coffee-room at a Metropole Hotel. For each one was a little table, presently spread, with more than club or hotel speed, with the English breakfast or the French *déjeûner*. West Dean is popularly regarded as having eclipsed Goodwood as the resting-place of royalty at the close of the season. To an earlier generation of sportsmen and sportswomen Goodwood House, as we have seen, seemed a social paradise on the rising of Parliament. When fashion and smartness began to be synonyms, something less remote from the modish caravanserai came into request. One of the special providences of polite life had established Mr. and Mrs. W. James at West Dean, a place socially so characteristic of the Edwardian age that it might have seemed the sudden growth of a single season. As a house, however, it existed in Stuart times. On the site of the present building there stood, at the opening of the seventeenth century, the family home of the Lewknors. By the usual vicissitudes of which the reader has seen so much, the estate went to the Peacheys while George IV. held his Court at the Pavilion. In 1804 West Dean was acquired by Lord Selsey, completely rebuilt by him and furnished with a frontage of three hundred feet. Through Lord Selsey's daughters it passed to the Vernon Harcourts, of Nuneham; by these it was sold to a China merchant, Frederick Bower, who in turn disposed of it to its present owner. Mr. W. James has made many improvements and additions. The original plan of the building, however, is still preserved; all the living rooms open one out of another on the same floor. If from some points of view a blamelessly refined fulfil-

ment of the best Pavilion ideal, this home of sweetness
and light is also a museum of beauty and art. The
pictures are good, the carpets and tapestry are the
union of rich magnificence and educated taste.

The host was famous with the big game of South
Africa long before Cecil Rhodes had exploited its
mines. The hall with its panelled ceiling and the
minstrel gallery are decorated with Libyan trophies
of the chase and, like the rest of the house, furnished
in the Louis XV. style. West Dean may be a more
perfect specimen than many others of the class to
which it belongs. Neither it nor they would have
achieved their reputation as mere monuments of
wisely expended wealth alone. Taste, tact, intelligence, accomplishments, and continual thought on the
part of the hostess form equally essential conditions of
their fashionable renown.

Mr. Michael Grace's Battle Abbey was conceded,
even by the historian Freeman, to occupy ground over
which Senlac Fight raged. Lord Brassey's Normanhurst looks down upon the entire length and breadth
of the authentic field, from the point where the
standard was set up to that where Harold fell.
Normanhurst, as may be gathered from its name,
marks the position occupied by the invading force.
Battle, on the other side of the little valley which
separated the two armies, more especially indicates the
Saxon ground, confronting the Norman positions, and
beyond them the long blue line of the Channel. No
situation could be more interestingly picturesque than
that of Normanhurst, or by its international associations better suited to the home of a family created by

The Fashionable South Downs

a man who has left his impress in characters equally clear upon all parts of England and France. The Cheshire farmer's son, the Thomas Brassey whose iron roads had become his enduring monument before the Victorian age began, died at Hastings in the last month of 1870. Thus the Sussex palace which, inhabited by the son, has acquired, within and beyond seas, a fame corresponding to that of the father's labours that formed its foundation, was to be viewed by the elder Brassey only in his dreams.

Twelve years before his death an event, equally interesting to France and England, had powerfully impressed the popular mind with the world-uniting influence of Thomas Brassey's work. On the 4th of August, 1858, the royal yacht *Victoria and Albert*, exactly at noon, came up with the French squadron that was to form the royal escort some six miles out at sea from Cherbourg breakwater. This visit of the Queen and the Prince-Consort with the future Edward VII., then a boy of seventeen, had long been looked forward to and was in all minds and lips. On his way from Paris to meet his English visitors Napoleon III. had opened the railway between Mantes and Cherbourg. In that line the Queen's subjects had taken an interest from the first, for, like the railway from Rouen to Havre, it had been designed by an English engineer and constructed by an English contractor; the former of these was Joseph Locke, the latter the founder of the Normanhurst family. As if to complete the line of communication with all parts of the earth, Thomas Brassey the second steered his yacht, the *Sunbeam*, into every

A New House as a Political Force

creek and corner of the oceans unfolded on our planet. It was not enough for him to bring home mementoes of his voyages that have given to 24, Park Lane, and to Normanhurst the look of annexes to the South Kensington Museum.

In due course, when the *Sunbeam* was again riding at its anchorage in English waters, Sir Thomas and Lady Brassey received in London, or more frequently on the south coast, the Empire's remotest citizens, who recognised in the Brassey name and its associations the emblem and the earnest of solidarity of the Anglo-Saxon race. With these mingled, of course, a crowd of other guests. In the summer of 1885 Mr. Gladstone had been cruising with the Brasseys in the North Sea. At this time suspicions of the Liberal leader's Home Rule proclivities were beginning to be rife. His letters to Lord Hartington filled that statesman with misgivings lest his own conviction of Irish affairs should result in a severance from his political chief. During this period Normanhurst remained in a ferment of agitation, and, like other of the new political houses, less splendid, the source of ceaseless rumours concerning compromise or arrangement between the leader and the led. At Normanhurst the Liberal stalwarts declared the party would be saved, and in 1886 the "Grand Old Man" made Tom Brassey a lord. In 1895 immediate danger to Imperial unity seemed to have blown over. The State could spare the master of Normanhurst for a time to the governorship of Victoria. Whatever his party ties or Imperial preoccupations, the owner of the south coast palace never neglected the duties of a literary and

The Fashionable South Downs

artistic Mæcenas. The older generation of writers was represented among the Brassey guests by the reputed original of Warrington in " Pendennis," George Stovin Venables ; by Augustus Hare, of the Hares of Hurstmonceux, already described, then settled at Holmhurst, Hastings, the most variously accomplished, the most socially omniscient of the country-house " tame-cats " of his time, ready wherever he might meet her, at Normanhurst or elsewhere, to cap the venerable and voluble Mrs. Duncan-Stewart's best peerage stories and personal reminiscences ; by " Big Higgins," otherwise Matthew, the " Jacob Omnium " of the *Times*, of the *Cornhill Magazine* in its infancy ; by John Ormsby, the Spanish traveller and scholar ; by two other pillars of the *Saturday Review* under Douglas Cook—H. S. Maine, the author of " Ancient Law," and Charles Austin, some-time Fellow of St. John's, Oxford, who, in one of his Saturday articles, had devised for the *Daily Telegraph*, when an infant print, the adhesive label of " Jupiter Junior." At Normanhurst also Laurence Oliphant made one of his occasional reappearances in society, and a younger author, in something like Oliphant's vein, Mr. W. H. Mallock, philosophically wearing the laurels of his " New Republic," showed himself as the literary lion of the London season. Never did so much of visible delight beam forth from the features of an aged artist as when at Normanhurst, like the " Ancient Mariner," he held spellbound by his glittering eye a knot of ladies captive to his tongue. J. R. Herbert, R.A., had really persuaded himself that his native land was not Wales, but Gaul. He pronounced his name in the Gallic fashion, as if "Air-bair," and affected a broken English in his talk. A fervently devout Catholic, he had recently seen in the Oxford Bodleian an old manuscript on the Magdalen. This discovery hurried him off to the mountain hermitage of St. Maximin in Provence, where, according to tradition, the sainted sinner died. In a glass case on the altar was the Magdalen's skull; by special favour Herbert was allowed to take it in his hand. He thus adoringly saw the outline of the profile of "our Lord's dear friend herself." A vivacious young lady among the artist's listeners at Normanhurst wanted to know how one could be sure of all this. "How can one help it," was the pained reply, "when it is all written in the Acts of the Apostles?"

"Will make the best maiden speech of his year, have his pockets clean picked by the Turk, and die in a Paris slum without a sou in his pocket." So, as he rode down to a Harrow speech-day, did Lord Palmerston prophesy to his companion concerning a young Oxford man who had got into Parliament in 1857. The prediction fulfilled itself nearly to the letter. H. A. Monro Butler-Johnstone, shortly after taking his seat for Canterbury, received Disraeli's congratulations on his oratorical *début* with the cleverest discourse about foreign policy which the great man had heard for many a long day. He squandered his princely wealth upon the Sultan and his *entourage*. Towards the close of the nineteenth century he did breathe his last, not in an absinthe shop, but in a pharmacy on the boulevards, with nothing about him to pay his funeral expenses. The

subject of this literally fulfilled prediction at the time
of its making was a young man with an intellectual
countenance, not otherwise particularly well favoured,
with narrow chest, almost indeed none at all, and
generally with the physique of the thread-paper.
During the earlier seventies he was a frequent guest at
another Sussex country house, not far from Normanhurst. This was Sir Julian Goldsmid's Fairlight.
Owning a substantial slice of Brighton, Goldsmid
reserved his hospitalities at his house in Adelaide
Crescent in that town for the most distinguished of
his political friends and sometimes even of his foes. It
was upon one of those visits that Lord Beaconsfield,
revisiting, after many years, with his host, the Old
Steine, remarked : " Every great city is the embodi-
ment of a great idea ; every town of pleasure should
be the expression of a caprice ; but," he added, "for
me, like most people of maturer years, the memories
of this place make it rather too like a cemetery by
the sea." As the pair extended their ramble westward, the guest stopped for a moment before the
house in Brunswick Terrace, where he mentally
located the card-party—one of his most powerful
bits of descriptive writing in " The Young Duke."
"Yes," he said, in meditative reference to the scene,
" there it was that, for two days and two nights on
end, the Baron de Berghem sat ankle-deep in cards,
no one speaking a word or showing any sign of
emotion till Temple Dice could not prevent an
expression of disgust when he found that a false
tooth had got loose." At Sir Julian Goldsmid's,
the Etonian Butler-Johnstone met a Parliamentary

Ralph Earle and Disraeli

contemporary whose Harrow promise rivalled Johnstone's own Eton performances. This was Ralph Earle, a prodigy of political precocity and Parliamentary promise while a sixth-form boy at Harrow ; Earle, however, had too strong a suggestion in him of the Randal Leslie, in " My Novel," for the prejudices of his time and too much ambition of independent initiative to suit his chief ; he really possessed something of his master's aptitude for turning fact into fiction by the employment of qualities that recalled the Italian state-craft and conspiracy of the Middle Ages. " If intellectual power, decked out by subtlety and finesse, could have made a great career, Ralph Earle," said Disraeli, " would have been a success, instead of being as brilliant a failure as his friend Lord Henry Lennox, without Henry's eloquence." No man was ever less fitted for a deliberative assembly than Ralph Earle ; none had ever sacrificed so much to get there. Disraeli, the object of his early idolatry, chanced to meet him when an *attaché* at the Paris Embassy, took a fancy to him, and eventually found him a seat in the Commons, a place at the Board of Control, and made him his private secretary. The last of these positions realised Earle's fondest dreams. Those were the days in which the " Coningsby " series of novels filled clever and showy lads with Parliamentary ambitions, just as Thackeray's " Pendennis " sent others into journalism, or James Grant's, Charles Lever's, and Captain Marryat's romances impelled others into the army or to sea. The acute attack of Disraeli-on-the-brain eventually proved fatal to Ralph Earle's career. The months occupied by the Derby-Disraeli Household Franchise Bill of 1867 were a period of plot and counter-plot, of secret machination, of open desertion by followers from leaders on both sides. As a relief to the uncongenial rough-and-tumble work of Parliamentary warfare, Earle's temperament impelled him to negotiation with the malcontents, Liberal as well as Conservative. These connections brought him into hostility against the scheme of democratic enfranchisement, and so into conflict with his patron as one of its authors. At last he got up in the House and openly denounced Disraeli for his betrayal of Tory principles. Disraeli, sitting in contemptuous silence, took no notice whatever of the attack. Leaving the place soon afterwards, the great man met one of his private secretaries, a peer. " I am not," was his sole comment on the incident, "surprised at the moral aspect of the thing, for I knew the man too well ; I confess, however, to have been taken a little aback by the stupidity of the performance." The statesman, who had withdrawn Earle from the diplomatic employment, which exactly fitted his powers and tastes, to the entirely unsuitable Parliamentary field, could, of course, politically crush his former *protégé ;* he could not, however, crush the brilliant personality of the versatile rebel, nor prevent his finding a new and pecuniarily profitable career in which Earle's diplomatic and Parliamentary experience were turned to good account. At the time of his being a guest at Fairlight he had bested all competitors as a negotiator of concessions from foreign Governments to English capitalists and contractors for public works. Helped, it may have been, by the great mercantile position of the Liverpool family whose name he bore, he amassed in this way a small fortune, leaving behind him not much less than half a million, greatly to his friends' and family's surprise. It was characteristic of the man's curious reserve that, with large sums at his bankers', when, in his last illness, going off to a German spa, as if to allay any suspicion of his real resources he asked his father to lend him £50.

To a younger generation in politics or diplomacy represented among the Fairlight guests, belongs the most intelligent, resourceful, and *répandu* of Foreign Office clerks of his day, now on the staff of the British Embassy in Paris, and a member of the Suez Canal Board, Sir H. Austin Lee, as well as the shrewdest and most genial of Scotch baronets, successively secretary to Lord Goschen and Mr. Gladstone, Sir James Carmichael. Other guests presenting a gravely picturesque contrast to the cosmopolitan company, sometimes surprised the Fairlight visitors. Doctor E. M. Goulburn, the Balliol contemporary of Jowett, Lake, and Stanley, a former Rugby head-master, afterwards Dean of Norwich, passing his last days at Tonbridge Wells, with his silver hair as a veritable crown of glory, was tempted more than once to the Fairlight dinner-table. To keep him in countenance came another cleric of his generation, the Rev. James Pycroft, erectly bearing the burden of his many years to the last, whose book, "The Cricket-field," made him a father of nineteenth-century literature on the game. Both these clergy-

men, during the years they lived at Brighton, had
first known there Julian Goldsmid as their ground
landlord. Additional variety was given to these
parties by two or three of the most remarkable old
ladies who, in unabated vivacity, ever survived
their generation. One of these, a dowager Lady
Donoughmore, abounded in Irish stories. "My good
woman," said a very stiff and starched, severe-looking
English settler in Galway to a Connaught mendicant,
"I haven't a penny to give you." "No, but your
honour looks like to die soon ; you've an awful ugly
face, I pity the poor worms that will have to eat
you." From Brighton, where she might be staying
with Mrs. Aïdé, occasionally came over a lady whose
apparition reminded many of Cinderella's godmother
or of some other good old fairy. This was the
Mrs. Duncan Stewart, who invariably opened her
anecdotal series with a Disraelian story really in the
great man's manner. "I hope you are quite well,
Lord Beaconsfield," she had said. "No one is *quite*
well," responded the oracle ; "I am tolerably well."
Mrs. Stewart piqued herself on being of the present
as well as on having a memory articulate with
phonographs of the past. Among her most modern
acquaintances were the actress, Miss Genevieve
Ward, and her mother. "Strange," some one had
said, "that this handsome and stately actress should
remain single." "She is nothing of the kind," put
in Mrs. Stewart, "and this is the story of her
marriage. A Russian nobleman, Count Guerra,
had made her an offer, had been accepted, but
indefinitely delayed or point-blank refused marriage.

Mrs. Duncan Stewart on Miss Anderson

The Czar, appealed to on the lady's behalf, induced his noble to prove himself faithful to his troth. "Good," was the Count's comment; "but my wife shall suffer for it all her life." On the day of the ceremony, the bride, as if dressed for a funeral, entered the church with her mother. On leaving the church after the nuptial service had been gone through, the newly made wife was hurried into a carriage by herself, a titular countess without her count. She never saw her husband again." An undercurrent of more or less serious thought seemed to flow beneath Mrs. Stewart's show of conversational frivolity. She often talked about her interest in a future state. "Whichever it is to be, I have," she would say, "good friends in both places." Another of the Fairlight guests, old Lady Airlie, united something like Mrs. Stewart's years with conversation of a very different kind. "As a child," she said, "I was one of a decidedly quarrelsome family, but we were taught that it was ill-bred towards Heaven to complain, even of the weather." This lady had known the Carlyles intimately, Unlike some, she had never found the Chelsea sage other than agreeable with his acquaintances and pleasant to his wife. "To know," she continued, "Lady Ashburton was to adore her; I, like others, worshipped her. So did not only Carlyle, but Mrs. Carlyle, jealous of her though she was." Occasionally the Fairlight drawing-room supplied a specimen of the æsthete as Dumaurier was then drawing him in *Punch*. His dress was a complete suit of black velvet and salmon-coloured stockings;

The Fashionable South Downs

he joined the shooting party, but he generally fell down when the gun went off.   That, however, did not prevent his charming the ladies.   " You do not look well, Mr. Maudle," said one of these. " Thanks; I am not ill, only tired.   The fact is I picked a primrose in the wood yesterday; it seemed sick, and I have been sitting up all night with it." It may have been one of the divines already mentioned who contributed an episcopal story which seemed new to the Fairlight conversation.   The Bishop of London, having given a cabman only sixpence over his fare from St. Paul's Churchyard to Fulham, was asked by the driver whether St. Paul, if he came again, would be living in that palace.   " Certainly not," came the answer, " he would be at Lambeth, and it would be a shilling fare."   The already mentioned Mrs. Duncan Stewart, one of the most regular among the Fairlight guests, posed as a patroness of writers and painters, but uttered sharp criticism about both.   James Whistler was then at his zenith.   "His pictures," said the lady, "always look to me as if he had upset the ink-pot and left Providence to work out the result." One little entertainment always provided for the Fairlight guests was unique.   The excellent cook, an Italian, had also a perfect mastery of sleight of hand.   After dinner the chef, attired as a conjuror, performed with hats, handkerchiefs, watches, rings, and playing-cards tricks that recalled the Egyptian Hall in its prime.

CHAPTER IV

ERIDGE AND THE KENTISH GANG

WHAT the Bloomsbury Gang was under George III., the Kentish Gang became and remained during the second half of the Victorian age. The earlier *côterie* took its name from the

Eridge and the Kentish Gang

Duke of Bedford's London house ; the later from the fact that its rural headquarters were at Eridge Castle on the Kent and Sussex borderland, and that the most active of its earlier members were connected with the county of hop-fields and cherry-orchards. The most strenuous spirit of the Bloomsbury cabal, the Marquis of Stafford, survived to 1823. Three years after that date the light was first seen by the *generalissimo* of the Eridge division, the fifth Earl of Abergavenny, who, appropriately enough, in the year of Benjamin Disraeli's transformation into Earl of Beaconsfield, 1876, became the first Marquis of Abergavenny. " Burgeny " was the way in which Lord Burleigh wrote it when penning his account of Queen Elizabeth's six days' stay, in 1573. For more than five hundred years the ennobled Nevills have been settled at Eridge. The first marquis of his line is also the first of his name since George Nevill, third Baron of Raby, to append the initials K.G. to his name. Just a century before the present owner of Eridge attained his majority, his ancestor, the earliest of the Abergavenny earls, filled his family at home with sore misgivings during a certain Easter vacation. In the April of 1747 a disagreeable incident occurred at the Oxford college, in which Lord Abergavenny was passing his rackety undergraduate-ship. At the foot of the staircase on which were his lordship's rooms, there was found one morning the dead body of a servant with a fractured skull. " Wilful homicide " was not alleged against the noble student and his companions—the chief of these being Lord Charles Scott of the Buccleuch family. Every one seems to have been more or less tipsy; the probability is that one of the noble gownsmen kicked the fellow downstairs. The man was too drunk to fall discreetly, and so his end. Without any reference, however implicit, to the Oxonian from Eridge, the coroner's jury brought in the verdict of "wilful murder, against a person or persons unknown." The head of the family took, however, rather a severe view of the escapade; his son and heir did not keep the next University term; his college days, indeed, seem to have come to an abrupt end. The "My Lord Burgeny's house," visited by the great Tudor queen, was, of course, not that inhabited by his successors in the family honours. The aspect of the present nineteenth-century built castle contains no suggestion of the Nevills' feudal greatness. The castellated tradition is perpetuated by the square tower that surmounts the dwelling, rather than by an imposing front of battlements. That which most impressed Burleigh when attending his royal mistress at Eridge was the grand variety of its park scenery. This remains its most commanding feature to-day, and the Eridge rocks are as perfect and imposing to-day as when they where first admired by the Elizabethan courtiers.

Before the first Marquis of Abergavenny became the master of Eridge Castle, he had taken under his special protection the renascent Conservatism of his time. Asked by a neighbouring Sussex agriculturist, in sympathy with the Eridge politics, whether his lordship had a good head on his shoulders, a Kentish farmer replied he could not

Eridge and the Kentish Gang

tell, for he had only seen that nobleman twice in his life, and that out of doors. On both occasions, it seemed, the master of Eridge was kneeling down, and had thrust all his person above his shoulders into a rabbit-hole, for ascertaining whether a ferret was doing its work properly inside. From earliest boyhood a working sportsman in every branch of out-door amusement, Lord Nevill had mingled with tenant farmers and their men in every kind of open-air sport. In this he did but follow the example of his family's founder, the mediæval king-maker. To win the commonalty on any subject to his own patrician side he believed, with the "last of the barons," that there was nothing like letting his inferiors know and feel the great noble to be of the same clay as themselves and a sharer in their tastes. Long before the Conservative Household Suffrage Bill of 1867 became law, or had even been introduced, the heir to the Abergavenny earldom never for a moment doubted the existence of the Conservative working man. The 1868 elections gave the Liberals a majority of nearly 130 for disestablishing the Irish Church. Disraeli's resignation had scarcely been followed by Gladstone's instalment in the premiership when Lord Nevill, frequenting the London music-halls for the better observation of the political signs of the times, saw conclusive evidence of the reaction being already fairly on foot. For the peerage generally " the press " used to mean the *Times* alone. Enlightened on these matters by its most serviceable guest, Mr Markham Spofforth, Eridge

Genesis of the Junior Carlton

Castle first discovered that "the party" had a natural ally and a most effective instrument in the penny newspaper. By this time Lord Nevill had developed into the fifth Earl of Abergavenny. Eridge became as much the symbol and the shelter of the new and progressive Conservatism as Mr. Markham Spofforth's Inverness cape. Yet it really seemed but the other day that the fourteenth Lord Derby had appealed to Eridge to remonstrate with the Kentish Gang on its lukewarm loyalty to Benjamin Disraeli. "Pity that you could not find an Englishman," grumbled the Nevill division. "He is exactly like the new ostler at the Tunbridge Wells inn," who was, of course, afterwards always known as "Dizzy." As for the real Dizzy, Eridge had begun by cold-shouldering him; it was there, however, that he was first recognised by the party Brahmins as the one man whose genius could convert the new democracy to the old Tory faith. Throughout these operations the political master of the ceremonies at Eridge, the already named Mr. Spofforth, the Conservative election manager had made himself invaluable. Equally good with the gun and the billiard-cue, this clear and level-headed lawyer had shown his good Yorkshire wits in mastering the urban democracy created by the 1867 Bill, as thoroughly as his fellow-countrymen know the points of a horse. One product of the Spofforth visits to Eridge was the foundation of the Junior Carlton Club. It happened in this way. The steady spread of the new Conservatism brought a flood of applications, chiefly from country solicitors, for membership of the Carlton. That club was then overcrowded. The Conservative Club in St. James's Street closed its doors against "gentlemen of the long gown." Coming up from Eridge one morning, Mr. Spofforth called on Disraeli, then leader in the Commons, at his house in Grosvenor Gate. "A capital idea," was the verdict; "see Lord Derby" (then Premier). To St. James's Square the visitor accordingly at once went. "I approve," were the peer's words, "on condition that the curtain does not rise before the house is full." At first members came in rather more slowly than might have been expected. The applications soon increased by leaps and bounds. As Mr. Spofforth had foreseen, the completed new institution soon furnished Conservatism with the most powerful corporation it had known since, in 1832, the efforts of an earlier Tory wire-puller had been instrumental in bringing into existence the parent Carlton itself.

For some years later than the time now referred to, Eridge maintained its old authority; the Kentish Gang parted with none of its power. A Kentish baronet, Sir W. Hart Dyke, of Lullingstone Castle, was one of the whips. Mr. Spofforth, indeed, had for some time given up the work of election management. It was a Kentish member, Mr. J. E. Gorst (Chatham), who ruled in his place, himself to be followed by another Kentish organiser of victory, Mr. R. W. E. Middleton. The master of Eridge continued to play a chief part in all matters touching the internal discipline of the party down to the last quarter of the nineteenth century. Dissatisfaction with Sir Stafford Northcote's languid leadership began to organise itself below the Conservative gangway in 1880, while Lord Beaconsfield still lived. Eridge in council decided that discipline must be maintained. From the Castle issued to Lord Randolph Churchill the mandate that those who aspire to rule must first learn to obey. Not that the master of the Kentish pack objected to a reasonable amount of sport. In 1884 it was the Castle henchmen rather than the Whitehall or even the Carlton contingent which put pressure on Lord Salisbury to insist upon having the scheme of county suffrage before him in its entirety as a condition of accepting the principle of the Bill. How the Eridge ultimatum was met by the Longleat negotiations will be seen in the Wiltshire visits that we are about to make. The authority thus exercised by Eridge in modern politics may have been enhanced by the dignity of age belonging to its associations, if not to the actual edifice. Before the Norman conquest its ten thousand acres of park land had belonged to Earl Godwin, King Harold's father. Afterwards it remained a royal possession till Edward III., who granted it to Hugh Despencer. His heiress, by her marriage with Richard Beauchamp, Earl of Worcester, brought it to the Nevills. To-day the Nevill domain extends almost uninterruptedly to Lewes and Brighton. Of this vast tract, a large slice came, not from the Despencers, but from the De Warrens, whose daughters " acred up to the chin " their respective husbands of the Beauchamp, Howard, and Sackville name. The commandership-in-chief of

Eridge and the Kentish Gang

the Kentish Gang comes to the owner of Eridge originally from the Norman Conqueror's brother, Odo, bishop of Bayeux, whose endowment with the Kentish manor of Birling gave him that foothold in the county which was to form the territorial germ of the political suzerainty of Eridge.

The place of Kent in English politics had been a distinguished one long before the Eridge pheasant covers became famous. The organisation of a Kentish Gang had indeed begun while the Bloomsbury Gang was yet in the plenitude of its power. The political antidote and rival to Bedford Whiggism proceeded from the Kentish country house just out of Bromley village. Hayes Place, dear equally to both the Pitts, was united by the closest links with the life or death history of Chatham and his son ; it enjoyed a celebrity with eighteenth-century Englishmen rivalling that attached by the religious Greek to Delphi or Dodona. "The oracle at Hayes," writes Horace Walpole (March 26, 1778), "has been consulted, but shrouds its dignity in ambiguity ; the god himself takes the form of his own Pythoness, enveloped in flannels, that are the symbols of vast vigour of mind beneath." This was the period in which there were being submitted to Chatham names for vacant offices of State. " Whether Lord Rockingham shall go to Ireland, the Duke of Richmond shall be this, Charles Fox shall be t'other, Mr. Burke shall be something else, &c., &c., after, of course, Lord Camden, Lord Shelburne, the Duke of Grafton, Barré and Dunning have been appointed to the essential posts." Chatham bought Hayes from the

Holwood and the Pitts

Harrison family in 1757; the new house that he built is the plain structure in white brick still standing. Originally, however, the walls were of stone. The outer brick shell was the work of Thomas Walpole, who possessed the place for a few years, but restored it at a price, in 1767, to its original owner. His own improvements of the grounds so endeared the place to the first Pitt as to grow into his very being. The belts of trees, with which he surrounded the dwelling, have not yet disappeared. The story of these plantations is familiar. They were raised with a rapidity till then unknown. Night was not allowed to interrupt the work. With the help of torches, successive relays of labourers continued their toil through the hours of darkness to the dawn of day. Associations of Chatham's son are not confined to Hayes, where he was born, bred, and lived. At a distance of two miles, close to Keston village, are the grassy undulations and woods of Holwood Park. Here was the scene of the birds'-nesting expeditions of the younger Pitt, recalled to the poet Rogers by Lord Bathurst who used to take part in them. Here, too, it was that, walking with his son, Chatham impressed on him the need of prudence, with the remark, " Recollect when you have grown up, it is not you, but your brother, who will be Lord Chatham "; " But," rejoined the spirited lad, " I shall be William Pitt." " That," pointing to Holwood House, " is the place I mean some day shall be mine." Such had been the words of Chatham's second son to Bathurst. It was not, as has been said, at a tea-table on the Holwood lawn that the second Pitt, then living in the house, had discussed slave-trade abolition with his friend William Wilberforce. William Wilberforce's son, the bishop, who will afterwards appear in these pages, pointed out to the present writer in Holwood Park, where it begins to descend into Keston Vale, the very oak-tree beneath whose shade the outlines of the measure were settled between the two friends in 1788. At a later date, in 1863, when occupied by Lord Cranworth, Holwood was the scene of many conversations between its then owner and his guest Lord Westbury about the " Essays and Reviews " judgment. Westbury was then Chancellor ; before delivering his judgment on ʿthe subject, he talked it over with Cranworth under the Holwood trees. A later tradition identifies the same place with the spot on which Benjamin Disraeli and W. E. Gladstone met for the last time as personal friends. A more authentic tradition, however, gives Lord Derby's house in St. James's Square as the site of the incident.

The most famous of country houses in this neighbourhood is connected by the ties of personal association and family connection equally with Hayes and Holwood. Chevening Park was the home of Lord Chatham's daughter, the third Countess Stanhope, the wife of the democratic Earl, known indifferently as " Citizen Stanhope " and " Citizen Charles." It was thus the haunt of her daughter, the famous Lady Hester Stanhope, before the future Queen of the Lebanon began to keep house for her uncle, William Pitt the second,

Chatham Memorials at Chevening

in Downing Street. The picturesque road, winding
through the Park up to the brow of the opposite
hill, was made at Chatham's suggestion. The
house inside contains some Pitt relics not yet
catalogued in the guide-gooks. Thus there is the
elder Pitt's portrait, painted for Chevening at the
instance of Sibyl, the second Countess. Of
Chatham's son there remain the despatch-box in
which his papers were always carried to the House,
the original manuscript of a play in blank verse,
"Laurentius," written by the future statesman at
the age of thirteen, and twice acted at Chevening
exclusively by members of the Pitt family. There
is also a locket containing the younger Pitt's hair,
which formerly belonged to his devoted niece,
the imperial Lady Hester; of her, however, most
of the Chevening memorials have disappeared.
One link of union between Chevening and the
outside world was severed in the last quarter of
the eighteenth century when the road traversed
by Chaucer's wayfarers was closed and the Pilgrims'
Trackway, running westward across the Park,
ceased to be trodden by the general public.
Among the Chevening parties given by the historian,
the fifth Lord Stanhope, none surpassed in eventful
interest that with which the New Year opened in
1860. Three days before, the historian Macaulay
had died at Holly Lodge, Kensington. Of all
Lord Stanhope's friends he had been the most
intimate. The Chevening influence at once set
itself in motion therefore to secure for the dead
writer a place in Westminster Abbey. Henry Reeve,

editor of the *Edinburgh*, Abraham Hayward, Goldwin Smith, George Grote, the historian of Greece, with his irrepressible wife, were among the first to sign their names in the Chevening library to a round-robin, begging the dean to assign a place within the august precinct. There, on the following 9th of January, the funeral took place. Under three dynasties, like the London roof of the family in Grosvenor Place, Chevening has been famous as a guest house throughout Europe and on both sides of the Atlantic. Its cosmopolitan renown began before the then Lord Mahon had finished his history. It was augmented after he had come into the title. It was perpetuated by his successor; under him, indeed, the interest of the Chevening hospitalities was widened ; his brother, Edward Stanhope, when Colonial Secretary, brought with him to the place a constant succession of visitors from Greater Britain.

As regards both antiquity and diversity of historic interest or personal association, the neighbouring Knole does not yield to Chevening. Almost a part of English literature, Knole specially connects itself with the revival of English poetry and poetic genius, after having been almost crushed out during the Marian persecutions. To that depression, indeed, other than religious agencies contributed. English literature was then strongly under Italian influence. The spirit of melancholy, breathed by Petrarch and his most widely-read disciples, possessed the charm of congeniality for an age steeped in the religious gloom, or at least in the sombre pensiveness

Knole as an Intellectual Force

of the Reformation. In England, too, the air was heavily charged with the moral issues of theology as well as of politics. The lighter forces of the renaissance had spent themselves. The fates and furies rather than the muses seemed the presiding divinities of the period. Even thus might not a popular appetite be created for poetry which, while not less historically representative than Chaucer's, should adapt its music to the sterner tune of a vexed time. Such were the considerations and questions often present to the mind of the then owner of Knole. The very murmur of the trees in his park, during his solitary rambles, seemed, in his own words, "charged with strange, sad melodies." Could he but interpret and express these aright, the result might be verses which should form a link between Chaucer and Spenser, which his contemporaries would be compelled, and which posterity would be instructed or delighted to read. He had already made for himself a place among the dramatists of the day. Thomas Sackville now conceived the idea of essaying for his own time, in the Chaucerian stanza, what had been done by the father of British verse for an earlier age. The ideas, the aspirations, the lessons. and the chief personages of Tudor times were to be reflected by the Elizabethan minister in his book, which was to be a link between "The Canterbury Tales" and "The Faerie Queene." Thomas Sackville, afterwards to be known as Lord Buckhurst, High Treasurer, had, in 1562, won literary fame at Court by his "Gorboduc," the earliest English tragedy in blank

121

verse. It was then the fashion for noble and wealthy
courtiers to entertain their sovereign with theatrical
representations beneath their own roofs. Queen
Elizabeth is known to have witnessed and admired
this play. The performance, at which she assisted,
may therefore have been given at Knole, then,
as for years afterwards, the finest country house
in Kent belonging to a commoner. Spenser knew
it well; having, as he courteously said, got the idea
of his " Faerie Queene " from the " Mirror for
Magistrates," he pleasantly spoke of his own great
poem as in a way a product of Knole. For the
sixteenth-century owner of the place, Sackville's
father, though holding high financial office under
Henry VIII., was not noble, either by title or even
associations. He had married the daughter of
Lord Mayor Bruges. His Kentish home was famous
as a resort of city magnates or of State officials
with city connections before, in his son's day, the
founders of English prose, Francis Bacon and
Walter Raleigh, among poets, Ben Jonson and
Edmund Spenser, met at the Knole dining-table.
The place then acquired some of the special
distinction already belonging to Penshurst. Not
overvaluing themselves on their large share in
the great transactions of their time, the masters of
Knole were pleasant and kindly hosts, fond of
having their neighbours of all degrees about them,
specially interested in young people, ever making
friends among posterity by their kindness to children.
The sixteenth - century country houses may have
known no formal visitors' book. Famous guests

were in the habit, for the instruction of future ages, of leaving behind them some tribute to their host's qualities. This might take the form of an epigram, a stanza, or a prose sentiment. Sir Philip Sidney, on leaving Knole, attached to a copy of his host's "Mirror for Magistrates" a prose compliment to its notable morality. Spenser, a more frequent visitor, dropped a metrical panegyric on the private virtues of "its truly noble author." "Who," he exclaims, "more loving to his wife, more tender to his little ones, more fast to his friend, more moderate to his enemy, more true to his word?" Buckhurst died the first Earl of Dorset. His grandson must have degenerated from the cool, practical sagacity of his Tudor ancestors. The third Lord Dorset was conspicuous among the country hosts of his time for two things—the magnificence of his life and the frequency of his duels. The former brought him to poverty ; the latter to his death. He had already sold his Kentish estate to a certain Smith of Wandsworth. By a process that has been euphemistically described as repurchase, but that seems to have been merely a resumption due to favour in high places, his grandson, the fifth Lord Dorset, restored Knole to the family. Afterwards he became the first representative of the short-lived Dorset dukedom. The third Duke's widow married Lord Whitworth, successively English ambassador to Russia and France. This marriage made the modern Knole the resort of diplomatic society. From Knole first went forth Whitworth's account of his interview with Napoleon, which produced an explosion of national feeling against the French Emperor. Napoleon's insults had been levelled personally, not only against the ambassador whom he charged with complicity in the murder of the Czar, Paul I., but against the English people.

"I find you've got Delawarr on your list; pray don't lick him, for he is a brother peer." So, with a Harrow monitor named Wildman, interceded the youthful Byron, vainly of course; for the poet's luckless friend promptly received a double dose of the monitorial cane. Byron's chum was George John, the fifth Lord Delawarr. Another of the poet's school-fellows of Knole associations was the fourth and last Duke of Dorset, often visited at Knole by Byron. This final wearer of the dukedom, killed by a fall from his horse (1815), left the estate to his sister, Lady Mary Sackville. Dying in 1864, she bequeathed all share in the property to another sister, her co-heiress, Lady Elizabeth Sackville. This lady not only became by marriage Countess of Delawarr, but was created Baroness Buckhurst. Her son thus added the barony of Buckhurst to the Delawarr earldom. That peer, by his brilliant service in India under Lord Gough, as well as during the Crimean campaign at Alma, Balaclava, and Inkerman, associated the modern Sackvilles with the chivalry and diplomacy of his own age, after a manner becoming to their sixteenth-century traditions. His brother and successor was a clergyman, with a sober but sincere loyalty to the picturesque ancestral genius of his house. Benjamin Disraeli, when visiting Henry Hope at the Deep Dene in Surrey, frequently went on to his friends the Sackvilles at Knole. Thus, perhaps, he became familiar with the name he selected for one of his characters in "Coningsby." The " Buckhurst " of that novel was, in fact, none other than the Baillie Cochrane who died Lord Lamington, and whose daughter became seventh Lady Delawarr. In, and for some years after, 1850, no resort of society in the Sevenoaks district was visited by more variously interesting guests than Knole. A Lord Cantelupe of that period had died of rheumatic fever. A frequent visitor at the place, Lord Malmesbury, the Foreign Secretary, stricken by the same malady, had recovered on a country doctor treatment of calomel and strong alkalis—the heir of Knole having been plied by the fashionable medicine-men with acids, principally lemon-juice. Dr. Quin, the skilfully eclectic and unprecedentedly popular physician, was then at his fashionable zenith, curing patients, more by the charm of his manner and the wholesome suggestiveness of his talk, than by his prescriptions. He seldom missed a week's end party at Knole. The gatherings in which he took part and the beneficent practical interest of the hosts did much to bring the modern cult of the doctor and the nurse into fashion. At the same time Knole gradually became a recognised social rendezvous for critical experts of foreign policy on both sides of the House. Whiteside, overflowing with animal spirits and Irish humour, meditated his oratorical *coups* in Knole Park. Here the future Lord Cairns had for the companion of his morning strolls the cleverest and most animated Irish member of the day, Seymour Fitzgerald, who sat for Horsham, and who primed the most brilliant *frondeur* of his period, the third Sir Robert Peel, of the trumpet-like voice and the magnificent gestures, with the latest news about the Danish duchies or the annexation of Savoy and Nice. With Peel was "Eothen" Kinglake, ever preparing the most subtle and dainty studies on these subjects, to be poured forth as resonantly effective declamations by that son of his first leader, whom Gladstone credited with the finest organ in the St. Stephen's of his day. Penshurst and Raby have never fully renewed the hospitable splendours of their mediæval meridian. Knole, however, throughout the Victorian age, continued to be a social centre as interesting in its way, if not as illustrious, as in Elizabethan days. Ismail Pasha failed, indeed, to induce his host to give him the opportunity of meeting either Lord Beaconsfield or Lord Salisbury. But, as Lord Delawarr's guest in the last century, that astute and agreeable Oriental delighted his fellow-guests at Knole with a humorous acceptance of ill-luck and a debonair gaiety which never failed him in the darkest moment of transition from splendour to obscurity or shame during the parti-coloured melodramatic course that might have been a plagiarism from the stage of opera-bouffe. That happy quality elicited from another guest at Knole, Sir William Howard Russell, the remark: " Behold an Oriental whose philosophy blends the fatalism of the Koran with the resignation of the New Testament."

Social contrasts, as dramatically different and ex-

tending over about as long a period as those of
Knole, have been witnessed at another Kentish
seat, Hever Castle, the birthplace of Anne Boleyn.
Hever at some points of its history illustrated the
sanguinary cynicism which was among the moral
endowments of Anne's royal husband. Waiting till the
death of his father-in-law, Sir Thomas Boleyn, then
Earl of Wiltshire, Henry VIII. claimed the property
in right of the wife he had beheaded. Having
thus possessed himself of the estate, he settled it
upon one of Anne Boleyn's successors in his con-
jugal affections. In the last quarter of the eighteenth
century and in a very different connection, Hever
Castle became a familiar name to visitors to the
Royal Academy of Art and to readers of *Punch*.
Attracted by the unique preservation of its most
ancient and characteristic features, by the diversified
beauty of the building, by its portcullised entrance,
above all by the surrounding moat, so redolent of
mediævalism, a little company of artists, including
at least two future P.R.A.'s,—Millais and Poynter—
rented the place for their summer holiday. Among
their visitors, two were conspicuously frequent.
One of these was Charles Dickens, then dividing
his time between Broadstairs and Gad's Hill the
other was one of Mark Lemon's latest recruits on
the *London Charivari*, who afterwards succeeded
to his chair. While looking one Saturday evening
before dinner, with Millais at his side, into the moat
Dickens conceived the idea of that mystery of
"Edwin Drood" which he did not live to solve.
About the same time, F. C. Burnand, then writing

or meditating " Happy Thoughts " for *Punch*, found inspiration for droll paragraphs with the natal stronghold of Queen Elizabeth's mother as their centre. The contrasts of owners and visitors witnessed at Hever are typical of those experienced by more than one equally historical and picturesque house in the southern counties. Hever of late years has been so often let, notably to the artistic tenants already mentioned, that one cannot be surprised at the periodical, though as yet unfounded reports of its being for sale. The same thing is, however, said about another Kentish mansion that has seldom or never been in any occupancy, except of its owners. Leeds Castle, near Maidstone, resembles many or most of the south of England fortresses in its past associations with English queens. Before her imprisonment at Pevensey Joan of Navarre, wife of Henry IV., found herself a compulsory guest at Leeds. Among other queens, Katharine of Aragon lived here. The unsolicited hospitalities of the place were also extended by its tenant, the diarist Evelyn, to six hundred Dutchmen, made prisoners of war. From Charles II.'s friend Lord Colepepper, through the Fairfaxes, Leeds passed to the member for Rochester, Mr. Philip Wykeham Martin, who, in the May of 1878, died suddenly in the library of the House of Commons. In the hands of its present possessors, the place is less widely known for its house-parties than for the attraction it constitutes to visitors of all classes when the building and gardens are thrown open at flower shows and upon other such occasions. The date of its first known hospitalities vindicates

Leeds Castle from Wyckliffe to Jowett

the claim of Kent to be considered the cradle of the country-house system. In the fourteenth century Leeds Castle was crown property, and belonged both to Edward III. and Richard II. The former of these sovereigns appointed William of Wykeham Surveyor of Castles. That statesman did the honours, Leeds among them, for the monarch. Under his administration the ancient structure near Maidstone received among its regular guests not only Chaucer, who, from his position as Surveyor of Works, might in any case have been free of such buildings, but the historian Froissart and the reformer William Wyckliffe, both before and after 1360, when he became Master of Balliol. In connection, therefore, with Leeds two facts establish themselves beyond doubt. The antiquity of its social gatherings belongs to the same remote epoch as those of the Chaucerian franklin. In his references to each, the father of English poetry, as a country-house chronicler, was drawing as directly from the life as in the case of his other Canterbury portraits. Secondly, it is interesting to learn that, five hundred years before Benjamin Jowett came into request as a guest beneath rural roofs of all degrees, his fifteenth-century predecessor at the master's lodge in Broad Street was as much in demand with the same rural hosts as Jowett himself.

"Namquae Mars aliis, dat tibi regna Venus." The old couplet on Austria's marriage-made prosperity might have been written about a country house in the now suburban Beckenham, belonging to the eighteenth- and nineteenth-century Burrells. Peter

Eridge and the Kentish Gang

Burrell, M.P. for Haslemere eventually, *viâ* knight-hood, reached the peerage as Lord Gwydir, in 1796. Meanwhile, from his Kentish villa, his eldest daughter had married the wealthiest commoner of the time, R. H. Bennett, who had first seen his future wife when examining at a neighbouring country house, Shortlands, the embalmed head of Oliver Cromwell. The second daughter found a husband in his future Grace of Northumberland (Duke Algernon). The youngest daughter also became a duchess by captivating the eighth Duke of Hamilton; he was succeeded by, as her second husband, the Marquis of Exeter. The father of these lucky young ladies had set them a good example in marrying the Duke of Ancaster's daughter, subsequently, by her brother's death, left a peeress in her own right. The beauty of the Gunnings resolved itself into a combination of fault-less features with queenly bearing. There was little of classical loveliness about the Burrells; they were merely sweet girls with pretty faces, perfect figures, and the most winning manners in the world. "I have just seen," said Bennett, recounting to a friend the meeting over the Protector's skull, "the most captivating woman, from whatever point of view you regard her, human eyes ever beheld." Even the fastidious George Selwyn, one of the guests at the Shortlands wedding-feast, admitted that Mrs. Bennett was "well enough." Less ancient, generally very different in kind, is the repute enjoyed by another Kentish roof, long since a landmark in modern science. Till his death in 1882 Charles

Kentish Homes of Science

Darwin's home at Downe, Farnborough, was to men of science from all points of the compass what Lord Stanhope's Chevening was to men of letters. Downe, to this day, attracts the pilgrims of science. The author of " The Origin of Species " had Sir John Lubbock (Lord Avebury) at High Elms as his neighbour in life. The entomological peer may affect the Kentish squire less than Darwin did ; he shows all Darwin's interest in Kent's flora and fauna. " Same as I shot Captain Marker," Rawdon Crawley's description of the pistols in the inventory of his effects, was pleasantly used by a former Lady Lubbock, when pointing out a certain pair of hand fire-locks in the High Elms armoury. The other "specimens" in this little Kentish museum include curiosities of nature from every land or sea, as well as insect life at various stages of its progress towards human civilisation. The great attraction is, or used to be, a room upstairs where one was permitted to smoke at night ; it contained the celebrated ants. Here the industrious little insects, with the naked eye or through a glass, were seen in discharge of every domestic duty, from giving their young a bath to teaching them how to earn their living and set up house for themselves. The High Elms investigations morally rehabilitating the unpopular and unamiable wasp, belonged to another period, and also had their memorial in the collection. At Downe, Darwin was never better pleased than when mistaken for an ordinary country gentleman of an observant and meditative turn. Visitors who looked a little below the surface, saw in their Downe host a touching simplicity of character, which reminded those who could recall the author of " The Christian Year " of Keble in his Hursley vicarage.

That quality which in Darwin at once ripened casual acquaintance into affection, was replaced by an attribute, kin to it rather than like it, in the most celebrated among Sir John Lubbock's guests. Of all the country houses at which the present writer frequently found himself with him, none seemed to supply so happy a framework and so humanising an environment for Herbert Spencer as High Elms. Nowhere did he expand more genially, talk with more freedom and pleasant freshness, or reveal himself according to his nature, transparent in honesty, free from whatever might verge on affectation or pose. Huxley, often his fellow-guest, was charmed by his intense and glowing personality. What chiefly attracted and impressed one in Spencer was the lack of effort to conceal his essential humanity. " But," I recollect his saying, " for a certain knack of co-ordinating and generalising the facts of everyday life, I do not know in what I should have differed from others born into and educated into English Nonconformity of the middle-class." Such in the High Elms garden was his confession to his old friend Edward Smyth Pigott, who, when the two were young men together, had given the philosopher of the future his first literary opening in a paper called the *Leader*. At the time of these Kentish visits Spencer seemed unusually pleased with himself and the rest of the world. Our host had induced him to come out of his shell a good deal, to join, if I recollect rightly, the committee not only of the London Library, but of the Athenæum Club. At this time the last novel of his old friend, " Daniel Deronda," had just appeared. Apropos of it and of its author's recent visit to High Elms, Spencer remarked : " The papers, I see, charge me with spoiling George Eliot's style by inoculating her with scientific phraseology and a love of metaphors from my own studies. They forget that she is actually my senior in point of age, and immeasurably so as regards knowledge and power. If either of us has been the other's pupil, I have found a teacher in her. As for the diction, if one wishes to put Lewes on one side, let them look back to Vico, Helvetius, or Lamarck. She was always much more widely read and better informed than myself. Those," he continued, " who think science an enemy to style had better look at Huxley, a clear and pure writer if there ever was one." That brought back to some of those present a little piece of dialogue between the typical man of letters and the typical scientist. James Hannay, the blood-and-culture journalist of the *Pall Mall Gazette* in its early days, had been a midshipman in the same period that Huxley became a naval surgeon. Years after the two met each other on the steps of the British Museum. " Huxley," said Hannay, " I care nothing for *homo* except as a creature of historical tradition." " Nor I," was the answer, " for him except as a compound of gas and water. But if we were each of us better educated men than we are, we should know how to respect each other's studies more." Few people can have had a sincerer contempt for the superficial infidelity and the crass unbelief which to-day boast of Spencer as their master. "All I say to those who assert or deny a personal Creator and a Divine Revelation to man is, 'You have no evidence on which to discuss the subject.'" To such effect at High Elms did Spencer express himself, when pacing the grounds in company with J. A. Froude. "You see," I remember the historian turning round to say to the present writer, "as Wilkes was never a Wilkesite, so nothing can less bear out the vulgar idea of Spencerianism than the author of the system's own words."

Lord Avebury's dwelling in the Farnborough district forms Kent's social citadel of the new learning. The older culture and the still older politics both possess representative houses elsewhere in the county. In the winter of 1903–4 Oxford University would have lamented very many vacancies had any serious accident happened to the trains freighted with an academic cargo to the railway station at Hawkhurst, Kent, from the Isis. On reaching their railway destination the Oxford delegates at once went to Seacox Heath, Lord Goschen's country house on the Sussex frontier. The building itself stands on Sussex soil ; the outskirts of the woods, part of the gardens, and a few cottages are in the adjoining shire. The boundary line between the two counties runs through the garden. On the occasion now mentioned the academic visitors were preceded by the official Poker. Then came the two Proctors, without their "bull-dogs." These were followed by Canon Ince of Christ Church, then Regius Professor of Divinity, formerly, in Lightfoot's Rectorship, a well-known classical tutor at Exeter College, by Professors Gondy and Gotch, by the Master of Pembroke, by the President of St. John's, by the Master of University, by the Warden of Wadham, by certain distinguished Dons from Balliol, Oriel, University, and New. Lord Salisbury had recently died ; Lord Goschen had been chosen as his successor in the Oxford Chancellorship. The delegates, on reaching his country house, were shown into the library ; the spokesman saluted his host, in official Latin, as the visible head and chief guardian of the University whence he came. The visitors epitomised and symbolised in their own persons characteristic phases of Oxford development from its mediæval and cosmopolitan infancy down to its periodically revolutionised present. The Chancellor's deputy or vice is the product of a period in which Gown professed to live in bodily terror of Town. The most famous of the early Chancellors, Grosse-teste, Bishop of Lincoln, could no more be in regular residence than were any of his busy successors. Hence the need of his deputy to protect the collegers against the citizens. " Proctor " used to have a protective as well as a disciplinarian meaning. The fact of two of these officials having visited Seacox Heath, takes one back to the time when the different interests of students from the south and from the north of England called for separate championship and regulation. One of the colleges, Pembroke, represented by its head at Seacox Heath, counted among its seventeenth and eighteenth century undergraduates respectively John Pym and Samuel John-

Eridge and the Kentish Gang

son.   The place had been known as Broadgates Hall
in Pym's day ; it had scarcely become habituated to
the newer style in Johnson's.   Two other Pembroke
men of later distinction were the younger Tom Hood,
Mr. J. Chamberlain's class-mate at University College
School, London, and Dr. Birkbeck Hill, some time a
fellow official of Anthony Trollope at the General
Post Office.   Hill's sufficient title to fame is his
classical edition of the biography in which Boswell has
familiarised all time with the personality of Pembroke's
greatest alumnus.   The younger Hood, during twenty
years in the literary London of the Victorian age,
exercised a refining influence upon all the departments
of journalism in which he worked.   As for the new
Chancellor, Lord Goschen enjoyed the rare distinction
of having won a first class in the earliest examinations,
both for Classical Moderations (1852) and in Classical
Greats (1853), ever held.

Among the various intellectual interests served by
the younger Hood just mentioned was the stage.
The Kentish country house was, in the sixteenth
century, a creative and didactic force in English letters.
Especially in Elizabeth's time had it allied itself with
the English drama.   Knole was only one of many
private roofs beneath which Crown and Court witness
theatrical performances, professional or amateur.   The
county whose attractions have detained us for some
little time had acquired a reputation dear to the player
at the beginning of modern history.   Canterbury,
with its adjacent district, may fairly style itself the
cradle of the non-professional stage.   The Canterbury
cricket week in the early forties of the nineteenth

century originated a movement that communicated its impulse to amateur acting in halls, manor houses, and rectories far and wide. In their beginnings the "Old Stagers" were only cricketers seen in another aspect. The best known member of the group was Sir Spencer Ponsonby-Fane. He and his friends had been playing the national game all day and every day. There was, therefore, little time for rehearsals ; such preparation of scenes as there could be took place in corners of the cricket-field, in the dressing-tent, at any odd moments that could be found. The stages of development were much as follows. What was afterwards known as the Beverley Ground, Canterbury, had been first the lawn or paddock of a country house. On this Beverley Ground, in 1841, an eleven of England in a return match, played earlier during the same year at Lords, beat the Kent Club. The match proved a great social success ; the brothers John and W. de Chair Baker and Mr. F. Ponsonby, afterwards Lord Bessborough, each of them more or less "stage-struck" as well as "cricket-struck," took in hand the establishment of an annual meeting in the cathedral town, that should combine the attractions of cricket by day with theatricals by night. The country houses of the neighbourhood united in supporting the idea and in promoting its organisation. Among its friends none were warmer than the family at Harbledown Rectory, between one and two miles out of town. To that household belonged the future Anglo-Indian statesman and poet, Sir Alfred Lyall. As years have gone on the regulations of the "Old Stagers" may have become more elaborate. The rules were finally drawn up at a meeting held about 1852 at the Canterbury Hotel, so exclusively the resort of county dwellers in the neighbourhood as to be little more than an urban annex to the country house.   Archer, Butler, Bentinck, Seymour, Grimstone, Hartopp, are names that, constantly figuring in the amateur dramatic chronicle, proclaim the closeness of the connection between the "Old Stagers" of the cricket week and the country houses of Kent.   In 1855 the Canterbury "Old Stagers," recruited from many a rural home in the country, took in hand the business of amateur pantomime.   Just a quarter of a century later, the idea was revived and actively adopted by a little company among whose members were Mr. A. S. Wortley, Corney Grain, Augustus Spalding, F. C. Burnand, and Montagu Williams.   From the Canterbury amateurs in their country-house setting proceeded that histrionic afflatus which, animating Mrs. Charles Crutchley, Mrs. William James, and Miss Muriel Wilson, justified so expert a critic, himself so good a stage artist, as Mr. William Yardley in giving these ladies a place among the most accomplished of non-professional players.   Harbledown Rectory, a few miles out of Canterbury, at times formed a recruiting ground for Kentish country-house theatricals.   It was the birthplace of the distinguished Anglo-Indian official Sir Alfred Lyall.   His father, Dean Lyall, was the most hospitable of his cloth and, as a host, the most appreciative of theatrical talent.   Amongst the "stars" of the Kentish country-house stage whose radiance owed something to his encouragement, were Allan Ayresworth, Alan Mackennon, Holman Clark,

The Derings of Kent

Bromley-Davenport, T. Jeffcock, George Neugent. The Kentish actresses came from the professional stage, and often found their local experience the best school for success on the public boards.

Some ten or fifteen miles from Canterbury, in the Ashford neighbourhood, are two abodes whose associations suggest that the Kentish country house of the nineteenth and twentieth century has not degenerated from its earlier distinction. Dering, of Surrenden-Dering, cut his name deep in the Long Parliament as well as elsewhere. Among the independent Parliamentarians of his time, none was more importunately critical of his associates or more quick to discover weak points in his rivals and opponents than Sir Edward Dering. His nineteenth-century namesake inherited something of his ancestor's controversial intractability and passion for intellectual dissidence ; alone among the under-graduates of his time, he could not be cowed by the terrible E. A. Freeman at the *viva voce* examination in the Law and History schools. His success in the entire ordeal was due to a force and facility of expression, also ancestral gifts. His youthful pen was equally happy at criticising a picture show or describing a prize-fight. On April 17, 1860, the Anglo-American combat between Sayers and Heenan took place in Dering's county at Farnborough. The best account of the battle was that written by Edward Dering, in the *Saturday Review*. Delane might have liked it for the *Times*. It was, too, as a guest at a Kentish home not far from Surrenden-Dering that the *Times* man, Nicholas Woods,

Eridge and the Kentish Gang

composed his story of the battle, appearing, as it did, the next morning, before the *Saturday* was out. This was the much-talked-of article, to which the *Times* editor gave the finishing stroke by one of his happiest touches : " Restore the prize-ring ! as well try to re-establish the heptarchy !" Another *tour de force* of a very different kind achieved itself some years later in the Ashford neighbourhood. At Old Swinford Manor, a pretty house in a perfectly delightful garden, lives, at this moment of writing, Mr. Alfred Austin ; he lived there in 1870, and in that year made a notable addition to the feats of writing well against time, achieved beneath the rural roofs of Kent. Mrs. Beecher Stowe's " Lady Byron Vindicated " involved an abominable charge against the poet. The future laureate was then among the most important and regular political writers for the *Standard.* Telegraphically instructed as to his subject from the editor in Shoe Lane, he daily sent off by train his leader for the newspaper's next number. One morning the editorial order came, not for a leader, but a three or four columns refutation of Mrs. Beecher Stowe's calumny against the author of " Childe Harold." The pamphlet, to be elaborately answered at such short notice, only reached Mr. Austin simultaneously with his literary brief, at 8 or 9 a.m. Before a late lunch, he had not only mastered every detail in the indictment against the poet ; he had collected a triumphant legion of rebutting witnesses. The testimony furnished by Byron's private life, by his vices as well as his virtues, by his family relationships and by the references to

140

Mr. Alfred Austin's Home and Exploits

these in his poems, amounted, it was shown, to moral proof that Mrs. Beecher Stowe's story was the morbid product of her own imagination. Never were the details of circumstantial evidence more ingeniously and effectively marshalled than in the long and practically conclusive answer sent off from his country house by Mr. Austin. It reached London that evening, and was published in the newspaper the next morning. Adjoining Swinford Manor is Hothfield Place ; its park was the scene of Jack Cade's death, at the hands of Sheriff Iden, as described by Shakespeare. Lord Hothfield, a successful player at many games in his Christ Church days, used to be the poet laureate's most successful opponent on the lawn-tennis ground. In this game King Edward the Seventh's laureate formerly found the same mental relaxation which the object of his own youthful idolatry and of the Countess Guiccioli's passion discovered in pistol-shooting, the boxing-gloves, and swimming. Near Hothfield and Swinford is another social centre of rural Kent, scarcely less rich than its rivals in varied associations. This is Scott's Hall. The sixteenth-century head of the family, Sir Thomas Scott, was to be the leader of the Kentish militia when there seemed a danger of the troops landed by the Spanish Armada over-running the country. Appropriately enough, in view of the later celebrity of their line, the Scotts of Scott's Hall could boast descent from William de Balliol ; for the master under whom the College of Jowett began to achieve its modern pre-eminence had the blood, as well as bore the name, of the Kentish

Eridge and the Kentish Gang

Scott.   Born in Devonshire, Robert Scott, who in 1870 became Dean of Rochester, was connected with Kent, by residence as well as family, when he died. At the Kentish country house bearing his name it was that, in his student days, he conceived the idea of the famous Lexicon which, in early manhood, he was to execute with his friend H. G. Liddell.   The hospitalities of the district now being traversed used to be largely literary, and were not confined to a single host.   Among Mr. Alfred Austin's guests, two great novelists, Anthony Trollope and Charles Lever, were both often to be found at the same time.   The host had done much foreign correspondence for the *Standard;* he had sent home letters descriptive of the Franco-Austrian campaign, of that between France and Austria which opened the way to Italian independence, and of the death-struggle which, three years later, placed Germany at the head of the European system.

The present chapter opened at the local residence of the man who, for something like half a century, ranked as the generalissimo of the Kentish forces of the Victorian age.   It will, therefore, appropriately end with a flying visit to the Kentish homes belonging to pillars or ornaments in the Conservative system, long presided over by the master of Eridge.   In Kent, if anywhere, the personal extremes, so far as age is concerned, of the Tory corporation domiciled in the county, certainly touch each other.   An earlier chapter, mainly occupied with the Sussex dukeries, revealed an ancestor of Lord Milner, General Ready, among the Duke of Richmond's henchmen at Goodwood. Among Lord Goschen's most regular guests beneath his roof in the Hawkhurst district were two of his private secretaries, trained by him into becoming serviceable or famous as Conservative officials. One of these was the late Sir Clinton Dawkins, whose familiar record of achievements, in Whitehall first, in Egyptian administration, on the Viceroy's Indian Council afterwards, formed the complete fulfilment of ambitions which, with less of love and capacity for work, his premature death would have left only visions. Among his fellow-visitors at Seacox Heath used sometimes to be another Balliol man, though of a little earlier generation, who, at the time these lines are written, is Lord Chancellor in the new Liberal Administration; this was Lord Loreburn, better known still to many as Robert T. Reid. For another reason than the constant meeting of the two men at Seacox Heath, their names may appropriately be mentioned together. When, in the sixties, Mr. Reid began his Oxford course, it was as a demy of Magdalen. He had never, like other of his Cheltenham contemporaries, stood for the Balliol. Even when established in his Magdalen rooms, it was not, however, too late to do so. On one condition for such candidature the Magdalen authorities insisted. The demy must first absolutely resign the smaller prize already in his hands. It was a severe risk. The young man confidently took it, and carried off, with flying colours, the blue ribbon of Oxford freshmanship. In the same way Dawkins, having done brilliantly in the open competition for the English Civil Service, gained a high appointment, though not in the India Office, on which he had set his heart. The only way of obtaining a transfer was to be absolutely first in the next competition, Flinging up the appointment he had already won, he once more submitted himself to the examiners, with the result that, coming out at the top of the list, he had only to walk into the department he coveted. Another of the then Mr. Goschen's guests, exactly Dawkins's contemporary, was that descendant of the General Ready of Goodwood associations, as accomplished a Balliol scholar as the future Lord Chancellor himself, and whose name in later years was to become a controversial synonym for a particular school of South African and Imperial statesmanship generally, Mr. Chamberlain's High Commissioner.

Among the patriarchs of the Kentish Gang, one, who chiefly charged himself with its intellectual health, survived till 1887. This was a son of the Surrey house, the Deepdene, presently to be visited. A. J. Beresford-Hope, the life-long acquaintance of Benjamin Disraeli, in his later years asserting some independence of his leader, became the butt of the future Beaconsfield's sharpest satire : "Batavian grace" was Disraeli's way of alluding to the Dutch origin of the Hopes. "The contortions but not the inspirations of the Sibyl," contained a pleasant reference to Mr. Beresford-Hope's habit of swaying his body to and fro in exciting moments of Parliamentary debate. This representative of Cambridge University in the nineteenth century's later years was also the chief restorer of St. Augustine's, Canterbury ;

where he rivalled in the munificence of his art patronage and the cost of his ecclesiastical structures the splendour of the Florentine Medicis. He was also the first great prototype of the nineteenth-century newspaper founder. The neighbourhood of Goudhurst, within which Bedgebury stands, abounds in those traditions of smuggling that were often effectively worked up by the formerly popular novelist, G. P. R. James. Bedgebury Park in the seventeenth century formed a great meeting-place for those Parliamentarians who, resisting the malignant influence of Strafford over the king, were not yet prepared to go all lengths with his enemies, and who, in several cases, eventually joined themselves to Charles. Colepepper was himself a Kentish man ; the lords of Bedgebury Manor were his relations. Their house became the rendezvous of Colepepper's political friends. Chief among these was Falkland. The old house that, like Eridge, among others in this region, had often received Queen Elizabeth on her progresses, disappeared in 1688, to be replaced by a building in whose erection Falkland had a share. " When next I come to Bedgebury," had often been the farewell words to his Kentish hosts of Clarendon's "incomparable young man," " I hope to find you have done something towards recovering the precious flotsam and jetsam on your Kentish coast." The allusion was to a Spanish treasure ship, sunk on the southern shore at no great distance from Goudhurst. At last the submerged treasure was brought safely to land. It proved to be so valuable that all the funds wanted for the new Bedgebury were at once forthcoming.

Eridge and the Kentish Gang

Where had formerly stood the moated house was now the park lake. By 1688 Sir James Hayes had completed the creation of the modern building, which, in Mr. Beresford-Hope's hands, was to grow into an imposing specimen of Louis XIV. architecture without and of Louis XIV. decoration within. The Bedgebury visitors' book suggests an entire chapter in the modern narrative of periodical literature. The Peelite *Morning Chronicle* was an outlying portion of the Bedgebury Park estate. The Lord Robert Cecil of those days, afterwards Marquis of Salisbury, Abraham Hayward, and a rising young barrister, William Vernon Harcourt, were amongst its regular writers. The editor was John Douglas Cook, a choleric Aberdonian, with a round, red head, a bull neck, a *bon-vivant*, a man of pleasure, but also a first-rate man of business, with few or no real literary tastes, but with a quick, almost infallible, instinct for the literary article that would take with his public. Bedgebury acquired a reputation for its hospitalities in the Peelite interest, with the illuminating presence of the literary lights, who reflected their brilliancy upon the Bedgebury newspaper. At the end of the forties, the fulfilment of the Peelite programme left the *Chronicle* without any special work to do. There, however, was an exceptionally able journalistic staff available for a weekly print of an entirely new and stirring sort. At Bedgebury were settled, between Mr. Beresford-Hope and Douglas Cook, the details of the *Saturday Review*, whose first number appeared in 1855. Douglas Cook edited it from his rooms in the Albany, where he interviewed his chief writers on each successive Tuesday. The personal tastes of the proprietor at once impressed themselves on the new weekly with far more distinctness than they had at any time done on the deceased daily. Among Mr. Beresford-Hope's high Anglican friends was the Rev. William Scott, then or afterwards the clergyman of an East-end parish, at one time concerned in the management of the High Church *Christian Remembrancer*, with which the leading men of the "Oxford Movement" had much to do. A considerable scholar, accomplished, accurate, sure-footed as a mule, "Parson" Scott afterwards became Douglas Cook's assistant in the editorship. At first, however, he was only one of the writers. H. S. Maine, in the middle of the nineteenth century, had been tutor of Trinity Hall, Cambridge; he became one of the chief *Saturday Reviewers*, bringing with him his most promising pupil, the Vernon Harcourt, known to Cook from the *Chronicle* days. These, together with Scott, G. S. Venables, and one or two more, composed the early staff of the *Saturday*, and were among the most frequent guests at Bedgebury, while the early numbers of the paper were planned.

Through several generations, in the hands of many owners, Hempsted Park has been among the Kentish Tory houses. Since its occupation by Lord Cranbrook, the Gathorne-Hardy of earlier days, it has been periodically resorted to by Conservative leaders and their followers, for obtaining the practical counsel of one who, in his day, combined dash and judgment in debate, and who only left the House of

Eridge and the Kentish Gang

Commons to become the sage and shrewd counsellor of those for whom and with whom he formerly had fought so well. Some ten miles to the north of Hempsted is the home of one among the rising hopes of that party which had its patriarch in Lord Cranbrook. Chilston Park was bought by a family named Akers, enlarged and beautified by money made by successful years of West Indian trade. An inheritance in the Scotch border country involved the second surname of Douglas. Owned by Mr. Aretas Akers-Douglas, the pretty little property of Chilstone, traversed by a gleaming trout stream, has annexed itself to the estates of the Kentish Gang. Selected by Lord Randolph Churchill as Whip of the Fourth Party, the squire of Chilstone rose to be the useful auxiliary and often, in his absences from St. Stephen's, the representative of Mr. Balfour. To that minister Mr. Akers-Douglas gradually played something like the part of Dundas to the younger Pitt. Chilstone thus became a premier's week-end haunt, where he took council with his second-in-command, and often was provided with the opportunity of using his charm of manner as a spell for the recall of incipient seceders to personal loyalty. To a use not unlike this had, in earlier days, been put the Kentish castle, where dwelt and dwells one of Mr. Akers-Douglas's predecessors in the patronage secretaryship. Sir William Hart-Dyke, in respect of historical position, stands midway between the Cranbrook and the Akers-Douglas periods. A contemporary and athletic rival at Harrow of Fred Burnaby, who rode to Khiva, he did more than most of his younger compatriots towards strengthening and enlarging the authority of the county coterie which has made the shire of hops a political force of the first order. Brighton, as has been seen, owes its first start in fashionable and civic life to its notice by Stanmer. Tunbridge Wells is under a similar obligation to Eridge, one of whose royal guests, James I., detected the chalybeate in the waters of the Kentish spa. The fish dinners of the lower Thames might never have come into vogue, but that a party from Lullingstone chanced to dine at a Gravesend inn, afterwards know as the "New Falcon," in the whitebait season.

CHAPTER V

THERE has purposely been reserved for a
separate chapter the first Kentish roof beneath
which were united the best features of country-
house society. The English constitution, as Disraeli
once put it, was born in the bosom of the Chilterns ;
the country-house system was cradled in the valley of
the Medway. For about two centuries—at least,
from the reign of Queen Elizabeth to the end of
the Stuart era, whose closing incidents were planned
in the home of the Sidneys—the higher possibilities
of a rural home were continuously illustrated at
Penshurst. Thence, in virtue of the Pembroke

Penshurst and its Early Owners

marriage, to Wiltshire first, to other parts of England afterwards, radiated influences associating the Kentish Sidneys with the higher activities—social, political, intellectual, even physical—of the age. The place thus became a school of breeding of manners and of mind—a pattern for other country houses of that and of succeeding ages. What the Sidneys were among the actors in the drama of English affairs and letters, their habitation became to the scenery amid which the plot of the play was unfolded. The Penshurst house has for some time been restored to the appearance it wore when its halls and galleries began to be trodden by guests more various and brilliant than had before assembled beneath any Kentish roof. Time, tempest, and the woodman's axe have dealt gently with the trees in the park. The twentieth century therefore sees, within an hour's journey from Charing Cross, unchanged in all essentials, the place that from 1547 to 1704 formed the most variously interesting panorama of character and conduct. From its first Anglo-Norman possessors it passed to the Bohuns, Dukes of Buckingham. Of these thirteenth-century owners, one fell in battle, two died on the scaffold. Its name was a corruption of that borne by its Norman possessors—Pencestre or Penchester. Between 1216 and 1377 Sir Stephen Penchester, lord of Penshurst, was also Warden of the Cinque Ports and Constable of Dover Castle. Famous for his learning and accomplishments, he became a presage of those Sidney successors who were specially to impress their character and fame upon "the castle on the hill." Such was the meaning of the term, abbreviated as years passed by, to its existing form. Fortifications, of a kind, the ancient Penshurst had. Its defences, however, were trenches, mounds, and wooden palisades, such as may be seen in the Bayeux tapestry. It never boasted a Norman keep or moat. From the absence of all stone remains the old house must have been entirely of timber. The fourteenth-century owner of Penshurst, Sir John de Poultney, four times Lord Mayor of London, obtained special licence from Edward II. to embattle the structure. After belonging successively to the family into which Poultney's widow married—to the Duke of Bedford, who was regent, to his brother Humphrey, Duke of Gloucester—in 1447 Penshurst passed to the Staffords. A little later, in 1521, it was possessed by Edward, Duke of Buckingham, who, having gratified Henry VIII. by the splendour of his assistance at the Field of the Cloth of Gold and, in other ways, humoured the royal whim, incurred the royal jealousy, and after a mock trial went to the block. "God have mercy on his soul, for he was a most wise and noble prince, the mirror of all courtesy"; so ran the popular verdict as the crowd saw Buckingham walk with quiet courage to his death. Penshurst once more reverted to the Crown. In 1550 Edward VI. granted it to Sir Ralph Fane, who, in less than two years, lost his head for alleged complicity with the Protector, Somerset. Sir William Sidney had fought at Flodden, had been Edward VI.'s tutor, chamberlain, or steward. His wife had been Edward's nursery governess. To William Sidney therefore the young king now granted Penshurst.

What Happened in Sacharissa's Walk

Authentic knowledge of the Sidney family begins
with its knightly representative, Sir William, in
the twelfth century. But the Sidney marriages
had connected the Penshurst family with many of
the chief English houses, amongst them with the
Egremonts, with the Harringtons, with the Fitz-
walters and the Fitzwilliams. William Sidney's son
Henry, became the husband of the Duke of
Northumberland's eldest daughter, and by her the
father of Sir Philip Sidney as well as of two other
sons, one of them Robert, afterwards first Earl of
Leicester, and of Mary, eventually the wife of Henry
Herbert, Earl of Pembroke, and possessor of Wilton.
With its succession of grassy quadrangles—the ambassador's court, the baron's court, the president's
court, and others—Penshurst presents an aspect
which is rather that of an Oxford college than of a
private dwelling.

It is a many fronted house. The longest façade
of variously shaped windows looks out upon a park
whose picturesqueness comes even more from its
singularly graceful undulations than from the massive
symmetry of its trees. The grounds still have the
" Sacharissa's Walk," where, for the last time, the poet
Waller knelt at Lady Dorothy Sidney's feet and
received his decisive dismissal. On a bowling green
nearly parallel to what was afterwards " Sacharissa's
Walk," the poet Spenser often matched himself at
a rubber with his brother guest, Sir Walter Raleigh.
By what stages the property reached its most famous
possessors has been already seen. Their family
name, a corruption of the patron saint of France,

St. Denis, points to their having come from the Paris suburb called after the saint. The name, originally written " Sidenie," was always spelt by its possessors with " i," not " y," for the second letter. The Sidneys, as has been seen, became a political family under the Tudors. Their reputation survived the Stuarts ; they were a national force in the revolution of 1688. Their men are all brave and their ladies all pure. That, at each successive stage, formed the traditional character of the Sidneys. The Sidneys of the original stock were not indeed confined to Kent. Four centuries before the grant of Penshurst to William Sidney, an earlier ancestor of the same name, who had come to England with Henry II., founded country houses in Surrey and Sussex. The Sidney women were at least not less remarkable than the men. Four daughters were born to the sixteenth-century owner of Penshurst. Of these three became the respective ancestresses of St. John, Viscount Bolingbroke, of Lord North the statesman, and of Lord Byron the poet, belonging by birth to the third George's reign. Judged by modern standards the Sidney portraits show the beauty of the men to have been rather that of mind and character than of person or face. The great Sir Henry Sidney (1529–1586) has a countenance not wanting in strength, but as featureless as that of an infant in arms. His grandfather Nicholas had married Anne Brandon, widow of Louis XII., aunt to Charles, Duke of Suffolk, Henry VIII.'s sister-in-law. The grandson, in character and bearing, was not less of a purely Tudor product than by descent. This Henry

The Making of Philip Sidney

Sidney, by marrying (1551), the daughter of John, Duke of Northumberland, united Penshurst with the family which, from the fall of Somerset to the death of Edward VI., gave the country its real rulers. The shadow of death now fell heavily on the Kentish mansion. Northumberland was beheaded in 1553. Worn out with anxiety and ailments, his eldest son, Lord Warwick, passed away next year in the welcome quiet of Penshurst. During the troublous period that followed, Lord Guildford, Lady Jane Grey, and the Duke of Suffolk all perished. While his relatives played a part in the great transactions of the time and perished, Sir Henry Sidney, never leaving Penshurst, preserved his head and his health. Of all his line he showed himself the most cautious and fortunate. Even during the Popish revival under Mary he found a friend in Mary's husband, Philip II. Henry Sidney's third daughter, by becoming Countess of Pembroke, connected the life and letters of Penshurst with those of Wilton. Her famous brother was the idol of his own generation and the perplexity of the next. How was it that in an age crowded with great men and great achievements, Sir Philip Sidney towered above his contemporaries? Horace Walpole's answer suggests probably the true explanation. The cause of his fame was the unique combination of merit and learning in a man of that rank.

Like others of his name, Philip Sidney learnt at Shrewsbury more than he forgot at Christ Church. He had, however, been personally trained by his father with the same care that Chatham bestowed on William Pitt. The most famous scion of this

Penshurst as a Parent Country House

Kentish house was, therefore, above all things, the moral and intellectual product of Penshurst Place. In the park may still be seen an avenue of trees, under which the father, in his afternoon walks with the boy, tested his recollection of the morning's lessons conned with the tutor. Here, too, it was that he impressed on the lad those maxims for the conduct of life, afterwards emphasised in the correspondence still extant among the Penshurst archives. "Not empty of some advices" was the family description of the letters that, during the half-year, found their way from Penshurst Place to Shrewsbury school. Philip was to begin every day with lifting up his mind to the Almighty in hearty prayer, as well as feelingly digesting all he prayed for. He was also, early or late, to be obedient to others, so that in due time others might obey him. The secret of all success lay in a moderate diet with rare use of wine. A gloomy brow was, however, to be avoided. Rather should the youth give himself to be merry, so as not to degenerate from his father. Above all things should he keep his wit from biting words, or indeed from too much talk of any kind. Had not nature ramparted up the tongue with teeth and the lips with hair as reins and bridles against the tongue's loose use. Heeding this, he must be sure to tell no untruth even in trifles ; for that was a naughty custom, nor could there be a greater reproach to a gentleman than to be accounted a liar. *Noblesse oblige* formed the keynote of the oral and written precepts with which the future Sir Philip Sidney was paternally supplied. By his mother, too, Lady Mary

Irish Visits to a Kentish Park

Dudley, the boy must remember himself to be of noble blood. Let him beware, therefore, through sloth and vice, of being accounted a blemish on his race. "Your loving father, so long as you live in the fear of God." So ended the epistles from home, received by Philip Sidney at Shrewsbury School, and duly answered in Latin and French, as well as in his mother-tongue. Stationed at Ludlow while Warden of the Marches, the father frequently visited his son while pursuing his studies. Of the Welsh whom he had been sent to keep in order, he warmly said : " Better people to govern, Europe holdeth not." Henry Sidney's life was spent in the service of the State, within or beyond the four seas. After he had regulated the affairs of Wales he went on a mission of help to the Huguenots in France. That business won him the Garter. An errand to Ireland for coercing or conciliating the native chiefs proved less successful ; he began with losing all his stuff and horses during the voyage to Dublin (1566). From the Penshurst point of view the Irish episode proved prolific of interest. By way of cementing the improved relations between the English Crown and its Celtic vassals, Henry Sidney invited some of the Irish chiefs to visit him at home. Moved to admiration by the natural beauties of the Kentish park, by the brilliantly polished suits of steel armour almost covering the walls of the chief rooms of the house, and especially by the gallery for the musicians, looking down upon the great baronial hall, they were appalled by the store of books and manuscripts which had always been features of the place. Long before the

Penshurst as a Parent Country House

Irish visit this country house had won fame as the great letter-writing depôt for the western world. In later years Algernon Sidney, after the death of his father, Robert Sidney, second Earl of Leicester, could point to shelves groaning beneath the weight of forty quires of paper written by his father, but never published. The Sidney correspondence had, however, assumed formidable dimensions during the sixteenth century. The heads of the Sidney house had a trying fondness for reading selections from the family papers aloud to their guests. After some hours occupied by this ordeal, the Irish visitors (1568–71) implored their host not further to tax his voice. The specimens he had already given them were enough; the rest might be taken as read. Many of these compositions were in the handwriting of the author of "Arcadia"; for Philip Sidney accompanied his father on most of the diplomatic travels, and himself copied as well as drafted the more important despatches. All, in fact, that a reading-room well supplied with foreign newspapers is now, that for successive generations, three centuries ago, the Penshurst muniment-room was. From the reign of Henry VIII. onwards, the Sidneys of Penshurst figured actively in the Court life, in the domestic and foreign politics of their day. In every part of the habitable globe was a resident or travelling Sidney, who transmitted his epistolary narrative of all that passed around him, not only to his relatives at the old home, but to his acquaintances at every capital or Court. Copies were generally kept. Copious extracts were read to the Penshurst guests.

The Penshurst Letters and Leicester Earls

Those selections must have contained the pith and marrow, the quintessence and cream, of the European chronicle of the period. This tradition did not die out while Penshurst preserved its historic character. Sir Philip Sidney's younger brother, Robert (1563–1626), united in himself the Lisle viscountcy and the Leicester earldom. His son Robert, second Earl of Leicester (1595–1677) added to the family documents papers containing the secret history of Charles I., Charles II., and Oliver Cromwell. The chief value of these lay in their disclosures of foreign opinion about each stage in the events that ended with the king's execution. Penshurst, in the first Lord Leicester's ownership, had indeed been a literary rather than a political centre. Among the papers that descended to his son were notes of conversations with master-minds which only needed publication to become a part of English literature. The letters written by him in his library, overlooking the park, reflected the best thought and the freshest information of the time. The first Lord Leicester's epistles spread this knowledge from the Medway to the Ganges. In every branch of literature, in all abstract studies, especially mathematics, this nobleman seems to have been equally at home. Concerning the second Earl of Leicester, Sir William Temple was afterwards to write : " He was the most observant and learned person of his day, and only fell short of being a very great man by reason of the staggering and irresolution of his nature." That description, with a few little changes, might equally have fitted the first Earl also. Under

Penshurst as a Parent Country House

his *régime* the Penshurst housekeeping book, still or till recently extant, shows the high-water mark for that age of country-house hospitality. Had there come down to us any companion volume, containing the names of the visitors, we should have had a catalogue of guests unrivalled for the brilliance and variety of their genius. When the musicians, in the minstrel gallery looking down upon the baronial hall, were tuning their instruments for the evening's entertainment, William Harvey, who discovered the circulation of the blood—the most famous physician of St. Bartholomew's Hospital and the greatest consulting doctor who ever took double fees from wealthy patients—was discussing in one corner with Francis Bacon the recently formulated Third Law of Kepler. In a window recess close by stood a little gentleman of academic manner and dress, fresh from his Oxford common room, mathematically precise in his ideas and diction. This was the genial and kindly author of " The Anatomy of Melancholy " —Robert Burton of Christ Church, whose allusive prose was afterwards to be copied by Algernon Sidney himself in the " Discourses on Government." In the Penshurst hall now Burton apologises to a brother clergyman, also an author, Giles Fletcher, for not quite understanding certain lines in " Christ's Victory and Triumph." Fletcher notoriously took Spenser for his model. The poet of the " Faëry Queen " himself, when in England, seldom missed the Penshurst parties. Leicester's life-long hope was to bring about a meeting between the great singers of the day and the most variously accomplished friend of his youth, his comrade in military and political service, who had found solace for imprisonment as well as lettered fame in writing the "History of the World." But Sir Walter Raleigh was always prevented by adventures abroad or imprisonment at home from paying the repeatedly promised visit to the Kentish country house. Ben Jonson stayed there for weeks together. Was a greater than Jonson—the myriad-minded creator of "Hamlet" and "Macbeth"—ever among the Penshurst guests? Local tradition, after careful sifting, prompts an affirmative answer. The idea is also encouraged by a fragment of documentary evidence which some wind of chance has blown, it would seem, from Penshurst itself to the present writer. It is merely a two- or three-line memorandum about notes for future use, made at Penshurst by William Shakespeare. All the sixteenth- and seventeenth-century owners of Penshurst, during their civil and military employments, had combined an interest in letters with the part they had played in affairs. The first Lord Leicester, like his grandson Algernon, had an enthusiasm for the stage. Some time before 1616, the year of Shakespeare's death, he had made Penshurst an intellectual as well as fashionable resort. That character it never afterwards lost.

Robert Sidney, second Earl of Leicester, had succeeded Strafford as Irish Viceroy. Penshurst, we have seen, received its earliest visitors from Ireland in Sir Henry Sidney's day. These were to be followed by others of a very different kind in the second Leicester's time. Ready and even eager to make his predecessor's policy his own, he packed his Kentish seat with visitors whom he thought likely to promote his project of rallying English and Irish Catholics round the king against the Parliament. At one time it seemed as if loyalty to his sovereign would earn him the same reward as Strafford. Warned by that example and distrusting Charles in good time, he broke with the king soon enough to save his life but not his estates. Marriage connections had ever been a bulwark of the Sidneys. His alliance with the Dudleys and the Lisles secured Leicester the restoration of his estates first and Parliamentary favour afterwards. Between 1644 and 1650 the country folk noticed two strange children playing in the park and keeping entirely to themselves. Curiosity was aroused as to who they could be. Their dress, it was thought, indicated high birth ; but their manner and countenance bore signs of depression. Their eyes were often red, as if from weeping. Not till the little boy and his sister had disappeared from the place in 1650 did the neighbours know that they had seen the late king's son and' daughter, the Princess Elizabeth and the Duke of Gloucester. The children might never have exchanged Penshurst for the Isle of Wight at all but for money disagreements between Leicester and the Commons. The custodian of the two little Royalties was a keen bargainer. He received an annual allowance of £3,000 for his royal charges. Applying for an increase and failing to get it, he informed his wife that, by way of indemnifying himself, he must deduct, from her housekeeping

Sacharissa and her Brother

allowance, a sum equal to the desired but denied augmentation. At the same time he found himself engaged in an undignified squabble with Parliament on the subject of a jewel, a present from one of his little guests, and now claimed by the Commons. To this Leicester the Sidneys chiefly owed their great cash resources. He found a Court life little to his liking ; he hated the town as much as he loved the country. Especially dear to him were the autumnal tints on the Penshurst trees. On the plea of health, he soon obtained leave to pass most of his time at his old home. An absurd story represented his son, Robert, as father of the Duke of Monmouth. The paternal favourite was beyond doubt Algernon, who perished for alleged complicity in the Rye House Plot, and whose treatise on " Government " was partly thought out and planned in Penshurst Park as he lay on the grass. Another son, Henry, after having served as Viceroy of Ireland, died Earl of Romney. The same Irish office was also filled by his heir Philip, who sat in Cromwell's House of Lords. Of his daughters, one, Lucy, by her marriage with John Pelham, became progenitress of George II.'s Duke of Newcastle. His daughter Isabella married her relative, Viscount Strangford. But, in that generation of the Penshurst ladies, Dorothy Sidney eclipsed all her sisters. She was the " Sacharissa " whom her rejected lover, the poet Waller, immortalised. Born under James I., this lady lived throughout the entire reign of Charles II. to be one of the few gifted, as well as absolutely spotless, beauties of the Restoration. The eldest of a family of thirteen, born at Sion House, Isleworth, she was, by her mother, Dorothy Percy, a granddaughter of the Earl of Northumberland. To-day she is claimed as the genius of a Sussex, not less than a Kentish, country house. Her time, indeed, was almost equally divided between Petworth and Penshurst. She had become a reigning beauty at the age of sixteen. In her own words, she fell in love with a sweet, old, moated manor house, whither some friends had taken her on a visit to the family of Edmund Waller. This was Groombridge Place, famous as the abode in his captivity of the Duke of Orleans, who had been made a prisoner at Agincourt. At first sight Edmund Waller fell in love with Dorothy Sidney. The passion was not reciprocated and was discouraged by the lady's parents. The poet's position and appearance lacked the charm of romance. Twelve years Dorothy's senior, he had now become a rather corpulent and sleepy widower. No rebuffs prevented his addressing to the Penshurst beauty the series of love lyrics which, celebrating her as "Sacharissa," have made her name a synonym for every conceivable charm of person and of mind. In the Penshurst grounds is still pointed out the spot on which the lover for the last time knelt at the feet of the obdurate fair. In the house is still seen the original of his farewell stanzas. The poet contrived to live on with a broken heart for some half a century after (July 20, 1639) Sacharissa had married at Penshurst the young Lord Spencer. Lady Leicester was the cleverest matrimonial diplomatist of her day. For a time she had favoured " my lord of Devonshire's " pretensions to her daughter, but soon rejected him for another suitor, the gay Lord Lovelace. Eventually he too was passed over in favour of the lucky Sunderland. In addition to farewell verses to Sacharissa, the dismissed poet wrote a congratulatory letter of the bitter-sweet sort to Lady Leicester on the coming Spencer marriage. He wishes the bride the like passion for him she has preferred to the rest of mankind that others have had for her. May this love, he adds, before the year go about, make her taste the first curse imposed on womanhood, the pains of becoming a mother. May her firstborn be a son, resembling her lord as much as herself. May she that always affected silence and retiredness have her house filled with the noise of her children and of her grandchildren. May she arrive at that great curse, so much declined by fair ladies—old age—living to be old, yet seeming very young; be told so by her glass, and have no aches to tell her the truth. Four years after his marriage, Lord Spencer having been created Earl of Sunderland, fell, together with Carnarvon and Falkland, at the Battle of Newbury. Sacharissa now settled down to pass her peaceful widowhood at Penshurst. She was still but twenty-six, in the full flower, therefore, of her famous loveliness. She was, of course, besieged by suitors; for a long time she showed no sign of favour to any.

At last one of the most indefatigable among the Penshurst neighbours and visitors, a Kentish squire, Sir Robert Smythe Boundes, having vainly attempted to amuse her with his vivacity and impress her with the fineness of his equipages, suddenly fell into a state

Penshurst as a Parent Country House

of distressing despondency.   His family lamented his
gradual consumption by the fever of a hopeless and
fatal love.   Shortly it became known that Sacharissa
had accepted him out of pity.   The match did not
gratify her own family.   Lord Leicester abruptly
quitted Penshurst rather than be present at the
wedding.   The evil omens attending the second
marriage were not unfulfilled.   Sacharissa once more
became a mother.   Of the son thus born there is
little record.   Her chief delight was in her brother
Henry and her son-in-law, Lord Halifax, the famous
"trimmer" of a later day.   She had a constant source
of trouble in the love affairs of her son, Sunderland,
culminating as these did in his marriage with the
friskiest beauty of the time, Lady Anne Digby.
Other causes of unhappiness were the second Lord
Sunderland's quarrels with his uncle, Algernon
Sidney, the latter's long years of suffering exile
followed by his execution in 1683.   That calamity
she only survived three months, dying in 1684.
Algernon Sidney had been attached to his sister by
ties of intellectual sympathy as well as family affection.
His "Discourses on Government," as a piece of
literary mosaic, in miscellany of interest and fresh
variety of illustration, may almost be classed with
Burton's "Anatomy of Melancholy."   It may well,
indeed, have been that Algernon's acquaintance and
conversations with Burton, as his father's guest, gave
him the idea of his political treatise.   That work
may have been roughly drafted by its author in the
intervals of his diplomatic employments abroad.   It
was put in order for publication during his sojourns

Shakespeare's Penshurst Book

at Penshurst with his widowed sister. "A keen critic and a perfect sister" is Algernon's description of the lonely Lady Sunderland. To her, during the summer afternoons at Penshurst, he read specimens of his morning's work. Other literary subjects were suggested by the associations of the place to Sacharissa and her brother. Algernon Sidney did not, indeed, come into the world till six years after Shakespeare went out of it, but the tradition of the poet having been his grandfather's guest lasted throughout Algernon's time. While Algernon was working at his Discourses, the Penshurst library still contained a book that may have been handled by Shakespeare. This volume is a translation into Latin verse of all the plays of Sophocles by George Retaller, described as a councillor in the Royal Belgian Senate at Mechlin and a Master "libellorum supplicum"; it also contains Henry Stephens' notes on Sophocles and Euripides, an essay on the imitation of Homer, another on Sophocles. It was published at Antwerp in 1570.[1] Such a book may well have found its way into England at once. And there were many agents on the Continent retained by the lords of Penshurst for collecting important publications. Such a work, therefore, may have been consulted by the poet in the Kentish manor house, when he was the first Lord Leicester's guest. Ben Jonson was so frequent a visitor of the Sidneys that, in any conversations between Shakespeare and

---

[1] The only extant copy, so far as I know, is possessed by Mr. T. Herbert Warren, President of Magdalen, to whom I am indebted for this description of the book.

Penshurst as a Parent Country House

his Kentish host, the author of "Every Man in his Humour" probably would have been mentioned. Jonson's remark about the scantiness of Shakespeare's classical knowledge had been made in conversation before it was put into a poem. The present writer chances to have seen a manuscript fragment which, so far as it can be deciphered, seems to refer to some conversational protest by Shakespeare himself against the notion of his not being thoroughly at home in Latin versions of Greek plays. Sacharissa possessed literary interests before she captured the heart of the poet Waller. That experience and the loneliness of widowhood deepened and widened her intellectual tastes. She prized all records of the higher life that from time immemorial had found a centre at her Kentish home. She often talked about them with her favourite brother, Algernon, who took a greater interest than any other of his generation in the family papers. As regards these documents, I have already mentioned a fragment of manuscript that originally seems to have come from Penshurst. So far as its writing can be deciphered, it favours the idea that Shakespeare conversed with his Penshurst host about the Greek drama, and may have improved his knowledge of the subject from the Penshurst bookshelves. What, therefore, is antecedently more probable than that, in their talks on literary subjects, Algernon and Dorothy Sidney should have discussed the Shakespearian associations of their Kentish home? In the literary traditions handed down by their grandfather, the first Lord Leicester, their family pride might have enabled them to detect a proof that, from

Shakespeare's Debt to the Sidneys

Penshurst itself, the poet of all time had derived some first-hand knowledge of the masterpieces of the Attic stage. In 1623, seven years after Shakespeare's death, Ben Jonson, in the verses written by him for the first folio, had in the famous phrase mentioned his great contemporary's "small Latin and less Greek." That, the brother and sister might have said, was an old charge. Had not the Lady Dorothy herself heard from her literary lover, the poet Waller, of Greene's taunts aimed at Shakespeare as one who owed nothing to learning, but everything to native wit, and as having only fed on the crumbs from the translator's trencher. What, Algernon might indignantly have exclaimed, did this mean except that the mightiest intellect of his age had not been nourished on academic food? Our grandsire's friend, Ben Jonson, he might have added, brought from Westminster School a ripe scholarship which ranged him with the professional academics who always derided Shakespeare. And, as for Shakespeare himself, let us remember his master at Stratford School—Walter Roche—had come from that home of the new learning at Oxford, Corpus Christi College, and taught his boys to read Latin like their native tongue. Algernon Sidney himself, a man of action rather than of books, would have made it a special point to maintain the sufficiency of Shakespeare's learning for all his practical needs. But such references as his Discourses contain to the place of education in national polity suggest a familiarity with the school and college curricula of his time, at home and abroad. Contemporary observation would be likely to have acquainted him with the same details as, at the present day, Mr. Churton Collins has gathered by research for continuing what was practically Algernon Sidney's argument.[1]   One must not, indeed, read into the slender memoranda of the Penshurst dialogues between the brother and sister too many results of Mr. Collins' Shakespearian research.[2]   To Algernon and Dorothy Sidney, converse with the scholars met and the books read at Penshurst seemed abundant compensation for Shakespeare's lack of a public school or university training.   Moreover, speaking from his own experience as to the acquirements of seventeenth century schoolboys, the brother would have reminded his sister that, by the age of sixteen or seventeen, Shakespeare must have possessed a good colloquial knowledge of Latin.   Our poet's acquaintance with Plautus, Algernon might have added, was shown by his transformation of the " Menæchmi," of which no translation then existed, into the " Comedy of Errors." Whether or not Algernon Sidney used his acumen and knowledge to anticipate any of the other positions taken up by Mr. Churton Collins, the views now attributed to ·him were merely those of the unprejudiced and thoughtful criticism of the time.   In the seventeenth century the intelligence of the modern middle-class public had still to be organised.   On a rather higher level, such as that of Penshurst, country house table-talk reflected higher interests and covered more edifying themes than those which, in the same circles,

---

[1] " Studies in Shakespeare," pp. 14 and 15.
[2] " Studies in Shakespeare," but especially pp. 6 and 7.

"Waiting till you are Young Again"

have since become popular. The rural home of the
Sidneys registered the high-water mark of literary
knowledge and insight known to an age that saw in
intellectual culture and taste a note of social breeding.
In that part of the grounds looked down upon by
Sir Henry's tower may still flourish the nut-tree
planted on the day of Sir Philip Sidney's birth. The
Sacharissa memorials are not confined to Penshurst.
Althorp and Petworth both possess some of her best
portraits. Nor does it seem quite certain that
Penshurst and not Petworth or Lady Wharton's
place, Wooburn in Buckinghamshire, witnessed the
well-known meeting between Sacharissa and the
rejected poet in later years. "Why," asked the lady
of her former lover, "have you not written verses
about me of late? Surely you are growing old?"
"I am waiting rather," replied Waller, "till you are
young again, and as lovely as ever." Dorothy
Sidney's beauty had its monument in palace small
talk as well as in poet's lay. At Queen Anne's
Court it was still the theme of the grand old ladies.
"To us," they said, "who have seen Sacharissa, her
graceful motion and her winning attraction, the finest
women nowadays are merely pretty girls." The
mercurial Waller long haunted the scenes consecrated
by the divinity he had vainly wooed. It may not
have been in the old Kentish mansion that the poet
met his former flame, when Lady Sunderland. It
was certainly the Penshurst drawing-room which
heard his witty rejoinder to Charles II., when
both were Penshurst guests. Waller, after long
oscillation between the royal and republican parties,

read to the second Charles at Petworth an ode on the Restoration. " But," said the king, " your masterpiece, I am told, is your panegyric on Cromwell." " Ah, sir," came the ready reply, " we poets never succeed so well in truth as in fiction." Penshurst Place, in Algernon's earlier days, had become a hotbed of royal enthusiasm for the South of England. Lisle's lukewarmness in the reaction against Cromwell seriously compromised him with his brother-in-law, Algernon. The latter indulged his passion for private theatricals by getting up a performance at Penshurst of " Julius Cæsar." Casting himself for the part of Brutus, he embellished the dialogue with an abundance of anti-Cromwellian gags. The county guests who witnessed these performances recalled, in their talk between the acts, how, some years earlier, Algernon Sidney, then among the most brilliant figures of European society, in his home letters sketched from life the chief personages on the stage of continental politics. These epistles were written in cipher. The second Lord Leicester, after a day or two spent in mastering their contents, read the long, unforgotten descriptions of Cardinals Albizi, Azzolini, Barberini, Borromeo, Gizi, and others, to a company not unlike that which now applauded Algernon's improvisations against Republicanism.

Penshurst long maintained the political character stamped on it by the second Lord Leicester. The Henry Sidney, much younger than any of his brothers, who became Earl of Romney, remarked to his friend Halifax, some time after the events of 1688, " I always curse the hour in which I brought Billy to

England." Others, of equal authority on such a subject, though less partial to the Sidney clan, only saw in the Penshurst king-maker the fly on the wheel. Dean Swift denied him any part in these, on the ground of his being an illiterate and frivolous old rake. The invitation to William of Orange was, however, first conceived by Romney at Penshurst. Its details were arranged at Hurley on the Thames. The conspiracy against James had already got wind. Romney, considering his life unsafe in St. James's Square, took refuge in a Thames-side cellar until the new dynasty was established. Penshurst now became a Whig house. Afterwards, as a provincial rendezvous for supporters of the Hanoverian *régime*, it lived socially on its early reputation, but gradually lost distinctive character and interest. The first great display of English fireworks was arranged in its grounds by Romney to welcome William III. on the return from one of his absences in Holland. "To Penshurst, but oh, how fallen! It is forlorn. Instead of Sacharissa's cipher carved on the beeches, I should sooner have expected to find the milkwoman's score. There are loads of portraits, but most of them seem christened by chance, like children at a foundling hospital." So, in 1752, Horace Walpole. The visit prompting this description was paid nine years after the last Lord Leicester's death. Through marriages of the Sidney women, the place had then become the property of some people named Perry. From those possessors it found its way to the Shelleys. These, adding the Sidney patronymic to their own, soon became known exclusively as Sidneys. Their de-

Penshurst as a Parent Country House

scendants have furnished Penshurst with the third
Lord de Lisle and Dudley, who is its present possessor.
Walpole, like others of his time, had been wearied by
the extravagance of the conventional panegyrics
bestowed upon Penshurst and its Sidney owners.   In
the latter he saw men at least as noticeable for their
shrewd adaptability to the social and political conditions of the time as for chivalry and patriotism.   With
regard to the place, he admittted the unique interest
of some of its likenesses—especially those of Languet,
Sir Philip Sidney's friend, of the first Lady Leicester
with a vast lute, of Sacharissa herself, of the
primate, Fitzallen, of Wentworth, Lord Strafford, of
Humphry, first Duke of Buckingham.   These portraits
were pronounced by Walpole as old as any extant in
England.   He believed also in the genuineness of the
table and seats in the hall as the oldest of their kind in
England, and of the alleged specimens of Sir Philip
and Algernon Sidney's light-brown hair.

CHAPTER VI

TWO CENTURIES OF WILTON

Success of Sir Philip Sidney's "Arcadia" compared with that of Lewis Carroll's "Alice in Wonderland"—Wilton House—The Pembroke Herberts—William, third Earl of Pembroke—Henrietta de Querouaille, wife of seventh Earl—The "architect" (ninth) Earl—His widow's marriage with Captain Barnard—The tenth Earl's elopement with Kitty Hunter—Lady Pembroke, her pretty sister and smart contemporaries—English peeresses masquerading as Greek girls—The Wilton visitors' book from Horace Walpole to George Payne—Palmerston at Wilton and Sidney Herbert.

"A LITTLE pamphlet of Sir Philip Sidney's in defence of his uncle (Queen Elizabeth's Earl of Leicester) gives me a much better opinion of his parts than his dolorous 'Arcadia.' I don't think he could have been warmer about his family if he had been of the blood of the Cues (Montagues)." It was, indeed, a standing marvel with Horace Walpole that the pastoral romance about Musidorus and Pyrocles should have recommended Sir Philip to the Crown of Poland, as in our time the fifteenth Lord Derby's sagacious and detached statesmanship secured him the offer of the Greek monarchy. The best idea of the sort of vogue secured by the

175

Two Centuries of Wilton

" Arcadia " in the sixteenth century will be gained if one recalls the special kind of popularity won by Lewis Carroll's " Alice in Wonderland " three hundred years later. Both books immediately coloured and enlarged the social vernacular of all classes. The " Arcadia " at once influenced the colloquial dialect of Court, Cabinet, and town. Its phrases, expressive of compliment and love, passed straightway into the conversational currency of the time. This place they held till they were incorporated into the dialogue of the polite comedy of the Restoration. In Horace Walpole's time, the patience of a young virgin in love might not be able to wade through Sir Philip Sidney's romance. On its first appearance and for some time after, Musidorus, Pyrocles, and the Kalender were as often on the lips of the polite world as, in the Victorian age, were the Jabberwock, the Walrus, the Carpenter, and Alice herself, and the sayings of each were quoted on the croquet lawns, by curates and undergraduates, between 1865 and the outbreak of the Franco-Prussian war.

At Wilton, nature has crowded the beauties of half a dozen shires into the park and grounds. Money and art have crammed the house itself with the feudal lumber of Wardour Street. Next to the marble statues inhabiting the hall and galleries, the chief characteristics of the Wilton interior are the complete suits or mediæval armour and weapons of war that, hung against the wall, form an effective background for more modern works of art. George Payne, Charles Greville's Newmarket friend, who could be as pungently epigrammatic as Greville

176

himself, and who made the remark just quoted, hit off at least one feature of the place. The unique beauty of the exterior consists in the three rivers that run through the gardens, the Palladian bridge crossing them, not unlike that spanning the Serpentine in Hyde Park, and the cedars, now, unfortunately, disappearing from age. What George Payne when visiting Wilton together with Greville and Palmerston wished to convey is historically true enough. Wilton is an old place. The Pembroke Herberts are an old family. They are not, however, descended from William Marshal, the Pembroke Earl of Magna Charta celebrity. They derive their lineage from a stock of Thomases, Herberts, and Fitzherberts, who held Court offices under the Plantagenets and who, in the time of the Tudors, acquired large estates in a county wherein, before then, they held not an acre. One of these sixteenth-century ancestors, William Herbert, became territorially enriched under Henry VIII., and stood so high in that monarch's favour as to be appointed one of the executors of his will. That distinction gave him the further honour of sharing a seat in the funeral conveyance to Windsor with Sir Anthony Denny. By his marriage with Mrs. Gam, the widow of Sir Roger Vaughan, he introduced the Christian name of Gladys to the ladies of his family. By 1580 Sir Philip Sidney's sister had become Countess of Pembroke. With the opening of the seventeenth century Wilton began to share the intellectual distinction already enjoyed by Penshurst. William, third Earl of Pembroke, then master of the place, was that nephew

Two Centuries of Wilton

of Sir Philip Sidney apostrophised in Ben Jonson's well-known lines. In person he was the handsomest of his race. As a host, he had no rival since his uncle the first Lord Leicester of Penshurst. The third Lady Pembroke, the granddaughter of Sir William Cavendish of Chatsworth and of " Bess of Hardwick," was famous for the taste, the splendour, and the economy of her entertainments. The dramatist, Philip Massinger, a son of Pembroke's retainer, brought up, if not born, at Wilton, acted as her major domo, and secured both Shakespeare and Spenser among the guests. Her best known, but not next, successor as Wilton's chatelaine was the sister of Charles II.'s Duchess of Portsmouth, Henrietta de Querouaille, who married the seventh Earl of Pembroke. The next generation gave Wilton its greatest beautifier. The " architect " Earl, as he is generally known, did not limit his operations to his Wiltshire home. One at least of the new lodges in Windsor Park was designed by him. So, too, were the river-side home of Horace Walpole's neighbour, the Countess of Suffolk's Marble Hill, Twickenham, and the waterhouse in Lord Orford's park, Houghton. A more national monument of his structural accomplishments survived to the nineteenth century in the bridge spanning the Thames at Westminster. That dates from between 1739 and 1750. The design was that of the Swiss architect, Labeyle ; but all the arrangements were made by the ninth Lord Pembroke.

In the eighteenth century Wilton became the most fashionable and conspicuous country house south of the Trent. That position was chiefly due to the ladies of the Pembroke family. These began to be in modish evidence in 1751. Then it was that Rigby, the Duke of Bedford's man, as gossip-purveyor to his patron, reported the latest feminine sensation from Wilton. This was the marriage of the ninth, the architect-Earl's widow to Captain Barnard of the Blues. A studious, reserved, thinking sort of a philosopher, the bridegroom differed from most guardsmen of the period. There seems, however, to have been little about him that explained his capture of the "stateliest dame of quality of the day." The most self-interested of great ladies, as Captain Barnard's bride was accounted, filled her house, out of the London season, with an unending succession of smart guests. The glades and galleries which had heard the talk on great subjects of the sixteenth century's master-minds, now echoed with the cancans that frivolous letter-writers were to distil into sheets of cream-laid post, con- stituting the *chronique scandaleuse* of the period. " Have you," writes one of these gossip-loving ladies from Wilton, " heard about the Duke of Queensberry's visit to Alnwick ? Receiving his guests at the gate, the Earl of Northumberland said, ' Now is the first time that ever a Douglas and a Percy met here in friendship.' And this from a Smithson to a true Douglas ! " The Wilton company were particularly interested in and communicative about the marriage and coronation of George III. From distant Wiltshire, Horace Walpole hears at Strawberry Hill the echoes lamenting that there will be missed at the ceremony two brightest luminaries of fashion—Lady Walde-

grave for beauty and the Duchess of Grafton for
figure.   When the day of the royal ceremony arrived,
Wilton sent, at the head of the Countesses, Lady
Pembroke, who, looking the picture of majestic
modesty, shared the palm of loveliness with Lady
Kildare.   Each of these ladies had consulted Horace
Walpole himself.   " No profession, you see," he com-
placently writes, " comes amiss to me, from a tribune
of the people to a habit-maker."   As for others who
assisted at these functions, the verdict of the Wilton
critics was that the ancient peeresses held their own.
Thus Lady Westmorland looked still as handsome
as any and with more dignity than all.   Nor could
anything be more charming than the Duchess of
Queensberry, though her locks were milk-white.
Lady Albemarle impressed every one as "charmingly
genteel."   Middle age had good reason to be proud of
its representatives in Lady Holdernesse, in Lady Roch-
ford, and in Lady Strafford, the last " the perfectest
little figure of all."   Soon after the incidents mentioned
in these letters, early in George III.'s long reign,
Wilton became associated with a painful escapade.
The tenth Earl, a major-general and a bedchamber
lord, had married one of the most beautiful creatures
in England, Lady Elizabeth Spencer, sister of George,
Duke of Marlborough.[1] The lucky husband, however,
as he was accounted, had been overcome by the charms
of Miss Kitty Hunter, a daughter of one of the
Admiralty lords.   An elopement with her took place
from a ball at Lord Middleton's.   Society, when it had
recovered composure after the shock caused by the

[1] She died in 1831, at the age of 93.

"Something of Nelly Brien for the Eyes"

news, sympathised with Lady Pembroke, the more
so as her husband cynically justified himself by saying
that, having failed to make his wife hate him, he had
no other course but this.   After having deserted her,
Pembroke wrote apologetically to his wife, offering
to return.   The lady briefly replied " she had no
wish to see him till he had redeemed his character."
Subsequently, however, a reconciliation was effected,
and the couple lived together at Wilton almost as
comfortably as if nothing had happened.   Miss Hunter,
with whom Pembroke had run away, showed on her
part a spirit that went far towards condoning her
offence.   Her father had offered to receive her home
on condition of her returning to Lord Pembroke his
money and the child that had been born.   The former
she readily parted with ; as for the latter, it was, she
said, all now left her to live for.   Lady Pembroke's
sister, Lady Bolingbroke, also a reigning beauty of
the period, sat to Sir Joshua Reynolds for her portrait.
Lady Pembroke it was who, coming to the studio,
whispered in the artist's ear a message from Lord
Bolingbroke : " You must be sure to give the eyes
something of Nelly Brien."   That lady, as Horace
Walpole reminds us, was the frailest beauty of the
day.   Her portrait, also by Reynolds (1763), was in
the Manchester exhibition of 1857, and afterwards
found its way into the Hertford collection.   This
seventeenth century Lady Pembroke was the leading
spirit in the smartest section of the polite world of
her time.   She was, in fact, the typical predecessor
of the ladies who, in the latter half of the Victorian
age, were known as professional beauties.   Together

with Frances, Lady Brown, who loved laughing, she formed one of the jury of matrons who insisted upon George Montagu taking a house near Walpole at Strawberry Hill. In conjunction with the dowager Countess of Fife, she organised the first masquerade ever witnessed in Edinburgh, and gave to the canny Scot, Almack, the idea of starting the rooms that, a little later, were the fashionable feature in King Street, St. James's Square. " But for Lady Pembroke," is Walpole's comment, " the masquerade would never have been known in that northern land where no masquers were before." This was the Lady Pembroke who, having first delighted her guests by rehearsing the part at Wilton, appeared a little later as a pilgrim in a fancy ball at Richmond ; the Duchess of Richmond on the same occasion being a Persian sultana, the Duchess of Grafton Cleopatra, Mrs. Fitzroy the pride of a Turkish harem, Lady George Lennox and Lady Bolingbroke Greek girls in "the most piquant costumes you can imagine." The scene on which, on the close of the eighteenth century, the curtain fell at Wilton was one of fashionable cosmopolitanism. The eleventh Lord Pembroke had married (1784) Elizabeth, daughter of Dr. Johnson's Topham Beauclerk. On her death in 1808 he took, as his second wife, Catharine, daughter of Count Woronzow. That Russian diplomatist, during the years in which Anglo-Russian relations were embroiled by such questions as the ownership of Malta and the right of search at sea, had been repeatedly sent by the Czar to England. Having for a time acted as permanent ambassador at the Court of St. James's, he left the

Wilton, Woronzow, and Wraxall

Russian service, settled down to a country gentleman's life in Hampshire, and, as has been seen, saw his daughter become the eleventh Lady Pembroke. The twelfth Earl also took to himself a foreign wife (1814), a daughter of the Duke of Lorraine and widow of the Sicilian prince, Buttera. Wilton thus became the most fashionable rural rendezvous of Europe as well as of England. Among its English guests was one who contrived grievously to compromise himself with its foreign connections. This was the diarist, Nathaniel Wraxall, who had attributed to Woronzow's authorship the report of the Prince of Wurtemburg having connived at malpractices which had brought his wife to her death. Lord Pembroke himself was not only an influential Russian's son-in-law; according to Wraxall, he had other family connections with highly-placed Russians.[1] It is not, therefore, surprising that the next time the diarist visited Wilton he thought his welcome less warm than usual. The institution of legal proceedings soon explained to him the reason. For some time to come the week's-end guests at Wilton talked of little else than the great *cause célèbre* of the day. In much the same fashion, seventy years afterwards, country-house companies in several parts of England were to discuss the proceedings against Edmund Yates of the *World*, ending as these did with Lord Coleridge's sentence of imprisonment at Holloway. Wraxall was condemned to a fine of £500 and six months loss of liberty. The money having been paid and half the term served,

[1] "Wraxall," vol. i. p. 150. Note Raikes' Journal, vol. i. p. 34.

the Anglo-Russian agencies, organised in the Wilton drawing-room, set him at liberty.

Throughout the entire Victorian era Wilton remained the chief social rallying ground in the South of England for the political forces gradually being raised against Whiggism. In 1839 the Melbourne faction had disgusted and alarmed the fashionable Tories by coquetting with the Radicals. In those days the very charge of being a Radical was bad enough. It was in the Wilton drawing-room that a fine lady, hearing the unsavoury word mentioned, languidly. asked what it might mean. Then, remembering herself, she said, "Ah, I think I have heard. They are a sort of people who go about with Dissenters, vegetarians, homœopathists and other uncomfortable persons." If the mere suspicion of Radicalism were a disgrace, the fact of not being clean shaven grievously aggravated it. G. F. Muntz, who had just got in for Birmingham, was not only the first member of the House of Commons to wear a beard ; he was also charged with Chartist associations. The company at Wilton could scarcely contain itself for disgust and alarm. When this same gentleman was put on the commission of peace by the Government, the Lord and Lady Pembroke of the day thought that the reign of law approached its end. Nothing remained, they said, but to consign their art treasures to the cellars of Coutts' Bank, to shut up their houses in town and country, and to live abroad till the Whig tyranny were overpast. While such was the con-versational strain of the Wilton drawing-room, news came first of the odious charge, due of course to Whig malignity, against one of the Duchess of Kent's suite, Lady Flora Hastings. A little later Charles Greville or George Villiers brought the news of Lady Flora's death. The Whig ministers were, of course, as directly responsible for this as for the bad seasons, agricultural depression, and the big blue-bottle flies in the butchers' shops. The attack on Whiggism, from the social side, was ingeniously planned beneath the Pembroke roof. Their connection with the Radicals easily enabled the Wilton emissaries to represent Lord Melbourne and his colleagues as not less the enemies of humanity than the instruments of the Revolution. These were the men who wished to see the monarchy broken, provided they could hurl its fragments at the head of their opponents. Such were the sentiments uttered across the walnuts and the wine at the Wilton dinner-table. They were really echoes from the *Times*, whose slashing leaders were then talked in country houses much as they have been from that day to this. Things would not be so bad were there any restraining force on the other side. But, alas! the Wilton quidnuncs who were behind the scenes knew of course for a fact that the Duke of Wellington's powers were failing. At Wilton, too, it was that, some time subsequently to this, W. E. Gladstone, as the guest of his friend's sister-in-law, was to hear the first misgivings expressed about the then Tory leader. Sidney Herbert told Gladstone at Wilton that Peel's temper, though kept under thorough discipline, was naturally so violent as to render him liable to break out and do untold mischief at any moment. Among several commentators on that estimate, the fourteenth

Two Centuries of Wilton

Lord Derby's Foreign Secretary was perhaps the best informed critic. As a boy, the third Lord Malmesbury used to spend his winter holidays at Wilton with the Pembroke children for his playfellows. Agreeing with his friend Greville as to Sidney Herbert being a "smart fellow," not without some reason, as it proved some years later, he spoke of Sidney's innate and impulsive violence. The incident in question occurred in 1846 ; it arose out of the ministerial secessions that eventually left Sir Robert Peel and Lord Derby the respective leaders of rival factions. On March 15, 1846, at one of Lady Palmerston's Cambridge House receptions, Sidney Herbert excitedly told Malmesbury that his conduct in leaving Peel was unworthy a gentleman ; all the Protectionists, he added, were a set of fools, Lord Stanley was " the greatest fool of all, and Peel was delighted at having got rid of us." Subsequently the two disputants met amicably at Mrs. Norton's tea-table ; before the week was out they were visitors together at Wilton, reunited as they rambled through the grounds in the same friendship as when they had played there together in their childhood. The non-political visitors at Wilton had always been among the most interesting. In addition to those already mentioned, there came in the sixteenth and seventeenth centuries the clerical kinsman of the house, the poet George Herbert, from his neighbouring rectory Bemerton, with his friend Izaac Walton, who often angled successfully in the streams that flow through the park. The most interesting figure in the category of gentle and gracious visitors belongs to our own time and, at the present moment of writing, still survives. Florence

Florence Nightingale and Palmerston

Nightingale, though born in the Italian town from which she takes her name, is the daughter of a Hampshire neighbour of the Wilton family. The accident of locality had made her name familiar to Sidney Herbert, long before he went to the War Office. When little more than thirty, as Peel's secretary at the Admiralty, he had heard that the Squire of Embley's daughter was inspecting the European hospitals and contemplated training herself as a nurse at Kaiserswerth. Shortly before her visit, in 1856, to Queen Victoria at Balmoral she was more than once a guest at Wilton. At Wilton, too, was organised, in 1855, the national testimonial to Miss Nightingale, whose details were first explained by Sidney Herbert himself at a Willis's Rooms meeting, presided over by the Duke of Cambridge (Nov. 29, 1855). Of Sidney Herbert's statues, that in Pall Mall by Foley seems in all respects better than Marochetti's work in Salisbury market-place. Between his tall, handsome presence and that of one who had borne the same surname before him, Lord Herbert of Cherbury, as well as between the chivalrous characters of both, something like a family resemblance exists. Among the contemporaries of the statesman who died Lord Herbert of Lea, none visited Wilton more frequently than Lord Palmerston or more pungently put on record a sense of the moral value to public life of his example and influence. Politics, he said, threaten now, as they never did before, to degenerate to mere thimble-rigging or the three-card trick. If, in the next century, they do not reach that level, we shall have to thank men like Sidney Herbert. A year or two later, on Herbert's death, Palmerston

Two Centuries of Wilton

delivered in the House of Commons perhaps the one
entirely pathetic speech he ever made. " I had
trusted," said the aged Premier, "that after I was
gone, he would lead the gentlemen of England." As
he said the words his voice trembled; he turned
aside to conceal the tears which had risen. Wilton,
indeed, abounds in Palmerston memories of the
pleasantest kind. Here, looking out upon the cedars,
is the schoolroom, in which the present fourteenth
Lord Pembroke and his brother were reading with
their governess. Suddenly the door opens, Lord
Palmerston enters, takes up the book, which happens
to be " Robinson Crusoe," and curtails the morning's
studies by talking to his young friends for more than
half an hour about it. Presently, rejoining another
visitor, Sir Thomas Acland, he goes down to the
grounds, and, under the cedars themselves, sees
a third young Herbert puzzling over some Latin
"longs and shorts," set him as a holiday task and
keeping him from his fishing. "Acland," says
Palmerston, " do that boy's verses for him." The
exercise is finished in a moment as by magic; within
ten minutes the released captive is dropping his line in
the stream spanned by the Palladian bridge.

CHAPTER VII

MARSTON AND LONGLEAT

THE autumn of 1904 witnessed the revival of associations, equally interesting in society and politics, at two country houses which may be described as in the direct line of progress from Salisbury to

189

Marston and Longleat

St. Michael's Mount. The ninth Lord Cork's death
in the later months of the year not only deprived
Somersetshire of an adroit and active Lord-Lieutenant,
but closed a rural, as well as urban, rallying centre of
orthodox Liberalism. As Mr. Gladstone's some time
Master of the Buckhounds, the ninth Lord Cork,
essentially assisted by his wife, a daughter of the
house of Clanricarde, one of the wittiest as well
as most highly endowed of the great ladies of her
day, had been for many years among the entertainers of his party, both in his London house and
at his Somersetshire seat. His ancestor in Elizabethan times was the younger son of an incon-
siderable Herefordshire squire. That was the period
when England sent her impecunious gentry to make
their fortunes in Ireland. The founder of the Cork
earldom first settled on Irish soil in 1588, with, to
quote his own inventory of his possessions, less than
thirty shillings in cash, a diamond ring, a gold bracelet,
a taffeta doublet, a pair of black velvet breeches,
competent under-linen, other little unnamed neces-
saries, a rapier, a dagger, and two cloaks. He had
the knack of transmuting whatever he touched into
gold. Apart from real estate, houses and parks, he
soon could reckon his income at £50 a day. The
basis of these fortunes had been a marriage with a
Limerick heiress. His success made enemies, who,
among other unkind things, said that he was in the
pay of Spain. Summoned to England to answer
these charges, he soon found himself in the Tower.
Restored to liberty by the Queen, he obtained a
snug Irish sinecure—Clerk to the Council in Munster.

The Rise of Marston

The confiscations following the Earl of Desmond's rebellion further enriched this fortunate Boyle, who also made a wise investment in buying Sir Walter Raleigh's Munster lands at a bargain. At the beginning of the seventeenth century the first Lord Cork held most of the Irish property now possessed by the Duke of Devonshire, and worth not much less than £50,000 a year. About a generation later, Boyle, now squire of Marston in England, supplied Charles I. with £20,000 for the expedition against the Scots. In repayment he received his earldom a few years later. The extent of his dominions and influence, the stately profusion in which he lived, his power with the sovereign he had helped so lavishly, caused him to be known as the great Earl of Cork. In Ireland, he led the movement having for its object the extinction of Romanism, the extension of Protestant faith or authority, and the substitution of English settlers for aboriginal peasants on the fertile soil of Leinster. He succeeded in converting his clerical brother into an episcopal pluralist as Bishop of Cork, Cloyne, and Ross. Other relatives became respectively Archbishop of Tuam, Archbishop of Armagh, and Bishop of Waterford. The head of the family died Lord Chancellor of Ireland, bequeathing to his eldest son his estates and the now extinct viscountcy of Blesinton. Other sons, inheriting their father's good fortune and brains, became peers. The most intellectually distinguished of the number refused a peerage. The eldest son, Viscount Boyle, afterwards second Earl, made great additions to the family property in the North of England by marrying into the Cliffords of Cumberland. His daughter's marriage united the families and the estates of the Boyles and the Cavendishes. The son of that marriage has left a memorial of his building tastes in Cork Street, in Burlington House, Piccadilly, and in Chiswick House, afterwards known as the Duke of Devonshire's cottage on the Thames. Upon the death of the fourth Earl of Cork, the title passed to the fifth Earl of Orrery; he thus became the fifth Earl of Cork and Orrery. The second of these titles is perpetuated by the astronomical instrument which its inventor, Graham, named after his Oxford friend and fellow student; for Graham's contemporary, the fourth Lord Orrery, had won a high reputation at Christ Church before becoming involved in the controversy about the Phalaris Letters. This was the dissertation which first made Bentley's fame world-wide. Marston abounds in memorials of these episodes. They have always formed the centre of literary interest. It would have been well for Anglo-Irish relations if all Saxon adventurers who have achieved prosperity on the other side of St. George's Channel suggested to the Celtic mind associations not less agreeable than those grouping themselves round Marston. Jonathan Swift was only one of many distinguished visitors from the sister kingdom to the Somersetshire home of the Boyles. There he met his pet aversion—the Hanoverian apologist, Burnet, the tame cat of the place, and the poet diplomatist, John Gay, a Barnstaple man by birth, but in whose veins his Boyle hosts had discovered some Irish blood to flow. Gay's sojourns at Marston proved sufficiently eventful. It was here that a suggestion of Swift sowed in his mind the seed of the " Beggar's Opera." Twelve years later, in 1728, the play made its immediate and extraordinary success. The Lord Cork of the period assisted at its first performance. In a letter, written after leaving the theatre, to his wife, he spoke of the audience as not at once recognising in Captain MacHeath, the highwayman, Sir Robert Walpole. It was not, he said, the Peachum and Lockit dialogues or song which saved the piece and made its fortune, but Lavinia Fenton's impersonation of Polly. This actress, he adds, is not particularly pretty, but she has the most piquant face and manner, as others than his Grace of Bolton think, of any young female now on the stage. The Duke of Bolton, a handsome scapegrace, recently separated from his wife, first made the " Polly " of the play his mistress and afterwards his wife. The several children she bore him all came before marriage, the youngest, a clergyman, dying in 1809. As Duchess of Bolton the actress visited at Marston, and created among the company a perfect enthusiasm by her finished manners, her bright intelligence, and her delightful conversation. Lord Bathurst and Lord Granville, each of them then between seventy and eighty, nearly let their jealousy about her provoke a duel between them in Marston park. The Bolton peerage, belonging to the main line of the Paulet family, died out with Harry, the fifth Duke, in 1794. Lavinia Bolton was the second lady described as an actress whose posterity belonged to the peerage. The first was the progenitress of the Beauclerks—Nell Gwyn. Another was Miss Farren, the twelfth Earl of Derby's second wife. She became the ancestress of the Earls of Wilton, but not of the later Earls of Derby, who sprang from the twelfth Lord Derby's marriage with Elizabeth, daughter of the sixth Duke of Hamilton and Brandon. The seventh Countess of Cork, to whom Marston chiefly owes its hospitable reputation, was by birth the first Viscount Galway's daughter. The ninth Lady Cork could have had no more appropriate precursor than this hostess, who not only made her husband's social fortune, but, in the political circles of the last quarter of the eighteenth century, prepared the way for the position, taken a little later by Mrs. Crewe, with her favourite toast of "True blue and all of you." Curiously enough, speaking of the seventh Lady Cork, as she afterwards became, Boswell uses the words "the lively Miss Moncton who used always to have the finest bit of blue at her parties." Born April, 1746, she died at the end of May, 1840.

That curious whole length at Longleat of Frances, Duchess of Richmond and Lennox, came from Easton Neston, the Earl of Pomfret's seat. The best picture of her is in Wilson's "Life of King James," and very diverting indeed. Horace Walpole's words suggest the dominant characteristic of the Longleat galleries. Their contents are, in a special degree, pictures with a history. The country home of the Corks, though close to the Wiltshire frontier, is within Somerset by two or three miles. That of the Baths

Longleat's Story

belongs to Wiltshire rather more decidedly than Marston does to Somerset. The place takes its name from the leat or watercourse which feeds the fine lake in front of the house. A priory formerly stood on the ground to-day occupied by a palace. Its inmates first made the conduit for the stream, that it might turn their mill. After the dissolution of the monasteries the place was sold by Henry VIII. to Sir John Horsey; he, eleven years later, in 1540, parted with it to Sir John Thynne, a favourite of Protector Somerset. The two men had first become acquainted when they were prisoners together in the Tower. Escaping his patron's end at the block, Thynne became controller to the Princess Elizabeth during her sister's reign. According to tradition, in the fine house built by him Thynne had for his architect John of Padua. The masons employed were, however, entirely Wiltshire workmen. The structure had not been long finished before, in April, 1567, it was destroyed by fire. The rest of Sir John Thynne's life was occupied with building the house that exists to-day; he left it incomplete. The work was not fully done before the fourth Thynne (Sir James) secured the services of Sir Christopher Wren, whose personal contribution to the fabric seems to have consisted of two stately staircases. In 1670 the inheritance passed to the nephew of Sir James, Thomas Thynne, the "Tom of Ten Thousand," whose shooting by Count Königsmark in Pall Mall is depicted on the well-known memorial to him in the south aisle of Westminster Abbey. The next owner of Longleat was Thomas Thynne, the first

Marston and Longleat

Viscount Weymouth.   During his proprietorship the
place contracted the earliest of those ecclesiastical
associations that continued to the nineteenth century
its social characteristic.   On entering the library at
Longleat attention is at once fixed by the portrait, in
an old frame, of a keen, ascetic face, whose penetrating
eyes almost seem to follow and look through the
visitor in whatever quarter of the room he may be.
The dress worn consists of full canonical robes, whose
priestliness is brought out in stronger relief by the
black silk skull cap surmounting them.   This, of
course, is the famous seventeenth- and eighteenth-
century Bishop of Bath and Wells.   The Kens had
been settled in East Somerset before the Thynnes
were known in Wiltshire.   The religious tradition of
Winchester School, which Warden Barter at a later
day did so much to revive, was less that of its founder,
William of Wykeham, than of Thomas Ken.   If it
was not in the groves and galleries of Longleat that
Ken first meditated his Evening and Morning Hymns,
he certainly here impressed upon them the final shape
in which they have become classical.   Here, too, it
was that he began to set both compositions to music,
singing them to his lute before rising in the morning
or retiring to rest at night.   A little dark oak box
in the Longleat library used to contain, and may contain still, not exactly the musical score for these compositions, but a memorandum by their author of his
ideas about their rendering.   Ken, who was Fellow of
New College in 1657, came to Oxford, an ardently
devout and impressionable youth, some two years
earlier, matriculating in the same term as his con-

Ken and Thynne at Oxford and Longleat

temporary and life-long friend, the Thynne afterwards
Lord Weymouth. The shock of discovering the
University so little like their pious anticipations of it
drew still closer the sympathetic ties of the intimacy.
Instead of being a holy cloister, the place seemed a
pandemonium of Antinomian Puritanism and Republican profanity. The Book of Common Prayer was still
forbidden. The proctor was a boisterous fellow, great
only at cudgelling and football. The vice-chancellor
went about in Spanish leather boots, huge ribbons at
the knee, and his hat mostly cocked. The two fresh-
men were proof against the moral contaminations of
the academic atmosphere. With the future bishop
disgust only sealed the resolution to become an
educational reformer. "With God's help I will lay a
foundation now to make the next generation better."
The remark was addressed by him to Weymouth at
Longleat. Meanwhile, since their Oxford days, the
Churchman had shown his independence of royal
patronage with consequences to himself that were
more creditable to Charles II. than Ken had expected.
The Court of the Restoration was passing the summer
at Winchester while Ken belonged to the capitular
body. A fragment of dialogue between Canon Ken
and Lord Weymouth, relating to this period, has
been preserved : "They are going, I hear, to billet
Madam Eleanor Gwyn upon your prebendal residence." "They will do no such thing," Ken replied.
And when Nell announced her impending arrival
beneath the canonical roof she received the polite but
firm reply that no accommodation could be offered.
"This fellow," remarked the King to Thynne, "may

be a hypocrite, but is not a sycophant. Od's fish, I must make a bishop of him." Very shortly after the royal mistress had almost seen the prebendal door closed in her face, the see of Bath and Wells fell vacant. It was at once offered to and accepted by Ken. The only time Charles appears to have seen Ken was on his death-bed. "That prelate of mine," murmured the moribund sovereign, "has spoken to me like a man inspired." Yet a little later, Bishop Ken and Viscount Weymouth are once more at Longleat together. The latter beseeches his friend not to sacrifice his career by refusing to humour James II. "Surely," observes the nobleman, "we Catholics of all schools ought to rally round the Throne against Presbyterians, Brownists, Muggletonians, Fifth Monarchy men, Sixth Swingers, and Atheists." Bath and Wells did not find this argument convincing. He accordingly was one of the seven diocesans whose acquittal formed the signal for the landing of Orange William. But though the good Anglican prelate distrusted Romanism, he retained his loyalty to the Stuarts. He refused the oath of allegiance to the usurper. He thus became the most illustrious among the episcopal nonjurors whom William ejected from their sees. "A noble and faithful friend, even like a brother born for adversity." Such was Ken's description of the old college comrade who now made Longleat the dispossessed prelate's home. Near the old library stood the rooms assigned to the bishop. Throughout the Thynne period the mansion had been a hospitable centre for the fashionable and famous who found their local metropolis at the neighbouring city of

Uncle Izaac Walton

Bath. It now became the resort of a theology culture and learning, whose influences radiated throughout the country and even coloured the religion and the philosophy of the time. Izaac Walton, a native of Staffordshire, after thirty years of business as a London linen draper, had married a great-grand-niece of Archbishop Cranmer. Some twenty years later he found a second wife in Bishop Ken's half-sister Ann. The son of this marriage, Ken's nephew, the Reverend Izaac Walton, was vicar of a neighbouring village, Poulshot, and a frequent guest at Longleat. Another clergyman, the family chaplain, Doctor Harbin, and a Nonconformist divine, who lived at Frome, Singer, with a widowed daughter, Elizabeth Rowe, who kept house for him, completed this little company, whose literary relics remain among the Longleat archives. These contain hymns of Ken's as yet unpublished, the most pathetic being an anodyne for pain, in which occurs this verse :—

> "One day of pain improves me more
> Than years of ease could do before ;
> It is by pain God me instructs,
> And so to endless bliss conducts."

At Longleat the good bishop remained for twenty years. When in tolerable health he was excellent company. A habit of drowsiness seems to have grown upon him, but so long as he could keep his eyes open he held the table in a roar. Dying at Longleat, Thomas Ken, according to his wish, rests in the nearest parish church within his old diocese, St. John's, Frome.

The secular associations of Longleat in the sixteenth century, like its ecclesiastical connections a little later, are memorialised in the portraits that adorn its walls. The most famous personage round whom these political memories group themselves lives still on Holbein's canvas, wearing a black jewelled cap, the Order of the Garter, and the George. This was Protector Edward Seymour, first Duke of Somerset. Sir John Thynne, beginning as his confidential agent and secretary, became his most intimately trusted friend, as well as, at Longleat, his habitual host. "After my services in the army and at Court," said Somerset on one of these occasions to his friend, " I became esquire to the King, much pleasing His Majesty by my prowess in the Greenwich tilt-yard when the Court kept Christmas there." From being Viscount Beauchamp, Seymour became, in 1537, Earl of Hertford. Wulfhall, the house of Seymour's father, is in the same part of the county as Longleat. Both places were visited by Henry VIII. about the time that he made himself Seymour's brother-in-law. The tradesmen's bills and other documents relating to such occasions, preserved at Longleat, show the magnificent scale of these hospitalities, as well as the exact cost at which a barn at Wulfhall was fitted up as a ballroom for Jane Seymour's wedding-dance. Longleat, too, witnessed some of the interviews held by Jane Seymour's royal husband with Somerset, Paget, and Thynne about the succession and the future Edward VI.'s training. Somerset's letters, still extant at Longleat, abound in language prophetic of the writer's fall. It was the " *ego et rex meus* " of Wolsey over again. " Edward, Protector by the

grace of God," grandiosely sends greeting to his
"well-beloved Mr. Thynne." In other places the
royal plural is employed : "It is our intention," &c.
In the January of 1552 the end came on Tower Hill.
It was met with the courage and piety to which the
Longleat papers contain a testimony. Having presented his sword to the Lieutenant of the Tower, he
handed his money and rings to the headsman. That
did not ensure the skilful performance of the work.
Having risen up once to remove his doublet, he laid
his head on the block a second time before receiving
the death-stroke.

Another historic ghost of the Seymour family and
name, also depicted by Holbein's brush, haunts Longleat. This was the fourth son of the Wulfhall house.
Thomas, Lord Seymour of Sudeley, had inherited all
the ambition of his line. His skill in seamanship had
fairly won him the place of Lord High Admiral. He
aspired to the hand of the Princess Elizabeth (the
future queen). Edward VI. would not hear of this,
but offered him a surviving stepmother, Anne of
Cleves, though preferring his uncle should take the
Princess Mary with a view to converting her to Protestantism. Eventually Seymour of Sudeley married
Queen Katharine Parr, to whom he had been attached
while she was yet only Lord Latimer's widow. The
marriage was kept a secret. It only, indeed, became
known after Katharine's death. The disfavour of his
brother the Protector brought Sudeley, after a mock
trial, to the scaffold. The doomed man requited the
fraternal hatred, and occupied the last days of his life
with an attempt to incite his sovereign's two sisters to

Marston and Longleat

rebellion against the Protector. The portrait in the
Longleat library shows him as a remarkably handsome
and powerfully made man. Beneath the painting are
written the words : " A subject true to king and
friend to God's truth." That was not the universal
estimate. Admitting him to have died with a courage
worthy of a better cause, Bishop Latimer calls Sudeley
"a man furthest from the fear of God that ever I
heard of in England. Whether he can be saved or
no, God in the twinkling of an eye can save a man
and turn his heart. When a man hath two strokes
with an axe, who can tell but between the two strokes
he doth repent ? "

Among Longleat's *habitués* during the last quarter
of the seventeenth century, the most interesting and
pathetic story belongs to the original of the finest
Vandyke possessed by the place. This was Thomas
Wriothesley, last of the Southampton earls. The
best Longleat portraits belonging to this period are
all of Royalists. Under circumstances recalling those
which inspired Tennyson's " In Memoriam," Southampton's father was returning from the Low Countries
to England. He had gone thither in the hope of
bringing back his eldest son for the recovery of his
health. The lad died during the journey. The
second son, Thomas Wriothesley, now his heir,
hastening to the English coast to welcome his two
relatives home, was so overcome by the shock of
finding his father in charge of a dead body, as to be
seized with an illness that for some time threatened to
prove fatal. He lived, however, to be Charles I.'s most
constant supporter as well as an active promoter of

Charles II.'s return. One of the four courtiers permitted to pass some hours by his master's bier, he
supplied his son with money. His loyalty to the
Stuarts never wavered; it did not, however, ensure his
approval of all the Court measures. Even under
Charles I. he had dissented from the policy of
Strafford, but had been confirmed in his opposition to
the democratic faction by Pym's declaration against
plots and conspiracies, which all the members of both
Houses, except himself and Lord Robartes, had
signed. His second daughter by his first wife found
a husband among his political opponents. As Rachel,
Lady William Russel, she has her place in the catalogue
of England's heroic matrons. The third Lady Southampton was the kinswoman of her lord, the second
Duke of Somerset's daughter and Lord Molyneux's
widow.

Among the artists who, not less than the divines
and thinkers of the seventeenth century, found a
home at Longleat, was the Dutch Cornelius Janssen.
A Londoner by birth, he almost lived with the
Thynnes till his settlement at Amsterdam in 1643. In
the studio set up for him in the Wiltshire house he
executed his finest portrait, that of Henry Rich, first
Lord Holland, himself the founder of the suburban
mansion whose fame does not yield to Longleat.
The handsomest as well as the most polished
and agreeable man of his age, he is seen in the
Longleat portrait as he was when he accompanied
Buckingham on his Spanish mission for negotiating
the marriage of the then Prince of Wales with the
Infanta. After that errand had miscarried, Holland

conducted the transaction which gave his future king a French wife in the Princess Henrietta Maria. From the first the lady showed herself more impressed by the grace and good looks of the envoy than by her destined lord. Holland himself found a wealthy wife in a London heiress, Sir John Cope's daughter. Taken prisoner by the Parliamentary army, he fell a victim to Cromwell's dislike of Presbyterians; these, influenced by his brother, Lord Warwick, were for sparing his life. Holland, however, suffered death on the same scaffold and in the same year that two months earlier had received a more august victim in Charles himself. Before Lord Holland knelt down to the block he had seen the head of his friend the Duke of Hamilton severed at a single blow. To the last he had retained his courtesy as well as his loyalty and courage. When going through the form of trial he scarcely answered his accusers, preferring, as he said, to receive his life from their favour rather than from the strength of his defence. Of his four sons, the eldest, Robert Rich, succeeded not only to his father's title, but also, on his uncle's death in 1672, to the Warwick earldom as well.

Near the portraits of Ken and Holland in the Longleat library is one of several counterfeit present-ments of Lucius Carey, second Viscount Falkland, executed by Vandyke during his five years' stay in England very shortly after he had finished his most famous painting of Charles I. The unique interest belonging to the Falkland likeness in the Longleat library comes from the fact that it represents its original, not in his brighter and more prosperous

A Death Suit to the King of Heaven

period, but during the time of his despair for his country, when the colour had left his face and all care for his appearance and dress had departed. In the chapel corridor is the Vandyke of Falkland's brother peer, also mortally wounded in Newbury fight. Bearing a title best known to-day for its revival in the Herbert family, the Earl of Carnarvon, contemporary with Falkland, was a Dormer by birth, successively created by Charles I. Viscount Ascot and Earl of Carnarvon. His cosmopolitan interests presaged those of some among his Herbert successors. From diplomatic missions abroad, he brought home some foreign vices, and liked high play as much as he loathed hard drinking. In the field he charged with the impetuosity of Rupert himself. Asked on his death-bed whether he had a last wish for the king, he replied, " I will not die with a suit in my mouth to any king, save the King of Heaven." The handsome wife, who in the Longleat picture holds Carnarvon's hand, was a daughter of the Pembroke Herberts. The most interesting among the Longleat family portraits are not in the library, but in the dining-room. Here is Lely's Henry Coventry, whose London house was in the Haymarket, on the very spot where Joseph Addison afterwards had a lodging, and whose name is perpetuated by a well-known street close by. Coventry's property went first to his nephew, James Thynne, afterwards to another descendant. The real founder of Longleat was this " Tom of Ten Thousand." He, having made his Wiltshire home the most famous house of the countryside and taken a wife who posed as a *femme incomprise*, found a favoured rival and his own assassin in Count Königsmark ; the actual death-shot was fired by a Pole, hired for the business. Königsmark was acquitted ; the bravos in his pay were hung. The chief of them on his way to the gallows complained of dying for two men and a woman, on none of whom he had ever set eyes. The Duke of Monmouth, Thomas Thynne's great friend, in whose arms the murdered man died, brought the conspirators to justice. Some there were who thought the fatal shot had been intended for Monmonth and not its actual victim. The surviving physiognomy of the Thynne family, the square, broad forehead, the clear-cut features, especially the fine nose and the firm chin, as well as a certain winning expression of face and grace of manner, were brought into the family by "Tom of Ten Thousand," or by his father, Sir Thomas of Richmond, who had taken a wife with Stuart blood in her veins. Not far from the unfortunate "Tom of Ten Thousand," the Longleat table is looked down upon from the walls by another Thomas Thynne. By inheritance the third Viscount Weymouth, he so delighted George III. by the delicate considerateness as well as magnificence of his hospitality, that before bidding adieu to his host and his 125 fellow-guests, the royal visitor insisted upon bestowing a marquisate upon the princely owner of a place whose reputation for beauty was altogether surpassed by the reality. Beside this nobleman is the first marchioness, who, together with her dower, brought to the Thynne family a connection with two historic houses. The second Duke of Portland's daughter, Lady Elizabeth Cavendish Bentinck, had for her mother the grand-daughter of Queen Anne's minister, Harley, Earl of Oxford. The alliances made by the daughters of this marriage formed links connecting Longleat with the Ashburnhams, Aylesfords, and Chesterfields.

Longleat's most interesting political associations are connected with the latter half of Queen Victoria's reign. " If in private business two men were to come to a breach when standing so near to one another in aim and profession, they would be shut up in Bedlam." So at Longleat, in the late summer of 1884, observed the eighth Duke of Argyll to a fellow-guest, his former Cabinet chief, W. E. Gladstone. The occasion of the remark was the difference between the two Houses developed by the Liberal scheme for giving to country householders the electoral rights conferred seventeen years earlier by the Conservatives on householders in towns. On the object of the measure, both parties to the controversy were professedly as nearly of one mind as the Duke had put it. In his dislike of political change, the fourth Lord Bath showed himself a true descendant of his Tory ancestors. He shared, however, the Gladstonian view that it would be impolitic and futile for the peers to use redistribution as a death weapon against franchise. Agreeing with the Liberal leader upon the impracticability of successfully dealing with the two subjects in a single Bill, he did not condemn the fifty-nine senators, gradually falling to fifty afterwards, who, in the Gladstonian phrase, had " put an effectual stoppage on the measure." Like many others of his order, he was now chiefly concerned to prevent the agricultural labourers' enfranchisement being turned into an

Marston and Longleat

agitation against the veto of the Upper House. The essential details of this episode are given in the third volume (pp. 125–130) of Mr. John Morley's monumental biography. The fourth Lord Bath's ecclesiastical sympathies were those of his titular leader, Lord Salisbury, on the one hand, and of his personal intimate, Mr. Gladstone, on the other. Resistance without quarter to Gladstonianism was the cry that had gone forth from Lord Abergavenny at Eridge. The politics of the early eighteenth century seemed reproducing themselves ; it was daily becoming more and more a war of country houses.

From Balmoral to Goodwood, and thence to Hatfield, the sovereign's conciliatory counsels had been carried by the Duke of Richmond. It was Lord Bath and one of his clerical guests, well known to Mr. Gladstone, who laid the first plank of the golden bridge across which there sounded from Hawarden the note for a movement, if not of surrender, at least towards compromise. The fourth Lord Bath was one of the few Tory High Churchmen whose continuance of personal relations with Mr. Gladstone qualified him for a mediatorial part between that statesman and his own leader, Lord Salisbury. Throughout the negotiations occupying the next few weeks, he was well served by one of his most frequent clerical visitors, Canon MacColl, then the depositary of many communications to and fro between Longleat, Hawarden, and Hatfield. Nothing now remained but for the principals in the transaction to select their representatives in the discussion about the lines on which redistribution should proceed. The Longleat nominees could be none other than Lord Salisbury's nephew, Mr. Arthur Balfour, then a private M.P., and Lord Hartingdon, then Liberal Secretary of State for War. The Longleat county franchise treaty of 1884 was fraught with consequences more far-reaching than then seemed likely. It promoted between the master of Chatsworth and the representative of Hatfield the habit of political co-operation which was to grow into an agency for the joint control of Unionism. It educated a future premier in that re-allotment of Parliamentary seats which in the next century he was to take up on his own account. Nor in that century was Longleat to find itself disconnected with the public service of the country, though in a different sphere of usefulness. The fifth Lord Bath is the chairman of King Edward's Commission for ascertaining the best treatment of painful diseases arising out of existing conditions of industrial life. In the autumn of 1904 he gathered at Longleat his colleagues in this benevolent work and the medical specialists, competent by their experience to advise and direct in such a matter. The eighth Duke of Marlborough used humorously to anticipate the time when Blenheim Palace would be utilized as a school of hygienics. That was before the Health Congress at Longleat.

CHAPTER VIII

A MORE notable *chef d'œuvre* by Sir Peter Lely
at Longleat even than the "Tom of Ten
Thousand," is his painting, in the library, of the most
famous among the founders of the Dorsetshire
country house first reached after leaving the adjoining
county. The tiny man, gorgeous in a Chancellor's
coloured robes, looking down upon Lord Bath's writing-table from above the storeys of bookshelves, is the
leading spirit of the Cabal ministry, the "Ahitophel"
of Dryden's satire, "for close designs and crooked

A Chancellor's Childhood

counsels fit," known to history as Anthony Ashley Cooper, first Earl of Shaftesbury. His paternal ancestors, the Coopers, lived at Rockbourne in Hampshire. His father, Sir John Cooper, married Anne, daughter and heiress of another baronet, Sir Anthony Ashley, of Wimborne St. Giles. Here, while his parents were his grandfather's guests, the future Lord Chancellor was born in 1621. The child's physical dimensions were a maternal inheritance; for his father, Sir John Cooper, is described by his son as lovely and graceful in mind and person; his mother's father, Sir Anthony Ashley, as having a large intellect but his person of the lowest. That relative had, in the year just named, himself married a young wife. The fact did not diminish his delight in his new grandson, who he insisted should find a home beneath his own roof. Ashley Cooper, therefore, was bred where he had been born. When only ten years of age the boy lost, nearly at the same time, both his parents and his grandfather. Under the latter's will he became heir to large but encumbered estates and to the persistent ill-will of litigious relatives. In his autobiography he has described his life with Sir Daniel Norton, one of his trustees, in London. Afterwards he found a home with a relative named Tooker, near Salisbury. Meanwhile little Ashley Cooper had given precocious proof of a tactful prudence which was to checkmate his domestic enemies. His territorial rights were assailed by his relatives. At the age of thirteen, being in London, he contrived to see Noy, the Solicitor-General, and appealed so successfully for his assistance that, without any fee, a suit in the Court of Wards was at once decided in the boy's favour. At the time of his birth there had been among his grandfather's guests an astrologer, who foretold for the infant a great career in troublous times. The prediction, remembered throughout life by its subject, explains the lawyer's partiality for planetary lore. "Stars," in his own words, "told perhaps more truth than may at the time have been thought." The first part of the horoscope was fulfilled by performances at Exeter College, which won him the reputation of the most prodigious youth in the University. There came a further correspondence of prophecy to fact when, as an undergraduate of eighteen, the young man married Lord Keeper Coventry's daughter. The pair lived in London but made frequent country visits. Once, falling ill at Tewkesbury, Ashley Cooper displayed a patience and courage, so much admired by the electors for the borough, or their wives, as to secure him the Parliamentary seat. His opponent was a wealthy and unpopular Sir Henry Spiller. While absent from the place, the rising light of the law was chosen and unanimously returned as its member without a single penny of expense. By a second marriage he became the Earl of Exeter's son-in-law, thus connecting the Ashley Coopers with the Cecils. Going with the times, he aspired to a third wife in Cromwell's daughter. He urged the Protector to take the title of king. Popular feeling declared for the Restoration. While serving Cromwell, Sir Anthony Ashley had been intriguing with Charles; he had received the exiled prince secretly as his guest at Wimborne

The " Poor Man's Peer " at St. Giles'

St. Giles. He now led the Presbyterian faction that
promoted the renewal of the monarchy. He formed
one of the Parliamentary deputation of twelve sent to
Breda to bring back Charles. To Ashley Cooper it
was that, back in England, Charles said with a smile,
" Od's fish, man, they all seem so glad to see me,
'tis a pity I did not come before." The lady actually
taken by the first Lord Shaftesbury for his third wife
was a daughter of Lord Spencer, a niece of Lord
Southampton, who, Clarendon says, it was hoped
would restrain the slippery humour of his nephew-
in-law.

Wimborne St. Giles had belonged to the Ashleys
since the days of Edward IV. The different parts of
the long, rambling house group themselves round a
quadrangle. It was while strolling here with the
seventh Lord Shaftesbury as his host, that the
present writer heard the foregoing and many other
details about the ancestor to whom his descendant of
the Victorian age presented a contrast so dramatically
complete. The Lord Chancellor had a confidential
servant, in face and person curiously like himself.
Hence of course frequent mistakes and several of the
practical jokes to which this Keeper of the Royal
Conscience was much given. With much quiet
humour in the recital, would the good Lord Shaftesbury of our time recall his seventeenth-century
progenitor's doings, and especially a certain escape
from arrest abroad by pushing the valet, who was so
like him, into his place. In those days another
frequent and famous guest was the artist for whom
his host had obtained the promise of the baronetcy

that came nine years after his own death. In the last eighties Burne Jones was still busy with his designs for the memorial window to Lady Shaftesbury. Other visitors on the occasion now referred to were the late Lady Strangford, Mr. Gladstone, Messrs. Moody and Sankey, and, if I remember rightly, General Booth and Dr. George MacDonald. Of all the sights and associations connected with St. Giles' House, the chief interest for the host and often for his company lay in a paddock, where a prettily marked donkey passed its time between dozing and grazing. This was the animal which, a few years earlier, the costermongers of the East-end had clubbed together to give "the poor man's peer." Instances of this animal's intelligence and virtue only for a short time interrupted the flow of anecdotal tradition. One memory in particular of the first Lord Shaftesbury, recently disinterred from the St. Giles' archives, was dwelt on with humorous gusto by his descendant; it was also enlivened by quietly droll comment and gesture as accompaniments to the recital. The personal contrast between the Shaftesburys of the present and of the past gave the story, as it was conversationally told, a flavour not to be reproduced in print. Its substance was as follows. The Lord Chancellor had received from Mordaunt, at his London house in Aldersgate Street, warning of imminent peril. Taking with him a young nephew, he started for Harwich *en route* for Holland. The two were disguised respectively in the dress of a Presbyterian schoolmaster and his pupil. The severe garb, however, did not conceal the comely countenance and the long, yellow, chevalier

A St. Giles' Romance

ringlets of the lad. "As for me," said the hostess of
the wayside inn, "I shall ask no questions and tell
no tales. But perhaps this fair young sir had better
occupy the time of waiting for your ship in making
love to the maid ; for the hounds are already on your
scent." At this moment there seems to have arrived
Shaftesbury's servant who so closely resembled his
master. He was actually seized. The capture
enabled the fugitives safely to take ship. The exile's
stay at Amsterdam, where he had taken a large house,
proved shorter than he had expected. Gout in the
stomach came on. In the January of 1683 his dead
body was conveyed to Poole. The whole county
attended the funeral at Wimborne. The nineteenth-
century Wimborne St. Giles is charged with associations of Palmerston as well as with memories of the
exemplary relative who was regarded as the jaunty
premier's bishop-maker. The French seizure of
Savoy in 1860 added greatly to Palmerston's diplomatic worries, and caused him often during the week
to seek change of scene and air. Many of these
short holidays were taken at St. Giles' House.
Excusing himself for a late arrival, the minister on
one occasion said to his host, "The fact is Count De
Flahault (the French Ambassador) wanted some talk
with me before going to Paris. To kill two birds
with one stone I took him down to the station in my
brougham." "What was he to say to the Emperor?"
"In answer I could only refer him to John Russell's
words in the Commons. That speech, he said, was
offensive to his master. 'It was not,' I said,
'intended to be so.' He went on to speak of his

215

country as wishing to avoid but not fearing war. That was too much for me, so I said my historical reading taught me that a conflict between French and English on anything like equal terms would not be unsatisfactory to us. Flahault said he had been at Waterloo, and that his country's soldiers were much better now than they had been then. I rejoined by reminding him of the dialogue between Marshal Taillard and Marlborough after the former had been made prisoner at Blenheim. 'You have just beaten, my lord,' said Taillard, 'the best troops in Europe.' 'Always excepting,' the Duke added, 'the conquerors of the best troops.'" A little later in the evening the subject of Mr. Gladstone came up. Said Palmerston, " He will soon have it all his own way. Whenever he gets my place we shall have strange things." Other subjects mingled with the political talk at St. Giles in those days. The old statesman, known in former days as Cupid, did not think he had outgrown the name. Lady Shaftesbury remonstrated with him on his too marked attentions to young married women. " In the first place," she said, "it is very wrong ; in the second, it is most ungentlemanlike ; in the third, it is very stupid, for it can never succeed." Said the statesman in reply : " As to the religious aspect, I admit the practice of the Churches differs. As regards the taste, that is a matter of opinion. I think it most gentlemanlike. With reference to its results, your ladyship is totally misinformed, for I have never known it fail." In the place of any reminiscence like that just given, Lord Shaftesbury showed his visitors family memorials other than those belonging to the first peer of his line. Of these, if I remember rightly, the most remarkable was literature, personified by a female figure in the dress of the period, mourning for her most famous son, the third Earl, who wrote "The Characteristics." There was also a miniature reproduction of another effigy in the adjoining church, the three Fates unwinding the thread of the fifth Lord Shaftesbury's life.

The marriage of Richard Nevill the king-maker with a daughter of the then Lord Salisbury gave him, on the south of the Trent, a territorial sovereignty not less extensive than that which came to him from birth in the north. His chief southern residence was in the heart of that Cranbourne Chase district where we have been lingering. The exact spot may be identified with the site of another of Dorsetshire's rural homes to be visited before leaving the county. Part indeed of the older house, including fire-places and chimneys, seems to have been built into the existing Canford Manor. Before the ground was covered by any secular abode, it was occupied by a convent, whose lady-superior came from Belgium. The manor-house of to-day dates partly from the last half of the eighteenth century, but mainly belongs to a later period. Externally the great feature of the place is the pine-woods, into which the elaborate gardens open and the drives through which remind one of Archachon or Biarritz. These woods stretch in one direction nearly up to Poole, the Dorsetshire seaport that once formed part of the manor. The most ancient among the definitely ascertainable owners

of the estate was John of Gaunt, whose name has
perpetuated itself in certain details of the building.
The feudal forerunner of the patrician borough-
mongers of a later day, Gaunt frequently received
beneath his roof here his nominees in the detested
" nether house," to confer with them during the recess
on the steps to be taken for crushing his particular
opponent who had baffled so many of his designs,
John de la Mare, the indomitable chairman and
Speaker of the Commons. Geoffrey Chaucer, for a
short time knight of the shire for Kent, had been
placed under personal obligations by Gaunt; the poet
probably sympathised with his patron's aristocratic
ideas on Parliamentary polity. Local tradition still
points out the spot in the grounds on which the
haughty and ambitious Plantagenet used confidentially
to converse with the bard of " The Canterbury Tales."
Till 1765 Chaucer's room was the name given to one
of the Canford guest-chambers. The first five or six
decades of the nineteenth century possessed no better-
known specimen of the new type of commercial and
industrial M.P. than the then owner of Canford, Sir
John Guest. As member for Merthyr - Tydfil or
Glamorgan he had a seat at St. Stephen's for nearly
a quarter of a century. During part of the time his
discriminating hospitalities made Canford the most
influential of Dorsetshire socio-political centres. His
most frequent visitor during the Crimean epoch was
H. A. Layard. Those were the days in which
Palmerston (February 15, 1855), writing to his
brother, contrasted the improbability of a month
ago with the fact of his having become since Prime

Canford Antiquities and Politics

Minister. The Peelite coalition Government had fallen like straws before the wind. Of the politicians who had secretly laboured for that result, the honours belonged to Mr. Layard. Sir John Guest, an independent member of the Liberal party, distrusted the Russell faction as much as Mr. Layard disliked and plotted against that faction's chief. At Canford had been suggested or considered every move in the game whose object was to keep the Radical Russellites out and to get in the Palmerstonian Liberals, or, failing that, the Tories. Hence Lord Derby's overtures to the Peelites generally as well as to Palmerston in particular. If these would only take service under him, Lord Derby pledged himself that Disraeli would acquiesce in Palmerston's leadership of the Commons. The Canford Manor influence had signally helped Layard in becoming a political personage. At every stage of his progress the wealth of the Dowlais ironmaster had helped him. Thus on going to Ceylon in 1840, Layard had been able to take the valley of the Tigris in his way. Five years later the same support promoted the excavations, whose finds made him the celebrity of the moment and the first of acknowledged experts and authorities on every branch of the Eastern question, in connection with which specialism was at that time imperfectly developed. The Derby ministerial project failed. Palmerston came in. Layard remained for the rest of his time scarcely less acceptable to Conservatives than Palmerston himself. Most of this he owed directly to his Dorsetshire patrons. The prominence in the Canford gallery of some Assyrian sculptures, Layard's gift, remains the fitting and abiding testimony to the fact.

The political flavour acquired at this epoch by Canford has clung to it since. During the five years of his Under-Secretaryship at the Foreign Office, afterwards as Chief Commissioner of Works, next as a social and political leader of the Turcophilism which was the vogue in 1868, till his dispatch as Turkish Ambassador in the next year, Canford supplied Mr. Layard's backers with their organisation. Half a generation later the place performed a like office for the brother of its mistress and his Parliamentary friends. Lord Beaconsfield's Irish Viceroy, the seventh Duke of Marlborough, was the first Lady Wimborne's father. More certainly and uninterruptedly than at Blenheim he found at Canford the repose which was a periodical necessity in the few intervals of rest allowed to his upright and industrious career. Presently the chief political activities of the family became centred in Lord Randolph Churchill. His two principal henchmen as well as trusted and able advisers were already well known to his father. In this way Sir John Gorst and Sir Henry Drummond Wolff found themselves frequently the guests of their chieftain's brother-in-law. Throughout the late summer of 1885 the relations of Lord Salisbury and of Lord Randolph Churchill respectively with the Conservative Associations of the central union supplied episodes of chronic importance in the inner life of the Tory party. What Whitehall, Pall Mall, or Hatfield itself was to Conservative ministerial orthodoxy throughout the whole of that period, Canford remained to the Tory democrats of the Fourth Party. To them, in fact, it was what it had been a generation earlier to the little Palmerstonian group which, thanks chiefly to Sir John Guest's good offices, gathered itself round the fluent, florid, self-assured, and irrepressible Layard. Canford was not one of Delane's country houses. But later editors of the *Times* have been among the most frequent of its guests. No newspaper writer who dealt appreciatively with the second brother of its mistress was long left without an invitation to Canford. In 1895 the occasion for these attentions ceased to exist. In their place Lady Wimborne found in her Dorsetshire home the opportunity first for strengthening the social resources of Anglican Evangelicalism against the increasingly fashionable organisations employed by the Romanising agents of both sexes. In earlier days the programme of the Primrose Club had been considered and arranged under Randolph Churchill's eye, amongst others, by the then Sir Algernon Borthwick and Sir William Marriott in the Canford drawing-room or library. The whirligig of time works its revenges and Wisdom is justified of her children. Deviating from the Randolphian lines originally laid down for it, Primrosery, it was thought in Dorsetshire, inclined too much to become the instrument of fiscal reform. The Canford house-parties were therefore so arranged as to provide the adherence of orthodox Cobdenism with such a meed of recognition in Dorsetshire as well as in Arlington Street as would take away from it the reproach of only finding a home to-day beneath shabby genteel or at best middle-class roofs.

From Wilts through Dorset

The commercial territorialism which won its first recognition in the peerages bestowed by the second Pitt, has domiciled itself on ground even more ancient than that appropriated by it at Canford. The pedigree of Milton Abbey has its social roots in the earlier part of the tenth century. After having been the home successively of secular priests and Benedictine monks, it was bought for £1,000 from Henry VIII. Tregonwell himself had acted as the king's proctor in the divorce from Katharine of Arragon. He was also the progenitor of Tregonwell Frampton, popularly known as " the father of the turf." In this part of the county, indeed, horse-racing is still sometimes spoken of as an institution due to Dorsetshire. Tregonwell Frampton was certainly born near Dorchester, in the seventeenth century, and was employed as trainer at Newmarket by two of the Stuart kings. He was also employed by or associated with Godolphin, owner of the famous Arabian horse called after his name, of Tom Killigrew, and in their early youth two of Charles II.'s natural sons, the Dukes of Richmond and of Grafton ; his name is also remembered in connection with an act of barbarity to a high-mettled horse, too horrible to be mentioned. From the Tregonwells and the Framptons the place passed first to Sir Jacob Bancks, a member of the Swedish embassy to England, afterwards to the Damers, who became Earls of Dorchester. From the day that it found an owner in Baron Hambro it has never ceased to be the smart place of the district. Its best known earlier guests under this dispensation came from Eton, Trinity, Cambridge, or

George III. as Squire

Merton, Oxford. Visitors from this last named college soon made a discovery that the Dorsetshire Abbey church and the Oxford College chapel are built on the same lines. In each case the nave, though begun, was never finished. The Hambro restorations have been carried out at Milton with a perfection afterwards reproduced in a like work at Tewkesbury. Crichel, during the Victorian age, had, as a Conservative country house, something of the importance that in Kent belonged to Eridge. The first Lord Alington was then Mr. Sturt. His shooting parties in his Dorsetshire home, especially during the "jingo" period of 1868–70, were often worth several votes in a division to Disraeli. Nor, it was observed by those who knew him best, and in the country saw most of him, did the garb of an English squire seem anywhere to sit so naturally upon the Asiatic statesman as at Crichel.

During the summer of 1788, for the first time since succeeding to his grandfather's throne, George III. transformed himself from a sovereign into a country gentleman. His whole progress in that year through several southern counties, whether on the journey or at some temporary halt, was that not of a monarch but of a squire, to whom fresh air and exercise were necessities of daily life. Never before had he gone so far from Windsor as to Cheltenham. Here Bayshill Lodge was fitted up for him as a country house. His small suite consisted chiefly of the treasurer of his own household, Lord Courtown, his queen's vice-chamberlain, Sir Stephen Digby, and General Manners. Even these courtiers were left behind when the king took his long walks through fields and lanes. Nor did he perfunctorily go through his cure at the Gloucestershire spa. Indeed, he drank the Cheltenham waters too assiduously for his good. The copious draughts were thought to have set up an irritation of the nervous system, conducive to the later mental maladies. Lord Bathurst, celebrated by Pope, was visited at Oakley Grove. So too were Lord Fauconburg and one or two other hosts of that kind. The king liked, he said, their society ; he disliked being fêted, and stipulated that there should be no State entertainments. Crichel lay almost in his line of march but was not visited. It had been burnt rather less than half a century earlier. It was then being rebuilt by its Napier owners, afterwards to be much enlarged by the Sturts. It then received more than one royal visitor, notably the Prince Regent, who brought with him his daughter, the Princess Charlotte, for her temporary establishment here with the Dowager Countesses of Ilchester and Rosslyn. George III. however, on his progress through Dorsetshire, noticed an architectural work of the Sturts in the then just built Observatory, 200 feet high, surveying the entire interval of varied space between Dorchester to the west and on the other hand to the Needles. He was also much interested in the personal associations of the entire Crichel district. Here in the Woodlands district, belonging to Lord Shaftesbury, the unhappy Duke of Monmouth was taken by the soldiers of James, in a field known to this day as Monmouth's Close. A little more to the south every inch of the Sturt domain

Crichel's White Farm

is strewn with traditions about the wanderings and escapes of the second Charles. Among that Prince's local friends was a seventeenth-century lord of a great Dorsetshire manor, Squire Hastings, son of Lord Huntingdon, the most scientific sportsman of his day and district, whose example and instruction did much towards securing for the Crichel coverts their future fame. "Was not," during this ride inquired George III., "Joseph Addison born in these parts?" "He was," came the answer, "at a village hard by Crichel—Milston. Here the essayist's father, originally a chaplain at Tangier, became rector." Had the king been traversing the district a generation later he would have found it enriched with fresh literary associations. In the first half of the nineteenth century no Dorsetshire country house was more of a literary and generally intellectual centre than the rectory of Alton Priors, held by a former fellow of New College and public orator, W. Crowe, a poet considered in the running for the laureateship. A little later than this, at the neighbouring village of Nether Avon, the king would have found Sydney Smith in his first curacy, dependent for his food on the precarious weekly visits of the butcher, who often could not spare him meat, but left him to dine on potatoes flavoured with mushroom ketchup. The twentieth-century characteristics of Crichel date entirely from the first Lord Alington, so long the popular "bunny" Sturt of the House of Commons. Helped by his brother, Colonel Napier Sturt, he made what he called his "blanche" paradise a feature of his estate. It consists or consisted of a farm on which the colour of all the animals,

225   P

and so far as possible everything else, was white. " I hope the consciences of men and visitors," Lord Alington would sometimes add, "are of the same complexion." In Sussex, if I mistake not near East Grinstead, another white farm at this moment exists. Such are the wayside interests and associations of the country traversed by George III. on his journey through the Crichel country to the Dorsetshire watering-place, Weymouth. During the ride thither the king gave signal proof his kindliness and courage. He had recently visited, amongst other Gloucestershire spots of interest, Berkley Castle ; in conversation with his companion on Edward II.'s murder in that building the king seemed wholly preoccupied. A minute or two later, with the remark that he would ride on a little by himself, he spurred his horse and met a labourer briskly riding by the side of a wagon. Attempting to steer his horse between the equestrian and the cart, the king was somehow hit on the leg by the other rider and nearly precipitated into the wagon. Manners, seeing the accident, quickly rode up. Doubling the thong of his hunting crop, he lifted it against the man, exclaiming, "You scoundrel ! don't you see it is the king?" The countryman, petrified with surprise, remained speechless and in imminent peril of the courtier's lash. "Don't strike him on any account," suddenly exclaimed the sovereign ; "my knee is hurt a little, but it was altogether an accident, and will do me no real harm." On reaching the next stage, his majesty insisted on himself applying the liniment, then known as arque-busade, which had been procured. It proved to be a severe and painful contusion ; but the king would not confess himself disabled, and continued the journey as if nothing had occurred to interrupt it. Weymouth might almost be spoken of as an annex to Milton Abbey, already visited. The future home of the Hambros was enlarged in the eleventh century by a grant of the watering-place whither George III. went on horseback in 1788. The exact point in the esplanade to-day occupied by the royal statue marked the limit of the walk taken every morning before breakfast to and fro by the royal patron of the place. Some among the king's happiest days were passed on the Dorsetshire sea-coast. It was here that his second and favourite son, Prince Frederick, paid monthly, sometimes weekly, visits. On one of these the prince ceased to be known as titular Bishop of Osnaburgh, received the ducal titles of York and Albany, as well as the colonelcy of the Coldstreams, vacant by the third Earl of Waldegrave's death. In these days spies from Carlton House were suspected of being always secreted about the royal residence at Weymouth. The monarch's eldest son, impatient for his succession, was thought to have agents about his father's person, who sent daily reports as to the sovereign's health. The future George IV., before and after his instalment in the Brighton Pavilion, paid duty visits to Weymouth. Upon one of these, the prince somehow brought with him one of his own circle. Somewhat to the king's disgust, but infinitely to his son's amusement, the stranger mimicked the Parliamentary manner of a pretentious and often absurd M.P., one Fonblanque. Tears of vinous laughter ran down the prince's face as he repeatedly almost roared himself into a fit. This artificially heightened the effect of the wine. " With all his faults," exclaimed the king, " my son is not a drunkard. If he is tipsy now it is " (pointedly addressing the unasked visitor) " your fault." In a general way the chief object of the prince's dutiful journeys to the Dorsetshire coast was to bring back to his boon companions ludicrous accounts of his father's state. It was not enough to recount these infirmities ; the affectionate son insisted upon acting them too. Thus he showed to his convives how the old king had become so blind as to fall into a hole in Lord Dorchester's ground, and to step into the Weymouth waves, mistaking them for his pleasure boat. If, however, the son had his spies at Weymouth, the father certainly contrived through some subterranean channel to hear a good deal of the Pavilion table-talk. On the occasion now mentioned, the anecdotes with their histrionic accompaniment caused little laughter. One parasite, more cautious than the rest, said in a very serious and audible tone, " Poor man, sir ! " The prince took the hint, and the Weymouth stories stopped.

An earlier king than George III. possessed, though he seldom inhabited, a country house at Weymouth. James I.'s visit to Bath in 1613 proved the occasion for a Court progress from Wilts to Dorset. In the former county the clergy then passed for the most musical in England. One of their number, named Ferrabey, had entertained the king and queen with a masque performed at his vicarage. In the dress of an old bard, surrounded

Waiting for the Empress

by choristers in shepherds' weeds, he escorted his royal visitors with a musical accompaniment, for several miles of their journey to Weymouth. The queen, Anne of Denmark, had an extreme dread of the plague then threatening London, if not actually present in it. Hence the southern counties tour now referred to. The same building that received James was prepared for his grandson, the second Charles, during the pestilence that came five years after the Restoration. More historic among Dorsetshire country houses than any of the monarchial abodes at Weymouth, is a country house some little way out of the town that has sheltered princes of more countries than one and their suites. This is Lulworth Castle. The last occasion on which it sheltered an European sovereign was in 1830, when the second French revolution drove Charles X. and his family from their capital. More than a generation later, however, other royal visitors from the opposite side of the Channel were expected but did not arrive. In the July of 1870 the second empire fell with the fall of Sedan. The Tuileries it was known would not long retain the imperial occupants. On the English side the matter of speculation was less whether the Empress Eugénie would. flee, than what point on English soil she would first strike. Even while she was about to enter the Kentish watering-place that received her, a letter from the Parisian Englishman, Sir Charles Blount, to his Dorsetshire friends and fellow-religionists, the Welds, held out some chance of her actually landing at Lulworth. Thus it was that, during the month just mentioned, there had assembled at the old castle a little party of English sympathisers with the French imperialists. These included the majestic presence of the sixth Duke of Rutland, who had known the third Napoleon while an exile in England, and lodging at 13, King Street, St. James's. The Empress Eugénie he had first seen during her girlhood at Clifton, Bristol. He remained to the close of his life in 1888 a reverential worshipper at the shrine of that deity. Others who waited in Lulworth Castle to welcome the fugitives were the late Sir William Fraser, two or three Howards, the late Frank Lawley, a former London associate of Prince Napoleon at Crockford's Club, then a chief writer for the *Daily Telegraph*. Another newspaper man who had been even more intimate with the Napoleonic entourage was there also in the then stalwart, handsome Thomas Hamber, editor of the *Standard*, and at that time in the full maturity of vigorous and fearless manhood. Before there arrived the announcement of the possible visitors having already disembarked at Ramsgate, the expectant circle at Lulworth was reinforced by the third Sir Robert Peel, son of the minister, and by the Richard Monckton Milnes, recently transformed by Palmerston into Lord Houghton. Naturally enough, Napoleonic and Bonapartist reminiscences largely covered the conversation of the Lulworth party on this July afternoon. The twentieth century had arrived before a grandnephew of the great emperor, as a naturalised subject of the United States, in succession to Mr.

Lulworth Expects Eugénie

Morton, Secretary for the Navy, became one of President Roosevelt's Cabinet ministers. Nor in the last seventies had *la belle Americaine* risen to be a princess of society in London. Even the Chicago duchess had yet to exist. These developments were, however, confidently predicted by Lord Houghton, after he had recalled the establishment in the States of Jerome Bonaparte and his marriage to Elizabeth Patterson, a Baltimore merchant's daughter. "In the next century," prophesied Houghton, "this marriage will be looked back upon as the foundation of the American cult on this side of the Atlantic." A greater than Houghton, Sir Walter Scott, we were reminded on that afternoon at Lulworth, had made the same sort of anticipation. Mrs. Jerome Bonaparte's father had been known equally to Monckton Milnes and to Sir Walter. He had, indeed, always passed with the novelist's friends for the original of "Old Mortality." His other daughter, Mrs. Bonaparte's sister, Frank Lawley or Sir William Fraser informed us, did actually marry into the English peerage. In 1825 she became the second wife of the Duke of Wellington's brother, the Marquis Wellesley, during his Irish lord-lieutenancy. Houghton, and no doubt others present at Lulworth on this occasion, could recall how, four years after the *coup d'état*, while yet a bachelor, through his ambassador Walewski, the third Napoleon asked for the hand of Princess Adelaide of Hohenlohe. To Sir William Fraser the Emperor had confided his opinions on Benjamin Disraeli. "Not the head of a statesman; like all

231

literary men, from Châteaubriand to Guizot, ignorant of the world, talking well, but nervous when the moment of action arrives." A little later, when settled at Chislehurst, Napoleon III. paid a flying visit to Lulworth, attended by his secretary, the ever faithful Bonapartist, Pietri. Apropos of that estimate of Disraeli, his host ventured a mild dissent. "My remark," came the rejoinder, "applied to the literary character generally when transplanted into affairs. The Jew is always an exception. But substitute the brilliant writer whom I first knew as Lord Robert Cecil, since three years Marquis of Salisbury; my opinion, I think, will be verified by the event." "The truth is," I recollect then remarked Mr. Weld, "Louis Napoleon can have seen next to nothing of Disraeli since the two, as young men about town, used to meet each other in Lady Blessington's drawing-room at Gore House; he might just as well have called Disraeli, what in those days he certainly was, a common looking lawyer's clerk, converted by gorgeous waistcoats into a bad specimen of a Jew swell." The career and personality of the man who made that remark were enough to confer distinction upon the modern representatives of the ancient Lulworth family. Few things have benefited the English colonies more than the immigrants to them somewhat above the average social position. Such are the cadets of great houses, whom the changes in our social constitution may not have permitted to find a suitable career at home. Competitive examinations have barred the way to the public service. Brains themselves cannot always command success in the law courts. Pocket boroughs no longer give the Heaven-born statesman his first Parliamentary start. Such was the situation faced some two generations since by a young Dorsetshire man who might have considered himself qualified by position and birth for advancement at home. Frederick Aloysius Weld, of Lulworth, had been educated at Stonyhurst, a college standing on land once owned by his family. In his own county his people had bought castles and lands from the Howards. Loyal to the old faith in its darkest days, they married and inter-married with Arundels, Cliffords, Petres, and Sturtons. Many sons and daughters did they give to the service of their Church. Of the latter several took the veil. The former numbered a squire of Lulworth, who made the vows and afterwards as a cardinal became a powerful member of the Roman conclave. Frederick Aloysius Weld, in 1843, had gone direct from Stonyhurst to New Zealand. From the first his new life proved a success because he could turn himself to anything, and work equally well with his head or hands. He became the greatest explorer of those early days. The eager, investigating spirit that had come to him from his ancestors, prompted him to visit great portions of the uninhabited interior in the southern or middle island of New Zealand. His physical researches, recorded in the Geological Society's journals, form the earliest scientific account of the volcanic phe-nomena of the Sandwich Islands. The establishment of constitutional government brought him into politics.

From Wilts through Dorset

He was one of the small band of shrewd statesmen who at once saw the needs of the colony, and set to work to start fairly the coach of representative rule. Having recruited his health by a journey home, and by a long stay at Lulworth, in 1869 he went as governor to Western Australia, the first, if not the only, colonial politician who had achieved a viceregal position. What he accomplished in Western Australia he did afterwards in Tasmania. Throughout that part of the world, this product of a Dorsetshire country house will always be remembered as a man who succeeded beyond the seas because he omitted to carry out with him none of those attributes, in virtue of which for between two and three centuries, Lulworth has never wanted a Weld to do his duty at home. In an earlier chapter it has been mentioned that Arundel in the twelfth century was held for the Empress Maud against King Stephen. Near the spot where we have now been lingering there stood, many centuries ago, a fortress, attached, like Arundel, to the same intrepid woman who so long and bravely maintained her sovereign right against her usurping kinsman. Another spot of the Dorsetshire coast, devoid of historic interest like that of Lulworth, abounds in country-house reminiscences worth giving here. Even in the short memories of polite society, Abraham Hayward still lives as conversationalist and guest. In the latter capacity he has been much misrepresented; for throughout the second half of his life he accepted comparatively few dinner invitations, and made no experiments in strange dishes. In his own words, "Cold beef if you like, but good claret and plenty of it," had become his theory and practice. What he was in Belgravia or Mayfair, he was also in the smart country houses of the day. In Dorsetshire at West-hill, Lyme Regis, he had a sister whom he often visited. Here he would bring with him his most intimate friend and contemporary, A. W. Kinglake. In general society, except now and then at a club dinner, Hayward indulged the anecdotal vein. "A story," he would say, "may sometimes be permitted if it really illustrates, but then, as always, it must be cut short." His narratives of literary reminiscence of late were kept entirely for Westhill. Such was his account of taking a Semitic savant from Bonn to visit S. T. Coleridge at Highgate. Always absent-minded, the "damaged archangel," as Wordsworth used to call him, was, that day, in a dreamy and almost half-unconscious state. The introduction of the Hebrew stranger woke him up to a soliloquising monologue on the misdeeds of Israel. "A stiff-necked, evil people, accursed of the Lord," &c. Meanwhile, with arms meekly folded and head bowed, the Hebrew whom Hayward had brought with him, took it all resignedly as part of his racial chastisement. Miss Hayward, allowing for difference of sex, his exact likeness in the flesh, had much of her brother's memory and biting wit. From her, and not from him, came the story of her uncle who, having received a living from Lord North, took for the text of his first sermon, "Promotion cometh not from the east, nor from the west, nor

yet from the south." The little gatherings at
Westhill were most pleasantly assisted at by the
local clergyman, Dr. Parry Hodges, a courtly, highly
polished, but perfectly unaffected divine of the old
school, who had been everywhere, known every one,
and who, accompanied by his nephew, Sir Bruce
Seton, drew forth from Hayward his very best talk.
At Westhill it was that Hayward gave his often
quoted account of Garibaldi and the social promotion designed for him by his English admirers :
he was to marry the old Duchess of Sutherland.
On its being hinted that the patriot already had a
wife, Hayward at Lyme Regis was responsible for
the rejoinder, " Gladstone must be put up to explain
her away." Always a serious politician, Hayward
had been consulted in his time by Cobden as well
as Palmerston. At his sister's house he told her
friend, the rector of Lyme Regis already mentioned,
" In the end I think I shall succeed. But I look
for nothing within twenty years." On the same
occasion, too, speaking of Lord Justice Cockburn's
passion for music, " It is," said Hayward, "a professional taste. Lord Tenterden once pointed out
to me a man we had heard in Canterbury Cathedral
with the remark, ' He is the only man I ever
envied ; we were both competitors for a chorister's
place. He got it, and is where you see him. I
consoled myself for failure by going to the bar,
and have become Lord Chief Justice.' "

CHAPTER IX

FROM TRESCO ABBEY TO POLWHELE

The Scilly Islands—Their place in legend and history—Tresco
Abbey—"King" Augustus Smith—John Douglas Cook on
the identity of the islands—Other Tresco guests—Douglas
Cook at Tintagel—Details of the history and "government" of
Tresco—Miss Rhoda Broughton—"Only just eighteen!"—
Charles Reade—H. S. Stokes—Pencarrow : Sir William and
Lady Molesworth — Literary and political visitors — David
Urquhart—Captain Gronow—J. A. Roebuck—Mr. Leonard
Courtney — Tom Hood, the younger — Theatrical guests—
Foreign royalties at Pencarrow—Stow—The genealogy of the
Granvilles and Baths—Stow formerly a Royalist centre—The
house as it used to be—Lord Lansdowne's advice to his
clerical nephew—The Moncks of Cornwall and Devon—Berry
Court—Werrington—The Rev. H. A. Simcoe at Penheale—
His encouragement of village industries—The Rev. R. S.
Hawker at Morwenstow—Tennyson—The sermon and sack of
potatoes — Lord Falmouth's Tregothnan — The Laureate's
recognition of a Homeric precedent in the park—Carnanton :
its Disraelian and other associations—Boconnoc : its story and
its cricket week—Polwhele a type of the smaller Cornish
country house—The descendants of Maria Theresa's favourite
noble.

THAT he may not outstay his welcome in the
country houses to which he has been introduced
on or near the south coast, the reader may now

From Tresco Abbey to Polwhele

proceed to the extreme point to be touched in his westward journey. By a tolerable sailor the distance is easily accomplished by sea without land being touched from the time ship is taken in Poole harbour till the foot is planted on the Scilly island, Tresco. Such was the route taken for the first time by the present writer late in the nineteenth century when on a visit to Tresco Abbey. In no other way can so characteristic a panorama be secured of the Dorset, the Devonshire, the Cornish coasts, as well as of the western archipelago itself. Here, as in Sussex, the track of British royalty, victorious or fugitive, may be traced ; for the guide-books should tell us not only to identify the ten miles of sea separating Land's End from the nearest Scilly with the Lyonesse, before its submergence by the ocean, the scene of King Arthur's last battle and death ; they should relate how the islands themselves, having been first annexed to his realm by the Anglo-Saxon Athelstan (938), and by him peopled with monks, sheltered a Stuart prince between seven and eight hundred years afterwards ; how, in 1645, the Parliamentary ships, entering these remote waters, drove the future Charles II. from his insular asylum. Four years later the Scillies became the headquarters of the Royalist *revanche*. Sir John Grenville, as good a servant of the Crown on sea as on shore, fortified so strongly every one of the hundred or so Scilly rocks projecting above the water as to render them the nearly impregnable home of Royalist privateers. Nor could the Parliamentary admirals, Ayscue and Blake, reduce the stronghold till 1651.

Tresco and King Smith

Those who may have been the present writer's fellow-guests at Tresco Abbey, first in the days of the hospitable, benevolently despotic Augustus Smith, will recollect their rooms to have borne the name of Sampson, Bryher, and of other Scilly islets habitable by human beings as well as by sea-birds. They may also remember dinner-table discussions about the etymology of the modern name and the identification of the islands themselves with their reputed names in Greek and Latin. No less a person than John Douglas Cook, the first editor of the *Saturday Review*, had happened conversationally to speak of our host's sea-girt realm as the Phœnician Cassiterides or the Roman Sillinae Insulae. Among those who heard the remark were the two most interesting and intellectual of Cornishmen then living. One of these was R. S. Hawker, of Morwenstow ; the other was a clergyman also, Mr. Kinsman, of Tintagel, whose not infrequent parishioner the *Saturday's* founder then happened to be ; for in those years, when not from the Albany, where his London chambers were, the *Saturday* was edited from the site of the palace famed in Arthurian legend. The straggling highway of which Tintagel village consists contains the little Cornish home of those whom it still seems natural to call Sir Arthur and Lady Hayter. It was bequeathed to them by the friend and literary servant of their uncle, the *Saturday's* proprietor, Mr. Beresford-Hope. Hither Douglas Cook came at each successive break, however short, of the London season or session. Here he entertained a grand acquaintance or two, notably the Duke of Newcastle, with a few others of

From Tresco Abbey to Polwhele

the Pelham Clinton family.   At Tintagel also he
maintained a crew of fishermen, whose sole business it
was to keep his London dinner-table supplied with
the delicacies of the deep.   This, too, was the locality
that cradled a literary libel action which made some
noise in the period looked back upon.   Walter
Thornbury, a genial and clever Bohemian of the
nineteenth century, had been making a holiday tour
on the western side of the Tamar.   Accidentally
encountering the London editor on the Atlantic coast,
he resented, and afterwards in a novel called "Great-
heart," he caricatured, Cook's assumption of local
sovereignty.   "A Napoleon of editors indeed, but,
mercy on us, what a temper!"   So of Cook,
whispered to me a contributress who once stayed at
Tintagel, Mrs. Lynn Linton, who wrote the "Girl of
the Period" article in the *Saturday*.   "Has he not,"
she would almost tearfully go on to say, "stormed at
me, cursed me, on one occasion actually hit me, on
one of his bad days!"   At the Tresco Abbey dinner-
table where we have just met him, Douglas Cook, a
choleric Aberdonian with red hair, a bull neck, the
gourmet and epicure shown in all the lines about his
mouth and double chin, blandly took his friend
Kinsman's correction, and only so far asserted the
prerogative of editorial autocracy as to pooh-pooh a
suggestion that Scilly could possibly have anything to
do with the sun-god Sulleh.   "Is it really necessary,"
put in Hawker, "to give the lie to local tradition?"
The Scilly waters are particularly fruitful of a despised
fish that, properly dressed, however, makes very
tolerable eating.   The old Cornish fishermen, in their

aboriginal dialect, called the conger-eel "silya," and would have spoken of our host's dominions as the "conger isles."

The Tresco table-talk formed the conversational condensation of antiquarian research or theories about "King Smith's" ocean realm; the Tresco gardens were an epitome of flowers and fruits indigenous to the different zones, but, whether their first homes were the temperate or the torrid, perfectly domesticated under the Italian blue of the Scilly sky and in the perennial spring of the Scilly climate. The house inside is a library and museum of local record. Prehistoric Scilly has, or used to have, its monument in some human bones excavated in 1812. Near these were found brass and copper plates of horse-shoe shape, conjectured to have been the musical instruments of primitive man. All were in good preservation, though their antiquity was fixed by the experts at some thousands of years. The subterranean finds of Scilly have, however, not been many. The ancient deluge which annexed the land of Lyonesse to the sea, destroyed everything reared by human hands upon the islands. Of the genuine aborigines not a family was left. The modern inhabitants all came from the Cornish or Devonian mainland. There are, or there were, Tregarthians, Crudges, and Bampfields in Scilly. The first name is obviously and purely Cornish. The Bampfields, or Bampfylds, belonged to Devon as well as Cornwall. As for the Crudges, they had, by frequent intermarriages, connected themselves so closely with the Godolphins as to become absorbed in that house. The pictures

and relics most conspicuous in the Tresco collection
are so many different witnesses to the fact that the
beginnings of inhabited Scilly, as of other outlying
fragments of Britain, were ecclesiastical. Hence the
very name given to one of the group, St. Nicholas.
Not only this islet, but whatever had belonged to the
monkish rulers in the whole archipelago were, as the
contents of the Tresco muniment-room show, given
by Henry I. to the Abbot of Tavistock. A local
artist, discovered for or by Augustus Smith, endowed
Tresco with a portrait of the earliest clerical sovereign
recognised by the islands. This was Burgold, Bishop
of Cornwall. In the twelfth century the ecclesiastical
rulers had not been dispossessed ; by their side, however, a secular rule had grown up. The same brush
that limmed Burgold also added to the Tresco
collection the lineaments of the earliest governor of
Scilly, Robert de Wick. Of these island kinglets
nothing is known before the member of an ancient
line, Ralph de Blanchminster. That once famous
stock disappeared with the fourteenth century.
"King" Augustus Smith's predecessor in 1484 was
Sir John Coleshill. After an interval of occupation
by Katharine Parr's fourth husband, Lord Seymour
of Sudeley, the islands fell to the Crown. Thomas
Godolphin in the sixteenth century was the most
famous of the Scilly viceroys ; he was followed by the
Duke of Leeds. In 1800 the Scillies became incorporated into the duchy of Cornwall.

The insignia of local empire and the instruments
of authority and discipline, still preserved at Tresco,
show the administration to have been mainly

Scilly under King Smith

military.   Augustus Smith disliked tobacco more
even than he did dogs.   Smoking, however, was
allowed in a summer-house occupying an obscure
angle of the grounds.   Here were hung specimens
of the whips formerly used to chastise offences which,
on the mainland, would have been visited with
imprisonment or perhaps transportation.   Near the
scourges was a pile of copper coins, representing
the fines levied under successive lord proprietors on
culprits of various degrees.   Its actual exercise was
never, of course, in question ; but the power of life
and death almost invested itself in " King Augustus."
Throughout Mr. Smith's thirty-eight years of amiable
absolutism, ended only by his demise in 1872, none
of his subjects dreamed of questioning his sovereign
right or of demurring to any of his imperial edicts,
chiefly directed as these were against overcrowding
and violations, great or small, of his ideas of order
or propriety.   Long before a questionable character
reached a criminal development, it disappeared from
the islands.   Ludicrous stories were formerly current
concerning Augustus Smith's despotism as a host.
With the single reserve that he discouraged or forbade
the diffusion of cigar or pipe odours through his house,
his guests knew of no restrictions on their enjoyments
or their ease.   He expected, indeed, his visitors to
feel and perhaps display an interest in the polity of
his island kingdom, in its fauna, flora, and history.
A bachelor, he also insisted on punctuality at breakfast
and dinner ; he never bored his friends into excursions
by water or land.   There were well-manned boats,
belonging not to himself but to his people, to take

his guests to any point of interest they liked. Numerous and miscellaneous this company used to be. Whenever a yacht was seen in the offing, or the steamer plying between Penzance and St. Mary's had landed its passengers, Mr. Smith heard of all the arrivals on his shores. Any person whose name was at all known received an invitation to the Abbey. Some of these visitors have been already mentioned. Among others whom I can recall were the novelist, Miss Rhoda Broughton, with her friends of the Tower family. Miss Broughton had then recently achieved her first great literary success with " Not Wisely but too Well." She deprecated congratulations on it, and was humorously satirical on the reports representing the much talked about author as " being only just eighteen, you know." On her journey down she had, it seemed, overheard herself discussed by fellow-passengers in the train, who, after compliments or criticisms on the work, added, " And fancy, those who know her well tell me she has refused three millionaires." The charm of Tresco Abbey in " King " Smith's day was the delightful uncertainty as to what guests might be opposite or next one at any coming meal. There were no carefully composed house-parties; but every fresh steamer which reached St. Mary's seemed pretty sure to bring some one whom the host thought worthy of a summons to his court. Among these unexpected arrivals I recall that of Charles Reade the novelist. It was the first occasion on which the present writer, or indeed any of the company, met this remarkable man. He was then occupying always during the long vacation, his Oxford rooms

Rhoda Broughton and Charles Reade

at Magdalen, where he still retained his fellowship.
"An ox-eyed, benevolent countenance," was the
description he had recently given of himself. No
portraiture could have been more exact. Very fresh,
unconventional, often agreeable his conversation
proved—especially when, as generally happened, he
was in the critical vein. Admiring Miss Broughton,
till then a personal stranger to him, in the course
of the agitated strides up and down the room which
were the accompaniments of his talk, " Pity the little
minx should be so fond of going so near to cheeking
her Creator." There appeared to be one other condition besides perambulation necessary to Reade's
colloquial flow. He declined alike wine and coffee ;
directly dinner was over he begged for a large
breakfast-cup of tea. That inspiration once provided,
kept his tongue active throughout the evening.

Other guests, less known to fame, used to be
equally interesting figures at Tresco. At the period
now looked back upon, the present writer abounded
in the interest of inexperience in literary personages
and subjects. Whatever concerned the inner history
of the craft he had adopted was very welcome. He
could scarcely have anticipated meeting at this remote
country house two remarkable links between the
journalism of the eighteenth and nineteenth centuries.
One of these was a lady, the wife of a naval officer,
then Captain, shortly afterwards, I think, Admiral Sir
William Gore-Jones. The daughter, if I rightly
remember, of the first representative possessed by
Finsbury in the House of Commons, Serjeant
Spankie, she had seen as a child all the most famous

From Tresco Abbey to Polwhele

newspaper men who flourished in pre-penny press days. Her father, eventually Attorney-General at Bengal, had assisted Perry in the editorship of the *Morning Chronicle*. Charles Reade, in his good-natured, boisterous way, had been pleasantly grumbling at the journalistic ascendancy of the Hebrews in London. " Unprecedented, wholly mischievous, and entirely abominable," were the mildest words used by him on the subject. "As a fact," gently observed the lady, " I think you will find the power of the Jews in the press to have diminished rather than increased during the last hundred years. I can just remember," she continued, "being taken by my father to Mr. David Ricardo's at Gatcombe Park, Gloucestershire. There the exception was to see an influential publicist without Semitic blood or not of Nonconformist descent." Ricardo himself was the son of a Jew stockbroker, whose adoption of Christianity cost him his entire patrimony and made him look to his pen only. Hence the articles on the principles of finance in the *Morning Chronicle*, then largely controlled by Serjeant Spankie. There were many more of the children of Israel, then highly influential in newspaper London. One of these did the lady now mentioned recall. This was a certain Lewis Goldsmith who, first attracting notice by scurrilous attacks, impartially upon the English and French Governments, having founded two papers, the *Anti-Gallican* and the *British Monitor*, eventually did good and respectable work for the *Chronicle*. After this conversational excursion into the coulisses of primitive publicism, it seemed according to the fitness of things that Augustus

Before W. H. Russell, Finnerty

Smith should casually mention a new-comer expected by him for at least a few hours during the week. This was a young man named Finnerty, then one of the sub-editors or chief reporters of the leading Plymouth journal, the *Western Morning News*. The name was at once recognised by Serjeant Spankie's representatives. An older Finnerty had been employed as Parliamentary shorthand writer for the *Chronicle* during Spankie's association with its editorship. Accompanying Sir Home Popham on the Walcheren expedition, the elder Finnerty was justly described by his son, who reached Tresco in due course, as the pioneer of W. H. Russell and other special correspondents of a later day. He was, however, not quite so successful ; for the authorities on shipboard had no sooner discovered his real errand than they landed him at the first shore they touched. " In those days," said Finnerty junior, " the greatest sailors did not always know their true interests." This casual remark roused a violently contradictory spirit in the great novelist, who was then engaged in one of his many wars with specialists, medical and other. " Ignorance," he burst in, " is the badge of the tribe of experts. No persons are so incompetent for affairs as the reputed men of business known as lawyers. None think so little of healing as doctors. Who can possibly show such ignorance of the theory and practice of religion as clergymen ? " Some time before this there had appeared some anonymous newpaper verses about the dramatic version of Charles Reade's " It is Never too Late to Mend " on the London stage. They were not too

From Tresco Abbey to Polwhele

complimentary to their subject, but they amused Reade ; he insisted on repeating them to something like the following effect :—

> " Mr. Reade you've written stories
> By the dozens, and your best
> Goes to show ad bonos mores
> Via sera nunquam est.
> Well, there may be something in it,
> But I always shall contend
> That in life there comes a minute
> When it is too late to mend," &c.

Some years later, by the bye, apropos of our meeting in the Scillies, Charles Reade mentioned he had ascertained the poet whom he had quoted to be Henry S. Leigh.

Among the local celebrities met by the Tresco guest was one who, before his death on the eve of the twentieth century, had become not undeservedly known as "Cornwall's grand old man." This was Henry Sewell Stokes, liked and respected by the whole countryside, eventually County Clerk of the Peace, but, when I first knew him, holding high Municipal office at Truro, where, as a lawyer of much experience and wide connection, he had done not a little to secure Augustus Smith's repeated returns for that borough. A man of fine presence, with a most striking lion-like head, at his Truro house in Lemon Street or Strangways Terrace, he had been the friend and host of Alfred Tennyson during the Laureate's repeated visits to the West, for the purpose of steeping his imagination in the local colour which picturesquely tinges so much of the " Idylls of the

Cornwall's Grand-Old Man

King." "A highly cultivated and noble-minded gentleman for whom I had special regard," as Mr. Leveson-Gower, so long a Cornish M.P., describes him, Mr. Stokes united the taste and temperament of a poet with much poetical performance of his own. At his Bodmin home, Hill Top, he kept open house for visitors of all kinds, especially for men of letters and lawyers going the western circuit. In this way one frequently met at his table Herman Merivale and Mr. Leonard Courtney. Appreciated by Lord Granville as well as by his brother, Mr. F. L. Gower, Mr. Stokes' verses were chiefly known to readers attracted by the force of local or personal connection. Mr. F. L. Gower has recorded his question to the London bookseller whether he had sold many copies, with the bookseller's reply, "A fair number, but all to you."

As regards literary associations, a pre-eminence among Cornish houses belongs to Pencarrow, the cradle, as without exaggeration it may be called, of colonial self-government and of philosophic radicalism. Originally belonging to the Stapletons, the place in the fifteenth century came by purchase to the ancestor of the modern Molesworths. At Pencarrow House, Sir William Molesworth, formerly a fellow-student with Lord John Russell under Dugald Stewart, while at home on vacation from Cambridge, became by inheritance the eighth baronet of his line. Here he entertained Jeremy Bentham and James Mill. Here, too, were arranged the negotiations for his purchase of the *Westminster Review*, the earlier numbers of which, as his property, were planned and edited by him in

From Tresco Abbey to Polwhele

his Pencarrow library.   At Pencarrow, too, it was that, from Lord Aberdeen, in 1853, he obtained his earliest start on the official ladder, the Commissionership of Public Works, to be followed two years later by the promotion to the Colonial Secretaryship.   Six years (1839–45) and sixteen volumes were occupied with his edition of Hobbes.   Much of the labour of compilation, all the business of proof-correcting, were done at Pencarrow.   During those strenuous years his Cornish home was more like a London publisher's office than a country house, crowded with experts in political philosophy, literally overflowing with matter just arrived from, or about to be dispatched to, the printer. The sum expended by him on this enterprise, from beginning to end more than £5,000, did not prevent his making many improvements in his house and grounds.   It did, however, somewhat contract the scale on which those works were carried out.   The hospitable traditions of her husband's family and home were carried on by his widow, Lady Molesworth, so well known and still so unforgotten a figure in London and in country-house society in the Victorian age.   It was in 1869 that a peerage given to a great Cornish squire, Mr. Robartes, produced a vacancy in the representation of Bodmin and an interesting call at Pencarrow House.   The visitor was the new Liberal candidate, Mr. F. Leveson-Gower.   " Not at home, sir," was the servant's prompt observation on opening the door, and seeing, as he supposed, one of the county callers whom he knew his mistress did not desire. " Her ladyship's ill in bed," the man continued, seeing the stranger hesitated to depart.   When he had departed the servant was speedily sent after him. The Liberal candidate and his companion and brother-in-law, Lord William Compton, took their places at the Pencarrow luncheon-table.

As the widowed hostess of Pencarrow Lady Molesworth displayed a constant, an unstudied, and, because of its unaffected sincerity, a touching devotion to her husband's memory. After lunch, which in later days became more and more the first set meal of the day, she went into the library with her guests. These continued to number, so long as any of them remained, Sir William Molesworth's principal friends and literary or political associates. No break whatever did she allow in the continuity of the intellectual traditions of the house. She took an interest indeed in the dogs, the horses, in the frequently renovated and enlarged stables, and especially in the gardens, whose perfect state and proportions at her husband's death admitted of no improvements or additions. The gardens, therefore, always remained much as he left them. But the library was hallowed by exceptionally endearing memories. When the hostess took her friends into it a tender solemnity, as of one entering a shrine, sometimes seemed to come over her manner. In that corner of the room Sir William had held his earliest conversation with Charles Buller, the real author of the " Durham Dispatch," constituting, as it did, the earliest charter of that colonial self-government which was not to be fully established till 1856, the year after Molesworth's death. This was the conversation in whose course Buller first struck out the phrase often used by him afterwards of " shovelling the paupers out of the country and shovelling the convicts into the colonies." In another part of the same room had Sir William Molesworth and his visitor, Gibbon Wakefield, drawn their chairs together that they might not miss a syllable of each other's sanguine talk about an autonomous, an industrial, a peaceful, a progressive Greater Britain beyond seas. On these occasions Lady Molesworth may not have been present herself. She had, however, personally welcomed to Pencarrow Joseph Hume, and had heard him almost rehearsing those financial criticisms on State expenditure which, as she recollected, generally wound up with, "The *tottle* of these figures of wastefulness, Mr. Speaker, is ——."

At Pencarrow were also occasionally to be met three more public men, each belonging to different eras, representing views of his own, sharply challenged by the others, but each in his different way full of interest to his fellow-guests. David Urquhart, first returned for Stafford in 1847, had identified himself so closely with the Turk against the Russian, as with Asiatic interests generally in the Near East, that many who first met him beneath the Molesworth roof expected to see a specimen of the Orientalised Briton, if not turbaned as to his head, yet with the jet black eyes and dusky complexion proper to a Turcophil. Instead he proved to be of purely Saxon type, with lint-white hair and face untanned by the sun. At least once Urquhart stayed at Pencarrow at the same time as one who had preceded him by fifteen years as member for Stafford. This was the "dandy guardsman," probably the last surviving specimen of

Gronow, Lever, and Pencarrow

the Regency "buck," the diverting diarist, Captain Gronow, whose anecdotes of Peninsular experiences, and especially of the "hundred days" in Paris, first heard by a fellow-visitor at Pencarrow, Charles Lever, supplied that novelist with some of the most dramatic incidents in "Harry Lorrequer." Pencarrow also occasionally received the best known of David Urquhart's later disciples, Joseph Cowen, of New-castle-on-Tyne, who, soon after taking his seat at St. Stephen's in 1868, electrified the House by his fervid and finished declamation against Gladstonian Russo-philism, breathing the Urquhart inspiration in every sentence. In private life this born orator was the most reserved and shrinking of men, with a voice soft, low, and at times a little lisping, rather suggestive of a shy Oxford don. Touching Disraelian policy in foreign affairs at one extremity, Joseph Cowen, at the other, belonged to those intellectual Radicals who, till the sect had quite died out, were seldom unrepresented beneath this roof. Twice did the present writer behold in the flesh John Stuart Mill, the logician and son of the earlier Pencarrow guest already mentioned. The first time was at Dean Goulburn's church in Oxford Square, London, when he followed the service and the sermon with a manifestly devout attention that must have prepared all who noticed it for the gravitation towards orthodox Christianity shown in his posthumous essays on religion. The second occa-sion—the only one of my finding myself at the same table with him—was at Pencarrow. Nor was he then the only guest of the same political and intellectual communion. John Arthur Roebuck might have been

From Tresco Abbey to Polwhele

Lady Molesworth's visitor long after her widowhood began, for he lived on till 1879. It was quite early in the seventies that I saw him at Pencarrow, his table-talk and presence generally leaving upon those who met him the impression of a wasp in oil. Two of Roebuck's contemporaries, one a Cornish member, Disraeli's "superior person," the stately and dogmatic Horsman ; the other, the Parliamentary wit of his time, were often of the Molesworth parties. Bernal Osborne's racy electioneering stories first told at Pencarrow would fill a volume. Here, too, many made their earliest acquaintance with Horsman's successor as Liskeard M.P.—Leonard Courtney, a Penzance man by birth, whom, I believe, one might have met at " King Smith's " Scilly court. In the Pencarrow days Mr. Courtney's second wranglership seemed a comparatively recent honour, and London had not overcome its early surprise at the capacity for intellectual and physical exertion which had caused J. T. Delane to say : " After Courtney has walked for three hours, ridden for three more, and been leader-writing for six, ordinary mortals can deal with him on something like equal terms." Since another and earlier of the Pencarrow guests, Henry Reeve, the foreign policy mentor of the *Times*, no one, perhaps, impressed Delane more powerfully than Mr. Leonard Courtney. Roebuck, indeed, must have been, not long before his death, at Pencarrow ; for at the Molesworth breakfast-table he received the offer of the Privy Councillorship, and, when he had divulged the official letter's purport, the congratulations of his fellow-visitors on being the first person not having held office to be the recipient of an honour vainly asked by the historian as an alternative to the peerage he had refused. In an earlier generation than mine the Molesworth hospitalities included, among women, Lady Canning and Lady Waterford, the two beautiful sisters of their day, but the daughters of two noticeably plain parents— Lord and Lady Stewart de Rothesay. Lady Waterford had no rival among amateur artists. Such of her pictures as came to Lady Molesworth may decorate the walls of Pencarrow under its present owner to-day.

Among the men of whose visits the place must still contain memorials were Abraham Hayward, of course; A. W. Kinglake; the two brothers Charles and Henry Greville, both diarists and professional diners-out, but both, in other respects, diametrically different the one from the other—Henry Greville, the musical and theatrical connoisseur, the Mæcenas of every sort of artist, always the hospitable master of a well-equipped house in town and country—Charles Greville (the Gruncher), who never gave a dinner to anybody, who regarded the opera and the playhouse as social pests, and who considered that society was going to the dogs when, at Pencarrow, " Billy Something," as he calls him, sat down at the piano and sang songs. The performer happened to be the amiable, accomplished Richard Corney Grain, one of Lady Molesworth's most habitual and welcome guests; for under that hostess Pencarrow witnessed the confluence of two distinct streams of hospitality. There were the celebrities, mostly public men, of early Victorian days. The latest and most acceptable of this group were the French ambassador, M. Waddington, who had been a Rugby

From Tresco Abbey to Polwhele

boy, together with the fifteenth Lord Derby, and Lord Kenmare, the most agreeable purely Irish peer of his day, Queen Victoria's Lord Chamberlain. The other current, whose waters sometimes, though not often, mixed with this had something of the smart Bohemian character. During his life Sir William, as well as Lady Molesworth, missed no chance of doing a good turn to men who wrote for their daily bread, though they might have nothing in common with the philosophic contributors to his own *Westminster Review*. Like many other country hosts, lay or clerical, Sir William Molesworth was attracted by the poetic genius and the heroically patient personality of Thomas Hood ; his influence secured from Sir Robert Peel a pension for the humourist's family. Tom Hood, the younger, had no sooner ceased to be a child than the Molesworth connection concerned itself to secure him an education at London University School, where he had for his class-mate Joseph Chamberlain. After he had gone through Oxford, Tom Hood owed to the same friends a War Office clerkship. Pencarrow itself continued to be his second home. There he sometimes met his father's two comrades, Thackeray and Dickens. In the Pencarrow parties, however, of that time, and more particularly after Sir William Molesworth's death throughout the sixties, or beyond them, the theatrical element predominated—E. A. Sothern ; Charles Mathews ; his brother, Frank Mathews, with their respective wives ; the best Lady Teazle of her time, Miss Herbert, and Alfred Wigan stayed at Pencarrow only less frequently than at the two other fashionably Bohemian, artistico - sporting country houses of the time—the Duke of Beaufort's Troy, near Monmouth, presently to be visited, and the present Duke of Fife's parents' Duff, Banffshire. The kindly hostess of Pencarrow was sometimes carried by her hospitable instincts beyond the limit of her mansion's capacities. Among the foreign royalties who occasionally visited her in Cornwall were the Comte, the Comtesse de Paris, and the Duc d'Aumale. Company of this sort needed an amount of space which now and then necessitated less exalted guests being sent to sleep out in some of the cottages on the estate. Here the accommodation occasionally proved so imperfect that the sleepers out did not always turn up at the breakfast table in the best of humours. It was one of the guests, in Sir William's day, thus bedded out, who, soon after 1837, went back grumbling about the " mischievous crew," Molesworth, Roebuck, Macvey, Napier and Co., but rejoicing at their becoming " quite blown upon by their brother Radicals." When, however, Lady Molesworth's death after some few years followed that of Lady Waldegrave, a distinct department of the country-house system suffered a second loss, not made good to this day.

The rural homes of western England, to which we now pass on, possess much of their importance or interest as a heritage from Stuart times. One of them had been the cradle of two noble houses. A few words of genealogical explanation will prevent any confusion incidental to the names about to be mentioned. That portion of Cornwall now reached contains the site of the Battle of Stratton in the Parliamentary wars, the manors of Stratton, of Kilkhampton, as well as the great Royalist country house of that period—Stow. From the seventeenth century Marshal Stow are directly descended, through the female line, the twentieth century Marquis of Bath and Earl Granville; the latter name was indifferently spelt Granville or Grenville. Stow in 1685 had no rival for political importance among the greatest mansions in the West. The seventeenth-century master of the place was John Granville (born 1661), the son and heir of Sir Bevil Granville and his wife, a daughter of the Heavitree Smythes. John Granville inherited the monarchical enthusiasm of his father, killed at the Battle of Lansdowne. The mightiest and most magnificent of the king's Cornish friends during the appeal to the constituencies preceding James the Second's second Parliament, John Granville was known as "the grand elector"; he dominated the surrounding municipalities by importing into them officers of the guards who, sword in hand, saw that the countrymen voted right. The great squire of Stow attended Charles II. during his exile; he played an active part in the Restoration. He received his reward in becoming first Warden of the Stannaries, then Lord-Lieutenant of his county, after that Baron Granville of Kilkhampton and Bideford, subsequently Viscount Granville and Earl of Bath. Educated at Gloucester Hall, where some of his name resided in 1638, this Lord Bath maintained his university friendships throughout his life, and filled his Cornish home with scholars and churchmen, as well as with captains in war and politics. The only children he left behind him were daughters, of whom the eldest married Sir

The Cornish Granvilles

William Leveson-Gower. The second daughter, becoming wife of Lord Carteret, was created Countess Granville ; her son was the famous Lord Carteret, who at his mother's death became first Earl Granville. That nobleman left behind him only a daughter, Lady Louisa Carteret ; she, marrying Thomas, second Viscount Weymouth, became progenitress of the present Lord Bath. The mansion in which "the grand elector," the stately predecessor, as he may be called, of the later borough-mongers, repeatedly received his sovereign, and its outbuildings rise close by a little village called Combe ; they formerly presented an immense frontage, chiefly of brick. The interior exceeded the anticipations likely to be raised by the outside. The rooms had been constructed and decorated by the best English and foreign workmen of the day. Before that stately fabric came into being, a much simpler dwelling had sheltered the Granvilles of Stow during more than five hundred years. The splendid building which replaced this soon after the Stuart Restoration, flourished for more than half a century, was then demolished, and has not since been rebuilt. The last of the Granvilles who lived there, known as Lord Lansdowne, raised to the memory of his ancestor, the famous Sir Bevil, the pillar at the spot where he fell in Lansdowne fight, on the high plateau that overlooks the city of Bath. This was the Lord Lansdowne whose monument still exists in Kilkhampton church. Among his papers his descendants found a letter addressed by him to his nephew, another Bevil, a newly ordained clergyman. The writer begins by assuring the young divine that he could not have chosen a better Master, provided he had, after searching his heart, persuaded himself of fitness for His service. With earnestness in his new vocation let the youthful pastor combine politeness and sweetness as well as truth ; let him be humble without doing violence to his self-respect—because to be a cynic is as bad as to be a sycophant. Above all, let him not, with his sword, lay aside the gentleman, nor put on the gown to hide his birth and good breeding ; let him take as his model his uncle, Dr. Denis Granville, Dean of Durham—for he, too, had paid the Church of England the compliment of accepting office in it. Let him revere that pious relative's memory. So, too, may he in time become a dean himself ; finally, may the uncle's spirit descend upon the nephew as Elijah's upon Elisha. Above all, may the nephew, like the uncle, be cheerful, familiar, condescending in manner, in temper, in piety, strict, regular exemplary, as a clergyman apostolical, as a courtier well-bred and accomplished. Thus should Heaven's choicest blessings be poured down upon the dear nephew of his affectionate uncle, Lansdowne. That ends this kindly and characteristic epistle to his freshly surpliced kinsman from the peer immortalised by Pope as "Granville the polite."

Even where we are now in the far west, the principle of the decline and fall of ancient families is illustrated in the vicissitudes of their dwellings and the juxtaposition of the older territorialists by right of birth with the new by right of capital. John Granville was not the most famous agent in bringing back Charles II. produced by this neighbourhood. With the Granvilles of Stow were connected by marriage the Moncks of Kilkhampton in Cornwall, and of Potheridge in Devonshire. The general who declared for a free Parliament under the exiled Stuart was descended from Humphrey Monck of Potheridge, who, marrying a Champernowne, became a Cornish squire of hospitable tastes. General Monck's brother was a Cornish clergyman, rector of Kilkhampton. The West of England Moncks, and with them the one or two manor-houses at which they entertained, quite disappeared after the death of the great general's son. The Cornish and Devonshire Moncks disappeared as entirely as the houses which had been connected with them. Not far from the ancient home of the Granvilles are two houses equally representative, in their different ways, of distinct epochs and dispensations in English politics. The picturesque remains of Berry Court, Jacobstowe, mark a sixteenth and seventeenth century of hospitalities, always in the interests of Church and Crown, arranged by the widely extended Berrys. Close by spreads the trimly kept park of Werrington with the modern and comfortable house in the background, which, occupied by successive members for Launceston, Colonel Deakin first, his son afterwards, did duty as a western stronghold, about a generation ago, for the Conservatism, informed and guided by the genius of Disraeli, but extended and supported by the wealth of Lancashire.

For many years during the first half of the Victorian age, one of the most picturesque among the human features in this Cornish landscape was an old-world clergyman, perhaps the last of the socio-theological

From Tresco Abbey to Polwhele

school to which he belonged. His costume was noticeably archaic then. It is not to be seen at all, out of Madame Tussaud's gallery of engravings of eighteenth-century dress, now. He always wore Hessian boots, with a tassel exceptionally long and full suspended from them in front ; thus shod he stood considerably over six feet, with a figure, naturally powerful, developed by incessant pedestrianism to herculean strength. Belonging to the evangelical school (he had been a disciple, if not a personal friend, of Charles Simeon), he liberally supported by his purse and his voice, from West of England platforms and pulpits, far and wide, the Church Missionary Society, and kindred organisations. Much of his life passed in travelling from one country parsonage to another on errands of preaching. When at home the Rev. H. A. Simcoe kept the state of a squarson of high degree. Uniting ample means with hospitable instincts, he gave to Penheale Manor, Egloskerry, a character unique among the country houses of the time. The mansion itself formed an emporium for the elementary commodities of daily life. A youthful visitor, on arriving, found that he had omitted to put his clothes in his trunk before starting. The clerical lord of Penheale pulled the bell. The servant who answered it presently reappeared with all the articles necessary for a boy's toilet, not forgetting nightshirt, boots and shoes, neatly arranged on a tray. The reason why it seemed at Penheale as natural to ask for wearing apparel as for a cup of tea was that the host, not content with starting the villagers at some industry in cottages or work-

Penheale and Morwenstow

shops of their own, had established beneath his own roof separate departments for tailoring, bootmaking, and the manufacture of any other little utilities likely to be periodically wanted in a region where there were no shops. On the Simcoe property no boy or girl grew up without being able to produce almost anything absolutely required by decency or health. The manor-house at Penheale still stands. Its industrial accessories may have disappeared ; but in all parts of the world may be found British settlers who, or whose parents, leaving England in the nineteenth century's most distressful years, owe much of their success in a new world to habits acquired and handiwork learned at Penheale — in its day the uniquely beneficent training-school for emigrants.

Another clerical Cornish country house attracting, within the present writer's experience, many visitors, is Morwenstow Rectory. Here one used to be received by the writer of the spirited lines " And shall Trelawny die ? " which were actually taken by Macaulay when writing his history for ballad contemporary with the episode inspiring them. The Rev. R. S. Hawker had received beneath this roof Charles Kingsley when he visited Cornwall to acquire the local information about Stow, used by him afterwards in " Westward Ho ! " and many other guests less distinguished, often without the claim of personal knowledge or letters of introduction upon his hospitality. This loyal and eccentric Churchman only showed his profession to his visitors in the cassock that he always wore. For the rest his daily life and appearance were that of a country gentleman, scrupulously avoiding in his conversation any

From Tresco Abbey to Polwhele

approach to controversial topics, clerical or lay.
Directly there seemed a danger of such being
broached, he would rise from his chair by the table at
which he habitually sat, and leading one to the
window looking out upon the Atlantic, would say,
" There you have my views ; as to my ideas, they are
that, if the human eye could reach so far, you might
see right away to Labrador." Acquainted with most
of the great writers of the Victorian age, Hawker
delighted to talk of the visits payed him by Tennyson,
whom, in other than literary matters, he took as his
model. Only a West-country man, he declared, could
read properly his poems ; of these he considered the
verses about " the bells of Boscastle " to be his best.
Nothing pleased him more than to be asked to read
them. This he did always standing up in a rather
theatrical attitude, and in a deep-lunged, monotonous
chant exactly copying the Tennysonian method of
recitation. The congregation may have seldom
numbered more than the members of his own household. The daily service in the little church was never
or very seldom neglected ; it was frequently followed
by a fifteen minutes' sermon, characterised by a studied
avoidance of dogmatic theology, and a sufficiency of
moral admonitions purely practical in their tone,
sometimes dramatically personal in their application.
Having missed a sack of potatoes from his garden,
he took the Eighth Commandment for his text. " One
of our neighbours," he concluded, " has been robbed
of his vegetables ; the thief is now in the church ; can
it be that a piece of thistle-down has just alighted on
his head ? " Instantly the culprit brushed his hair with

his hand. The potatoes were restored in the course of the afternoon, and the offender dismissed with a threat of excommunication next time. On the occasion of going to Oxford for his D.C.L., the poet Longfellow also looked in at Morwenstow. I recall his prophecy of the rector's dying in the Roman communion. "Not," said Longfellow, "that he will doctrinally break away from the Church of his birth ; but he has so steeped his spirit in the Cornish legends of pre-Anglican Christianity that he is becoming unconsciously Romanised."

Another of Tennyson's Cornish country houses lies on the banks of the Fal, between Truro and Falmouth. This is Lord Falmouth's Tregothnan with the most quaintly diversified park, sloping down to the water's edge—a strip of shining shingle on which the fishermen are often to be seen mending their boats. That was the operation on which the poet, in company with his guide, the already mentioned H. S. Stokes, suddenly came. For a few minutes the poet gazed intently at the men thus employed. Then, with the air of one suddenly recollecting something, he produced a little Odyssey from his waistcoat pocket. He found the passage in which Ulysses repairs his storm-vexed craft. Alternately reading aloud extracts from the Homeric description and pointing to the work then being done under his eyes, he visibly exalted in the exact truth to modern life displayed by the Greek poet in his account of the process. Truro itself has often returned to Parliament a Willyams of Carnanton. Here is a house externally famous for the rich beauty of the woods that embed it, for the eighteenth-century artificialism of its gardens, and internally for its progressive transformation from a rendezvous of the king's friends in Stuart times into the impartially representative resort of celebrities, local and national, who have found both rest and inspiration beneath this typical roof. Originally possessed by Noy, the Attorney-General of Charles I., Carnanton provided that monarch's son with a resting-place in his western wanderings. Passing to the family which still owns the manor, it attracted visitors as various and as interesting as those whom we have already met at Tresco Abbey ; indeed most of those who reached Scilly had come on from Carnanton, whose owner, Mr. Brydges Willyams, in 1859, shared the representation of Truro with Augustus Smith. The twentieth-century master of Carnanton is the universally popular, because the uniformly courteous and kindly, hero of countless Cornish Parliamentary fights. With the already-mentioned H. S. Stokes for his agent, he first fought and won Truro in 1857 ; he repeated the victory in fifteen later contests. The Willyamses in all their generations have sweetened the Whig profession in politics with much social courtesy to those outside its pale. The late owner of Carnanton was a Liberal member at St. Stephen's in the future Lord Beaconsfield's time. In those days Disraeli frequently found himself a visitor in the West of England. On one occasion he took Carnanton on his way, going or returning. He might, indeed, never have penetrated to these parts but for a connection of the Carnanton clan. The aunt of Mr. E. Brydges Willyams of 1906, herself a Mrs. Brydges Willyams,

an exceedingly clever, intellectual woman, delighted by
Disraeli's literary genius, invited him to her house
at Mount Braddon, Torquay. He became almost
domesticated there, with such profit to himself as to
have received from his hostess in cash, jewels, pictures,
furniture, gifts amounting in value to about £60,000.
Fresh from a Carnanton excursion, Disraeli called
upon the original of his own Mr. Bond Sharp, then
living in Grosvenor Square. The interview was to
the following effect : " What security do you offer for
the £5,000 you asked me to lend you?" inquired
Henry Padwick. " My brains," was the answer.
Padwick accepted it. The money was lent immediately ; it repaid itself with interest some years later.

Throughout the Victorian age the smart country
house remained unknown between the Tamar and the
Land's End. The county had no more pleasant or
distinctive social characteristic than the rural home
justly proud of its combination of taste with comfort
and enjoyment. The union, of course, exhibits itself
in various degrees. Two instances, at opposite ends
of the scale, shall conclude our Cornish visits. The
great event in the rural hospitalities of Cornwall used
to be the Boconnoc cricket week. The place giving
its name to the function belongs to a group of
properties with which William the Conqueror endowed the earldom of Cornwall. Owned successively
by the Carminowes, the Courtenays, the (Bedford)
Russells, the Mohuns, Boconnoc was bought, in 1718,
by Thomas Pitt, Governor of Madras, Chatham's
grandfather. The last of the Pitt name to live at
Boconnoc was the first Lord Camelford. After him

From Tresco Abbey to Polwhele

the place passed to the Pitt cousins, the Grenvilles. Through these it came to its present possessors, the Fortescues. Architecturally the noticeable feature in the house is the skill with which the later additions have been incorporated into the original structure. So consistently at long intervals of time and by various owners has the leading idea of the first builder been adhered to, that even the expert can scarcely decide where the work of the Carminowes ends, where that of the Courtenays begins, at what point the white frontage of the Pitts passes into the later frontage of the Grenvilles. Boconnoc, too, possessed a deer-park which, as Disraeli somewhere reminds one, is a very different thing from a park with deer in it. Inside, the creative genius of Lord Camelford still has its monument in a gallery not less than 100 feet long, opening at one end into a drawing-room, at the other into a library. The walls of these, as of the fine and fanciful staircase, a great feature of the place, are hung with drapery in some parts, with paintings in others. Some of these pictures are interesting because of their artist, Gavin Hamilton, discovered by the first Marquis of Lansdowne at Rome, and by him introduced to the Grenvilles. In the " Prodigal Son's Return " and " Abraham's dismissal of Hagar," the freshness of the colouring and the expressiveness of the faces have delighted many generations of Boconnoc guests. The most interesting works are those forming part of Boconnoc's family history. Such are the first Lord Camelford, Governor Pitt himself, of the " Pitt diamond," the Duchess of Cleveland, presented by herself to her cousin, born

Boconnoc to Polwhele

Harriet Villiers, wife of Governor Pitt's eldest son, the first Earl Stanhope, the general, and Grenvilles innumerable. Sir Godfrey Kneller and Sir Joshua Reynolds are the chief painters. Several of the canvases attract connoisseurs because they are " kit-kats"; that is, they were originally commissioned, of a certain size (twenty-eight or twenty-nine inches by thirty-six), to suit the convenience of the Kit-Kat Club; this was the little society formed by Addison, Garth, the Duke of Marlborough, Sir Robert Walpole, and others in 1703, to promote the Protestant succession, deriving its name from the fact of its dinners being held at the house of Christopher Kat, a Westminster pastrycook. In its early days, Boconnoc was much of what Chevening was to Kent; it is now best known in connection with Boconnoc cricket week.

Other Cornish homes, having nothing else in common with Boconnoc, were formerly, on, however, much more modest a scale, associated with open-air games of all kinds. In the Victorian age Polwhele, near Truro, had for its occupants the English descendant of an Austrian family ennobled by Maria Theresa. Than Colonel Charles Liardet and his sons, there were no finer specimens of pure Saxon manhood. Mrs. Liardet, helped by her fair daughters, co-operated with the men of the family to make Polwhele an animating centre for other pastimes than cricket, especially archery. It was also the one house in the West which made itself the second home of Anglo-Indians, civil or military. Chief among these was Patrick Boyle Smollett, a lineal descendant of the novelist, with much of his ancestor's robust humour and full-flavoured fun, equally amusing in private life and in the House of Commons, where he sat latterly for Cambridge, and where he delighted to chaff the Irish members. To some of these he applied the expression " talking potatoes "—a phrase with which the Cornish air of Polwhele had, he said, inspired him.

CHAPTER X

A ROUND OF DEVONSHIRE VISITS

D URING the seventeenth-century struggle between Parliament and king, the Royalists had their social headquarters in the West at Stow, in which we have already seen the cradle of the Bath and Granville peerages. On the Republican side a corresponding position and associations equally interesting, belong to Port Eliot, some twenty miles further in the Devonshire direction. The house existing to-day is, of course, not that so dear to John Hampden's friend and colleague. The irregular frontage, formerly the characteristic that it shared with Penshurst and many other houses already mentioned, disappeared during several processes of restoration which it underwent. The new house stands nearly on the same ground as a priory that had existed from Saxon times. Parts of the monastic structure were embodied in the new building. Thus the dining-room was the refectory. It also became the picture gallery. Here, on canvas and in well compounded colours, is told the personal story of the place. John Eliot, the first master of the place, was painted in 1574. The presentment of the earliest Eliot knight, the great Sir John himself, is dated 1628. If that date be correct, the work must have been executed before Eliot's committal to the Tower in 1629. Port Eliot tradition mentions a portrait completed just before his death in 1632. It would therefore seem possible that there may exist somewhere a later likeness than that in Eliot's old home. The ennobled Eliots begin with the lord of 1783, by Sir Joshua. The first of the St. Germans Earls lives again in a portrait by the local artist, Opie. Another Sir Joshua, the first group ever painted by the artist, depicts Richard, the head of the Eliots in 1746 with his family gathered round him. Here, too, is the political philosopher John Locke, the scientific expositor and champion of the political settlement that, in 1688, embodied the chief principles contended for by the greatest of the Eliots and his friends. The collection suggests some dramatic contrasts. It contains the one authentic likeness of John Eliot's most famous friend and trusted colleague, John Hampden, with the open brow and fine features. Next to him is a mediæval master of Italian church-craft, Cardinal Bentivoglio, with the bald head and the clear-cut countenance expressive at once of intellectual subtlety and personal charm. Near Hampden, too, is the handsome Captain Hamilton, whence have sprung the even handsomer Dukes of Abercorn. Another picture, that of the Bel and the Dragon imposture detected by Cyrus, was pronounced by Reynolds to be the work of two very eminent hands; the head, he said, had been cut out of a painting by Quintin Matsys; the drapery and the background were pronounced undoubted Rembrandts. Later experts have detected in the drawing and the colouring proof that Sir Joshua was not wrong.

In the sixteenth century the Eliots, originally a very old Devonshire family, had been settled for some time in Cornwall. Their house occupied the same ground as an ancient priory, whose site, at the dissolution of the monasteries, had been granted to the Champernownes. These (1565) exchanged it for some of his Coteland property, with Richard Eliot, the famous Sir John Eliot's grandfather. From that day to this it has remained in the Eliot family. Throughout the Tudor period, towards whose close (1592) John Eliot was born, the hospitalities of Port Eliot were famous. The atmosphere of jollity and self-indulgence surrounding his boyhood developed habits and passions that seriously interfered with

young Eliot's career. Old Eliot would have agreed
with Sir Robert Walpole's father, that it did not
become a son to be the critical observer of a sire in
his cups. He therefore made the boy drink glass
for glass with him, till they both disappeared together
under the table. Before his Oxford days were over,
the lad had contrived to get into an ugly scrape.
Among those who visited at Port Eliot was a neighbouring squire named Moyle; between him and his
host's son no love was lost. Heated by wine and
argument, on one occasion, young Eliot thrust his
sword into the detested Moyle. The matter was
hushed up on the understanding that the young
swashbuckler should improve his manners by a
course of foreign travel. While on the grand
tour, he made the acquaintance of George Villiers,
the Duke of Buckingham, whom he afterwards
impeached. A morally reformed and a politically
educated character, he brought back to his Cornish
home a succession of guests, most of them English
or foreign diplomatists. Thus, by the time he
became owner of the place he had made Port
Eliot the most cosmopolitan country house in
the West of England. He did not live to co-
operate with his Buckinghamshire friend in organising the constituencies against the Court before
the ·Long Parliament met. John Hampden, however, was among the Port Eliot visitors. In the
Port Eliot library the host and guest laid down
the lines of the first Parliamentary campaign against
the king. The Port Eliot influence had already
given an international colour to English popular

Port Eliot Politics

politics. Unhappily for them Eliot's political friends and heirs violated, at certain fatal points, the Port Eliot principles. As the two friends paced to and fro on that portion of the Port Eliot grounds overlooking the Plymouth waters, "I would have you," said Eliot to Hampden, "avoid revolution if for no other reason than because of the reaction that is sure to follow." The physiognomy of the Celt showed itself strongly in him who thus spoke. Could there have been a better specimen of the prophetic power that has sometimes been a Celtic gift than this caution? Might it not be thought that Eliot had foreseen the libertine excesses of the Restoration after Puritanism, or in France the rise of Bonaparte and Talleyrand after Robespierre? This seventeenth-century precursor of the St. Germans peers, as his keen eye swept the horizon of affairs, saw that Cromwell would close what Pym had opened and Milton had sung.

Unlike some of those houses that have been visited, Port Eliot's reputation as a political country house comes chiefly from its association with an isolated owner who filled a large place in the public mind. In 1784 Samuel Johnson met at Sir Joshua Reynolds' dinner-table Lord Eliot, whose father, then Mr. Eliot, he had formerly visited at his country home. General Paley, Dr. Beattie, and other well-known personages of the periods were of the company. The Cornish host referred to by Boswell was Richard Eliot. His son became the first Lord Eliot; he exchanged his family surname for that of his mother; she was a daughter of Queen Anne's secretary, Craggs, a sister of Horace Walpole's friend, Mrs. Nugent. By their mother,

A Round of Devonshire Visits

Miss Santlow, the actress, Port Eliot had, in a remote degree, connected itself with the stage. And was it not at Port Eliot, after surveying John Eliot's picture, that Johnson conceived the sentiment banged out by him some time afterwards, "Patriotism, sir, is the last refuge of a scoundrel"? Mrs. Richard Eliot's portrait also, like others of her family, by Sir Joshua, is still in the Port Eliot collection. Hampden's friend, Sir John Eliot, had in him, as has been seen, something of the diplomatist not less than of the Republican. The international strain perpetuated itself more visibly among his descendants than did the political. During the competition between the son of Chatham and Charles Fox, the rival leaders at Westminster were privately represented by their own personal ambassadors at foreign Courts. John Eliot's ennobled descendant was employed in distributing "Pitt's gold" amongst the English allies against Napoleon. In this way, when the struggle between parties and factions was at its height, the Cornish Port Eliot supplied Toryism with the same sort of social stronghold as that which was possessed by the Whigs at Woolbeding or Stanstead in Sussex. Pitt himself, accompanied by the faithful Dundas, was an occasional visitor. On one of their journeys thither they had put up for the night at Exeter. A customer at the New London Inn, recognising the pair as they entered their carriage the next morning, said, "I see, landlord, you have had great company here, the Prime Minister and the Treasurer of the Navy." "I don't rightly know, sir, who they be, and bless me if I care," was the reply; "it is enough

A Port Eliot Contretemps

for me that they cleared out my best bin of port last night, each six bottles to his own cheek." It was one of their fellow-guests at Port Eliot, a Parliamentary opponent, Courtenay, who, being again at Lord Eliot's Cornish house after Pitt's death, effectively introduced Dundas into a conversational parallel between the English statesman and the Athenian Pericles. Both owed their command and position to the same power of speech and loftiness of character. Finally Pericles died heartbroken at the disgrace which had overtaken his friend Phidias; so Pitt's life was embittered and shortened by the impeachment of Dundas, when Lord Melville, for gross malversation and breach of duty.

On their journeys to Boconnoc both the Grenvilles, Thomas and William, Pitt's kinsmen, halted at Port Eliot. The contrast between the two brothers—the elder ponderous, pompous, saturnine, the younger quick, bright, and genial—excited much comment among the local guests. " As much as you like of Mr. William, but no more than the laws of hospitality command of Mr. Thomas," was the verdict of the Cornish squires on the two; still more of the Cornish ladies, who found the younger brother delightfully quick and entertaining in the give-and-take of tea-table talk, the elder surly as a bear till the second bottle was finished, and then disposed rather to slumber than to flirtation or compliments. With these came the pioneer of the modern business-like Conservatism. " Jenkinson," said Lord Eliot, " is the only man I know who talks better than any book, who can give Shelburne conversational odds and beat him." The future Lord Liverpool, if he chanced to be there at the same time as Pitt, was always singled out by the minister for companion in the morning walk. In all Parliamentary debates on commercial or industrial subjects, Pitt at Port Eliot used Jenkinson as a sort of holiday coach. If the rural colloquies between the two were unusually numerous and earnest, people knew that Pitt had cut out for himself some particularly hard work at St. Stephen's. Its nearness to the Plymouth quays and counters made Jenkinson specially in request at Port Eliot. "To-day, if you please," the minister would often remark overnight to this remarkably handyman, "we will have a look at the Mill Bay docks and Cattedown bonded-houses." One of Pitt's Cabinet colleagues, the Duke of Richmond, had then suggested plans for fortifying Plymouth and Portsmouth. At these signs of confidential intimacy between the chief and his subordinate, a look of anything but satisfaction seemed to come over another member of the Pitt phalanx, the Marquis of Graham, alluded to in words then often quoted from the "Rolliad," "the dark brow of solemn Hamilton." Whether at St. Stephen's or in the country house, the Pittites ranged themselves in a certain ceremonial order. Graham took his place at the head of the patrician wing. Next to him came John Villiers, Lord Clarendon's second son, called, from his good looks, his fine eyes, and his golden hair, "the Nireus of his party." At Port Eliot, as at other points of the country-house system, Villiers rendered Pitt the sort of service at a later date performed so tactfully in similar scenes for

Scientific Sailors at Port Eliot

Lord Beaconsfield by Montagu Corry (Lord Rowton). Among those called Pitt's business men after the future Lord Liverpool became an habitual visitor of Port Eliot, on his way to or from Sir Thomas Acland's Holnicote in Devonshire, was William Wilberforce, insignificant in person, with features concealing rather than suggesting intellect, but a clear and pointed talker, with whom Pitt paired in the after-breakfast walks when not preoccupied with Jenkinson. With these exceptions, Pitt at Port Eliot was seen to prefer for his companions any who were not professed Pittites. His consultative bodyguard in Cornwall as elsewhere, further comprised Pepper Arden, one of the law officers, Lord Mulgrave, and the Duke of Richmond, curiously reproducing the dark complexion and features of Charles II., but without his royal ancestor's sense of humour, quickness of repartee, and lavish recklessness. The Duke, receiving a large salary as Master General of the Ordnance, passed for the greatest screw of his time. His fellow-guests at Port Eliot often whispered to each other the lines in which the "Rolliad" had rallied him on his kitchen fire being always unlit. Two Port Eliot visitors with whom Richmond was often brought into contact were James Luttrell, Lord Carhampton's youngest son, and one who was the earliest specimen of a Naval officer equally at home with his ship and his pen. His brother sailor, though lacking Luttrell's grace and polish, Captain Macbride, combined with the nautical bluntness of the old school, clear, good, sound sense and a locally exact knowledge of the sea and shore whose projected fortifications so often

A Round of Devonshire Visits

brought distinguished State officials to Port Eliot. Courtenay, one of Pitt's most brilliant and bitter-tongued adversaries, in his capacity of West-country magnate sometimes mingled with these Tory guests. On one occasion a disagreeable contretemps occurred. A few days before, Courtenay in the House had made a personal attack upon the head of the Ordnance, the Duke of Richmond. With him he had contrasted his Grace's predecessors in the office—all men of tried bravery, military knowledge, and experience. When, on entering the Port Eliot hall, the Duke caught sight of his assailant in the company, he turned on his heel and disappeared; his Grace, it seemed, had gone to order his carriage for immediate departure. With no repetition of an incident of that sort, the Port Eliot house-parties have continued to the present day. The third Earl of St. Germans' daughter, Lady Louisa Eliot, married (1850) into the Whig family of Ponsonby. But though the twentieth-century Lord Bessborough and other guests of his political connection frequently visited Port Eliot, they escaped any experience like the Richmond-Courtenay meeting.

"Mount Edgcumbe," said Lady Ossory after a visit to the spot, "has the beauties of all other places added to peculiar beauties of its own." The combination of varieties, picturesque or impressive, that struck Horace Walpole's correspondent, distinguishes Mount Edgcumbe from other palaces by the sea. From the little peninsula formed by the Tamar and its influents, the panorama visible combines gentle sylvan landscape, broken by glimpses of rugged Dartmoor and

The Rev. Barter of Cornworthy

its craggy tors beyond. Where the park slopes down toward the water, one becomes aware in the distance of a sea swarming with the commerce of nations and the floating bulwarks of an empire on which the sun never sets. Before entering Mount Edgcumbe itself, let us glance at the earlier home of its possessors. This was Cothele; it lay within the Cornish frontier, but was chiefly Devonian in its characteristics, and in a neighbourhood memorable for possessing one of Sydney Smith's "squarsons," in his day not less of a personage than the Simcoe already visited at Penheale. This was Mr. Barter, rector of Cornworthy. Like other devoted parish priests of those days, he kept a private pack of hounds, showing sport equally good with hare and fox. In the first quarter of the nineteenth century, no western country house formed a more perfect microcosm than Cornworthy Rectory. Its inmates were known by many strangers to them in the flesh from some family verses, "The Cornworthiad," familiar to an earlier generation of Winchester and New College readers. The rector's sons, in whose company we shall find ourselves hereafter, were respectively Charles, William, and Robert. The eldest lived into the last quarter of the nineteenth century as Bishop Wilberforce's friend and unofficial right-hand man in the Oxford diocese. The second, William, fellow and tutor of Oriel, figured importantly in the Oxford Anglican movement. The youngest, Robert, died Warden of Winchester, leaving behind him a name still perpetuated in the cricket vocabulary of the school. Cornworthy was the ancient site of a monastery and an almshouse. On the front of the

A Round of Devonshire Visits

gallery in Cornworthy Church may still be visible the inscription, "Sir Peter Edgcumbe, Bart., gave by will to the parish of Cornworthy the ground on which the poorhouses are built." That benefactor lived at Cothele House. Cothele, therefore, contained the germ of the stately fabric which now looks down on Plymouth harbour. Of the parent dwelling few records, probably, have been preserved. Cothele was among the most famous houses of the West between 1485 and 1509; inside it was not more remarkable for the quality of its guests than for the antiquity of its furniture and fittings. These, as regards age and aspect, were in keeping with the time-worn exterior. All were at least as early as the two Tudor queens, Mary and Elizabeth. The immemorial age of the Cothele wardrobe passed into a local proverb. Some of its clothes, according to Walpole, dated from the time of Cain. "But Adam's breeches and Eve's under-petticoat were eaten by a goat in the ark." Relics of the Spanish Armada are familiar objects at most of the more ancient houses in the two western counties. The Spanish spoils that used to decorate Cothele were at least genuine. The eleven suits of complete armour, the arquebuses, the pikes, swords, halberds, bows and arrows, as regards the details of date and manufacture correspond to the description contained in the Spanish archives of the deadly equipments possessed by the "invincible" fleet which, under Medina-Sidonia, proudly sailed from Lisbon in the May of 1588.

The last half of the Tudor epoch added other Spanish spoils than these to the Edgcumbe store.

Cothele and Mount Edgcumbe

Cothele itself had come to the family by inter-marriage with the Cotheles in the fourteenth century. The old Cothele manor-house was small, inconvenient, interesting only from its prehistoric associations. Built of stone from the Dartmoor quarries on the west bank of the Tamar, the structure was conspicuous for a little quadrangle with an embattled tower in its midst, surrounded by buildings whose narrow, heavily barred windows spread a sense of captivity and gloom that suggested Giant Despair's Doubting Castle. The most curious of the Armada monuments transported from Cothele to Mount Edgcumbe is a figure, remarkable for the savage look imparted to the features by the artist, armed, *cap-à-pie*, in Spanish steel. This stands at the foot of the stone staircase leading to the room occupied by Charles II. during his wanderings. The drapery of this chamber is of Oriental workmanship, noticeable for the deep fringe made with knotted silk of many colours. The second Charles was followed in the next century by other royal guests at Mount Edgcumbe. On the 25th of August, 1789, the visitors' book records the king and queen of Würtemberg, with several of their daughters, to have passed a night or two at the place. Later visitors so coveted the honour of occupying the chairs in which these royalties had sat, that, to prevent them being worn out before the rest of the set, it became necessary to remove the labels recording the earlier illustrious occupants. Among the Edgcumbe portraits that may formerly have been at Cothele were an ancestress of the family so ancient as never to have been identified, Mary, Queen of Scots, and Sir Richard

A Round of Devonshire Visits

Edgcumbe. The last was the fifteenth-century head of the family, who left Richard III. for Henry of Richmond. Pursued in his own grounds by Richard's men, Edgcumbe, sheltering himself in a thicket, was in danger of being surrounded by his enemies. It was the work of a moment to fill his cap with stones and throw it into the water below. His pursuers, seeing the head-gear floating on the waves, thought their man had drowned himself, and at once took ship for Brittany. The fugitive commemorated his escape by building a chapel on the eventful spot. His lineal descendant, the first Lord Edgcumbe, restored the building in 1769. The original builder having been knighted by Henry VII. on Bosworth field, became first comptroller to the king's household, afterwards his ambassador to France. To-day his effigy is seen, devoutedly kneeling, in his own chapel. The paintings and other treasures of the modern Mount Edgcumbe are fully and exactly catalogued in all the guide-books. Those contents of the place which it has, therefore, only seemed worth while to mention here are such as have not before found their way into print.

Mount Edgcumbe, apropos of Chatham who had visited the place just before him, inspired Horace Walpole with his best known epigram, " This world is a comedy to those who think, a tragedy to those who feel." The younger Pitt has been met at Port Eliot. His father seldom came as far west as Bath without at least trying to secure a look in at Mount Edgcumbe. It was here that he unbent himself by hunting and by versification. The burden of his poetry was the hollowness of ambition. His best known lines in this vein addressed to the great actor are those beginning, " Leave, Garrick, the rich landscape proudly gay," &c. The Mount Edgcumbe atmosphere continued redolent of Chatham during at least two generations. Here, too, many of the most characteristic anecdotes about him first became current. In his frequent attacks of gouty fever, he could not tolerate a fire. Some of his colleagues, summoned on State affairs to his bedroom, were equally afraid of cold. Amongst these was the Duke of Newcastle who, when his fellow-peers were overcome by the tropical weather, insisted upon the House of Lords having all its windows closed. Calling upon Chatham in his fireless bedroom, Newcastle gave way to a violent but unheeded shiver. The great man was too much absorbed by the subject in hand, Admiral Hawke's movements against the French navy, to notice. The interview was unusually important and prolonged. At last the freezing minister espied an unoccupied attendant's couch in the corner opposite Chatham's. Thickly cloaked already, he escaped into it, pulling the bedclothes over him. Upon the issue of the interview hung the fortunes of two nations. The close and anxious discussion continued until Sir Charles Frederick came in and found the two States-men conducting an animated argument from beneath the coverings of their respective places of repose. Some weeks later Frederick related the experience at Mount Edgcumbe and made it public property. Memories of the Pitt family intertwine themselves with many more West of England country houses than readers of this book can be asked to visit. The fortune brought home by Chatham's grandfather, Thomas Pitt, the possessor of the famous diamond bearing his name, originally weighing 410 carats, sold in 1717 for £135,000 to the French Regents, still on sight at the Louvre, was expended in buying seats in Parliament and estates in the country. Some of these properties had belonged previously or belonged afterwards to the Cornish families of Tremayne and Grylls. Heligan is still one of the most hospitable houses in the West. Under John Hearte Tremayne, the father of its present owner, it was, during the first half of the nineteenth century, the rendezvous of politicians steeped in the personal traditions of Pitt or Fox, of their chief adherents or their most conspicuous adversaries. If they had not themselves heard the debate, they knew from those who had been present how John James Hamilton, afterwards Pitt's Marquis of Abercorn, when member for East Looe, opened the discussion of the Coalition East India Bill in what shared with Wilkes' attack the honour of being the speech of the night. They had heard the lively and facetious nonagenarian, Lord John Townshend's father, predict the fall of the Coalition, because, being at Court when Fox kissed hands, he had seen George III. turn back his ears and eyes, just like the horse at Astley's on being mounted by the tailor whom he had determined to throw. They had been at the same table as that at which Sir George Howard, the interpreter to the Lower House of George III.'s military ideas, had explained how it was that Pitt's Solicitor-General, Pepper Arden, was a good second to Dunning as the ugliest man of his time.

Nursery Etymology

Arden, when a child, had bought a tin trumpet at Stockport fair. Racing home against his brother, he fell down. The trumpet, running into his nose, deformed the whole lower part of his countenance. Howard, too, was with Lord Albany in his last illness and had helped to raise up the dying man in bed that he might write a few lines of gratitude to Pitt for a much tried and never failing friendship. The biography of Chatham, taken by Macaulay as the peg for his famous study of the statesman, was written by the Rev. Francis Thackeray, an uncle of the greater author of " Vanity Fair." The biographer is said to have been private tutor at the country homes of the two families just mentioned. As regards Heligan and the Tremaynes, I believe this to be a myth. Heligan, too, rather than Mount Edgcumbe, was probably the source of the freshest Court stories of the time. The Princess of Wales, mother of George III., in a state of more than usual dejection, was watching her two eldest boys, alternately at lessons and at play. " When we are grown up," said the second to his elder brother, the future king, " you may have a wife, I shall keep a mistress." " Peace, brother ! " came the answer, " there must be no mistresses at all." " Learn your pronouns," interposed the widowed mother ; " or stay, tell me what a pronoun is." " A pronoun," rejoined the Duke of York, " is to a noun what a mistress is to a wife, a substitute and representative."

> " Each art of conversation knowing,
> Highbred, elegant Boscawen."

This lady was the wife of Admiral Boscawen, the

A Round of Devonshire Visits

most universally coveted ornament of country-house parties in the West. " All herself—that is, all elegance and good breeding," was the general verdict on this guest of the evening. Some, however, whispered with an agreeing smile, Horace Walpole's nickname, " Madam Muscovy." If not Mrs. Montagu's equal in the management of a salon, Mrs. Boscawen proved a far more useful aquisition to the fashionable house-party of the period. What Mount Edgcumbe has always been among the great show places of the West, Langdon Court, the home of the Corys, has proved to more than one generation of visitors from all parts. A blend of fashion and intellect formed the speciality of both places. Of late the social citadel of fashionable exclusiveness, Mount Edgcumbe, as the haunt of the most modish blue-stockings, won fame not more for its state and splendour than for its austerity. No card-tables were brought out after dinner. Every one posed as learned or accomplished. A few succeeded in being really witty. Amongst that number was the Dowager Duchess of Portland. Mrs. Boscawen's chief rival, she was grand-daughter of Lord Treasurer Harley, first Lord Oxford. Her good looks were sung by Young, whose " Night Thoughts " were dedicated to her ; the bright talk of this original of Pope's " Narcissa " was worthy of her good looks. Her girlish beauty had been idolised and idealised by Jonathan Swift. Later her fame had survived the doggerel panegyric of Matthew Prior. Artistically this dazzling dowager may be called the progenitress of the whole race of amateur actresses, with Mrs. W. James at their head. In the

There may be Handsomer Women than I

piece then most in request for private theatricals, her costume and performance as Cynthia at Arundel Castle had filled the men with admiration and the women with despair. It was under a West of England roof that the Portland Duchess, anticipating a like utterance by Lady Foley, remarked, "There *may* be better looking women than myself. All I can say is, I have never seen them." Imagine a meeting in the same country house of a high-born British beauty of this overweening type and a modern American duchess, not less highly endowed! What would be the incidents of such a competition? Boswell's picture of Dr. Johnson, subdued to gentleness whilst sitting between the Duke and Duchess of Argyle at Inverary, often had its parallel in that group of rural homes now spoken of. Johnson and Garrick were both well known at Mount Edgcumbe in the same period as Chatham. The Duchess of Devonshire in the prime of her beauty hung on every syllable that fell from the sage's lips. The moralist became all smiles when her Grace had successfully contended for the nearest place to his chair. Here, too, Sir Joshua Reynolds, prevented by deafness from mingling in the general talk, holding his trumpet to his ear, invited to conversation those who stood or sat outside the central group. As a foil to the famous beauties, who regarded Johnson and the other men of mind as they might have done highly intelligent Newfoundland dogs, were Mrs. Vesey, a bright, clever, but not handsome woman, the positively plain Mrs. Chapone, and Mme. D'Arblay, with her father, Dr. Burney.

A Round of Devonshire Visits

The country houses now to be visited lie entirely in Devonshire. Conspicuous among them in the sixteenth century was, doubtless, Sir Walter Raleigh's birthplace, Hayes Barton. Here some have been shown the very room in which, to the terror of his household, who thought he had set fire to himself, the adventurous Elizabethan smoked the first pipe of tobacco that perfumed the Devonshire air ; not less well known is the board at which his visitors made their earliest acquaintance with the potato, brought with him from his Irish estate of Youghal. To-day, like so many other coeval mansions, Hayes Barton is a farmhouse. The Rolle estate, to which Hayes now belongs, is a typical instance of old acres benefited by new wealth and enriched by political or literary associations, investing it with the interest of a historical landmark. The Rolles were honourably connected with Devonshire long before the eighteenth century. That, however, was the period in which the modern Bicton was built. Two hundred years earlier the founder of the Bicton family, George Rolle, after a successful course of London commerce, became a Devonshire landlord first by the purchase of Stevenstone in the northern division. His descendant, Robert, whose general sympathies were with Parliament against the king, married Lady Arabella Clinton. The grand-daughter of this pair was the Margaret Rolle about whom Horace Walpole and Lady Mary Wortley Montague vied with each other in saying unpleasant things. Inheriting the Clinton barony, Margaret Rolle became the wife of the en-nobled Sir Robert Walpole's eldest son, Lord

Bicton and the " Rolliad "

Walpole. This marriage of the Rolle heiress into the family of the first great Whig minister explains the presence of Whig guests at Bicton. The obligation of the Rolles for their earliest title to George II.'s Whig minister had not prevented them from gravitating toward Toryism and supporting the second Pitt in the days of George III. To the leading spirits of the Whig connection, John, Lord Rolle, as he became in 1796, seemed a party renegade of the most thankless kind, and therefore fair game for the satire of their cleverest writers. R. B. Sheridan seems to have been Rolle's guest, not only in London but in Devonshire. He always denied any complicity in the burlesque whose central figure was the Bicton host. Adair, Burgoyne, Ellis, and Fitzpatrick were the chief writers of the " Rolliad," whose idea may or may not have suggested itself during their stay at Bicton.

The host appears to have incurred the ridicule of his former Whig friends by a fussy anxiety so to commend himself to his new Tory allies under Pitt, as to revive in his own person the peerage which was brought into the family by his uncle Henry during Walpole's premiership, but which had died with that relative. After twelve years' work in Parliament as one of the Devonshire members, his ambition was achieved. In 1796 he became Lord Rolle. His earlier friend, Fox, had begun under North by passing for a Tory. Like Fox, Rolle impersonated the political versatility of the age. Rather, perhaps, should it be said that the first of Bicton's ennobled owners loved society first, party afterwards. His fine face and handsome presence imparted a distinction to the homely manners of

A Round of Devonshire Visits

a plain Devonshire squire, imperfectly appreciated, as he thought, by Walpole's successors in the Whig management. Naturally, therefore, he turned to the Tory camp. His warm reception there involved no solution of continuity in his social and private acquaintanceships. His favourite guests at Bicton and elsewhere were still the bright spirits of fashionable Whiggism, the delights and the ornaments of the fashionable country-house system. Rolle, however, as a Whig renegade now found himself more than their host—their butt. His brand-new coronet only served to give fresh point to the satire of his most entertaining guests. These had formerly laughed with him ; they now began to laugh at him. It was, they said, as if Fielding's Squire Weston had covered his scarlet hunting-coat with a baron's robes. The "Rolliad" put all this so tellingly that it was no sooner out than it became the literary hit of the season. Rolle seems to have taken the joke with dignity and courage. The authors of the famous burlesque had satirised his claim to antiquity of descent by congratulating him on a lineage not only from the Norman Rollo, but from Adam himself. Other visitors at Bicton were Speaker Fletcher Norton, himself, as "Sir Bulface Doublefee," a figure in the pasquinades of the time; the jovial, unscrupulous Rigby, Paymaster of the Forces ; and the great admiral, Lord Rodney. It was at the Bicton dinner-table that Rodney explained to an admiring company the use of his manœuvre for breaking the line, and sometimes recounted his successes or failures in love and at play. Rolle's motion in Parliament against Rodney's recall by Fox, more than any other matter of public policy embittered Rolle against the Whigs.

Than Bicton Devonshire possessed no purer type of a high Tory house. There it was treason not to recognise revolution in Parliamentary interference with the king's choice of his ministers. "Those," said Rolle, "who wish to force their nominees on the Crown are foes of the monarchy as determined and dangerous as in an earlier century were General Ludlow or Algernon Sidney." In the April of 1780, the terror and indignation of these country houses were brought to a head by Dunning's motion against Dissolution or Prorogation till guarantees had been taken against an increase of the royal prerogative. "To Lord North, after His Majesty, we owe our preservation from republicanism if not from revolution." Rolle had often spoken to that effect in Parliament. He seldom gathered some neighbouring squires at Bicton without thundering the same sentiment across the walnuts and the wine. Next to North, the national salvation had come from the son of Chatham. The sinking fund in 1786, it was agreed at the Bicton dinner-table, by maintaining credit, commerce, and finance, had drawn the country back from the pit of ruin. "Whom, too, had we to thank but Pitt for those conquests on the Ganges, on the Coromandel and Malabar coasts, which had caused the sun of Britain to rise in the east as soon as it sank in the west?" To such effect expressed himself, both before and after his ennoblement, the Tory convert of Bicton. Sometimes he thus held forth standing at his mahogany and almost dinting it with the blows of his emphatic fists, causing the glasses and plate to rattle in chorus ; sometimes strolling through his beautiful park, where the oak and chestnut-covered glades slope down to the lake, whose iron fencing is to-day that erected by the hero of the " Rolliad."

Lord Rolle posed as, and might have piqued himself on actually being, the eclectic and cosmopolitan Mæcenas of his county. There were no men who then shone so brightly in the world of fashion as the more intellectual of the "macaronis" who then revolved round Charles Fox. Most notable of that group was the wit among dandies and the dandy among wits, Colonel Fitzpatrick, of the noble presence and the versatile pen that made him the life and soul of the "Rolliad" writers, the special adviser and confidant of Fox. A humbler but not less indispensable member of the group was a literary hanger-on of the Rolle family. A professional Grub Street hack, Dr. Wolcot (Peter Pindar) kept judiciously in the background and, meekly sitting below the Bicton salt, he corrected the mistakes of his noble contributors in grammar, spelling, and metre ; he polished up into drawing-room popularity some well-known lines, on the strength of which Fitzpatrick has been called the forerunner of W. M. Praed, beginning :

> " In seventeen-hundred-and-seventy-three
> My beloved Isabella first smiled on me."

Some time later they supplied Fox himself with a model for a composition of his own, with more real feeling, perhaps, if with less of the grace which Wolcot's editing infused in Fitzpatrick's halting lines :

"Of years, I have now half a century passed,
But none of the fifty so blessed as the last."

Meanwhile the Whig wits, who had found it a matter of political conscience to take this way of repaying their apostate host for his past hospitalities, had enjoyed the satisfaction of seeing the book whose idea Bicton had supplied obtain a vogue to be compared only with that achieved twenty-eight years later by another effort of the same description. "Rejected Addresses" (Horace and James Smith), were indeed confessedly inspired by the "Rolliad." The Bicton host, who suggested its title for the "Rolliad," lived till 1842. At Queen Victoria's coronation, when between eighty and ninety, he fell down in mounting the steps of the throne. On his returning to complete his homage, with the words "May I not get up and meet him?" the young sovereign rose and, by advancing one or two steps, saved the aged peer the trouble of the full ascent and the risk of another mishap. In the evening she sent to inquire after Lord Rolle. The "Rolliad's" birthplace thus associated itself with one of the most hopeful and touching auguries for the Victorian era. Her widowhood may have curtailed its hospitalities, but Bicton remained one of the show palaces of South Devon throughout Lady Rolle's life. The place had been sufficiently beautified by the "Rolliad" peer. The most impressive of Lady Rolle's Whig guests, Henry

A Round of Devonshire Visits

Reeve, editor of the *Edinburgh*, seems to have anticipated a retributive blight on the Rolle arboretum and gardens. He was constrained to admit that the desertion of plain Whig principles, notwithstanding the perfection of foliage and growth secured by Lord Rolle for Tory Bicton, must have marked an advance upon its outdoor beauties before it became one of Pitt's social strongholds. Between the Bicton of the eighteenth century and of 1906 a social continuity is preserved by its owner, the nephew and heir of the last Lord Rolle. Inheriting the conservatism of his predecessors, he divides his time chiefly between his Stevenstone estate in North Devon and Bicton in the south. The West of England has ever abounded in country gentlemen who, shunning the modern arts of advertisement, find they can perform their local duties most effectively without being weighted by a seat in Parliament. To that number belongs Mr. Mark Rolle, a Devonshire magnate because he is a Devonshire worthy. On a scale less stately than Bicton, but of associations equally interesting, are two other houses in this neighbourhood, now to be visited—Peamore and Pynes. During Keate's headmastership, two Eton boys, with features not unlike each other, were doing their form work; suddenly one of them said to his fellow, " D——— your eyes, Stanley!" To this at once came the rejoinder, " Damno tuos oculos, arboris accipiter." He who had spoken first became afterwards one of the most imposing and picturesque figures on the Conservative side in the Victorian House of Commons. The lad who had so glibly rolled off the pentameter

reply, then known as " Stanley," was to develop
into the fourteenth Lord Derby. His Eton class-
mate had the keen dark eyes, the hawk-like countenance belonging to the lord of Knowsley. Originally
coming from Essex, the Kekewiches have been settled
for four centuries in the West. The original connection
in the West of England of the Peamore hosts, as in
the case of some other now Devonian families,
was with Cornwall. The present Trehawke Kekewich,
son of Lord Derby's friend and supporter, is still a
Cornish landlord, in the parish of St. Tudy, as well
as the possessor of a slate quarry near Tintagel.
He is also descended from George Kekewich of
Catchfrench, near Liskeard, a sixteenth century
M.P. for Saltash. A later George Kekewich lived
hospitably at Peamore. His successors received
flying visits from several distinguished guests, who
for the most part seem to have taken Peamore
on their journey from Ralph Allen's Prior Park to
Boconnoc or some other house in the far west.
Amongst these were more than one formerly celebrated bishop. It was while visiting Peamore that
Archbishop Cornwallis received the royal intimation
that his wife's Sunday parties at Lambeth Palace
must cease. The good Lady Huntingdon had been
so shocked by these as to invoke the intervention
of George III. and Queen Charlotte. Hence the
royal epistle which, reaching his Grace in Devonshire,
restored the dullness of sabbatical decorum to the
primate's palace. Both Shipley diocesan of St.
Asaph's, the author of a fifth-rate ode on Queen
Caroline's death, and his less obscure son, Dean

A Round of Devonshire Visits

Shipley, were among the birds of passage who alighted at Peamore. The younger Shipley incidentally connects Peamore with an important change in the law of libel. A charge of libel against him was being tried at the Exeter Assizes, before the circuit judge, Buller, then being entertained at Peamore. A discussion between Buller and Shipley's counsel, Erskine, led to the legal change which established the future competence of juries to decide on the law as well as on the fact. Other Peamore guests were Hinchcliffe, who had risen from the livery-stable yard of his father to the prelacy of Peterborough, and Hurd, a farmer's son, who owed the see of Worcester to Warburton's patronage and his own tutorship to the Duke of York. This was the divine who incurred Samuel Johnson's suspicion that, though a Tory in name, he was a Whig at heart. In the nineteenth century there used to be no more frequent or honoured guest at Peamore than Robert Barter, Warden of Winchester. At Peamore, indeed, as well as at Pynes, a clerical element among the guests often blended itself with the political and the agrarian.

Great was the disgust at Peamore when London visitors brought word, in 1805, of Pitt having destined his friend and future biographer, Pretyman, for the succession to Moore at Canterbury. Proportionately fervent was the " Thank God, we have a king ! " when, a day or two later, Peamore knew of George III. bursting out to his Prime Minister, " No, no ; must have a gentleman at Canterbury."

One of the most characteristic possessions of

The Northcotes of Pynes

country houses in southern and western England is a dark-grey marble picquet-table, the cards and counters inlaid in white. At such a board as this was a certain South Devonshire manor won by Justice Northcote, the Elizabethan founder of the family indifferently called Norcot and Northcote, settled at Pynes for about the same period as the Kekewiches have occupied the neighbouring Peamore. The Sir Stafford Northcote of our day, who, in 1877, died first Earl of Iddesleigh, though fond of heraldry, took comparatively little interest in family antiquities. He carefully preserved, however, at Pynes, some papers shown to visitors but never published of the first baronet of his line who, as member for Ashburton, wrote the well-known diary of the Long Parliament. Among those documents were notes for the speech prepared by the first Northcote baronet, and delivered in the January of 1641 to diminish the king's jealousy of the house. The memorandum added that the speaker was fain to give over before he had intended by reason of bearish interruptions. Some of his visitors to whom Lord Iddesleigh showed this private record may have fancied they saw in it a presage of the annoyance to be inflicted in 1880 on John Northcote's descendant by Conservative malcontents below the gangway. Other family memorials suggested that the seventeenth-century Northcote had conceived the idea of promoting Charles II., then a boy, to the throne in his father's place. Sir John stands forth in these memorials as among the most loyal-hearted of the king's friends. He certainly, in Lord Iddesleigh's

299

words, "levied and led a regiment" during the first two years of the rebellion, at the defence of Plymouth. Among the most frequent guests at Pynes were the host's contemporaries at Balliol—Matthew Arnold, F. Temple, of Rugby, who afterwards passed from the see of Exeter to Canterbury. To Pynes also came Sir Charles Trevelyan, subsequently Governor of Madras, father of the present Sir George Otto Trevelyan and the late Lady Knutsford. These visitors were sometimes reinforced by another Devonshire man, Sir F. Rogers, permanent Under-Secretary at the Colonial Office, by the fourth Lord Carnarvon, and by a notable figure successively in the Oxford and official life of his day, Thomas Phinn, who sat for Bath 1852 to 1855. As a host in his Devonshire home, Lord Iddesleigh is still remembered for his amiability, his quiet fun, his chastened love of sport, and for his perennially fresh supply of Devonshire stories. In narrating these he seldom attempted the reproduction of the Devonshire accent, with which his only rival as a *raconteur* of ruralities, Archbishop Temple, spiced his equally copious store of West-country anecdotes.

CHAPTER XI

WHERE DEVON AND SOMERSET MEET

The West-country seats of the Acland family, Killerton Park and Holni-
cote—Holnicote the meeting-place of Wilberforce and his allies—
The origin of Grillion's Club—Ashley Combe—Byron's daughter,
Ada, first Countess of Lovelace—Robert Southey at Ashley
Combe—The Lovelace progenitors—John Locke—The seventh
Lord King, father of the first Earl—The connection of Ashley
Combe with the Byron name—Castlehill, a political country
house—The Earls of Fortescue—"A School of Manners"—
Pixton—The second Lord Carnarvon— Eggesford—The fifth
Earl of Portsmouth—His relations with Sir Thomas Acland—
Doubts and conjectures about Acland's speech—The Church
Militant in the Exmoor district—Canon Cook—Bishops
Wordsworth and Browne—The Greek Archbishop Lycurgus—
Sir George Williams — Orchard Wyndham — Sir William
Wyndham and his guests—St. John, Viscount Bolingbroke, &c.
—Atterbury Trelawny and Dean Swift—Dunster Castle—The
Luttrells—Colonel Luttrell—Temple Luttrell—Henry Luttrell
the wit—Gladstone and the ancient Greeks—St. Audries—
The two Sir Samuel Hoods—The Mallets and the Balches—
Sir Peregrine Acland's Fairfield—Dr. Johnson on the origin
of the word "Quantock"—The Acland-Hoods—"Shake an
ass and go"—St. Audries a centre of Unionism—A curious
memorial of the Palmers—Enmore Castle, the home of the
Egmont Percevals—Chapel Cleve—Thomas Poole—Words-
worth and Coleridge at Alfoxden—The last St. Albyn owner,
the omnibus driver—Quantock Lodge—Lord Westbury and
Lord Selborne—Country Houses round Quantock Lodge—
Sydney Smith at Combe Florey—Enmore Castle and Quantock
Lodge to-day.

Where Devon and Somerset Meet

THE two places, Peamore and Pynes, visited in the last chapter, have many associations in common with the country houses on the North Devon and West Somerset frontier. Killerton Park, the Acland seat, close both to Peamore and Pynes, was at one time without any rival residence belonging to its owner in the West. The earliest of the Acland country houses in the West was at Columb-John (Devon). The first baronet (1644), Sir John Acland, like many of the squires in these parts, served under Charles I., and repeatedly entertained his king at Columb-John. Holnicote, surrounded by a hamlet of that name, in the extreme West Somersetshire village of Selworthy, is the comparatively modern home of the Aclands. Their vast possessions in Devon and Somerset were acquired chiefly by marriages with heiresses. Nor is there much exaggeration in the West-country saying that an Acland may ride from Killerton in South Devon to Holnicote in West Somerset, without once finding himself off his own property. Holnicote's distinction among the country houses in this neighbourhood comes from its having been the neutral ground on which public men belonging to different parties, under at least two generations of hosts, met each other. Before the abolition of the Slave Trade, it was a favourite haunt of William Wilberforce ; in its then owner he had not only his most powerful supporters among the great landlords and Parliament men of the West, but a host beneath whose roof he met habitually the chief allies in his philanthropic scheme—among others Clarkson, the elder Macaulay, Dillwyn, and some-

The Genesis of Grillion's Club

times, not easily drawn out of her seclusion at Barley Wood, near Bristol, Hannah More. Holnicote, originally belonging to the great North Devon Castlehill family, had for Sir Thomas Acland's predecessor, in the first quarter of the nineteenth century, Matthew Fortescue. The intellectual interests of the Fortescues passed with the property to the Aclands. Some five-and-twenty years after its Emancipation gatherings, Holnicote witnessed the conception and execution of an experiment for bringing politicians of both parties into relations of social amity and goodwill. The idea had first occurred to a young Acland who had recently gone into Parliament. It was warmly taken up by his long-vacation visitors. As a result, soon after the friends had returned to their duties in London, Grillion's Club came into being. Its founders, in their talks about the matter at Holnicote, being for the most part as young as they were active, scarcely anticipated that the rival leaders of parties would meet each other at the weekly dinners. The institution was at once recognised and sought after by the leading members of the Whig and Tory rank and file. Before the middle of the nineteenth century, the Sir Thomas Acland, whom many can still remember, the grandson of one of its promoters, had the satisfaction of seeing among the most regular weekly diners the fourteenth Lord Derby, Lord Palmerston, Lord John Russell, Benjamin Disraeli, and W. E. Gladstone.

In this district, the headquarters of the Devon and Somerset stag-hunting, another social centre, Ashley Combe, stands immediately above the Ship Inn,

Where Devon and Somerset Meet

Porlock, where S. T. Coleridge, during a day and a night, wrote, "The Ancient Mariner." Almost invisible in the deep wooded glen, sloping down to the Severn Sea, Ashley Combe had for its former mistress Byron's "sole daughter of my house and heart," the Ada who married the Earl of Lovelace. In older days Ashley Combe was a settlement of charcoal-burners. Of the eighteenth-century house two rooms remain, incorporated into the first Lord Lovelace's enlargement of the earlier building (1846). That nobleman, as befitted the son-in-law of the most widely and enduringly popular of English poets, received many writers among his guests, especially Robert Southey who, on one of his West-country visits, had been at Ashley Combe before an expedition into the Quantock country. This was the expedition which first roused his enthusiasm for West Somerset, and taught him to see in the muddy waters of the Bristol Channel a tint more picturesquely harmonising with the contiguous landscape's special hues than the clearest azure.

Such literary pedigree as Ashley Combe possesses comes to it in virtue of a family connection with the Somersetshire worthy, who philosophically vindicated the political settlement of 1688. The ancestor of the Earls of Lovelace was the Lord King and Ockham ; he had for his mother John Locke's sister. Born at Wrington, near Bristol, practising in early manhood as a doctor at Oxford, while also lecturing on physical science at Christ Church, Locke revisited in later life his native Mendips; he may have extended his holiday trips further west, to the picturesque home of his collateral descendants. The seventh Lord King, an eminent authority on the subject of exchanges and currency, distinguished himself by his uncompromising resistence to paper money ; enforcing the strict letter of his leases, he insisted on his tenants paying their rent in the lawful coin. His monetary views long found a monument at Ashley Combe, in the shape of a numismatological collection. His son, the eighth baron, in 1838 the first Earl of Lovelace, was the peer who, as already said, distinguished his Somersetshire home by bringing to it as his bride Byron's daughter. This Lady Lovelace was asked by a visitor, pointing to the waves breaking on the coast below, how she liked the sea. Her reply clearly presaged a nineteenth-century æsthete's disappointment in the Atlantic : " I simply detest it, because it reminds me of an old governess of mine, who was my especial *bête noir*." Of the poet himself there never were, nor could have been, any associations at Ashley Combe ; for the first Lady Lovelace's father had died at Missolonghi in 1824, eleven years before her marriage. The local confusion once current on this subject may have risen from the fact that Lady Lovelace's ancestor, Admiral Byron (" Foul-weather Jack "), during one of his circumnavigations of the British Isles, put in under stress of weather at Porlock and may, possibly rather than probably, have been entertained at the house of which his descendant became the mistress. Nor was it the admiral, but his brother, the peer, who, having killed William Chaworth of Annesley, in a duel at a Pall Mall tavern, " The Star and Garter," was found guilty of manslaughter, but discharged on

claiming the benefit of the Statute of Edward VI.
The one naval officer of distinction whose name the
eighteenth-century visitors' book records, was the
Somersetshire seaman already met with at Bicton,
Rodney.

The greatest of all the political country houses in
this district, Castlehill, looks down on the little village
of Filleigh. Castlehill, in the heart of the red-deer
region, has supplied the West-country staghounds with
more than one master, as well as the local sport itself
with its most authoritative historian. From the time
when the second Pitt was Chancellor of the Exchequer
to that when the office had for its occupant Sir Michael
Hicks-Beach, now Lord St. Aldwyn, Castlehill has
opened its doors to eminent statesmen and officials
without any distinction of party. Pitt himself and his
friends were followed, among the Castlehill guests in
the next generation, by George Canning, with his
disciples, including the brilliant John Hookham Frere,
who first made Aristophanes intelligible to Greekless
readers, and who, in "Whistlecraft," gave Byron the
notion both for " Beppo " and " Don Juan." The
third Earl Fortescue, who survived till the present
reign, added to his Castlehill and other properties the
whole of Exmoor, purchased from the Knights. Like
Sir Stafford Northcote, at Pynes, he had been a
trained official before becoming a model landlord.
The grandson of one of Pitt's friends and colleagues,
he had himself been Lord Melbourne's private
secretary for four years after Queen Victoria's accession. His father, the second earl, had been Lord
Holland's host at Castlehill and his colleague in

managing the Whigs in the Upper House. He himself shared with Sir Thomas Acland the leadership of all county movements for educational and municipal reform. It was at the Castlehill dinnertable that, addressing his fellow-guest and kinsman, the third Earl of Carnarvon, the master of Holnicote uttered the oracle : " No one has a right to consider himself solvent who does not pay all his expenses out of the interest on his interest." " In that case," said another of the company, Sir John Lyon Playfair, " we must most of us be a disreputable set of bankrupts." " A good school of manners " was the description given by a frequent guest, the sporting clergyman, " Jack Russell," of the Castlehill interior. The words were true enough. With his intimate friends the third Earl Fortescue showed himself genial, vivacious, and a remarkably good talker. In general company at county gatherings and elsewhere he veiled his good nature under a cold and repellent reserve. Among the enemies of Whiggism, that was partly a studied trick of manner. Fortescue's own West-country neighbours, one, at least, of the Aclands and another of the Carnarvon Herberts, had modelled in early days their deportment after that of the cynosure for the better sort of early nineteenth-century youth, the younger Pitt. Nor at any other country house of the time could the grand manner of a more ceremonious age be illustrated more instructively than at Castlehill.

The two other socio-political centres influentially connected in this neighbourhood with the events of their age are Pixton, near Dulverton, and Eggesford, near North Molton. The exclusion of the second

Where Devon and Somerset Meet

Lord Carnarvon from the Grey Reform Cabinet had its natural result in making the master of Pixton the most bitter and violent adversary of the measure. As Lord Porchester he had figured prominently in the Whig action against the Tory Walcheren expedition. He had not, indeed, the oratorical power belonging to some of his predecessors as well as of his descendants ; but as a Whig territorialist he was a real power throughout the whole countryside. In whichever direction the squire, as long after his ennoblement he was called, led the way, the smaller landlords and farmers were sure to follow. At a Pixton tenantry dinner he uttered the stirring sentiment: " To vote for the Reform Bill means that a man has a fool's head on his shoulders or a traitor's spirit in his heart." His West of England home became the headquarters of resistance to the Grey measure. Lord Melbourne liked the Order of the Garter because, in his often-quoted words, " there was no ——— merit about it." For that very reason, as unworthy to receive it, the owner of Eggesford, who died in 1891, refused the distinction when offered to him by Lord Palmerston. He had, said Lord Portsmouth, done nothing to deserve it. Genial, country-gentleman-like, always clear-headed and shrewd, the fifth Earl of Portsmouth, in his relations with dogs, horses, and men, showed himself a keen, as well as a charitable, judge of each. He never said an unwise or an unkind thing. With the exception of an ancestral and altogether friendly rivalry with his neighbour, Sir Thomas Acland, he never had a difference with a human being. As the glimpse already given of him may suggest, the host of

Aclands, Herberts, and Wallops

Holnicote was a great squire of the superior and scientific kind. As little of a sportsman at heart as the guest and political master to whom his loyalty never failed (Gladstone), Acland distinguished himself among his neighbours for his farming politics. His economic views, which might have included the putting down of deer, were too much for the master of Eggesford. "No, no," he exclaimed, "don't do that; I find nothing so pacific as venison." The fifth Lord Portsmouth had only to take the field with his hounds, to show himself abroad, even to stroll through his own park, to elicit some unsought, but absolutely unavoidable, demonstration of popularity. On taking his place at any public dinner he was greeted with a chorus of "view-halloas," whose echoes seemed to float on the air long after the storm of noise had subsided.

Never since the Pixton denunciations of £10 suffrage in 1832 had the country houses we are now visiting been so fluttered as in 1877-8. That was the period of the Bulgarian atrocities agitation of deadly differences between Gladstone and Disraeli on the "Unspeakable Turk," of many Liberal secessions from the Gladstonian connection. The presentation of a portrait to Sir Stafford Northcote had been impartially promoted by West-country politicians on both sides. But, though the surface seemed tranquil enough, no one ever knew when or with what distressing results the volcano of strife might not show itself in eruption. What the masters of Holnicote or Eggesford might suddenly be moved to say—what blows might be dealt from the homes of the Aclands or the Wallops at

Where Devon and Somerset Meet

Castlehill for the Fortescue defection from Liberalism
—so were the speculations full of nervous apprehension
to the local mind, and rendering it at least a toss-up
whether a feast beneath any of these roofs might not
at any moment turn to a fray. Castlehill by this time
had become definitely a Conservative house. Its
social relations with Eggesford, with Holnicote, or
Killerton, continued generally as cordial as ever,
thanks in some degree to the conciliatory influence of
Pynes. It was at this time that Castlehill co-operated
with Eggesford, with Holnicote, or, more strictly, with
Killerton, to dine Sir Stafford Northcote. The Gladstonian Sir Thomas Acland joined. How he would
acquit himself on the occasion furnished matter for
amused conjecture at the country dinner-tables round
about. His political friends and kindred had nervously
urged the necessity of circumspectness and brevity.
" I will bet you what you like," Lady Susan Fortescue
had said to Acland, "you cannot keep your speech
under ten minutes." That the speech in question
proved about the right length and avoided controversial topics was attributed by the country-house
critics to the fact that before delivering his address Sir
Thomas Acland secured the advice and inspiration of
the then mistress of Eggesford, at this moment the
Dowager Lady Portsmouth, then and during some
years of the Gladstonian epoch eminent among the
town and country hostesses of the Liberal party.

As very young men, Gladstone and Acland had
founded something in the nature of a religious
brotherhood. Acland's interest in all things,
religious or ecclesiastical, like Gladstone's, lasted

On the Quantock Slopes

throughout his life. Holnicote and Killerton both abounded in clerical guests of all Anglican varieties, and indeed of all Christian communions. Among these clerical visitors who passed to and fro between the West-country homes now mentioned were Canon Cook, of Exeter, who had trained his Eggesford and Holnicote hosts into recognising Dean Church as the best writer of the day, who had edited the Speaker's "Commentary on the Bible," and who had been active in promoting the Bonn conferences between the English and Greek Church representatives. With him there occasionally mingled in the same company the two bishops who shared his anxiety for reunion, Christopher Wordsworth and Harold Browne. Dr. Dollinger, the "Old Catholic" champion, might, it was hoped, have been induced to travel to the hospitable land of the red-deer. In his place there actually came the Greek Archbishop of Syros, Lycurgus, accompanying Sir Thomas Acland certainly to Eggesford, perhaps in the fourth Lord Carnarvon's time to Pixton. Pixton, indeed, under one of this owner's predecessors, had associated itself with another movement, partly religious, partly philanthropic, of a very different sort. Sir George Williams, the founder of the Young Men's Christian Associations, a native of Dulverton, had visions of the institution that was to make his name a household word, in very early life. The Lord Carnarvon who then lived at Pixton often talked the subject over with him, and offered many hints for its organisation.

Where the Quantocks slope down to the Bristol

Where Devon and Somerset Meet

Channel still stands the most famous of all the eighteenth-century country houses.   Orchard Wyndham
has been, during many years, unoccupied.   Its owner,
now living at Dinton House, near Salisbury, Mr.
William Wyndham, is descended from the earlier
master of the place, Sir William Wyndham, in
whose possession it formed the most hospitable
centre of the Stuart cause in the county.   What
in the Victorian era the Kentish magnate, Lord
Abergavenny, has been shown to be to the Conservative cause, that some two hundred years earlier
was Sir William Wyndham to the Legitimacy and
Toryism of his day.   Marked now by the Egremont Inn is the exact spot in Williton at which,
periodically, the public conveyances used to stop.
Hither, from his mansion hard by, the Master
of Orchard Wyndham sent for those guests whom
he found it convenient to entertain, and who had
not posted the distance from London.   The handsomest and wealthiest of West-country baronets,
Sir William Wyndham, from being a local manager,
became, under St. John, Viscount Bolingbroke, a
national leader of the Tory high-flyers.   Eridge
Castle was at one time spoken of as the Carlton in
Kent.   During the eighteenth century's first quarter
Orchard Wyndham was literally the October Club
out of town.   Let us watch for a moment the chief
guests as their equipages drive up to the door, or
as they take their places at the table.   Clear the
way, if you please, for the patrician genius who poses
as the Alcibiades of his age, whom his disciples
call the greatest genius that has ever lived, who, to

his enemies, is the most unscrupulous scoundrel, whom women of all degrees, from the orange-girls hanging about the Court of Requests, to the great ladies of St. James's, are said to have found the most fascinating and irresistible of libertines, whom some practical men of affairs regard as the acutest of political philosophers, and whom friends and foes alike may agree to consider the most wonderful man of his age—St. John, Viscount Bolingbroke. With him are his equal in good looks, the Duke of Ormond, the stately and austere Sir Thomas Hanmer, some time Speaker, the representatives of extinct peerages, such as Bingley and Harcourt— the latter's features strikingly to be reproduced in his descendant, the Sir William Vernon Harcourt of a later day. Other and even more noticeable guests are the two Jacobite divines in their episcopal lawn sleeves, Atterbury Trelawny and an ecclesiastic; yet more notable Jonathan Swift, Dean of St. Patrick's, who, alone among the visitors, has accomplished the journey from the capital in a coasting vessel bound from London, *viâ* Bristol, for the neighbouring ports of Minehead and Watchet. Sir Roger de Coverley himself, while yet in the prime of life, did not realise a comelier picture of the country host than Sir William Wyndham, as, in the flower of his manhood, seated at the head of his table, he looks round upon the guests beneath a roof dearer to him than any other object except his wife and children. Thus looking round, he notices that Bolingbroke drinks two wines, champagne and Florence, and that Dean Swift never lifts his glass of port to his lips save after liberally qualifying it with water. "What a falling off is there," murmurs a local guest, Mr. Llewellyn, the high Tory rector of Wiveliscombe or Stogumber, "since Speaker Cornwall's fresh supplies of porter from Bellamy's, to quote the 'Rolliad,' or Harley, my lord Oxford, and his sixth bottle of port." With this fresh-coloured, blue-eyed squire, libertinism is but an affectation, a fashionable concession to the aristocratic weaknesses of the time. Some measure of profligacy is the high-bred veneer that so well became the ancestral *roués* who stood for the first Charles, and who helped to bring back the second.

The conventional description of Dunster Castle as the Alnwick of the West, fits the place better than could be done by any less unoriginal refinement of phrase. West Somerset possesses even fewer Liberal country houses than North Devon. In the nineteenth century, however, Dunster was as loyal to Mr. Gladstone as, two hundred years earlier, it had when, in the hands of the Luttrells, been to the Parliament. Five hundred years earlier, Dunster had been held by its founder, William Mohun, against King Stephen. By marriage, or by purchase, the Devonshire Courtenays and Tregonwells acquired a proprietorial interest in Dunster before it passed to its present owners of the Fownes Luttrell stock and name.[1] Among its eighteenth- and nineteenth-century visitors were Colonel Henry

---

[1] This East Quantoxhead manor-house, to-day occupied by a son of Mr. Luttrell of Dunster, is the oldest possession of the family in the county. It came, by marriage, to a Luttrell in the reign of

The Quantoxhead Luttrells

Laws Luttrell, who replaced Wilkes as member for Middlesex, and who amused the Dunster guests with the latest House of Commons gossip. Lord Nugent's house in Great George Street, Westminster, had been broken into by thieves. Among the articles carried off were certain portions of Court costumes. Colonel Luttrell, who eventually became the second Earl of Carhampton, asked whether Nugent had recovered his missing property, shook his head, adding, " I shrewdly suspect some of those laced ruffles are on the hands of the gentlemen who now occupy the Treasury Bench." In 1820 swords and lace were still worn on State occasions ; the fashionable Whigs of both sexes had not yet completely given up the use of hair-powder. Luttrell had been observed to be closely watching the new ministers reluctantly accepted by the king, as, fresh from Brooks' or their rather humble lodgings, they took possession of the seats recently occupied by Lord North and his friends. Another of the Luttrell tribe, sometimes received by the head of the Somerset-shire family at Dunster, was Temple Luttrell, a characteristic personification of the literary accomplishments then held in fashionable esteem, and of conversational diction, noticeable for its robustness even in that age of full-flavoured talk. " The Heroic Epistle to Sir William Chambers " produced on its appearance the same kind of sensation as had been

Henry III. Never having been for public sale since the Conquest, it probably stands alone as an instance of continuity of possession. The purchase of Dunster from the Mohuns by Elizabeth Luttrell took place at a much later date.

created by the "Rolliad." It was indifferently attri-
buted to Christopher Anstey of the *Bath Guide*,
to Temple Luttrell, and, among others, to Horace
Walpole. Walpole, though not its author, was an
admirer of the book, and even more so of its
reputed and perhaps most probable writer's gifts.
"Ten times more delicacy of irony, greater facility
than, and as much poetry as the Dunciad," was the
Strawberry Hill verdict on what the Strawberry
Hill critic believed to be Luttrell's *jeu d'esprit*.
About the same time Temple Luttrell and Lord
George Germain were scolding each other in public
like two oyster-women. The conversational fracas
had been, it seems, begun by Luttrell, who used
language worthy of Newgate; thus affronted, Germain's hand instinctively grasped his sword.
Whatever apology may have been given or refused,
no blood seems to have been spilt. Henry Luttrell,
the wittiest society talker of his day (1765–1851), of
an irritable and sensitive temperament, quite different
from that belonging to most of his name, gave some
little trouble to his Dunster hosts. His complaint
that the cream had a flavour of turnips caused the
issue of particular orders for the feeding of cows
against his next visit. "Well, how is it?" anxiously
asked the hostess. "Excellent," came the reply,
"— with boiled mutton!" A strange servant once
did not recognise him on his arrival. "I give you
my honour, sir," he said, "I am invited. If I am
not, you will have the pleasure of seeing me kicked
out of the door." Asked at Dunster why he lived
so much with Samuel Rogers, as great an expert

as himself in saying sharp things, he replied, "To prevent, at least for the time, Rogers' ill-natured words about me." Miss O'Neill, the actress, on a professional tour in the West, was met by him at Dunster. Not liking his looks, the lady markedly avoided him. His revenge was a remark to one of the Acland ladies, "I have seen fifty such girls in a cart in Kilkenny."

Dunster, the scene of many Gladstone visits, originated, on one occasion, a typically characteristic display of the Gladstonian universality of intellectual interest in things small, as well as great, of the perennially fresh, the enthusiastic and omnivorous thoroughness in whose vocabulary the word "trifles" had no place. The Dunster clergyman, in his Sunday sermon, had spoken of the Spartans as the bravest of the old Greeks. At the dinner-table some one contended that the palm for courage should be given to the Thespians. The great man said nothing at the time; the next day he returned to London to prepare the Budget which was then shortly due. The Hellenic subject proved to have a particular interest for a lady, one of the Clovelly Fanes, who, like Gladstone, had heard the sermon giving rise to the discussion. To Gladstone she accordingly wrote for his opinion. A week or so later, Dunster Castle was once more full of guests. Among them came, if not in the flesh, by letter, the then premier's private secretary (1880–1882) Mr. (now Sir Arthur) Godley, himself as a classical scholar the equal of his chief. From him the lady in question learned the effect produced by her

Where Devon and Somerset Meet

inquiry on the Downing Street staff. "When your letter arrived," said Mr. Godley, "it was handed to the three secretaries who happened to be in the room ; we could not agree ; we therefore took it to our master. Though then in the thick of his Budget work, he at once became so excited in the new subject that he threw up finance ; for three mortal hours he walked up and down, talking about nothing but Thermopylæ and the Spartans."

The place once filled in this corner of West Somerset by Orchard Wyndham, may to-day, socially and architecturally, be given to St. Audries, Sir Alexander Acland - Hood's. Among the country-house visitors in the South and West of England in the eighteenth century were two distinguished sailors. One served under Rodney, the other under Nelson. Both bore the same name. Each in his turn became Sir Samuel Hood. One, the Dorsetshire Sir Samuel Hood, Nelson's officer, died in 1815, a year before his Somersetshire namesake who had been with Rodney. Apart from his connection with the Bridport Hoods, the present owner of St. Audries may or may not derive his lineage from the Somersetshire clergyman in the Petherton district, who had for his son Rodney's Sir Samuel Hood. Or the St. Audries descent may be from the Nelsonian officer, the Dorsetshire Sir Samuel. All that is necessary to make plain here is that what has been spoken of as the twentieth-century equivalent of Orchard Wyndham, two hundred years ago, belongs to its present master by maternal right. While there were yet Wyndhams in the Williton neighbourhood, and when Henry Luttrell with other

318

fine London visitors was alternately amusing and bullying his Dunster kinsfolk, West Quantoxhead had yet to be overshadowed by a stately dwelling of the twentieth-century St. Audries type. The Mallets, indeed, or some earlier owners, had built a small manor-house which, in the eighteenth century, was the residence of a Bridgewater family named Balch. In 1754 Robert Balch was one of the Bridgewater M.P.'s, with one of the Egmont family for his colleague. In 1797 the St. Audries manor-house was in the possession of Miss Balch. At that time the chief social centre of the district was Sir Peregrine Acland's Fairfield, destined by the marriage of his daughter and heiress to become the parent of the new St. Audries of its Acland-Hood owners. About the family origins of these, something has been already said. The historic Fairfield of the present writer's childhood might, for genial and generous hospitality, have been called the Liberty Hall of the Quantock side. Other houses of the same character were Crowcombe Court and Cothelstone. At the last of these an eighteenth-century visitor, Dr. Samuel Johnson, took part in a conversation about the name of the surrounding hills. " If, sir," said the sage, " Julius Cæsar, as he well may have done, visited these parts, why should he not have exclaimed ' Quantum hoc ! ' " He knew indeed the more majestic heights of Alp and Apennine ; he had never seen among them such an undulating expanse of golden furze or purple heath." Sir Peregrine Acland's genial and generous reign at Fairfield overlapped the establishment of the Acland-

Where Devon and Somerset Meet

Hood dynasty at St. Audries. The first mistress of the present St. Audries reproduced the most amiable qualities of her father. From her marriage, in 1849, to her comparatively recent death, she showed herself the Lady Bountiful of the district, as well as the widely sympathetic hostess of house-parties most variously composed. Conspicuous at these gatherings were the patriarchal Sir Peregrine himself, still for the most part living in kindly, unassuming state at Fairfield, and a cousin of the Dunster Luttrells, noted for his fine presence, his frank manner, and his excellence in all kinds of sport—Colonel Henry Luttrell, a son of the East Quantoxhead clergyman, himself among the most popular and useful squires in the Mendip country. Sir Peregrine Acland, at St. Audries as beneath his own roof, abounded to the last in anecdotes turning upon the West Somerset vernacular. Slowly riding up to his son-in-law's newly finished abode, he heard two countrymen discussing the aspects of the place. Said one to the other, as if clenching the conversation, " Well, I suppose it's a case, as they say in France, of ' Shake an ass and go.' " A little inquiry identified the supposed Gallicism as " *Chacun a son goût.*" The hospitable fame of Fairfield had been for the most part of only local fame. The nineteenth- and twentieth-century St. Audries has been a social centre for Unionism, and rendered especial service to that Salisbury Administration in which Lord Knutsford, himself with Lady Knutsford a St. Audries visitor, preceded Mr. Chamberlain as Colonial Secretary. To-day Fairfield is inhabited

by the agent of the St. Audries owner. The old
Acland house at Fairfield was built by two sixteenth and seventeenth century Sir Thomas Palmers.
The memory of the early Palmer connection is
preserved at St. Audries not only by a portrait,
but by some baby clothes placed beneath the
picture. These garments belonged respectively to
John, Henry, and Thomas Palmer. These boys were
the children of Edward Palmer of Ightham, and
his wife, Alice, a daughter of John Clement,
Governor of Guisnes. According to the family
account, the three boys were all born with only a
fortnight's interval between the eldest and the
youngest. Amongst the visitors to the district as
well as to the house itself who brought away specially
pleasant memories of the late Lady Hood's kindness,
was one who had the same maiden-name as that
given by marriage to the former mistress of St.
Audries. The daughter of Thomas Hood, who
"sung the Song of a Shirt," married the clergyman
of Cossington in Somersetshire. Mrs. Broderip, as
she had now become, going for her health to the
Bristol Channel coast, reconnoitred West Quantoxhead for a suitable lodging. The news of her being
in the place brought an invitation from the great
house. The then Lady Hood insisted on the visitor
regarding St. Audries as her home till the necessary
accommodation could be found.

On the spurs of the eastern Quantocks, Enmore
Castle, the home of the (Egmont) Percevals may be
compared with Dunster further to the west. The
Percevals, in addition to other estates in southern

Where Devon and Somerset Meet

England and in Ireland, had received from William I. much land in the Quantock region as well as in the outlying districts. Just, however, where the Quantocks slope towards the Severn Sea, the Egmonts were not among the great territorialists. A Captain Perceval, who married Sir John Trevelyan's daughter, rented indeed the house of Chapel Cleve, subsequently for many years inhabited by the Hallidays. Its former mistress, Mrs. Halliday, still entertains her old friends in her home at Minehead, within manageable distance of those of her name and family who still live at Glenthorne, the hospitable and picturesque abode, from a deep hollow in the woods, looking down upon Lynton, well known to every Ilfracombe tourist. Any lands or houses in the Chapel Cleve neighbourhood now belong by purchase to the Dunster Luttrells. Originally rooted in Ireland, the Percevals were a family of tragic vicissitudes. The seventeenth-century head of the house, Robert, a noted duellist, while little more than a youth, was found under the may-pole in the Strand, dead, with a blood-stained sword at his side. How he came to his end remained a mystery. In 1812 Spencer Perceval, the Prime Minister, was assassinated by Bellingham in the Lobby. More recently a descendant of the statesman, with his wife and child, perished by a violent death in the wild west of America. Towards the close of the eighteenth century there lived on the Egmont estate in the shadow of Enmore Castle the most remarkable man in the neighbourhood, Thomas Poole, a born book-lover and critic, the friend and adviser alike of rich and poor. To him wrote the poet William Wordsworth, begging

Alfoxton, Wordsworth and "Nosey"

Poole's good offices with Cruickshank, Lord Egmont's agent, to enable the poet to take a small house at Adscombe, not far from the spot now occupied by Quantock Lodge. Wordsworth had been attracted to the neighbourhood by the fact of his friend S. T. Coleridge being already settled at Nether Stowey. Without some intermediary of unimpeachable respectability, Wordsworth had already received practical proof of the hopelessness of being suitably housed in that high Tory district. An application for Alfoxton had been, indeed, already made by him and refused, on the ground of his seditious sympathies. Thomas Poole brought forward evidence of his friend's real innocence and harmlessness. Thus eventually the poet secured the tenancy of Alfoxton for £40 a year, deer-park and all. The place thus became as important a landmark as Rydal itself in the evolution of the lake poets. At Alfoxton itself, as Wordsworth's guest, Coleridge wrote both his " Fears in Solitude" and his "Ode to Liberty." Wordsworth desired to continue his tenancy. The St. Albyn owners had been plied with renewed reports of the poet's revolutionary associations. Before renewing the lease, they sent down a detective to make inquiries. This officer of the law happened to possess a very long nose. Following Wordsworth and Coleridge in one of their frequent walks, he heard them talk about the philosopher Spinosa. To the keen ear of the Bow Street official, the strange word implied some uncomplimentary comment on his nasal organ. Thus wounded at a sensitive point, he reported so unfavourably of the poets that the non-renewal of the

Where Devon and Somerset Meet

lease prevented Wordsworth from prolonging his residence beyond the year. Since those days Alfoxton, still in perfect preservation, has been enlarged and improved into a capacious and capital modern mansion. Alfoxton has now passed from owners of the St. Albyn name. Its last St. Albyn occupant, while an Oxford undergraduate, lost at cards so much of his patrimony as abruptly to end all relations with his father. A good whip, he first became a coachman. The railways extinguished the industry of the road. The disinherited of Alfoxton obtained a position as driver of an omnibus between Sunbury on the Thames and the City. " Hurry up, St. Albyn, here's a old gent inside as says he's bound to be at the Bank in less than no time." This fragment of professional talk, overheard by the elder St. Albyn, when on business in London, formed the first intimation received by him for thirty years of the existence or the whereabouts of his cast-off son. As a child, the present writer first knew Alfoxton when inhabited by the elder and Mrs. St. Albyn, the stateliest couple that ever lived since the days of Chesterfield. The next time, after a decade's or so interval, I took my seat at the Alfoxton luncheon-table, the *ci-devant* Jehu of the knife-board was my host, a very kindly one, with no false shame about the vocation he had lately quitted, abounding in anecdotes about the Oxford and Cambridge boat-race, which he had witnessed for thirty years continuously from Barnes Bridge on the top of the 'bus he was driving across. From the Jenours, connections of the St. Albyns, this beautiful place has gone for the present to the cultivated and generous Archer family,—the greatest of the district's recent social acquisitions.

In the earlier days of Gladstone's Liberalism, when people still talked about Peelites, when Sir James Graham and Sidney Herbert both lived or had but recently died, Quantock Lodge, already mentioned, lately finished by Mr. Labouchere (Lord Taunton), received every summer a succession of guests representing the Liberal management. One rather striking contrast among these visitors may be recalled. It must have been in or about 1872 that, by some odd chance, one past and one future Lord Chancellor slept the same night beneath this roof. The former keeper of the monarch's conscience was Lord Westbury. Its future custodian was Roundell Palmer, afterwards Lord Selborne. It was Westbury who, at Quantock Lodge, described Selborne as a character unredeemed by a single vice. In the case of most of the houses now visited, the social life was agreeably reproduced on a smaller scale by adjacent dwellings that, to use the phraseology of Swiss tourists, were in effect "dépendances" of the chief building. Grouped round Quantock Lodge were Over Stowey Rectory, successively held by two of the Somersetshire Bullers, father and son. Near at hand were the charming houses of Mr. Robert Buller and of Mr. Robertson, Lord Taunton's agent, both fulfilling definite and delightful functions in the country-house system of the neighbourhood. Similarly Kilve Court, nearer to the Severn Sea, was for years inhabited by Colonel Luttrell, a Waterloo veteran, the father of Dunster's present owner, a master of fox-hounds and a keen sportsman. The intellectual life of the village had for its centre Kilve Rectory, then occupied by the Oxford Greswell, who had married, from the Muiravonside Stirlings, one of the brightest and kindest women who ever lived. Inland, on the other side of the Quantocks, Sydney Smith, in his Combe Florey library, composed and rehearsed his 1831 Reform speech with the Mrs. Partington-Atlantic simile, and made his rectory-house the intellectual adjunct to the lay social centres. In Sydney Smith's Combe Florey days the country houses with which he chiefly exchanged visits in the neighbourhood were not of his politics. They were for the most part Nettlecombe Court, where Sir John Trevelyan then reigned, and Hartrow Manor, where Sydney Smith lived to meet the Duke of Wellington, Sir Robert Peel, and Richard Cobden. As a territorial dynasty preponderating in West Somerset, the Egmont Percevals are no longer known. Enmore Castle belongs to the Broadmeads. Other parts of the former Egmont property are incorporated in the dominion of the present occupant of Quantock Lodge —still famous for its china and its curiosities—Lord Taunton's son-in-law, Mr. E. J. Stanley, member for the Bridgwater division, the most successful bric-a-brac hunter, the most expert of virtuosos and of cognoscenti in his county.

CHAPTER XII

IN SQUIRE WESTERN'S LAND

Halswell—The Tyntes—The Bridgwater elections: "the Man in the Moon"—Baron Tripp, the introducer of the waltz, and his colleagues—Bulwer Lytton's presence of mind—Brymore, the home of John Pym—Its connection with Francis Bacon—Pym's mother, Lady Rous, and wife, Anna Hooker—Lady Rous's funeral sermon preached by Charles Fitz-Geoffrey—Wentworth (Strafford) at Brymore—Pym and Hampden—Brymore's later owners—Guests at Brymore during Pym's life: Sir John Popham, Thomas Coryate—Cricket St. Thomas, the house of Sir Amias Preston—Ralph, Lord Hopton—Ralph Cudworth—Dr. Joseph Wolff at Ile-Brewers Rectory—Archdeacon Denison at East Brent Rectory—Freeman at Sommerleaze—Sir William Pynsent of Burton-Pynsent—His legacies to Chatham—William Pitt's childhood at Burton-Pynsent—Ralph Allen's Prior Park, standing in the same relation to Bath as Stanmer to Brighton—Allen, the original of Squire Alworthy in "Tom Jones"—Prior Park an open house—Its guests—Warburton—Literary visitors—Dean Swift—Bowood—First Marquis of Lansdowne—His descent from the Pettys and the Fitzmaurices—His grandparents, the Earl and Countess of Kerry—Bowood parties—Bentham, Dumont, Priestly—Lansdowne's household accounts—The third Marquis—Thomas Moore and other visitors—Bowood in the present day—The poet Bowles at Bremhill—Barley Wood, the home of Hannah Moore—Raikes, the founder of the Sunday Schools, and his Cotswold guests—Blaise Castle, the home of Wilberforce's friend, Harford.

327

In Squire Western's Land

STILL in the Bridgwater division of Somerset, about a mile from the eighteenth-century Enmore Castle, built by the second Earl of Egmont, now owned by Mr. Broadmead, is the rather earlier Halswell House of the Tyntes. This is a veritable monument in the struggles of local politics and the evolution of Society's fashions. Both the second and third Sir Robert Peels, Count D'Orsay, and the third Napoleon when a London exile, were among its former guests. The palmers' shells that some of the oldest families on Quantock-side are entitled to quarter in their coats-of-arms, imply an ancestor who took an ascertained part in the Crusades. The same distinction is conveyed in the very etymology of the name of the owners of Halswell. At the battle of Ascalon a young knight, conspicuous for his white armour and his white horse, bore himself so gallantly, as, with an appropriate heraldic device, to receive from Richard Cœur-de-Lion the motto : " *Tinctus sanguine infideli.*" With some verbal variation the legend was engraved under the armorial bearings of the family by that member of it who built Halswell, about the time that the last Stuart king ceased to reign. The Halswell politics were consistently Whig or Liberal. In the pre-Reform period Halswell House carried in its pocket the representation, not only of the neighbouring Bridgwater, but of Somerset itself. Those who remember "the old Colonel Tynte" can recall the most chivalrous and kind of Somersetshire worthies. He had himself been returned both for West Somerset and for Bridgwater before the Victorian age began. After the Queen's accession, as regards at least the neighbouring borough, his son became his Parliamentary heir. Before Bridgwater forfeited the right to a member of its own, Halswell remained the most active and important centre in local politics. The Parliamentary colleague of Colonel Tynte the younger was his friend and fellow—though not quite contemporary—Etonian, A.W. Kinglake, author of " Eothen " and historian of the Crimean War. The third Sir Robert Peel was staying at Halswell about the time of the French annexation of Savoy and Nice, of the indignation at which Kinglake had made himself the eloquent but, from his weak voice, the almost inaudible mouthpiece. The third Sir Robert Peel was receiving the congratulations of the Halswell visitors on the speech in which, a night or two before, in his magnificently resonant tones, he had denounced the French policy. Turning to his host and to Kinglake, he smiled significantly. " It was," he explained, " the exact oration, word for word, addressed in his delicate voice by Kinglake to the House, but only heard by Peel, who happened to be sitting next, and who had made the fullest notes." There existed a local tradition that Bridgwater liked to show its appreciation of aristocracy in returning a Tynte, and of literature in returning Kinglake. The constituency proved itself free and independent in giving its votes just as Halswell made it worth its while to do. Whatever other candidates may have been in the field, at the psychological moment before the polling, a mysterious personage, known throughout the constituency as "the Man in the Moon," became confidentially accessible to the freemen of the borough in a loft above the

In Squire Western's Land

Clarence Hotel. The exact details of the interview were a Punchinello secret. But the admirers of the principle of intellect in Kinglake and of birth and breeding in his colleague seemed to find it more convenient to pay their rent, or any other outstanding little claim, after a nocturnal visit to "the Man in the Moon," and invariably "went solid" for the Halswell nominee. Thus did the Halswell influence alone, and no other consideration, moral or material, from 1857 to 1865, continuously secure Bridgwater's representation by the accomplished literary stylist, whose book of Eastern travel exercised an abiding influence on the diction of English *belles lettres*, and as high-bred and courtly a man of the world as ever staked his money at Crockford's or set foot on the floor at Almack's. In the last days of William IV. the most indefatigable diner-out and country-house visitor of his time, Thomas Creevey, the diarist, coming up from Cassiobury (Lord Essex's), is in despair about a letter he had wanted to go by that evening's post. He has gone to Brooks'—not a frank to be had there for love or money. Disconsolately resigning himself to hard fate, as his foot is on the last of the club steps, whom should he meet coming in but one who at his West Somerset house had given him many a good dinner and many a good day's shooting. This was the Kemeys Tynte who in 1837 was the West Somerset M.P., the father of the Bridgwater member who sat with Kinglake.

Among those in the first half of the nineteenth century who had occupied Orchard Wyndham, already described, had been the bearer of the well-known

Halswell for Waltz

Somersetshire patronymic, Tripp. To his generation belonged an Anglicised Dutchman, Lord Anglesea's particular friend, who had become one of Society's pet oracles, Baron Tripp. The purely accidental identity of the names may explain the welcome received by the foreigner from many Somersetshire hosts. Among these was the Tyntes. The polite world at that time exercised itself severely about a recent novelty in ball-room programmes—the waltz. The new dance had for its introducer-in-chief this Baron Tripp. With him were the young Duke of Devonshire (the great Apollo in the drawing-rooms of his epoch), Tripp's compatriot and brother *emigré*, Tuyll, Newmann, Lady Castlereagh, and Lady Emma Edgcumbe, afterwards Countess of)Brownlow. As to Tripp, Society often seems to have laughed rather at than with him. Tuyll, however, commanded the same respect in all the English country houses of his time as he did in Holland, to one of whose best families he belonged. Thus it was that, with the help of his friends, rather than from his own influence, Tripp succeeded in bringing the waltz into fashionable repute. Country houses were divided in opinion about the dance. Gradually, however, it took its place at Almack's as well as in the best provincial ball-rooms. An occasional visitor at Halswell, Tripp, enlisting the Tynte influence in its favour, superintended the first waltz ever witnessed in the Bridgwater or Taunton rooms at a county ball. The younger Tynte, parliamentarily connected with the neighbouring borough, rather than the county, literally illuminated the old house of his fathers with brilliant guests. Never

In Squire Western's Land

before had been seen so many well-known Hyde Park or St. James's Street faces beneath a Somerset roof as at Halswell. Colonel Charles Tynte belonged to the dandies. Once at least Halswell received their queen, Lady Blessington, who, meeting there Louis Napoleon, then about to establish the second Empire, met his question as to the length of her intended stay in Paris with her famous *mot*: "*Et vous, monseigneur?*" To Halswell also came the then Sir Edward Bulwer Lytton. It was while a Halswell guest that he filled his host, his fellow-visitors, and the whole countryside with admiration for a surprising exhibition of presence of mind. By some mishap the fleecy wrapper covering his partner's shoulders at the public dance caught fire. Without saying a word, changing colour, or moving a muscle of his face, he took the ignited garment, in a moment smothered the last smouldering spark, and calmly returned it to its owner.

In its aspect as a historical monument, the Somersetshire country house, within an easy walk of Halswell, next to be visited, constitutes a constitutional landmark of the same kind as Port Eliot in Cornwall. The French Revolution of the eighteenth century was, as its latest historian has reminded us, the work of the professional middle class, especially of the lawyers. The English Revolution of the seventeenth century originated in the conferences at each other's rural homes of country gentlemen. The doctrines of royal absolutism were first framed by a Kentish squire, Sir Robert Filmer, of East Sutton, as well as, indeed, by Francis Bacon himself, when as a Hertfordshire squire entertaining

From Gorhambury to Brymore

James I. at Gorhambury.   From the home and birth-place of John Pym, Brymore, proceeded the first notes of a counterblast to the pretensions of prerogative, bluntly formulated by the Kentish baronet and philosophised over by the constructor of " The New Organon."   " The sum of my counsel to your Majesty," had in effect been the words of the future Lord Verulam to his royal guest, " is to take advantage of the Protestant depression prevailing abroad and in every way to humour the Protestant zeal of those who at home are ill-affected in the same degree to the Pope of Rome and to your own Sovereign prerogative."   In other words, the king was to employ the Protestantism of his Parliament as a leverage for raising money on the plea of supporting by arms the States hostile to Papal pretensions in Europe, and with that money to strengthen the out-works of the English throne.   Brymore therefore became the social headquarters of operations against the tactics matured at Gorhambury.   The stock of which the young Somersetshire squire came was old and opulent in the West.   His mother, by a second marriage, Lady Rous had seen much of Court society; she had gratified her social ambition by making her Somersetshire home the fashionable centre of the county.   Among her guests she had entertained a great peer of popular sympathies, the Earl of Bed-ford.   The fond mother had the further gratification of seeing that nobleman not only notice particularly her clever boy on his visits, but secure him a post in the Exchequer, as well as promise to bring him into Parliament as member for the borough of Calne.

In Squire Western's Land

The latter prospect realised itself in 1614. A little later Pym signalised the opening of his career at St. Stephen's by presenting Brymore with a new mistress in his wife, the daughter of a neighbouring squire, Anna Hooker. In 1620, above the old entrance-porch at Brymore, two hatchments were in quick succession displayed. Within a few months the master of the place had lost both his wife and his mother, Lady Rous. The most fashionable and eloquent Anglican preacher of the day, Charles Fitz-Geoffry, had been at Brymore in the days of Lady Rous. He now revisited the place in the room he had often occupied before, composed his funeral sermon, delivered afterwards in the parish church, of the deceased lady, and containing complimentary allusions to her promising son, referred to as " Phoebi Deliciæ." Of this discourse notes formerly existed among the Brymore papers. " He will never marry again" said the family mourners who had met at Brymore. Thanking them for their condolences, Pym himself, however, said nothing beyond the quotation, " It is good for a man to bear the yoke in his youth." Between "the Cock of the North," Wentworth (afterwards Strafford), and Pym, called in contradistinction "the Cock of the West," there always existed a rivalry, though at first of an amicable kind. Wentworth certainly visited Brymore. There may be good reason for the conjecture that in the large porch with the pointed Gothic doorway and pinnacles of Pym's Somersetshire home, the two men parted for the last time as friends, and that it was here, rather than at Greenwich, that Pym ominously murmured, as the visitor disappeared, "You are leaving us; we shall not leave you while your head is on your shoulders." The interest of Brymore to-day lies in the conversations between Pym and his visitors, of which it was the undoubted scene, rather than in the Parliamentary preparations which, in common with certain Northamptonshire seats, presently to be visited, it witnessed. To Pym, as to Hampden and to others of the Brymore parties, the foremost object of thought and fear was the fact that Henry VIII. was now shown by events to have done nothing more than put himself in the Pope's place. "We have," said the Brymore host, "to drill, discipline, and strengthen nothing less than Protestantism itself. For look beyond the seas. In Spain, the Inquisition and the Crown have combined to crush the political and religious movement against ancient authority. In France the past has triumphed over the present through Richelieu. In Germany and Austria Papal ascendancy has overwhelmed the Protestant States and restored the birthplace of Luther to the Infallible Church. At first Italy as well as Spain was well disposed to the new liberty, but now England and Holland alone are Protestant." "Therefore," rejoined Hampden, to whom these words were addressed, "now that so many friends of Gustavus Adolphus are visiting this country, let us draw closer the bonds of union between the Protestantism of the Continent and of this island." The religious and political settlement in the seventeenth century owed its essentially Conservative character to the moral influence radiating from houses like

In Squire Western's Land

Brymore. Hence alone the gradual elimination of revolutionary and destructive elements, Anabaptist, Fifth Monarchy, and other like propagandism which elsewhere than in England turned reform into riot. The sobriety, the good sense, that kept the spiritual zeal of the times from degenerating into mere extravagance, above all the moral earnestness, identifying the Parliamentary cause with the national convictions, were focused and mirrored at Brymore under the earliest of its famous owners. The appearance presented by the house to-day differs little from that it wore when John Pym's eyes opened on it for the last time. His grand-daughter married Sir Thomas Hales. Lady Hales was heiress to her brother, Sir Charles Pym, who died unmarried. By this line of descent, through the (Radnor) Bouveries, the place came to its present possessor, Mr. H. H. Pleydell-Bouverie.

Among the local visitors at Brymore during the Pym period was a Somersetshire squire, who eventually became Lord Chief Justice. This was Sir John Popham, of Huntworth, in the Ilminster district. He is not known to have had any family connection with the other Sir John Popham, a Hampshire squire, Speaker in 1449. The comic guest was as indispensable to the Brymore and to other Somersetshire house parties in the sixteenth and seventeenth centuries as in more recent times. The stock local jester of the Pym period showed himself in the person of Thomas Coryate. This gentleman, possessed of a small estate at Odcombe, on which his family had long been settled, from

A Travelled Comedian

an early age had determined not to incur the
reproach of the homely wits attributed to home-
keeping youths. Between the intervals of his
eccentrically extensive travels, no one seems to
have been in greater request with the smaller hosts
of his neighbourhood. The appearance of the
"Odcombian legstretcher," to give him his local
appellation, can scarcely have been less peculiar than
his habits of life. With a head like a sugar-loaf,
he carried, as the rural critics unkindly said, folly
in his face. He always slept in his clothes to save,
as he put it, the "labour and expense of shifting."
He was supposed to have only one pair of shoes
in use; these, however, must have been of excellent
quality, since he had walked in them nine hundred
miles through Europe. Among the treasures brought
back by him from this tramp, was the earliest
specimen of a table-fork seen in the West of
England, and used, according to one account, for
the first time at the Brymore dinner-table.

Not far from the modest rural home of the globe-
trotting Coryate was the house of Sir Amias Preston,
notable among the sailors of his time. The stock
of delicacies with which he had returned to Cricket-
St. Thomas, near Crewkerne, seemed so unfailing
that his guests spoke of them as "the widow's
cruse." His chief guest was Ralph, Lord Hopton
of Fosse, near Wells, born in Monmouth, but in
tastes and dialect as pure a son of Somerset as
ever drank sour cider. A devout warrior this, after
Cromwell's own heart, truly boasting that he could
pray as soon as he could speak, and read as soon

337   Y

as he could pray. His chaplain in the field was Thomas Fuller of "The Worthies," but with such an official Hopton could afford to dispense and, as commander of the Parliamentary troops, proved himself not less at home in the pulpit than in the field. Appropriately enough Hopton's most frequent fellow-guest at Preston's was the divine who had for his benefice the reputed original of the Arthurian Camelot. While rector of North Cadbury, near his Somerset birthplace, Aller, Ralph Cudworth, the chief of the Cambridge Platonists, planned the "True Intellectual System of the Universe." The treatise itself was written more than twenty-five years afterwards. His sermon before the House of Commons in 1647 was too latitudinarian for the Puritans generally; it won, however, the appreciation of Cromwell and the admiration of Hopton. To the latter, indeed, as the two paced in conversation, the lawn of Cricket-St. Thomas, Cudworth explained the central notion of his book, the reality of a Supreme Divine Intelligence and the existence from eternity of moral ideas. At Cricket-St. Thomas, too, some of Cudworth's papers were stored till their publication, long after his death.

Most of the low-lying level watered by the Bridgwater Parret, derives such attraction as it possesses from its country houses. Tolerably near the point at which the confluence of the Ivel and the Isle forms the Parret, was the hospitable home of the Wadhams, the founders of Ilminster School and the Oxford College which, bearing their name, stands to the school in something like the relation of Christ

Ile-Brewers and East Brent

Church to Westminster. A rectory house in this neighbourhood enjoys the distinction of having been inhabited by the father of an accomplished and agreeable diplomatist, still happily, as these lines are written, with us. The famous missionary, Dr. Joseph Wolff, signalised his incumbency of Ile-Brewers by rebuilding the church in 1861. Socially, however, he did much more than this. His hospitalities to all nationalities and all creeds made his rectory house the most cosmopolitan centre ever possessed by his adopted country. The clerical homes of this neighbourhood have been of at least as much importance as the purely secular mansions. Archdeacon Denison's East Brent rectory is itself no small part of modern Church and State history. The most impetuous and uncompromising of high Anglicans was the kindliest and most universal of hosts. It was the present writer's lot to witness his reception at lunch of a State inspector, whose right to enter his schools he had denied. Obtaining at last admittance, the official was greeted by the children singing—

"Old Daddy Longlegs wouldn't say his prayers,
Take him by the left leg and fling him downstairs."

The little scholars had been recently taught the verses, and, unconscious of their relevancy, chanted them to show their power of song. Denison, a squarson of the best type, an hour or two after the incident, with the easy kindness of perfect breeding, made the inspector perfectly at home beneath his roof. In 1856 came the proceedings against the Archdeacon of Taunton for his sermons on the Real Presence, preached in Wells Cathedral and condemned by the diocesan court. The ecclesiastical atmosphere of the whole neighbourhood was long electrical and agitated. Denison himself preserved his bonhomie, met and received friends and foes at the dinner-table as if no cause of clerical or social division were provoking a crisis. His brother who became Speaker in 1857, visiting him at East Brent, was so amazed at his novel serenity, that he remarked, " I shall have to reconsider my former nomenclature for him, ' St. George without the dragon,' and look up a new simile suggested by the St. Anthony whose peaceful preaching charmed the fishes." Almost next door to East Brent is Lympsham Manor, the ecclesiastical antipodes of Denison's rectory, but, under its late owner, the Rev. J. H. Stephenson, of more than diocesan fame for its all-receptive and refined hospitalities. Under the shadow of Ben Knoll Hill, on the very frontier of the sixth century Wessex, was the country house, Somerleaze, of the writer who provoked Thorold Rogers' clever epigram—" Where from alternate tubs Stubbs butters Freeman, Freeman butters Stubbs." To the host of Somerleaze were as applicable as to Swift himself the lines—

> "True genuine dullness moved his pity
> Unless it offered to be witty."

Freeman, at home, suggested to his visitors Samuel Johnson in Bolt Court. He was, that is, liberal with limited means, and with that touch of spontaneity and

Chatham at Burton Pynsent

unconsciousness that raises liberality into generosity. In Charles Isaac Elton Freeman had a congenial neighbour, of an erudition scarcely less than his own, and with the same fondness for improving at the same time the minds and bodies of his visitors, by taking them long walks to the accompaniment of always instructive and frequently interesting wayside lectures on the objects or associations that lay in their path.

"Somebody," writes Horace Walpole in 1765, "is dead somewhere in Somersetshire or Wiltshire." The person thus referred to was said to have left £200,000 to the first Pitt, Lord Chatham. As a fact the value of the legacy did not exceed £40,000, and it was the second that had fallen to its illustrious recipient, the first having been the Dowager Duchess of Marlborough's bequest of £10,000 ; her grandson entailed upon him, after his own son, the Sunderland estate. That son, however, afterwards Lord Spencer, cut off the entailment directly he came of age. The deviser to the statesman of Burton Pynsent was the head of an old Somersetshire family, Sir William Pynsent. His fame is compared by Walpole with an aloe, because " it did not blow till near an hundred." The subject of innumerable scandals in his own neighbourhood, he had quarrelled with Lord North over the Cider Bill, and with Lord Bute over the Peace of Paris (1763). He marked his indignation at Bute's surrender of Chatham's triumphs by the present legacy of his Somersetshire property. From Hayes, therefore, in Kent, to Burton Pynsent in mid-Somerset, the Pitt family removed at the time when Chatham's famous son was a child of some six years old. The most noticeable trace of Burton Pynsent's occupation by the Pitts is the well-known memorial pillar erected near the house, now a ruin, in honour of the original owner, the last Pynsent. There was, however, within living memory, in the stable yard, a little stone platform raised by Chatham to perform a double service for his famous son. From it William Pitt the second used to mount his pony and, as from a rostrum, to declaim those oratorical masterpieces which his father had set him to learn by heart. Hence the Whig taunt that "Billy Pitt had been taught speaking by his dad on a stool."[1]

The hereditary owner of Burton Pynsent was not Chatham's sole Somersetshire benefactor. Ralph Allen, of Prior Park, had little for which to thank the great minister. Chatham, indeed, had done much to discourage in his energetic and beneficent career the eighteenth-century worthy who, beginning life as a post-office boy, raised himself to be not only the earliest of postal reformers, but one of the creators of Bath as a social and polite metropolis. He showed his forgiveness of Chatham's affronts by leaving him a legacy of £1,000. "The greatest character in any age of the world," is the hyperbole in which War-

---

[1] For these details about the Somersetshire home of the Pitts, I am indebted to my venerable friend A. W. Kinglake. As she reminded him when he had with her the interview on the Lebanon, described in "Eothen," Lady Hester Stanhope, a frequent visitor of her grandparents at Burton Pynsent, knew Kinglake's family well; to them she imparted the substance of all now related by me concerning Burton Pynsent. "But for the inspiration directly or indirectly drawn by me from Burton Pynsent," Kinglake often said, "'Eothen' would never have been written."

burton expresses his admiration of the man whose hospitalities made Prior Park the most famous of East Somerset houses. The social obligations of Brighton to the accident of its proximity to Stanmer have been already noticed. The relations existing between Prior Park and Bath were much of the same kind. George III.'s daughter, the Princess Amelia, had, indeed, first become acquainted with the capital of Beau Nash in 1728. She did not, however, really know the place until, with her brother, the Duke of York, she revisited it as Allen's guest in 1752. On that occasion Allen gave up, for the time, his whole house to his guests, going himself to Weymouth, where he doubtless received in person George III.'s thanks for the attention to his children. Prior Park at this epoch was not so much the most miscellaneously receptive of country houses ; it was the most catholic of residential hotels, to which all persons of either sex who had made their mark, or who gave promise of doing so, were welcome. They came and went when and as they pleased. Horses and carriages were always in waiting, at a moment's notice, to take them on any excursions or convey them to any destination they chose. It only differed from a public institution in there being no bills to pay and servants on the look-out for vails. The picture in "Tom Jones" of Squire Alworthy watching from his terrace the sun rise in the full blaze of his majesty, himself thinking only how to prove himself acceptable to his Creator by benefiting his fellow-creatures, thus in point of nobility comparable with the sun itself, may very likely have been suggested by the master of

In Squire Western's Land

Prior Park. Many touches in the good genius of Fielding's novel are no doubt taken from Allen. The great difference, however, between the Prior Park landscape and the scenery in which Alworthy lives, prevents an absolute identification of Allen and his home with the stage on which the characters of the novelist first appear.

If Allen had been born without a real genius for business, he would not have become the greatest capitalist of his county, or made his Somersetshire home the kindliest and most inspiring among the social forces of his century. Allen's sources of revenue may be judged from the enterprises with which he is associated. He revived the Bath stone trade from the Claverton quarries, which formed a portion of his vast estates. Having begun as a child-messenger, he became not only the postmaster at Bath, but the contractor for carrying the mails in that part of the country. Till his time everything that went through the post was conveyed by boys precariously mounted on horseback, supplementing their scanty wages by habitual theft. From the commencement of Allen's administration the robberies ceased. He began by instituting three posts a week instead of one. In 1741 Bath had a post every day of the week except Sunday. Meanwhile he established himself at Prior Park. He had also founded the mineral water hospital at Bath, and generally brought into existence the place as it has since been known. Before his settlement in the demesne which looks down on the city, Bath was nothing—a centre, perhaps, of gambling, intrigue, and vulgar gossip, but with no apparent chance of succeeding to the fashionable vogue of Tunbridge Wells, then on its decline. "Nature and Providence may have intended the place for a resource from distemper and disquiet. Man has made it a seat of racket and dissipation, with the slavery of a ceremonial more stiff and formal than that of the German Elector." So, at Prior Park, said to Allen one of his visitors, Tobias Smollett, then meditating medical practice at Bath. Allen's friends did not so much visit Prior Park as live there. Warburton, of "The Divine Legation," regularly settled there on his marriage. He saw all the wits there more easily than he could have done in London itself, and he had not house-rent. There, too, were Gainsborough and Garrick. With these mingled Henry St. John, Viscount Bolingbroke, Charles Yorke, second son of the Earl of Hardwicke, Lord Chancellor, the most agreeable and amiable scamp of his time, Thomas Potter, second son of the Primate, a well-known figure at the Medemenham orgies, tall, handsome, polished, a reputed favourite with Warburton's pretty, merry wife. With Sarah Fielding, writer of "David Simple" and other stories, came her famous brother, then, as his literary friends were good enough to record, "too visibly past his prime—a poor, emaciated, worn-out rake, whose gout and infirmities had got the better of his buffoonery." Jonathan Swift, too, was as regular an *habitué* at Prior Park as we have already seen him at Orchard Wyndham. It was in the great saloon at Allen's house that Swift, after pacing restlessly up and down, stopped before an entire stranger with the words,

In Squire Western's Land

" Pray, sir, have you ever known in your life any
tolerable weather? I have always found it too dry
or too wet, too windy or too calm, too hot or too
cold. And yet I dare protest at the end of the year
Providence brings it in pretty well right." At Prior
Park, too, Swift having kept his room, from a slight
sickness, for a few days, signalised his reappearance
by one of the bitterest of his sayings, that whose
point lay in the impossibility of there being such a
thing as a fine old man. The stock guest was,
however, always Warburton, never more pleased than
when Allen put him into the pulpit in his private
chapel, or weary of abusing the incorrigibly im-
portunate member for Middlesex. "The blackest
fiends," he said, "would disdain to keep company
with Jack Wilkes, and I humbly ask pardon of
Satan for comparing them together." After that
outburst, Quin, in the drawing-room, called the author
of " The Divine Legation " a " saucy priest." Asked
to amuse the company with something theatrical, the
actor, looking hard at Warburton, recites from
Otway's " Venice Preserved" the passage in which
are the lines describing honest men as "the soft,
easy cushions on which knaves repose and fatten."

The next house to be visited is near enough to the
Somerset and Wilts boundary to be claimed by both
counties. Among the family portraits at Bowood the
most interesting are those of William Fitzmaurice, who
afterwards became Earl of Shelburne, and whose life
presented a series of contrasts more dramatic than
were common to the careers of most of his descendants.
After his birth in Dublin, May, 1737, his childhood

The Rise of the Pettys

was passed in the remotest parts of Southern Ireland under a tyrannical grandfather, Thomas Fitzmaurice, Earl of Kerry. That relative married Anne, the daughter of Sir William Petty, the most scientific economist of his time. Anne Petty's mother had become Baroness Shelburne. The brothers of the lady, made by Earl Thomas Countess of Kerry, had died childless. Through the Lady Kerry now spoken of, therefore, the Fitzmaurices added the barony of Shelburne to the Kerry earldom. The intellectual heritage of Bowood's modern possessors has not come to them entirely from the distaff side. If Anne Petty's husband, Earl Thomas, a bully by nature and by opportunity, lacked great mental endowments, he did not want for strong good sense nor for the iron nerves and dauntless perseverance without which genius itself may fail. The moral fearlessness, also a family characteristic, had conspicuously shown itself in Sir William Petty when, as Ireton's former secretary, he confessed after the Restoration his share in certain transactions with a fearlessness that won him the favour of Charles II. and his Chancellor, Clarendon. Soon after his marriage Anne Petty's noble husband retired from the Army, in which he had been trained, to his country home. Confessing his paramount obligations to his masterful wife, he laments making her an excessive bad husband. The lady enabled her husband to improve his fortune rather than his mind. She allowed no book in the house except an almanack, and no person to read it except her lord. This he did every evening, using it as a peg on which to hang anecdotes about famous friends, abuse of obscure

In Squire Western's Land

enemies or successful rivals. His eldest son and heir, Francis Thomas, third Earl of Kerry, wasted most of his money and invested the rest in French assignats. The fourth Earl of Kerry, brother of his predecessor in the title, also received the barony of Dunkerron and the viscountcy of Fitzmaurice. In 1753 he became Earl of Shelburne in the Irish peerage and, seven years later, Baron Wycombe in the English. His son, brought up, as has been already seen, chiefly by his grandfather, became Chatham's political heir, George III.'s Prime Minister, and Bowood's creator.

The future (1784) first Marquis of Lansdowne, like Sir Robert Peel afterwards, was trained from the first to become Prime Minister. Entering Oxford when only sixteen, he learned at Christ Church to appreciate good acquaintances, to see in Chesterfield and Granville the contrast between polish and simplicity, and to regard the Duke of Newcastle as "a hubble-bubble man." His studies ranged widely beyond the conventional curriculum. Under his tutor Holwell, or with the explanatory comment of Dean Conybeare and of Dean Gregory, both of whom gave him notions of people and things afterwards very useful, he studied not only the usual Greek and Latin classics, but Machiavelli and other modern authors who could instruct him on whatever pertained to the Law of Nations. The intellectual influence of a very remarkable Oxford teacher of his time, Dr. King, of St. Mary Hall, public orator, a Tory and Jacobite gentleman, did not prevent his growing up to admire Cromwell, but conveyed to him a dislike of William III. or of that king's enormous grants to favourites like

Bowood's Beginnings

the Bentincks and the Keppels. After leaving Oxford, as the guest of Lord Bessborough at his Roehampton villa, he made the acquaintance not only of Colonel Barré, his future political aide-de-camp and general Parliamentary factotum, but of "Capability" Brown, who, in consultation with Lady Louisa Manners, proved so useful in the construction of the Wiltshire palace. Through Bute he came to know the most famous of his guests, Johnson, Goldsmith, and Reynolds, to whom he sat for his portrait, perhaps more than once, between 1764 and 1776. On his qualities as a public man the verdict of his social intimates differs. Horace Walpole called him a good debater. Pratt, Lord Camden placed him as an orator only below Chatham. Jeremy Bentham, who found at Bowood a second home, described him as getting hold of an imperfect scrap of an idea, filling it up, rightly or wrongly, then with his imposing manner, dignity, vague generalities and emphasis, making the Lords think there was something in it when there was really nothing at all. "Shelburne," said the third Lord Holland, "wanted method, perspicuity, reasoning, judgment, and taste, making up for them by imagination, wit, sarcasm, and eloquence." At Bowood Bentham met the most submissive and useful of his foreign disciples, Dumont, the Swiss Protestant pastor at St. Petersburg, who had been tutor to Lansdowne's sons ; Joseph Priestley, Lansdowne's former companion in his foreign travels ; and a very remarkable Dissenting minister, Jervis, engaged by Lansdowne to superintend his boys' holiday tasks.

The most universal country host of his time was

In Squire Western's Land

also the most orderly and economical of country hosts.
"What folly," he exclaimed, "can be greater than
employing a lawyer or business man to audit one's
accounts? Dealers in money are like butchers, who,
dealing in blood, lose all feeling in their business."
"The host," was his maxim, "who looks into his own
affairs, can give his guests all they want for £5,000
a year." The first Wednesday in every month was
devoted by Bowood's earliest master to going through
his household bank-account. At 11 a.m. on every
Wednesday began the checking of the house and
kitchen expenses. Then came the examination into
details of estate management; for nothing was held
in greater abomination at Bowood than "the hoggish
farmer who grudges bread to every one under him, or
the illiterate manufacturer to whom wealth is a means
of insolence, and who leaves his labourers to die
through want, filth, and famine." In this way Bowood
became not only a great social, but an exemplary
educational, centre for rural entertainers of all degrees.
The earliest hospitalities of Bowood, indeed, were not
only on a larger scale than England had yet seen,
they also marked an entirely new era in the country-
house system. Hitherto, when the country squire,
small or great, went up to his Parliamentary duties in
London, he shut up his rural home and boarded out his
wife and children with small farmers. At all times the
entertainments were on the most modest scale. Thus
when, in the neighbourhood of Devizes, the country
gentlefolk exchanged visits, the men went upstairs to
the masculine apartments, the ladies to their hostesses'
bedrooms. The lords of creation eventually finished

350

Hosts and Guests at Bowood

their potations, for the most part in Wiltshire drinking nothing but beer. The ladies were then admitted to their presence. Passing to the Bowood of our own day, we see the type of an accomplished gentleman, wearing the old Whig dress, a blue coat with brass buttons and a buff waistcoat. With him, sitting or strolling through the grounds and rooms, is a visitor similarly clad in the uniform brought into vogue by Charles James Fox, and still perpetuated by the cover of the *Edinburgh Review*. The first of these is the Mæcenas of the nineteenth century's first half, the third Marquis of Lansdowne, who died in 1863. The other is the Mr. Stanley of that time, then full of the highest Whig promise, afterwards the Conservative Prime Minister, Lord Derby. Many of the visitors grouped round these are old enough to have heard and involuntarily to murmur the refrain of the old Whig ditty :

> " True blue
> And Mrs. Crewe "

—not omitting the lady's rejoinder :

> " True blue
> And all of you."

Between Lord Lansdowne and the distinguished guest who was to become Lord Derby, is the smallest gentleman then visible in polite society, Thomas Moore, the poet and musician. He has of late written several biographies ; Lord Lansdowne has just advised him to publish a series of nine such

351

lives by the title of " The Cat." Presently Moore
will sit down to the piano to sing his verses to the
accompaniment of his own melodies, with the perfect
taste and spirit that make him the delight of country
houses. At Bowood it was that, only a few years
ago, when the Regency debates were going on, he
brought down to the breakfast-table as neat an
epigram as the language contains, summarising the
Whig view of the conditions imposed on the Prince of
Wales's viceroyalty :

"A straight waistcoat on him, and restrictions on me,
A more limited monarchy could not well be."

At Bowood, too, Moore had been congratulated by
Sir Walter Scott on the honourable feelings that had
prompted the burning of the Byron memoirs ; and
Scott himself, referring to the report of Lady Byron's
possible marriage with Cunningham, said, " She must
never let another man bear the name of husband to
her." Under the third Marquis now spoken of, and
first famous as Lord Henry Petty, Bowood contained
visible links with the past, such as could be seen nowhere else in the world. Only a few days before his
death he showed Hayward a copy of Boswell's
" Johnson," presented to him by the author. The
third Marquis could appreciate the well-known lines
in the " Rolliad," about the Prime Minister his father,
and had some good stories as to his relative's
traditional want of frankness. His complaint to
Gainsborough about a portrait just painted of him
drew from the artist the words, "I don't like it either ;

Hallam, Macaulay, and Hook

I will try again." After a second failure, the painter flung down his pencil, saying "D—— it, I never could see through the varnish, and there's an end." Shelburne was nicknamed "Malagrida," after a Portuguese Jesuit of that name. "Do you know," said Oliver Goldsmith, "I never could make out why, for Malagrida was a very good sort of man." Bowood owed scarcely more to its master's and founder's wealth and taste than to the help of his wife (Lady Louisa Strangways), Lord Ilchester's daughter. "When we first came to Bowood," she used to say, "I had to borrow a rush chair from the lodge to sit upon." Hayward could congratulate her on possessing the best mounted house in Europe. Among the art treasures of the place is Olivia, in "The Vicar of Wakefield," brought back to her home, with her face hidden in her father's bosom, by Newton, an artist whom Lord Lansdowne discovered. "It is not very difficult," sneered Theodore Hook "to paint a figure without the face." "But it is very difficult," rejoined Constable, "to paint a sob. Lord Lansdowne saw, felt the sob, and bought it." "A right-divine gentleman," was Serjeant Talfourd's remark on his host, after a stay at Bowood. "He looks," said Sydney Smith, "for talents and qualities amongst all ranks of men, and adds them to his stock of society as a botanist does plants."

To-day the fifth Marquis of Lansdowne's guests may sit down to the same table at which Samuel Rogers, placed between Hallam and Macaulay, talked of their wrangling and fighting over him as over a dead body. They may lose themselves in the

In Squire Western's Land

crowd of grim statues as those amid which Adolphe Thiers once fell asleep, suddenly to be awakened by the Shakespearian critic, Payne Knight, and, rubbing his eyes, with a look at his marble companions, to fancy he had unconsciously passed into another world. Should they be fortunate enough to have for a fellow-visitor Mr. E. F. Leveson-Gower, they may hear how their twentieth-century host's grandfather, with exquisite humour, used to describe the poet Bowles when impatiently waiting till the ladies should make themselves ready for an afternoon stroll, remarking that the water from the lake had been for some time set on for the waterfall, and that he feared it would not last till they came (the point of this story was the fact of Bowles himself, when Rector of Brem-hill, near Bowood, expecting visitors, having been overheard by Rogers to order his gardener to set the fountain playing and to carry the hermit his beer); how Lord Lansdowne himself described calling at the artist Turner's Chelsea house on a foggy afternoon, being mistaken by the woman in charge for a cat's-meat man, and being told from the area, "Don't trouble to come again, for some rascal, perhaps yourself, has stolen my cat"; finally, they may hear from one who, in Mr. Leveson-Gower himself, heard it first hand, how Macaulay, asked as to the mount he would like for a morning's ride, said, "The only thing for me is an elephant." At the same party, and on the same day, Lord Palmerston, having said that, according to Darwin, a starfish, passing through the intermediate stage of a Bishop of Oxford, might become Archbishop of Canterbury, was gravely assured by the natural philosopher, Sir Roderick Murchison, " No such transmutation could take place."

The most famous among the Bowood company already mentioned, the historian Macaulay had as a child been patted on the head by the mistress of a country house in the south-west of England, very different from the Lansdowne palace. A great Somersetshire squire, Sir John Trevelyan, had in an earlier generation introduced Edmund Burke and William Wilberforce to the family circle in the district where Somerset and Gloucestershire almost meet, near Bristol, at Barley Wood. This pretty little place had been inherited by Hannah More and her four sisters from the Stapleton schoolmaster their father ; when occupied by them it became a humanitarian centre. At no great distance, though in a different county, near the town of Gloucester, lay on the slopes of the Cotswolds the villa of Robert Raikes, then the influential owner of the *Gloucester Journal*, to-day immortalised as the founder of the Sunday School. The habitual guests at his Cotswold home comprised Joseph Alleine, to be bracketed as an evangelical doctor with Richard Baxter himself, Alleine's colleague in good works and good writings, Thomas Stock, David Blair of Brechin, Theophilus Lindsey of Catterick, Yorkshire. The outcome of these meetings at the Cotswold villa was the successful adaptation to English eighteenth-century's needs of the machinery, first devised in 1580, by Cardinal Borromeo, at Milan, for providing children with suitable teaching on the first day of the week, and afterwards acclimatised at Ephratah, in Pennsylvania, by the descendants of those who had sailed to New England in the *Mayflower*. A more imposing and better known monument, formerly the actual scene of the meeting of these good men and holy women, may still be seen some four miles to the north of Bristol, in Blaise Castle, once the home of Wilberforce's chosen companion and biographer Harford, and still belonging to his family. An additional interest attaches to this place because the adjoining village contains the Harford cottages. These began to be built in 1810; they initiated the movement that soon spread for surrounding the manor-house with humbler homes worthy, in respect of cleanliness, health, and comfort, of English landlords.

The porch, the oven, and the tank became articles in the Young England scheme of peasantry reform, 1846. They had already been adopted and carried into effect by the Evangelical disciple of Hannah More and biographer of Wilberforce, at Blaise, between ten and fifteen years earlier.

CHAPTER XIII

SOUTH-EAST BY EAST

THE Wyndham name forms a connecting link between many social centres of rural England. And in this way. The Egremont earldom belonged to Algernon, seventh Duke of Somerset, with remainder to his nephew Charles, son of the Somersetshire Sir William Wyndham and of Lady Catharine Seymour. Thus the son of the man to whom Bolingbroke dedicated his best-known writings became second Earl of Egremont. George, the fourth and last Earl, died in 1845, leaving a life interest in his estates to his wife, who died at Orchard Wyndham[1] in 1876. After this, the possessor of the Orchard Wyndham estates and the head of the family became Lord Egremont's kinsman, Mr. William Wyndham, of Dinton, Wiltshire. Meanwhile an Egremont Wyndham had been created the first Lord Leconfield. He, as has been seen in the Sussex chapter, made the hospitalities of Petworth famous. His son, Mr. Percy Wyndham, an Eton schoolfellow of the fifteenth Lord Derby, formerly the supporter of Disraelian administrations in the House of Commons, survives to be to-day at Clouds, near Salisbury, conspicuous among Conservative hosts in the eastern corner of Wiltshire. The father of Mr. George Wyndham, formerly Mr. A. J. Balfour's private secretary first, Irish Secretary afterwards, he has made his Wiltshire home a favourite resort of the late Prime Minister and of the chief figures in the Unionist connection. Mr. George Wyndham's

---

[1] For an earlier mention of this subject see page 312. The house at Orchard Wyndham, though to-day unoccupied, is full of beautiful furniture, especially the Chippendale chairs and tables. And the secret chambers and mysterious passages which sheltered so many eminent Jacobites in the eighteenth century, are still what Atterbury and Swift saw them.

marriage with the Countess Grosvenor, the young
Duke of Westminster's mother, naturally affects the
composition of the Clouds house-parties. At these
gatherings, in addition to Mr. Arthur Balfour himself,
the former premier's particular friends are conspicuous
figures. The Cambridge senior wrangler of 1865,
Lord Rayleigh, Lady Rayleigh, Mr. Balfour's sister,
Lord and Lady Elcho, the host's son-in-law and
daughter respectively, are among the ornaments of
the Conservative intellectualism whom Mr. Percy
Wyndham's accomplishments and abilities qualify him
specially to appreciate. The head of an Irish branch
of his house, the Wyndham-Quins, Lord Dunraven,
found Clouds an agreeably neutral ground for discussing new departures in Irish policy with his party
chief when Mr. Balfour reigned at the Treasury, and
was irresponsibly maintaining an open eye and mind
with regard to possibilities of compromise between
the existing subjection of Ireland and Home Rule.
Close to Clouds is the great mansion of the district,
Knoyle House, whose Seymour ownership connects
it with the earliest source of the Wyndham ennoblement, the dukedom of Somerset. The historical
position of East Knoyle owes most of its interest to
the fact that long before the Stuart cause seemed in
serious peril, the Knoyle Seymours and their visitors
were privately discussing the signs of his disposition
and of his final purpose which they thought James II.
had given. That when the crisis actually arrived the
way had been cleared for the invitation to Orange
William, was due to the Knoyle house-parties of that
period. Lord James of Hereford has recently rein-

forced the Wiltshire hosts by the occupation of
Breamore. This place is within a short distance of
Salisbury. Its eighteenth-century owner, the first
baronet of his line, a great Court physician, sometimes
had for his guest, as well as for his patient, George II.
In the last days of the nineteenth century, Sir Edward
Hulse, the fifth baronet of his line, having many
relatives in the Army, made Breamore a military
country house. Before coming to the title, the sixth
of the Hulse baronets was among the pleasantest
young men about town ; he had no enemy but himself.
Dying in South Africa, he left to his infant successor
the much-encumbered estate, whose house has since
found, as has been said, a tenant in the sixth Sir
Edward Hulse's old friend, a keen sportsman, not
less than a great lawyer, still best known to many
as Sir Henry James.

More entirely of the past than East Knoyle is
another Wiltshire country house, the dismantled
palace of William Beckford, Fonthill. The father of
the man who built Fonthill, and for sixteen years less
than a century (1760–1844) maintained it as the most
magnificent and mysterious of private residences, had
been twice Lord Mayor of London ; he had not only
fêted officially Lord Chatham at the Mansion House,
he had privately entertained the great minister at a
country seat occupying much the same ground as that
on which his son's structure afterwards stood. The
younger Beckford inherited from his father a million
in ready money and £100,000 a year in income.
The story of his having written " Vathek " at Fonthill
in three days and two nights, unbroken by any rest in

With Beckford at Fonthill

bed, is pure fiction. The book, so far from being thrown off at a heat, was the slow product of laborious years. Equally apocryphal are many other anecdotes about Fonthill and its owner. The accidents of the present writer's childhood familiarised him early with the only true account of Beckford and Fonthill—that given by Samuel Rogers. This may be epitomised as follows. The death of Beckford's wife, Lady Margaret Gordon, Lord Aboyne's daughter, in 1786, left him a shrewd and intellectual victim of an eccentric melancholy. From 1784 to 1790 he had been member for Wells. As a widower he lost the little interest he may ever have had in politics, and immured himself in his Wiltshire museum. The only guest he willingly received was Samuel Rogers. On that visitor reaching the huge wall separating Fonthill from the outer world, he was told neither his servant nor his horse could be admitted inside. Mr. Beckford's stables and people would, it was added, supply all his wants. "Once in the place," Rogers used to say, "I could scarcely breathe freely for an overwhelming sense of surrounding splendour and virtual imprisonment." "Beckford told me," were Rogers' words to Kinglake, "that some little time earlier the Duchess of Gordon had insisted on quartering herself on him. 'But,' Beckford continued, 'the whole time she was here she never saw my face nor I hers.'"

Rogers, however, found the recluse a sufficiently courteous, and in his way, entertaining host. They only met at a late dinner. The master of Fonthill had the musical tastes of his family, and had himself found a music master in the great Mozart, the protégé of his cousin, Peter Beckford. During the short interval between dinner and bed-time, Beckford improvised melodies at the pianoforte, or read aloud from his unpublished works; these were astonishingly numerous. He also showed his guest hitherto unseen memorials of Wilkes, to whom his father had been so good a friend. During his few years of wedded life at Lausanne, he lived in the historian Gibbon's house, which, with all the books, he had bought. No son was born to him; he had, however, two daughters; these became respectively Mrs. Orde and the Duchess of Hamilton. By 1822 his riches had begun to melt away. The Fonthill establishment was broken up. "England's wealthiest son," as Byron called him, took a house at Bath, in Lansdowne Crescent, connecting it by a subterranean way with a tall tower which he had built on Lansdowne Hill, close to the scene of the seventeenth-century battle between the Royal and the Parliamentary armies. From that eminence, when the sun's rays fell at a particular angle, looking over the intervening valley, he could see beyond the spot on which the turrets of Fonthill had formerly risen. Beckford's Bath house is still inhabited. The grounds amid which he reared his Lansdowne tower are to-day a cemetery. Inside the lofty structure may yet be seen the red and purple decorations with which its builder fitted it, and, high up, a lonely room, wherein he once paid a man to undergo some weeks' or months' voluntary imprisonment, on condition that the captive should receive only just as much bread and water as might support existence, should neither wash his body nor cut his hair or nails. As for Fonthill itself, its social existence is wholly in the past. One anecdote, and one only, has been bequeathed to posterity by Fonthill's strange creator. Beckford's father, a sportsman and writer on sport, kept hounds. The huntsman had added to the pack a dog which the master heard him call "Lyman." "What means that name?" asked the employer. "Lord, sir," replied the man, "what does anything mean?" His vivid recollections of Fonthill's magnificence inspired Samuel Rogers in his last days with an apt illustration of the genius of an American poet, Edgar Allan Poe. "The only parallel," he said, "to the characteristics of Poe's imagination is that of the man who wrote 'Vathek.'" Beckford had the money that enabled him to translate his sumptuous and gorgeous visions into realities at Fonthill. Poe makes the human hero of his remarkable verses repose on cushions with velvet violet lining, start with terror at the rustling of purple curtains, and hear imaginary footfalls tinkling on the tufted floor. The poet's life was one long struggle with poverty. The conceptions of beauty embodied by Beckford in a palace, Poe tried to realise with alcohol or opium. With Beckford's money he would have satisfied his imagination by constructing the external reality of just such another palace as Beckford called into being on the Wiltshire weald.

Ford Abbey invests the Somerset and Dorset borderland with intellectual associations as interesting, if not as ornamental, as those bequeathed by Fonthill to Wiltshire. Ford Abbey, indeed, though often claimed by Somersetshire, stands rather in that Dorsetshire peninsula which juts out into the contiguous county.[1] While Beckford was concentrating his treasures and warning off inquisitive tourists with his bloodhounds at Fonthill, Ford Abbey witnessed the training for his life's work of the great logician and economist of the Utilitarian system. In the early years of the nineteenth century, James Mill rented a house in Queen's Square, Westminster, which had been Milton's, and which belonged to Jeremy Bentham. During the summer the tenant was invited to bring his son, John Stuart, on visits to his landlord's rural home. On this point let us recall what J. S. Mill himself had afterwards to say on the subject : " Nothing," were his words, " contributes more to nourish elevation of sentiments in a people than the large and free character of their habitations." And thus to young Mill the middle-age architecture, the baronial hall, the spacious and lofty rooms of Ford Abbey, so unlike the cramped and mean exteriors of middle-class life, gave the sentiment of a larger and freer existence. The literary associations of the Westminster house, duly pointed out by Bentham to his tenant's son, had already touched the poetic feeling systematically ignored by James Mill in the education of the sensitive boy. Residence

---

[1] As a fact Ford Abbey stands upon debatable ground, so near to the converging point of Devon, Dorset, and Somerset as to be said, with some plausibility, to belong to each of these counties.

Bentham and Mill at Ford Abbey

at the picturesque spot in the south-west of rural England was to prove a further training in the humanities. Ford Abbey, whose nearest town was Chard, had belonged, in the seventeenth century, to Sir Edmond Prideaux, Attorney-General to the Commonwealth. This really magnificent place stood in a large and beautiful park with many lakes and groves; through these a chestnut avenue, some quarter of a mile in length, led up to the building. It has been seen that in West Somerset, a century ago, Wordsworth paid £40 a year for Alfoxton Park. In 1814 the stately Ford Abbey was let to Bentham for £318, on condition of his quitting it, if desired, at one month's notice, taking particular care of the tapestry in the halls, of the gardens, and not using the deer in the park for the table. "The last provision," simply remarked the philosopher, "was quite unnecessary, for I always felt more disposed to caress the pretty creatures than to kill them."

Six months in every year were passed by the Mills with Bentham at Ford Abbey. During those annual periods the Dorsetshire paradise became a kind of Académie. The host rose about seven. With the break of an hour for breakfast, Bentham wrote till noon, for the most part in a spacious chamber, containing an organ, with furniture and decorations of the Commonwealth period. Here, after the morning's writing, the host played the organ for an hour, or sometimes battledore and shuttle-cock with his guest. The great event, however, of the day took the shape of long talks between the two seniors, listened to in silent admiration by the boy. It was during these conversations that Bentham, then chiefly occupied at Ford with his work on codification, told Mill that his early admiration for Hevetius had almost caused him to seek domestic service with the great encyclopædist. The only visitor, besides the Mills, was Francis Place, the Charing Cross tailor, whose recent biographer (Mr. Wallas) has claimed for him rather than for Lord Grey the true authorship of the first Reform Act. His guests were never allowed by Bentham to break in upon the afternoon's work with his amanuensis. The simple six o'clock dinner, at which water alone was drunk, was always followed by a brisk walk. There are stories of these philosophic hospitalities having been marred by a personal rupture between the master of Ford Abbey and his principal visitor, J. S. Mill's father. There was certainly long on view at Ford a letter to his dear friend and master from his most affectionate James Mill, in which the writer remarks that being too much in one another's company makes people stale to each other and is often fatal, without any other cause, to happiness in the most indissoluble of all connections. Nothing more dreadful, however, seems to have happened than that about this time Joseph Hume became a regular guest at Ford, and that the Mills' visits ceased to be a yearly institution.

In the century preceding the plain living and high thinking at Ford Abbey, another Dorsetshire house, already visited in these pages, Lulworth on the coast, the seat of the Welds, had been an asylum for famous exiles presenting a marked contrast to the society just quitted at Ford. The great French upheaval at the end of the eighteenth century had been preceded by years of trouble, unrest, and danger to many spiritual teachers in the country. Amongst those who, both then and afterwards, bowing their heads to the storm, found shelter in England was Jean Nicolas Grou. Born at Calais in 1731, educated by the Jesuit fathers, he had returned to Paris for a few days, only to see the enemies of religion burn in a moment a manuscript representing fourteen years of labour, undertaken at the request of the Paris archbishop. " If," meekly said Grou, " the work could have been used of God, He would have preserved it. Even yet, unprofitable servant though I am, He may employ my pen." The expectation was fulfilled at Lulworth Castle. Here the domestic chaplain, Father Clinton, had already, at the family's desire, invited more than one religious refugee from the Continent. Here now Grou became domesticated. Here, too, he wrote the well-known devotional book, "The Hidden Life of the Soul." So long as Parliament has existed, Trelawnys, Edgcumbes, and Bullers have come to it from Cornwall or Devon, Northampton has sent its Knightley, and Taunton its Portman. To Dorsetshire belongs the country home of the family last named. Bryanston, originally possessed by the Rogers stock, with which the Pyms intermarried, became the home of the Portmans about the time that constitutional monarchy was secured in England. Elizabethan in its design, but actually less than twenty years old, Bryanston, the periodical visiting place of royalties, is to its neighbourhood what Castlehill is to Devonshire—a house, that is, in its origins exclusively Whig, but detached from Liberalism to-day, its works and its personages, by the dissolving influences of Home Rule.

In Hampshire the best known of eighteenth- or early nineteenth-century houses lies in the district where afterwards the first pack of foxhounds was formed and the first cricket match played. On his way to Fécamp viâ Shoreham, Hambledon House received for the night Charles II. Subsequently this house passed to a certain John Tekell, best known as the husband of Lady Griselda Stanhope. She was one of those three Stanhope sisters, the eldest of whom was the Lebanon lady already mentioned at some length. Lady Griselda, herself scarcely less eccentric than her more famous sister, and her husband made their Hambledon house a rallying centre of the whole Stanhope clan and, of course, an emporium of family talk. From the Tekell country house it first went abroad that Lady Hester Stanhope had been proclaimed queen of Palmyra by the Arab tribes, and that, in 1839, she had died. Her memoirs, appearing in 1843 and 1846 respectively, were, at least in part, prepared for the printer at Hambledon. The Hampshire house richest in nineteenth century associations of general interest is that of Lord and Lady Ashburton in the Alresford district, the Grange. The period selected for the present visit is the first half of the Victorian age. Among the guests known to every one are Lord Lansdowne, Lord Clarendon, Lord Canning, Lord Grey, Lord Granville, Lord Houghton, Lord Elcho, Lord Aberdeen, Sir Henry Taylor, Twisleton, Brookfield, the contemporary and intimate friend of Thackeray and Tennyson, Sidney Herbert, and a personage more remarkable than any of these, wearing a long gaberdine, evidently a student and an author. Striking, indeed, is the contrast between the vaguely eloquent inspiration animating the talk of this last guest and the cynical, prosaic sagacity of another visitor, best known as " Bear " Ellice, who never misses a chance of pitting himself against Thomas Carlyle. It is the period of the Crimean struggle. The author of " Hero Worship " has forgotten that among the company is the then Secretary for War. At least Carlyle's face glows with approval as he thunders forth his version of the elder Pitt's reply to the Duke of Newcastle's objection that a expedition cannot be ready at the required moment : " If," quotes Carlyle, "the money and the men are not ready on Thursday next at ten o'clock, your Grace's head shall roll at your Grace's feet." " That," commented Carlyle, "is the way to speak to an incapable minister." Here the censor remembered who and what Herbert was, and apologised with a gruff laugh. The two men said good-night the best of friends. At the Grange, Carlyle constantly made blunders of this sort. On another occasion, pointing out to Prince Jerome Napoleon the perfection of English naval construction, he wound up, " If one of our ships meets a Frenchman of her own size, she blows her into atoms."

South-East by East

The host and hostess of the Grange were for many reasons the most remarkable couple of their set or their time. In mordancy and readiness of repartee Lady Ashburton was not surpassed even by Mrs. Grote. She spared no one, least of all her husband. " I trust that I," the poor Lord had once said, "have no favourite ology." " Indeed, my dear, if you only knew it you have, and its name is tautology." This because the unfortunate nobleman sometimes told the same story more than once. Lady Ashburton's earliest notice of Carlyle seems to have put some noses out of joint. Her criticism of the revolutionary tendencies she had discovered in a pamphlet by Monckton Milnes caused the writer in his own defence to say, " The writings of your friend Carlyle are much redder" (meaning, of course, of a redder republican tinge). The lady was prepared with her repartee : " You mean they are much more read." At the Grange it was that Carlyle, hearing that Mrs. Beecher Stowe had lately been there, set himself to scandalise the second Lady Ashburton by hotly defending slavery and abusing the abolitionists : " Mrs. Stowe !—a poor foolish woman who wrote a book of wretched trash called 'Uncle Tom's Cabin.' " That, of course, was Carlyle's way. Beneath the same roof he passed his famous verdict on Charles Dickens's friend the " *h*arbitrary gent," the historian John Forster—" Eh, mon, but you are a poor, weak, miserable crittur "—after Forster had to his evident satisfaction decisively disposed, in his most *ex-cathedra* manner, of several controversial historical points. On these occasions the general recollection of Mrs. Carlyle at one of the Ashburton country houses is that of a little woman busy with her embroidery in a solitary corner, silent and ignored. The Grange as a social institution flourished before the present writer's time. Froude's view is that Mrs. Carlyle was not happy there because, like the ladies of bishops, the wives of men of genius do not take the social rank of their husbands, and because the fashionable women who frequent the house understood how to make each other uncomfortable in little ways. Against that account may be set the reminiscences of the Grange parties given me by the late G. S. Venables, a regular *habitué* of the house. "Lady Ashburton," were the words to me of Mr. Venables, "had no little ways, saw that, at least in her house, the wives of literary men did take their husbands' rank, and did from my own knowledge inspire Mrs. Carlyle with a reciprocated attachment."

On the same social and intellectual plane as the Grange two other Hampshire houses became a little later social microcosms of their era. The Herberts of Highclere are identical in their origin with the Herberts of Wilton, for it was the third son of the eighth Earl of Pembroke who became first Earl of Carnarvon. This community of descent is picturesquely symbolised in Highclere Park by the stately Lebanon cedars, sprung for the most part from the older trees on the Pembroke property. Two at least, however, of the Highclere cedars have been grown from a cone which a Highclere clergyman's descendant brought from Palestine direct. The old house was the rural palace of the Bishops of Winchester, and formed the home during some months in every year of William of Wykeham. Under the Tudors the Highclere and Burghclere manors passed to the Fitzwilliams first, then to the Kingsmills, afterwards to the Warwickshire Lucys. The next owner was the Attorney-General to Charles II. and James II., Sir Robert Sawyer. His daughter and heiress became the wife of Thomas, Earl of Pembroke, Lord High Admiral. Their son, Robert Sawyer Herbert, inherited Highclere and Burghclere ; his nephew received property and became the first Earl of Carnarvon. The third earl, son of the peer who made Pixton the centre of resistance to the Grey Reform Bill, converted, with the help of Sir Charles Barry, the old house into the existing Highclere Castle. The social story of that dwelling begins with the fourth Lord Carnarvon, the Colonial Secretary, who anticipated Mr. Chamberlain in discovering the colonies, and who made his Hampshire home a social centre for the Empire. Late in the seventies of the last century the Jingo fever was at its height. Incompatibility of political temper with Disraeli, then Prime Minister, brought about Lord Carnarvon's resignation, and produced at Highclere a fusion of national, unaggressive Conservatism and patriotic, anti-militant, but not anti-Imperial, Liberalism. Sir Henry Norman, to whom Gladstone afterwards offered the Indian Viceroyship, and General Adye, both of them, as soldiers, opposed to Lord Beaconsfield's and Lord Lytton's scientific frontier, represented at the Highclere parties the ideas with which their host had

The Boers on Beer

identified himself. The purely political or economic aspects of this school of thought were displayed by Sir Louis Mallet, then permanent Under-Secretary at the India Office, formerly Cobden's right-hand man, as kindly and polished a gentleman as ever responded to a country-house welcome, tempering his Liberal economics with not a little of the old-world urbanity, learned by him in earlier years at continental Courts and chancelleries. With him were Thomas Bayley Potter, whose amplitude of snowy shirt-front, and whose geniality of spirit and bearing, gave a charm to Radicalism; Lord Sherbrooke, formerly R. Lowe, and Thomas Chenery, then editor of the *Times*. Both, as companions and conversationalists, disclosed at Highclere a charm not always discovered elsewhere. Once, if not twice, the parties thus composed were varied by immediate representatives from our over-seas empire. Such in the seventies were the guests from the Transvaal. The Boers had evidently resolved to repress every sign of appreciation and to remain impassively critical of all that they saw and heard. The Highclere library contained a shelf filled exclusively by writers of the Herbert name. "Pity," remarked a Boer gentleman on being shown the books, "that your relations had not something better to do." "One English institution," they considerately remarked, after having seen the Highclere cellars, "we can admire. The beer your butler gave us down there is undeniable."

The twentieth-century Highclere maintains all its old hospitable traditions. But the interests chiefly represented in these are now connected rather with fashion and sport. Of the great houses close to Highclere, Hurstbourne approached most nearly to Highclere's character. Whenever the mayfly season came round the then German ambassador, Count Munster, was pretty sure in the early morning to be seen whipping the trout stream which traverses the park. Lord Granville, when Foreign Secretary, was also a regular guest. It happened that after a tiring day in the open air he had gone earlier to bed than usual. Amongst the guests was a lady famous for her wealth of beautiful hair. Ignorant that her lord had already established himself between the sheets, Lady Granville entered the room with one or two more of her sister guests. These, sitting down, compared notes about their tresses. The lady already mentioned let her locks down for the benefit of her friends. The Foreign Secretary's slumber was broken, but as he said at the breakfast table next day, "It was a very little peep I gave from under the counterpane ; I felt like Clodius, and I had the presence of mind to slip down deeper into the bed than ever." Hurstbourne was among the few country houses visited together by George Henry Lewes and George Eliot. Here the novelist acquired the local colour and personal details for the country-house scenes in "Middlemarch." With these visitors were Meredith Townsend, of the *Spectator*, and Adams the astronomer, in whose hands Lord Portsmouth placed all his Sir Isaac Newton papers. These contained entries made before receiving the Communion on Whit Sunday, 1662, entreating the Almighty's pardon "for eating an apple in Thy house and for making a mousetrap on Thy day." This little fragment concerning the great man, related by their Fellowes connection with the Wallop family, was, with other memorials of the same kind, first brought to light by a frequent nineteenth-century Hurstbourne guest, John Cordy Jeaffreson, for years Hepworth Dixon's right-hand man on the *Athenæum*, also of invaluable service in innumerable country houses to the manuscript commission. To Hurstbourne, early in the nineteenth century, came Lord Byron, bringing, as he said, an olive branch to its owner, who, when both of them were children in 1799, had put the future poet into a passion by roughly seizing his head. " I will teach," said the boy Byron, suiting the action to the word, "a fool of an earl to pinch a brother noble's ear."

Hurstbourne stands as nearly as possible midway between Highclere and a country house rich in associations, very different from those grouped round the two other Hampshire houses just visited. The one feature in common between Hurstbourne and Tedworth, where we are now stopping, is the fact of the trout stream, the Wallop, in which Count Munster in the last century used to fish, watering also the country about the present home of Sir John Kelk, formerly the abode of the mighty Nimrod, Thomas Assheton Smith. The beginnings, however, of this branch of the Smith family were at Ashley Hall, Bowdon, Cheshire. The great hunter's grandfather, Thomas Assheton, adopted the patronymic of his uncle, whose property he inherited. This John Smith, in the early eighteenth century, had been both Speaker and Chancellor of the Exchequer. Born August 2, 1776, in Queen Anne Street, Cavendish Square, the man who made Tedworth a synonym for the national sport used, across the walnuts and the wine, to tell how, in 1783, the youngest boy in the school, he had at once been put in the Eton eleven, and how, in his first half, hearing a schoolfellow boast membership of a family which could ride, fence, play tennis, or fight against all England, he immediately challenged the boy to a duel of fisticuffs. The other combatant was also a coming Nimrod, the John Musters, who married Byron's Mary Chaworth. His early pugilistic laurels were still fresh when the future possessor of Tedworth heard his father, at a Leicestershire dinner-table, back himself and young Tom Smith, his son, against Sir John Peyton and his son, whom he had heard described as the first horsemen of their day, over from six to a dozen miles of fair hunting country. At Tedworth the riding-matches which followed were planned.

Very soon Assheton Smith was to have his own unique Leicestershire experiences, of the ring and of the platform as well as of the chase. "To relieve the *ennui* of a close week or two caused by a sharp frost in the shires, I thought," the young man said, " I might as well contest the then vacant seat for Nottinghamshire. ' No hunting M.P.s' was the welcome I saw on the placards that stared me in the face on approaching the scene of action. The next thing was to burn me in effigy in a red coat and fox's brush." The sporting candidate was unceremoniously shouted down. He managed, however, at last to edge in the

Blows like a Horse's Kick

challenge, "I will fight any man, big or small, directly I leave the hustings, having a preliminary round with him for love." After this a hearing was secured. The crowd indeed had reason to know that the unpopular candidate would show himself as good as his word. A few days before, Assheton Smith, going into a bank at Leicester, hitched his bridle over the iron rails outside. A coal-heaver, coming by with his cart, gave Smith's steed a cut with the whip that nearly caused the animal to jump into the window. " Defend yourself," said the reappearing equestrian, at the same time turning up his cuffs. The man from the cart at once began to strip, and the fight commenced. " I found," said Assheton Smith, " more than I bargained for. There was no flinching, however, on either side. At it we went, following each other up and down the street like a couple in a country dance. At last the constables came up. I left the brave fellow with, I think, the words, ' You will hear of me again.' I recollect, too, I went out to dinner that night with a beefsteak over my eye. The next morning I found out my opponent's abode—that is, I was told in answer to my question, ' He does live here, if he is still alive.' I sent the servant in with a £5 note and a message. This answer was brought back : 'The best man that ever stood before me ! God bless his Honour ! I duly earned the money, for his blows are like the kick of a horse. But to show my gratitude I'll fight him again, any day he likes, for love.' " The combined strain of hard riding and harder fighting necessitated a day or two's repose at Melton. He recollected that at Eton he had learned to clean a room

377

and to cook a chop, but not to do figures. He now, therefore, engaged the local post-mistress to teach him arithmetic. From a Midland hunting-field it was, too, that, hearing his father lay dangerously ill at Tedworth, he at once started on the ride to Hampshire, only stopping once or twice on the road to change horses. Smith's life as a Hampshire Master of Foxhounds followed his training in the shires, from 1824 to 1858. In both districts, long after his own hunting-days were over, he was remembered in the hunting-field as a disciplinarian, who was not, however, a bully, and as a horseman who, with a hand like Chifney's, then the first of English jockeys, mounted on his favourite horses " Radical " and " Big Grey," did all his riding from his legs. As may be inferred from these names, Smith affected democratic sympathies. He had, however, all the conventional patrician dislike of Canning. When, in the Tedworth dining-room, he heard of Canning's coming into power, but unaccompanied by any of his disciples, " Bad enough," he exclaimed, " to have that fellow brought in, though his infernal set are left out. Canning will still prove, to quote Falstaff, ' rotten as a stewed prune.' "

To the south-east of Tedworth, nearer to Winchester, still stands the house which, as Queen Victoria entered on the second half of her reign, was in Church and State what Assheton Smith's home was in sport. The Squire of Hursley, Sir William Heathcote, so long member for Oxford, was, as Disraeli said, one of those formed by nature to lead the country party. With his friend Keble, of " The Christian Year," at

Too Much for Sir W. Heathcote

the neighbouring rectory, as spiritual chief of his staff, Heathcote made Hursley the social citadel of the ecclesiastical Toryism that had for its chief champion his friend and frequent guest, W. E. Gladstone, his some time colleague in the representation of Oxford. It was when a guest at Hursley that an earlier University member, Sir R. H. Inglis, uttered a sentiment often attributed to Sir Robert Peel : " I respect the aristocracy of birth and of mind, but not the aristocracy of money." Not only a good Churchman, but a believer in the Oxford Movement's view of Apostolicity, Heathcote, entertaining at Hursley, in 1836, J. H. Newman's special friend, F. Rogers (Lord Blachford), impatiently exclaimed : " I cannot stomach his principle of economy, licensing, as to me it seems to do, any amount of *suggestio falsi* or *suppressio veri*." Since the Heathcote days the *personnel* of the hospitalities at Hursley has changed. Its present occupants have made it a pleasant, as well as a fashionable, rendezvous for the county balls at Winchester. The revival of these functions, like the revival of so many suspended race meetings, is largely due to the country-house influence of our time.

"Imagine the impossibility of living up to such a father." These words occurred like a refrain in the second Duke of Wellington's conversation as he pointed out to his Strathfieldsaye guests the memorials of the Waterloo hero, in which the place abounds. Every spot recalled its appropriate anecdote. Standing under this tree, " His Grace," as the second Duke always indicated his predecessor, dictated his reply to the tradesman who had applied to him for some debt of his son: " Field-Marshal the Duke of Wellington presents his compliments to Messrs. Smith and Jones, and begs to inform them he is neither Lord Charles Wellesley nor Messrs. Smith and Jones' debt-collector." A few yards off, some one stooping to pick up the great Duke's stick, accidentally fallen, received the stereotyped reprimand always elicited by any amiable little interventions of the kind, "Can't you be good enough to mind your own business?" On the other hand, just outside the grounds is the lane in which His Grace saw a little boy crying bitterly over a hedgehog, which he had to leave to go to school at a distance. The Duke not only took upon himself the charge of the animal during its owner's absence, but wrote to him once a week to say how it was getting on. On that garden seat the great captain, always precise about religious observances, received one of his guest's—a lady's—apology for not forming one of the party to church the next Sunday. She was a Catholic, and there was no Catholic church within a distance of twenty or thirty miles. " That," said the host, " need be no difficulty. My carriage and horses are at your disposal ; breakfast shall be ready a little after daybreak, and the thing can easily be done." " And," said the second Duke, " she had to go." The Strathfieldsaye host, who only died in 1884, reproduced many of his famous sire's features without, however, the impression of strength which these conveyed. It was the same kind of likeness which kinship often impresses on a smaller man to a greater—for instance, in Sir John Gladstone to W. E., or in Ralph Disraeli to his brother, Lord Beaconsfield.

Alfieri and Lady Ligonier

Shrewdness, however, as well as a dry, hard, sardonic humour, the second Duke of Wellington had inherited from the first. He had reason to believe two of his guests particularly wished their rooms to be close together. He placed them at opposite ends of the longest and most public passage in the rambling old house. Chuckling with delight at this arrangement, he simply remarked to a visitor to whom he confided it, " Diddled 'em, I think! " The recipient of this confidence was the nearly life-long friend, who, depressed by some domestic vexations, was thus rallied : " My dear Billy, I should have thought you would have been more a man of the world. Look at me ! I am old, I am deaf, I am blind ! All my farms are unlet. The young man in whom I am most interested has just married the wrong woman. I owe thousands at my bankers. And yet I am happy ! " Another spot of interest pointed out by the second Duke of Wellington to his visitors was the site in his park of the building in which Lady Ligonier carried on her intrigue with Alfieri, with the bough of the tree outside to which her visitor hung his horse's bridle.

The oldest of his friends, who lived nearly through the Victorian age, the Rev. G. R. Gleig, his father's biographer, afterwards Chaplain-General, lived at Winchfield, not far from Strathfieldsaye, and was expected to be in attendance when the second Duke entertained. The pair did not specially delight in talk of past days ; they simply found that their play at whist suited each other. Notwithstanding the irritability of age and gout, or of something more

381

serious, the Strathfieldsaye visitors only saw the second duke completely lose his temper once. Some-one, who said he had just come on from Hatfield, talked of having seen, in Lord Salisbury's stable-yard, the grave of " Copenhagen," the charger ridden by the Duke at Waterloo. " Copenhagen," of course, really rests in a Strathfieldsaye paddock, guarded by two quadrupeds of the zebra species, who have, or had, an unpleasant trick, on any stranger entering the enclosure, of seizing his arm. This inscription, by his rider, is on the gravestone :—

> " God's humbler instrument, if meaner clay,
> Must share the honours of that glorious day."

The great Duke's son, who then reigned at Strath-fieldsaye, impatiently grumbled out, " You humbug ! That story was not brought from Hatfield. You got it from a lying guide-book!" Then from the bookshelf he took down a topographical volume, and pointed out the identical blunder which might have misled his visitor. The best of the second duke's stories was one about the Duke of Malakhoff's shooting performance at Strathfieldsaye. During the battue Malakhoff had missed everything. To flatter his vanity and smooth his ruffled temper, the Duke of Wellington caused a pheasant to be tied by its leg to the top of a post, and put up Malakhoff with his double-barrelled gun some thirty yards off. In-stead, however, of firing in that position, the foreign sportsman walked close up to the bird, almost touching it with the muzzle, discharged both barrels into it with the words, " *Hé, coquin!* " " This," said the

Dizzy Risen from the Dead

Duke to his keeper the next day, "is the foreign general who smoked to death in a cave five hundred Arabs!" "Like enough, your Grace," was the man's reply, "he'd be capable of anything!" The second Duke of Wellington took the pride of a woman or a child in securing at Strathfieldsaye an occasional celebrity not belonging to his own world. Thus it was that visitors to the place were surprised once at the apparition in the drawing-room of Henry Irving, at the height of his Lyceum triumphs. "Surely," murmured another guest into the host's ear, "it is Dizzy come to life again!" And indeed the actor looked the part exactly. Those were the days in which the second Duke recruited his house parties from the company he met at Lady Dorothy Nevill's Charles Street luncheons. In addition to that hostess herself and her belongings, there came the late Duchess of Wellington's kinsfolk of the Taylour family, one at least of whom, a Crimean hero, had served under the great Duke himself. With these were one of the most agreeable London bachelors of his day, Mr. Newton, the police magistrate ; Lord Randolph Churchill, then in the prime of his social brightness and political enterprise ; Sir Henry Drummond Wolff, a guest altogether after his host's heart, the best *raconteur*, and the lightest in hand among conversationalists of his day.

CHAPTER XIV

FROM THE HAMPSHIRE AVON TO THE THAMES

Business-like Sport at Heron Court

THE social beginnings of fashionable Brighton have been circumstantially traced back, in an earlier chapter, to the Sussex home of the Pelhams, Stanmer, half-way between George IV.'s Pavilion and the scene of the first great victory won by the Barons against Henry III. The origin of the best known among Hampshire watering-places presents some analogy to the genesis of London-super-mare. In other words, the same parental relation filled by Stanmer to Brighton exists between Heron Court, the home of the Malmesbury Earls, and Bournemouth. On the eve of the Victorian age, what is now Bournemouth was an expanse of barren heath, broken by several cottages and half a dozen houses. The earliest associations of Heron Court, like those of Highclere Castle, were ecclesiastical. Highclere, as we have seen, belonged to the Bishops of Winchester long before it passed to the Herberts. The home of the Fitz-Harrises had supplied the Priors of the neighbouring Christchurch with a rural residence before the Earls of Malmesbury made it a rendezvous of politicians, dandies, and beauties. For ten months out of the twelve the second possessor of the Malmesbury earldom never moved from his Hampshire home, gathering beneath his roof relays of representative men and women for guests. The host was the keenest and, in a marked degree, the most methodical sportsman of his time. Dying in 1841, he left behind him a record of his prowess with the gun during nearly half a century. How many heads of game fell before every shot or were missed, were all entered day by day. Visiting at Heron Court his former colleague in the Derby Cabinet, the third Lord Malmesbury, Lord Beaconsfield was duly shown this book as a curiosity of the place. He carefully went through it, remarking, when he finally closed the volume, "The most extraordinary monument of patience and sturdy character I have ever seen." A sporting magnate of the old school, this second Lord Malmesbury was conspicuous among the most cultivated and broad-minded peers of his period. The staunchest of Tories, when he spoke of the English aristocracy as "the bulwark of the nation," he used the word in its strictly etymological sense, assuming the identity of an hereditary ruling class with whatever was best and strongest in the nation's life. "Who," at his dinner-table as well as in the House of Lords, he asked, "but an aristocracy trained from infancy in the hunting-field to fearlessness, would not have been discouraged when Napoleon's repeated success cowed Europe?" "I feel," said at Heron Court the third Lord Malmesbury, nineteenth-century Foreign Secretary, "something of a filial traitor, when, recalling my father's resistance to the £10 suffrage of 1832, I remember that, as a member of the Cabinet, I took my part in framing the really democratic measure of 1867, Lord Derby's leap in the dark."

"Here," said the third Lord Malmesbury to a Heron Court visitor, in the last years of his life, indicating a spot near the house, "I had a strange proof of the tricks that nerves may play upon the bravest man. A keeper was loading Lord Jocelyn's gun when the bursting of the barrel blew off two of

A Deal Extraordinary

the man's fingers. A doctor, who happened to be in the house, at once came out ; we stood round to see the operation and encouraged the patient, who never flinched. The only one of us who gave in at the sight was the hero of a hundred battles, Lord Raglan ; he was so overcome that he rushed into the house almost fainting." Of all the Heron Court hosts none can have excelled as a *raconteur* the one now spoken of. Whist being part of diplomatist's education, he had played the game with or against the best performers of his time, Lords Granville, Sefton, and Sir Watkin Wynn. Several hundreds depended on the rubber ; the decisive deal had just been made. Turning to take up his hand, Lord Granville found he had no cards. " I rather think," said Sir Watkin, " I have too many cards " ; he certainly had, twenty-six instead of thirteen, having inadvertently dealt himself two hands. On this occasion one of the players was Lord Alvanley, then connected with two incidents in everybody's mouth ; he had been publicly called by Daniel O'Connell "a bloated buffoon." Hence, of course, a duel, in which Morgan O'Connell represented his father. The Liberator's representative fired before the giving of the signal. Alvanley accepted the assurance of its being a mistake. Two shots were then exchanged. Having been withdrawn by his second, Colonel Damer, Alvanley, as he gave a guinea to the hackney-coachman, said, " This not for taking me, but for bringing me back." There had been several differences in the hunting-field between Alvanley and Lord Cardigan. On the opening day of the Quorn at Melton, Alvanley, with hat ceremoniously doffed, rode up to Cardigan and said, " I hereby beg to apologise to you, not only for any past offences, but for any I may commit in the ensuing season." At the Heron Court dinner-table of this epoch, the verdict in the Melbourne-Norton *cause célèbre* and the Whig rejoicings at Lord Melbourne's acquittal were among the topics of talk. " I really cannot see," drily observed a Tory guest, "why Lord Melbourne should be so cock-a-hoop at a verdict which only proves him to have had more opportunities than any other man and to have made no use of them."

Socially, at his Heron Court parties as well as in London, Lord Malmesbury led the Tory peers in recognising *la belle Américaine* as a princess in the polite world. He had first become acquainted with the representatives of this new social force in Rome. Here a smart American Mrs. Malaprop, living in the Via Babuino, near the Jesuit propaganda college, asked him to come to her reception "in Baboon Street, near the Pope propagating houses." Between two and three generations ago Heron Court was not more famous for its amusing table-talk than for the good looks of some among its guests. These included the Lady Pembroke of that period with her three beautiful daughters, afterwards respectively Lady Ailesbury, Lady Dunmore, and Lady Shelburne, also a future bride. This last was the daughter of Sir Lucius O'Brien, eventually Lord Inchiquin. She became the wife of the second Lord ·Malmesbury's youngest son Charles, who, having taken the bit between his teeth and decided on becoming a clergyman, died Bishop of Gibraltar in 1874. In the Heron Court company of the last century was one of Lord Malmesbury's former private secretaries, who, in a degree scarcely second to his chief, contributed to the fortunes of Bournemouth as a watering-place. This was the happily still surviving Sir Henry Drummond-Wolff, formerly Government Secretary in the Ionian islands, and as such concerned in the 1862 negotiations for giving the crown of Greece to Queen Victoria's second son. Meeting him at Heron Court, Disraeli at once recognised the serviceableness to the Conservatives of his pen and himself. A little later Sir Henry Wolff, at Boscombe Tower, possessed a Hampshire home of his own, where he entertained, among others, Dickens, who had long since recruited him as an occasional writer for *Household Words.* " So bright and clever a man, so neat a writer," said Dickens on leaving, "ought not to have wandered into Conservatism." At Boscombe Tower, Sir Henry Wolff, by his courteous hospitalities to political foes as well as friends, first secured the enjoyable popularity on both sides which made him an ever-welcome figure in public life. Thus his keen criticisims on Lord Granville's foreign policy in the Commons did not prevent his being a host with whom the Foreign Secretary's brother became especially intimate, if not at Boscombe, at Constantinople. " I looked upon these attacks," said Mr. Leveson-Gower, "as only in the way of business." At Boscombe, in the Fourth Party days, when Protestantism was fluttered by the so-called Errington mission to the Vatican, Sir Henry Wolff arranged the *mise en scène* for his

From Hampshire Avon to the Thames

appearances at Westminster as the champion of England against Rome ; the un-masquer of a Cyrenaic latitudinarian like Lord Granville, of a concealed papist like Gladstone, and of a professed Romanist like Lord Ripon.

Conspicuous also among literary hosts on the Hampshire sea-board was Sir Henry Wolff's neighbour, the registrar of the Privy Council, as well as the editor of the *Edinburgh Review*, Henry Reeve. In 1874, Reeve sold some thirty acres of land possessed by him at Winkfield for £6,000. With that sum he built his Bournemouth house, Foxholes. Completed in 1875, his Hampshire home continued to attract cosmopolitan guests, literary and political, till the close of its owner's active life. Here he received his most frequent visitors, Charles Greville, the diarist, whose journals he was afterwards to bring out ; Abraham Hayward, when a bird of passage between his St. James's Street lodging and his sister's, as already mentioned, at Lyme Regis in the next county ; and J. T. Delane, during the years in which Reeve's articles on foreign affairs, written for the most part at Foxholes, remained a feature in the *Times* of every Tuesday. At Foxholes, too, took place the animated discussion between Reeve and one of his innumerable foreign visitors on the then projected Suez Canal, regarded by the *Edinburgh* editor, among many others, as likely to be more than prejudicial, in fact, absolutely destructive, to English interests. At Foxholes he planned and partly executed the initial opposition to the project, and in 1875, chiefly with his own pen, denounced Disraeli's purchase of the Khedive's shares. The master of Foxholes had first improved any previous knowledge of Hampshire when a guest at the house of his proprietor, Thomas Longman. If Byron could call John Murray "the Napoleon of publishers," the nineteenth-century Thomas and William Longman were the social princes of their guild. Two more finished gentlemen were never seen at the covert side ; two more courteous and discriminating judges of writing never walked from Paternoster Row into the Athenæum Club. The Hertfordshire house of the latter will be visited in due course. The elder brother, outliving William by two years, continued his hospitalities at Farnborough till 1879. With the figure and seat of a neat horseman, he combined a taste for sport of every kind and kept for years, as well as himself hunted, a small pack of harriers. Henry Reeve, who owed to Thomas Longman and to the social opportunities that the Longmans provided not less than he did to his connection with the *Times* or to his position at the Privy Council office, was only one among literary guests representing the best thought and knowledge of the time. The local visitors were quite as agreeable as, and sometimes more interesting, than the metropolitan guests. Farnborough in the Longman days was the one place to which invitations were coveted by the contiguous Aldershot. The parties, made up from the camp to the frequent dinners and the occasional balls given at the Hill, were events in the military year. Among the civilian hosts in the neighbourhood, the most entertaining recalled by the present writer

From Hampshire Avon to the Thames

was the first Lord Basing, better remembered, perhaps, even now, as Sclater-Booth, one of Disraeli's House of Commons lieutenants. During the early seventies he happened to be among the dinner guests at Farnborough Hill. It was the period in which Dr. Kenealy, having got into the House of Commons as " Member for Orton," had at last found a day for bringing forward his motion of censure on Lord Chief Justice Coleridge. Disraeli's reply, a supremely happy performance of its kind, contained some compliments on his social demeanour to Coleridge. These, as reported by the newspapers, described the Lord Chief as not carrying into drawing-rooms an air of " adamantine gravity." " I was sitting," said Sclater-Booth, " only a place or two off Disraeli in the House ; the epithet I am sure which he used was ' Rhadamanthine '—a much better word." Another M.P., much Sclater-Booth's junior, with something like contempt, expressed his dissent from the emended version. " Pardon me," at this juncture, from a few chairs' distance, said a voice whose theatrical solemnity struck one's ear with an impressively familiar ring, " my right honourable friend is absolutely correct ; of course, I did say Rhadamantine." The speaker was Disraeli himself. Entering the room late, he had quietly taken an inconspicuous seat at the dining-table. Some of those who then heard his unexpected contribution to the table-talk and some of his subsequent remarks, must have mentally anticipated Mr. Arthur Balfour's description of Lord Beaconsfield's conversation— " a bronze mask talking his own novels."

An Empress in Exile

Farnborough Hill, in the last century the most refined and hospitable of genuinely English homes, to-day has long since been transformed into a French château. On the 9th of January, 1873, Napoleon III. died at Camden House, Chislehurst. Six years later, from Zululand, the same roof received the lifeless body of his son. The Kentish village contained for a time the remains of both. To-day these ashes rest in the mausoleum raised by the widowed mother at Farnborough Hill in 1888. Having purchased the estate from the present Mr. T. Norton Longman, the ex-Empress Eugénie' had already made Farnborough Hill her home. At the present time the palace built by an English publisher is therefore the monument of French Imperialism. The household presided over by the bereaved lady has always been suffused by an atmosphere of melancholy resignation. Its leading spirit till lately was the most brilliant among the former Napoleonic courtiers, the duc de Bassano, not less loyal in exile than he was superb in prosperity, Active and vigorous even in advanced age, he personally represented the Empress at any point in Europe at which evidence seemed desirable of her continued existence. He had the satisfaction of seeing his son, the husband of an English-Canadian, trained and ready to take his place in the councils of Farnborough Hill. With the elder Bassano were Madame Le Breton, the inseparable companion of her mistress on every journey, at Farnborough ever knitting by her side, and in harmony so exact that the click of the different needles fused itself into a single sound. The two ladies had known the same sorrows, for Madame Le Breton's brother, General Bourbaky, took her son Lucien, then under twenty, to the Franco-Prussian war, promising to protect him and bring him back safe ; in one of the first battles the lad fell.   Threatened with blindness, Madame Le Breton recovered sight sufficiently to resume her daily reading to the Empress.   The duc de Mouchy (Prince Victor Napoleon), his wife one of the Murat princesses, the former Bonapartist statesman, Rouher, the Bonapartist lawyers, Grandperret and Busson Billant, have been among the French visitors at Farnborough Hill.   The English have included the present Queen of Spain, with her mother and her aunt, Princess Christian.   The extremity of the Farnborough Park with its lake has been called by the ex-Empress her Compaigne.   Inside the house are other mementoes of vanished splendour, bronzes from Fontainebleau, miniatures from St. Cloud, an inlaid writing-table from the villa at Biarritz.   There, too, at the end of the central hall, an enclosure, consecrated to the Prince Imperial, contains a model of the room prepared at Chislehurst for her son's return from South Africa, to-day holding the young man's books, knick-knacks, his portrait, life-size, by a Viennese artist, and two paintings by Protais.   In one the Prince awaits the onset of the assegais ; in the other he lies dead among the tall grasses.

Reversing the track of the august apparition at the Farnborough dinner-table in the Longmans' days, let us now visit the point which Disraeli had left for the Longmans' dinner-party.   This place, Hazeley, near Farnborough, was then the rural home of the

Violet Fane and Lady Strangford

highly endowed lady who first won literary repute under the pen-name of Violet Fane. Amid the simple surroundings of her Hampshire house, her natural grace and unstudied piquancy of talk delighted a succession of visitors representing every kind of intellectual distinction. At Hazeley she wrote "Sophy : or, the Adventures of a Savage," the remarkable novel which to-day conveys, by the dialogues of its *dramatis personæ*, a better idea of its author's daily conversation than any formal memoirs or letters which may ever see the light are likely to do. Among her literary guests at Hazeley were A. W. Kinglake and Laurence Oliphant. Much converse with both these had influenced her style. " In the best talk," said a French visitor to Hazeley, Edmond Scherer, "there should be a certain delicacy of bitter-sweet flavour, leaving the same kind of after-taste in the mind that an olive with one's wine conveys to the palate. For observations pitched in the gentle key that gives that sweetened cynicism and softened satire, Mrs. Singleton is unrivalled among the well-bred *intellectuelles* of her time." The late Lady Currie herself recognised at least her conversational equal in one whom she met at political houses in London, who once at least visited her at Hazeley, but who as a talker will be best remembered in connection with Stonor, the Oxfordshire house of her most frequent host, Lord Camoys. This was the daughter of Admiral Beaufort, Emily, who as Viscountess Strangford lived till late in the last century at her house, Chapel Street, Mayfair ; her casual utterances on men and things blended epigram and insight. The talk had turned on Sir Henry Layard, then ambassador at Constantinople, and his earlier excavations in the Euphrates valley. Apropos of his discoveries on the site of the ancient Babylon, Lady Strangford, with the naïve demureness and in the subdued tone that gave an emphasis of their own to her remarks, said, "After all, when a man has a firman from the Porte and several pick-axes, it would be hard if he did not find something." The future Lady Currie was not less effectively inimitable in her way. Showing a visitor round her grounds at Hazeley, she stopped for a moment opposite a little wooden structure, inhabited by her favourite guinea-pigs. "A sad instance," she murmured, "of male selfishness. The fathers of the establishment, having devoured their wives, have resolved themselves into a sort of bachelors' club. I never saw them so happy before."

During the last half of the nineteenth century the Surrey and Berkshire district about Sunningdale abounded in social centres, forming the most agreeable and characteristic feature of the time. The present Lord and Lady Greville entertained political or literary friends at most week-ends. That was the period in which Matthew Arnold rurally recreated himself, after the labours of school inspection, at the summer home in the region which he loved with a life-long affection. Lady Violet Greville was the hostess beneath whose roof Arnold found social inspiration exactly needed to show him in his full charm. On one of these occasions he was sometimes tempted to indulge in the anecdotal vein that, as a

Matthew Arnold's Little Dinner

rule, he despised and eschewed. Soon after the Balliol function connected with the completion of the new hall in 1877, he met, at Lady Violet Greville's, one who, like himself, had assisted at the opening ceremony, but who, with a courage which he dared not imitate, had found a sitting place on the altar steps in the crowded building, during Archbishop Tait's sermon. "I wished," said Arnold, "I could have done it myself, but as a clergyman's son I felt it would not be the right thing." Arnold's other personal experience had reference to his official tour for reporting on the French educational system. His travelling expenses had not been calculated upon too liberal a scale. As the old saying has it, "Il faut être anglais pour diner à café Riche ; il faut être riche pour diner à café anglais." At one of these places Arnold determined to have a little banquet before he left Paris, "I had scarcely sat down to the good things," he said, "before I saw enter some one whom I at first took for Lord Granville" (then, as President of the Council, Arnold's official chief). "It turned out to be his brother, F. Leveson-Gower. When he came up to my table I showed him my little menu, with the remark that he would be able now to convince Lord Granville as to the insufficiency of the Government's allowance for my expenses."

In Surrey the historical place of honour among country houses belongs to Wotton, the home of John Evelyn, the diarist. Here his Tory dislike of the 1688 settlement caused him to retire six years later. It was his own birthplace, sweetly environed with delicious streams and woods. Here, with the leave of the actual owner, his brother, he created a fish-pond, an island, and other solitudes. Here he received socially congenial guests well affected to the Stuart cause. The house was partly destroyed by fire in 1856, but its most interesting contents, among them the prayer-book, given on the scaffold to Archbishop Juxon, by him presented to the diarist's father-in-law, are still to be seen. The brother of Lord Granville already mentioned, Mr. F. Leveson-Gower, in the second half of the nineteenth century added to the prettiest part of the Surrey hills one of the many charming and hospitable abodes which now dot this picturesque district. The view from Holmbury includes not only the entire range of the Surrey hills, but much of Sussex and Hampshire, with the outline of the South Downs plainly visible in the near distance. The Holmbury hospitalities formerly included a Derby party. No saving of distance was effected by making Holmbury instead of Pall Mall the starting point for Epsom Downs. The drive, however, took the visitors through a succession of delightful woodland scenes and along a road neither so crowded nor so dusty as the familiar cockney route. Not even from the Durdans, Lord Rosebery's villa, almost within sight of the grand stand, did there issue forth race-goers more distinguished than from Holmbury. The host himself, indeed, seldom assisted in person at what Palmerston called our national Isthmian games. Accompanying on horseback his guests some part of the way, Mr. Leveson-Gower generally found a quiet ride home through the cool lanes and the grass-bordered by-roads. Sometimes, when he met his

"No Place Like Home—bury"

returned visitors again at the dinner-table, he had some quaint experiences to relate. Once, he has recounted in his recent reminiscences, having turned his horse's head round from the carriage conveying Lord and Lady Spencer, the Duke and Duchess of Westminster, and others, he stopped to make a call at the Rookery, near Dorking, formerly the residence of the economist, Malthus, more recently the possession of Mr. Fuller. The men had all gone to Epsom. The ladies were at luncheon, and promptly found the visitor a place at their table. They mistook him, however, for a land surveyor named Simpson, who had been expected to call, and as such saluted him. Would Mr. Simpson take a cutlet or some chicken, and so throughout the meal. The guest, occupied in making himself agreeable, did not notice the mistake. Presently the hostess, whom he had never seen before, thought of looking at his card, discovered and declared his identity. " I am sure," said one lady, " he was so nice as Mr. Simpson that I scarcely like to know he is some one else."

" There is no place like Home—bury," said one of the many ladies (Lady Marian Alford or Miss Mary Boyle), who, at the time now recalled, were Mr. Leveson-Gower's guests. The opinion was shared by countless men as well as women. Among the former were, specially during the tenancy of Holmbury by Mr. James Kowles, Benjamin Jowett, W. E. Gladstone, Arthur Stanley, Dean of Westminster, and Alfred Lord Tennyson, poet laureate. " I like and love Gladstone," said Tennyson, "but I hate his politics and his dealings with the Irish, all of whom I

399

From Hampshire Avon to the Thames

wish were at the bottom of the sea." Among the famous talkers whom Holmbury knew well was Mrs. George Grote, the wife of the Greek historian, sometimes with, sometimes without, her famous husband. This remarkable lady affected a masculine manner, to some extent a masculine dress ; she set it all off by a more than masculine asperity of tongue. On one occasion she arrived at Holmbury driving a high dog-cart, with a coachman's cloak of many capes. " Good heavens ! " she had been a few minutes before overheard saying to a timid gentleman to whom she had given a lift, " don't speak so loud or you'll frighten the horse, and then Heaven only knows if he will ever stop ! " When in the house and talking, it was her habit to sit with one leg crossed over the other and both as high up as possible. In that posture she would lecture Dean Stanley on ecclesiastical history, Max Müller on Sanscrit epics, Count Saffi on Italian literature, any local expert in agriculture who might chance to look in on the growing of turnips or the breeding of Southdowns. The master of Holmbury, like others, noticed that years sensibly softened the Radicalism of both the Grotes, and quite destroyed Mrs. Grote's democratic preferences. The lady's favourite sport was the baiting of Mr. Henry Reeve. Your road," said the *Edinburgh* editor, after entering her house rather behind his time, " is so steep that the fly could hardly climb it." " That," she rejoined, " is because you had in your pocket the last number of the *Edinburgh*." A discussion between the two on some international question elicited from the gentleman the exclamation, " Another Grotius ! " The lady's response was imme-

Mrs. Craven on Everybody

diately, " Another Puffendorf ! "—a name happily suggestive of Mr. Reeve's majestic portliness of person and frilled exuberance of shirt-front. " Grota, whence the word ' grotesque,' " had been Sydney Smith's observation on this lady, who deserves to be remembered for some kind actions as well as many biting words. She never deserted any old friend of her own sex who had fallen on evil days ; she left Abraham Hayward £1,000 in her will.

Of conversational quality very different from Mrs. Grote, was another lady much in request under the intellectual roofs of the Surrey hills or the Thames valley in the last century. Mrs. Craven's chief host was Sir Mountstuart Grant-Duff, at whose hospitalities at York House, Twickenham, we have yet to assist. The daughter of the Marquis de la Feronnays, a famous French diplomatist, she had first cousins in all the great families of the Continent, and intimate friends at every social or intellectual centre of distinction in the world. Wherever congregated the Granvilles, the Cowpers, the Palmerstons, there was her home. The breeding of England, combined with the artistic temperament of Italy, found conversational or epistolary expression in the wit and epigram that are French. Some specimens of her talk and the personal estimates which were its most animated feature may be recalled. Palmerston she knew well, but failed, as many thought, happily or even correctly to appraise. Gladstone, his intellectual effervescence, his earnest rhetoric, and his Irish policy she hit off to the life. " Heaven," she exclaimed, "defend Ireland from her mortal foe and preserve to

401   CC

me my mortal friend." Gladstone's most confidential and sympathetic colleague, the inheritor of his political principles and his moral resolution, Mr. John Morley, personifies (she remarked) those traits of the English character, good sense, firmness, and honesty which Gladstone has done so much to obliterate. The enthusiasm which four-score-years-and-two had not extinguished expended itself in something verging on idolatry for General Gordon. Yet Mrs. Craven could understand the difficulty felt by English statesmen like Lord Granville in according entire confidence to one who seeks political and military guidance in the Book of Isaiah. It was the chivalrous simplicity of the man which fascinated her. As an instance of this quality, she never wearied of Gordon's excuse for refusing a late dinner invitation to Marlborough House : " I always go to bed at half-past seven." " La femme la plus spirituelle que j'ai jamais vu." The slight acquaintance with this remarkable lady possessed by the present writer deprives his own estimate of much importance. What, however, struck me most about her, as I know it struck some others too, was the evidence of an inner and deeper life, entirely different from the surface of her existence, which now and then in her talk seemed to well up from the depths of her soul. Her social life was a continual whirl. At the dinner-table people listened to one to whom the production of conversational effects had become second nature. If the company were theatrical, later on in the evening one witnessed an amateur actress of remarkable finish in some drawing-room selections from the repertory of the Comédie Française;

or perhaps, amid her most intimate friends, a well-bred imitation of the manners of different public men she knew. Such were her reproductions of Lord Granville apologising for his consanguinity with half the noble houses of England. Such, too, were her reminiscences of the great French Churchmen she admired heart and soul—some sermon of Dupanloup, some consultation between Lacordaire and Ravignan, over the spiritual remedies to be applied to her beloved but infidel France. Then would come her rendering of the thin, hard, professorial secularism of Paul Bert. In the hunting-field the most expert and fearless horsewomen are sometimes not above asking for a friendly lead over an exceptionally difficult fence. In the drawing-room Mrs. Craven occasionally did not disdain the same kind of initiative. On one occasion, apropos of Palmerston, Walter Bagehot had dwelt on that statesman's capacity for profiting by experience but inability to argue correctly outside his daily occupations. " Exactly," was Mrs. Craven's comment, " I have nothing but praise for his belief in England, but he should remember that elsewhere English methods have their risks as well as advantages, and that English institutions are more readily burlesqued than imitated."

Something might be said for discovering the earliest home of country-house talk as a fine art beneath one of Surrey's rural roofs. In the Dorking district lived, during the first half of the nineteenth century, at Fridley Farm, Richard (better known as " Conversation ") Sharpe. He might also have been called " Single-speech " Sharpe ; for having made a fortune in business with Samuel Boddington as his partner, he went into Parliament, caught the Speaker's eye, delivered his soul, and was never heard of at St. Stephen's afterwards. The most instructive friend ever possessed by the present writer, Abraham Hayward, had been of the company at Fridley Farm. Here the portraits in the dining-room were limited to the famous men with whom Sharpe had lived. Johnson, Burke, and Reynolds were all from the brush of Sir Joshua himself. To Sharpe, Reynolds had confided having taken from the print of a halfpenny ballad in the street an effect in one of his pictures which pleased him more than any he had produced. The Henderson at Fridley Farm was by Gainsborough, and by Opie the Sir James Mackintosh. Mackintosh, though in society as in political life too obviously didactic, too artificial in his manners and conversation, impressed all the Fridley guests as the most brilliant and instructive talker they had ever been acquainted with. " He had," said Hayward to me, "read everything, and could on occasion repeat most of what he had read." Pursuing our Surrey progress in a north-easterly direction, we make a short stop at a house, rich in diverse memories, standing in the prettiest grounds between Caterham and Godstone. Marden Park, more recently the property of the Clayton baronets, depends chiefly for its latter day notoriety on its yearlings sales. It was on one of these occasions that Lord Randolph Churchill, soon after he had fixed Parliamentary attention, first found himself pointed out as a personage by the crowd. Nearly a hundred years earlier the place had constantly received two Parliamentarians, some of whose opinions the Fourth Party leader inherited. The Marden host of the eighteenth century was William Wilberforce. His " Practical View of Christianity " had not long been out. It had at once become an extraordinary success. Its author, finding his home at Kensington Gore too close to Westminster for rest after his labours, bought a new country place, partly at least out of the profits of his book. Knowing from Chatham's contemporaries the authentic tradition of the elder Pitt, Wilberforce, at the house-warming dinner given to his anti-slavery colleagues at Marden, remarked, " I have no doubt whatever that as an orator Chatham's son is superior to Chatham." Bishop Samuel Wilberforce's mimetic and histrionic power is not yet forgotten. It was an inheritance from his father, the effect of whose anecdotes about the younger Pitt was heightened by the accompaniment of felicitous gesture and artistic intonation. During the first French Revolution, soon after Marie Antoinette's execution, an *emigré* called on Pitt in Downing Street. The talk was naturally on the horrors recently witnessed in Paris. The visitor, overcome by his thoughts and melted into tears, sobbed out, "Ah, Monsieur Pitt, la pauvre Reine, la pauvre Reine!" The Frenchman was still weeping, when a new idea seemed to possess him. " Nevertheless, Monsieur Pitt, you must see my little dog dance. Fanchon," he called out, "dansez, dansez." The man himself set the example, and further encouraged the animal with a little fiddle. The hilarity involved so much noise that a Treasury messenger, half expecting to find the stranger had assaulted the statesman, rushed into the room. What he saw was the minister struggling with convulsions of merriment. " It was all," observed Wilberforce, "the Gallic temperament." Thus the grave and holy Bourdaloue, appointed to preach before Louis XIV. and the Court at Versailles, had not appeared when the hour came. Messengers, sent to summon him, and finding the door locked and their knocking unnoticed, looked through a chink in the panel. What they saw was the good bishop skipping about his room to the sound of a musical instrument. Having effected an entry, they exclaimed, " Monseigneur, Monseigneur, the king waits for you." " Is it possible ? " replied the pious prelate, continuing his dance. " The truth is, I was so exhausted by fasting as to be unequal to preaching without some little refreshment of this kind first."

Marden has more associations of Pitt than this anecdote. The host and his political visitors had talked long and seriously overnight. In the morning, while awaiting breakfast, Wilberforce took Ryder, afterwards Lord Harrowby, round the garden. The early-rising Pitt had been before them. In a flower-bed they detected something which was not a flower. " It proved," said Wilberforce, " to be a portion of Ryder's very old opera-hat which Pitt had planted in the soil near the geraniums." A little later on the same day, walking with his host near the since celebrated Marden paddock, Pitt confided to Wilberforce his vain passion for Eleanor Eden, finishing the recital with the words " Perhaps in love, as in war, discretion is the better part of valour." At

Celebrities in Surrey Houses

Marden, too, Burke, on one occasion asked to meet Pitt, expressed to Wilberforce deathless gratitude for the instruction and comfort derived by him from the " Practical View," passing as the book had done to five editions in six months, and later through twenty-five editions in the United States. With the exception of the already mentioned Lord Randolph Churchill, the one nineteenth-century statesman occasionally to be met with in Marden Park was Robert Lowe, not yet Lord Sherbrooke, then occupying a little house in the adjacent village of Warlingham, and on Saturday afternoons often riding his celebrated white horse through the park. Another Surrey home, the scene of memorable meetings and tragic partings, lay at Merton. Here, on September 13, 1805— inauspiciously a Friday—his adieux were made by Nelson to Lady Hamilton, and among other friends to his brother William. A few days earlier, dining with Pitt in Downing Street, the great admiral, with the wetted end of a dinner napkin, had indicated the exact point in the Mediterranean at which he counted on coming up with the French and Spanish fleets. It was at Merton that he offered up his farewell prayer, committing to " the great God, whom I adore, the issues of Trafalgar and the protection of those so dear to me whom I leave behind. His will be done. Amen."

Among the subjects discussed at the most literary of the Surrey houses yet visited, " Conversation " Sharpe's Fridley, was Schlegel's " Critique on Flaxman's Designs for Dante." The sculptor, himself among the guests, showed a modest pride at his preference for Dante over Milton being commended by the leader of intellectual Germany. "If," said Flaxman, "I were to do my work over again it would be done far better. But in one thing I know I am right; my model for the drapery was the common cloak of the lower classes in Italy. Mr. Hope, for whom I executed these designs, the best possible judge on such a matter, confirmed my view of this garment as undoubtedly the same as that generally used in the days, not only of Dante, but of Virgil." Before descending upon the Surrey houses in the Thames valley, we pause for a moment at the famous and beautiful home of the accomplished and erudite patron who gave Flaxman the commission just mentioned. In the boudoir of that patron's Surrey house the Flaxman designs were placed. The Deep-dene belonged to Thomas Hope, the author of "Anastasius," the father of three sons, Henry, Adrian, and Alexander Beresford, all of whom afterwards became well known in society or politics. It then descended to the eldest of these sons, Henry; remaining the residence of his widow for life, it passed afterwards to her grandson, Lord Francis Clinton, whose mother, the Duchess of Newcastle, was Henry Hope's daughter. The place is now (September, 1906), let to Lily, Duchess of Marlborough, and was inhabited by that lady and her former husband, Lord William Beresford, the well-known sportsman, till the latter's death in 1900. Meanwhile some of the Deepdene's literary treasures had gone to Lady Hayter, since Lady Haversham. Amongst these papers was the manuscript of the well-known lines

Young England's Birthplace

on the letter H, often attributed to Lord Byron, sometimes to Maria Edgeworth, but really, it would seem, beyond doubt, the composition of Miss Fanshawe.

The foundation of Benjamin Disraeli's pecuniary fortunes has been seen in an earlier chapter to suggest associations with Carnanton, the Cornish home of the Willyamses. The literary and political movement resulting in the formation of the Young England party first shaped itself in the Surrey mansion of Henry Hope. Here met together the originals of the leading characters in the first novel of the Disraelian trilogy opening with " Coningsby " and ending with " Tancred." The poetical language conveying the dedication of the best known of these works only embodies an historical fact. The glades and galleries of the Deepdene did witness not only the conception but in greater part the execution of " Coningsby." It was Henry Hope, son of him who had written " Anastasius," and raised the lordly pleasure house of art in the Dorking district, that urged Disraeli's treatment in literary form of those ideas and themes frequently discussed by himself and his guests. The natural rulers of England were the aristocracy supported by the people. The territorial class formed the one stable element in the constitution. Capitalists were mushrooms, springing up in the early morn, disappearing as soon as the dew was off the grass. The owners of the land should and might be the objects of an unforced loyalty from farmers and peasants alike. A return to the old ways by the governing class would transform that traditional feeling into a principle of active life. Much of what could be done in this direction had been shown by the tractarian successes of Anglican Oxford. Such were the ideas whose systematic development began in the spring of 1844 at the Deepdene dinner-table and in the Deepdene library. At the time of his first becoming known to Henry Hope, D'Israeli the younger, as he was then styled, had achieved only an unenviable notoriety. His acquaintance with Lord John Manners, the Henry Sidney of "Coningsby," had not yet ripened into the friendship which led to and was cemented by the visits at Belvoir Castle. None of the great people who there first noticed the Jew lad had been met. But for the Surrey Mæcenas who first saw Benjamin Disraeli's great qualities and who made his beautiful house his guest's second home, the future Lord Beaconsfield might never have secured so much as a fair social start. The combination of Young England and Old Judæa, of visionaries in the State, and of dandies from the Alfred Club, was gradually dissolved. Its fruits remained. The popular Conservatism that throughout the last portion of the nineteenth century proved the greatest of political forces, had been cradled between fifty and sixty years earlier at the Deepdene, was indeed but Young Englandism transfigured to suit practical electioneering needs, just as the Deepdene politicians themselves were descended from Bolingbroke, who had sketched the outline of his "Patriot King," lying between the hay-cocks of his favourite suburban Tusculum.

The historical parent of the twentieth-century

smart country house has already been seen in the
Brighton Pavilion. Other royal progenitors of the
modern institution may be found in the Thames
valley of the same period. Oatlands Park, near
Weybridge, to-day the well-known hotel, when
occupied by the Duke of York till his death in 1827
became the stately pattern for fashionable hospitalities
on the banks of the Thames. The Chinese fishing
temple of George IV. at Virginia Water saw no
guests outside the little coterie with which his volup-
tuous retirement was passed. The visitors at Oatlands
completely mirrored the modes and mode-makers of
the day. The most imposing of the guests, the diarist,
Charles Greville, managed the Duke's stables. In his
account of the place he dwells rather too much on its
peculiarities and inconveniences ; he is almost silent
about those persons in the company who did not
belong to his own set. The Oatlands Park "week-
ends" brought together, as Raikes said, every one
who was anybody. A little before five o'clock p.m.
there started from White's Club, in St. James's, a
string of chaises so long as to monopolise the road.
Among those who thus journeyed down were two
distinct companies. The older group comprised
Lords Erskine and Lauderdale, the Duke of Dorset,
Warwick Lake, the richest commoner of his time,
Torrens and Raikes Currie, the father of the late
Lord Currie. Others, of junior standing, were Lords
Berkeley, Foley, Craven, Hertford, Worcester,
Charles Greville himself, his contemporary and rival,
alike in politics and society, Thomas Raikes, Sir
Henry Cooke, General Anson, afterwards Indian

Commander-in-chief, Alvanley, the witty *viveur*, and, towards the close of the host's life, Beau Brummell. When these fine gentlemen reached their destination they were sometimes surprised by the attention forthcoming from the royal hosts to a visitor who many of them had never seen before. This was a short, stout little gentleman, some five feet six inches high, with a very red face, very black hair, even blacker eyes, a countenance so animated and gay, a step so light and fantastic, that they might have been those of the most volatile and careless of mature striplings about town. This guest, however, was Francis Jeffrey, editor of the *Edinburgh Review*, which he had already succeeded in making a true reflection of the Whig character itself. Some time later he was to be the first British *littérateur* to contract a famous American marriage by finding a wife in the grand-niece of John Wilkes, Miss Charlotte Wilkes, of New York. The most magnificent of those invited had not yet come. The future Marquis of Hertford, then Lord Yarmouth, it was whispered, could not have started to time from Piccadilly, as he had previously accompanied Jackson, the pugilist, to see Harry Harmer, the coppersmith, at a prize-fight, then in every one's mouth, pound into a jelly the great "fancy" champion, Jack Ford. The belated peer was none other than the original of Monmouth in "Coningsby," of Steyne in "Vanity Fair," the husband of the *danseuse*, Maria Fagniani, the honour of whose paternity rested between George Selwyn and "Old Q."

Had the great gentlemen brought any of their womenkind to Oatlands? Among her own sex

A Kangaroo as a Pet

the Duchess of York seldom invited more than Lady Anne Culling and her three daughters. Of these, the eldest, having become Lady Worcester, died in the flower of her youth and beauty. Domestic effects of the pure womanly kind were not much in the Oatlands line during the York dispensation. No element of pathos, however, was wanting when, for the first time after her daughter's death, the bereaved mother found herself in the Oatlands drawing-room, pouring out her grief to the royal Duchess, in whom she had years ago learned to recognise not only the queen of a glittering set, but the most sympathetic and genuine of women. On the day selected for our present visit, no lady of any degree has yet made her bow to her Grace of York. There is still some time before dinner will be served. The Duchess takes Thomas Raikes, the silkiest of the Oatlands "tame cats," round her flower beds, paddock, and kennels. In the garden is a menagerie crowded with eagles and, the Duchess's special favourites, macaws. A herd of kangaroos and ostriches appear from another quarter; on the lawn before the windows of the royal boudoir these animals are soon joined by a troop of monkeys. To-morrow morning, soon after daybreak, a kangaroo and an ostrich will stroll together into " Dandy " Raikes' bedroom, awake him from his beauty-sleep and leave him in terror till " old Dawe," the footman, providentially appears. Raikes is far too finished a courtier to hint a complaint. At the breakfast-table he says, " If I like one creature more than another it is a kangaroo, and I prefer an ostrich even to a kangaroo; while there is nothing as a bedroom sentinel to equal a strong-lunged macaw." The good Duchess smiles pleasantly. When she dies she puts down Raikes for two macaws in her will. The explanation of Greville's slightly disparaging, if perfectly respectful, estimate of the Duchess of York is that this lady did not appreciate mere social smartness, however exalted and profligate, as highly as was done by some of those about her. She was even once, it is said, detected by John Wilson Croker and other of his lordship's parasites, laughing at the nickname of " Red-herrings," which his ruby whiskers and Byron's " Waltz " had fastened upon Lord Yarmouth, afterwards the Marquis of Hertford, the most magnificent of libertines who ever threw off a mistress or bowed before a king.

One lady, and she of world-wide fame, in addition to the already mentioned Lady Anne Culling, did occasionally visit Oatlands. The first Napoleon had recently instructed Fouché not to allow "that jade " Madame de Staël to inhabit Paris, or even come within forty leagues of it. That bitterness of hatred, entirely passing the power of words to describe, between England's arch-foe and the first French-woman of her time sufficed, of course, to open to the lady any English house she chose to enter. The Epicene, as the anti-Jacobin had styled her, herself the personification of aristocratic partialities, has to-day gathered round her a little circle of her Oatlands admirers, and is amusing them with a murmured caricature of Lord Yarmouth as the sensual personi-fication of patrician pomposity and pride. Presently, by some glowing tributes to the great qualities of the

From Villa to Asylum

Whig nobles, she draws John Wilson Croker, Yarmouth's *âme damnée*, who walks up to Sir John Bowring and says: "Shall I tell you where I last and for the first time saw that woman? She had received me early in the morning, sitting most decorously in her bed, writing, and with her night-cap on; her two bright black eyes smiled as benignantly as they could, but her face had not been made up for the day, and really looked as ghastly as the grave and as ugly as sin." Some years later, not at Oatlands, Croker, who had been in Paris while Madame de Staël lay a-dying, amused the country house visited by him on his return to England, with relating how the ruling passion proved strong in death. The lady, having begged that her last moments might be undisturbed, ordered the cards of every visitor to be brought her. Among these was the duc de Richelieu's. "And," she indignantly said to the servant, "you sent away the duc? Hurry, fly after him, bring him back. Though I die to the world, I live for him."

"Too small to inhabit and too large to hang to one's watch," was Hervey's well-known description of another among royalty's riverain homes, not less interesting in its way than Oatlands Park. This was the little building raised by Lord Burlington (the builder of Burlington House, Piccadilly), subsequently sold by the Duke of Devonshire to Dr. Tuke, the alienist, as a private asylum for the insane. The villa of Richard Boyle, Earl of Burlington, exactly copied from a Palladian building at Vicenza, by the addition of two wings in the middle of the eighteenth century, expanding itself into Chiswick House, became a social centre as famous as Oatlands and of associations more intellectual. Alexander Pope, from the neighbouring Twickenham, was its frequent guest. Another poet, Gay, was its laureate. The singer of "The Seasons," Thomson, celebrated the place and its company. Horace Walpole constantly inspected the Vandykes and curios with which the rooms overflowed. In 1767 one of the great artist's masterpieces, the portrait of Charles I., so impressed a foreign lounger through the gallery, that after musing for a few moments before the picture, he said, " Il a l'air du malheur." This foreigner was Jean Jacques Rousseau ; his exile in England was then coming to a close. Living in the village of Chiswick at the time, he had been shown over the great house by the Bishop of Peterborough. Among the portraits which were once at Chiswick House, and which are now divided between Burlington House and Chatsworth, is one bearing the legend, " Lady Dorothy Boyle, once the comfort, the joy, the pride of her parents, the admiration of all who saw her, the delight of all who knew her." The story of her life was a, happily short, tragedy. The picture was made from a sketch, drawn seven weeks after Lady Dorothy's death, by her mother. This daughter of the Boyles had, by an unhappy marriage to the Duke of Grafton's son, become Lady Euston. Her sister, Lady Charlotte, also, of course, represented in the family portraits, by a more auspicious union married Lord Hartington, became the mother of the fifth Duke of Devonshire, of Lords Richard and George Cavendish, of a daughter (afterwards Duchess of Portland), and brought to the Cavendishes not only their Piccadilly mansion but vast properties in Ireland. At Chiswick House, though not in the same room, died Charles Fox, in 1806, and George Canning, twenty-one years after. The catafalque-like bed in which Fox expired stood in a room opening upon the entrance-yard. Canning breathed his last in the upper storey of the left wing, full in view of the cedars on the lawn. Among nineteenth century celebrities often seen at Chiswick House was Sir Humphry Davy, the inventor (1816) of the safety-lamp, the pioneer of electrical science, the freshness of whose appearance suggested that he had solved the mystery of perpetual youth, a rapid and animated talker, the husband of a rich widow (Jane Apreec), ubiquitous in the smart country houses of her time, so dark a brunette as to be called by Sydney Smith "brown as a dry toast." Made a baronet in 1818, Davy owed not a little of his country-house popularity to his lectures on agricultural chemistry, opening as these did a fresh era in farming.

The social cult of the River Thames, as the instances already mentioned suggest, originated with a royal source and has been stimulated by Court exemplars. The stream itself has proved a distinctly democratic and levelling agency in the polite system. Its associations remain predominantly aristocratic till the middle of the Victorian age. The possession of the Duke of Westminster's Cliveden by an American millionaire symbolises the other social changes effected at several points on the Thames shore. After its erection by George Villiers, Charles II.'s Duke of Buckingham, the most notable incident in its story was the well-known meeting for the first time, caused by a shower of rain, of the prince who was to become George III. and his future minister, Lord Bute, at the card-table within its walls. Before its occupation by Frederick, Prince of Wales, George III.'s father, it had been improved by the Earl of Orkney, to whom the place had come as part of his wife's dowry. The terrace in front of the house, higher than that of Windsor Castle, was begun by Orkney and extended by George III.'s father. On the 22nd of May, 1795, between ten and eleven o'clock, through a servant's carelessness, burst out the fire which Lord Inchiquin, one of the house-party at the time, described in a letter still extant. The flames began just as he was going to bed. By the time they were extinguished the building was completely gutted, and Lady Orkney left "without a ring, a trinket, or a shift." The rebuilder of Cliveden in 1830 was Sir George War-render, one of the founders of the Garrick Club, best remembered to-day by Theodore Hook's punning allusion to his epicurean tastes and hospitalities, "Sir Gorge Provender." That *bon vivant* made his dinners the despair of contemporary hosts and the envy of the professional diner-out. After the term of its Warrender ownership, Cliveden became the possession of the Duke of Sutherland, whose hospitalities, refined by the grace, skill, and accomplishments of the Duchess, gave the Thames-side palace its modern fame and did something more than merely perpetuate the reputation for good cheer which first made it so desirable a resort under Sir George

Cliveden, Glenisland, and Fieldhead

Warrender. In 1845 the building once more fell by fire. It was raised up again by its ducal owner, himself to be succeeded by another duke, his Grace of Westminster, who in 1890 sold it to the inevitable money-king from the States. In Mr. Astor's hands Cliveden has become the riverside social centre for the fashion and intelligence of the Anglo-Saxon world. It may continue to be so now that it is the home of Mr. and Mrs. Astor junior.

Chief among the riparian hosts in this neighbourhood to carry on the Cliveden tradition have been General Owen Williams at the Temple, and the Oxford oarsman and athlete, Mr. W. H. Grenfell, at Taplow Court. These are but two names belonging to an innumerable and a well-known list. Sir Roger Palmer, one of those who charged at Balaclava, entertaining at Glenisland, Maidenhead, Sir George Wombwell, Harrington Trevelyan, and other old comrades in arms, popularised the stream with the Army, and so promoted the military clubs which are now among the features of its shores. The open house held by the kindly Hammersleys rather higher up the river, and the literary-aquatic gatherings of the accomplished Mr. R. C. Lehmann, at Fieldhead, have been institutions almost as historical as the Oxford and Cambridge training period or Henley week itself, to both of which, indeed, they had become indispensable as social accessories. As King Edward VII.'s Court has been moved to Windsor, so, between the beginning of spring and the end of autumn, in fine weather King Edward VII.'s society has collected beneath some of these smart and hospitable roofs. Throughout a portion of that period the Upper Thames at Marlow flowed past another house, the property of an owner not belonging to the Court set, but not on that account the less accessible to countless friends and, at his zenith, less sought after. During most of the years between 1876 and 1894, Edmund Yates, with his highly endowed wife, received, close by Marlow Lock, a succession of guests at least as interesting as, and not less representative than, any of the riparian companies already mentioned. Poerio and his fellow-captives in Neapolitan dungeons, still feeble from confinement and cruelty; Mrs. Beecher Stowe, of " Uncle Tom's Cabin"; Garibaldi, in his crimson blouse; David Livingstone; or, among those summoned to delight visitors with their art, Malibran, Lablache, Rossini, Donizetti; among philanthropists Lord Shaftesbury, the emancipator of the white slaves; Garrison, the emancipator of the black, have all ennobled with their presence the Thames-side house as well as the London palace of the Leveson-Gowers. The Boucicaults, the Bancrofts, Henry Irving, J. L. Toole, Francis C. Burnand, Arthur W. A'Beckett, Arthur Griffiths, Harold Power, the former colleague of the host at the Egyptian Hall entertainment in the middle of the last century, Edward Dicey, Louis Jennings, a *Quarterly Reviewer*, formerly a writer for Printing-house Square, afterwards editor of the *New York Times*, Bruce Seton, and Charles Wentworth Dilke, were only some among the intellectual workers for the public amusement or instruction who have brought away pleasant memories of good

Uncle Sam in Clover

cheer and miscellaneously animated talk from the riverside home of the man whose novels are as worthy a monument of his abilities as the weekly newspaper which survives its founder and literary creator. Many of those novels contain specimens of Edmund Yates's conversational smartness at its best, *e.g.*, "To pay a tradesman to whom a long account is owing a £5 note is like giving a wet brush to a very old hat. It creates a temporary gleam of comfort, but no more." With the money made by his American tour that helped to found the *World*, Edmund Yates brought back a large acquaintance with American cousins of every class. These included such typical persons as Samuel Ward, the chief of *bon vivants* at Delmonico's, the king of the Lobby at Washington, and the earliest of the Yankee "tame cats" in great English houses, from Dalmeny in Midlothian to the Rothschild palaces in Buckinghamshire. American smartness was then only beginning to be a social force in fashionable England. No Thames-side house was more useful to the Yankee visitors of that day than that of Edmund Yates and his highly endowed wife. Lower down the river than Wargrave, Goring, and Marlow, during the same period as the cosmopolitan hospitalities just recalled, was Lichfield House, Richmond. Here, after strenuous years of publishing work in Fleet Street, John Maxwell, at one time the literary adviser of James Johnstone, the owner of the *Standard*, settled down to the pleasant life of a Surrey squire. In 1874 he had married the lady whose novels crowned the edifice of his publishing fame, Miss Braddon ; as Mrs. Maxwell, she did the honours of his pleasant home on the borders of Richmond Park. Like her master in the art of literary romance, Bulwer Lytton, she enlarged her earlier reputation by a successful experiment in a new department of fiction (designed and executed at Lichfield). " Ishmael," a study of character under the Second Empire in France, was to the " Lady Audley's Secret " series what " The Parisians " had been to earlier works by the author of " Pelham," " Zanoni," and " Eugene Aram." Bulwer Lytton's son, the first Earl Lytton before he became Indian Viceroy (1876), Shirley Brooks, James Hannay, afterwards Consul at Barcelona, Mortimer Collins, the most musical Thames-side versifier of his time, George Augustus Sala, the most thoroughly trained of workmen in the Dickens school, and Charles Lever were among those who bequeathed literary associations to Mr. and Mrs. Maxwell's Surrey dwelling.

CHAPTER XV

FROM OSTERLEY TO ASCOT

AMONG country houses bordering upon the
metropolitan area, Osterley is neither less
famous nor interesting than Oatlands or Chiswick.
While the fashionable procession of chariots and

curricles, already described, was making its way from Pall Mall or Piccadilly to Oatlands Park, there drove up to some park gates not far from Oatlands a noble dandy, who habitually lived and moved in a state surpassed by none and approached by few even of the Regency bucks. He never left his quarters near St. James's Street before 6 p.m. When at that hour he moved abroad, he entered a brown carriage, drawn by brown horses, with servants in brown liveries. This was Lord Petersham, the inventor of a great-coat which, named after him, had lately cut out a garment of the sort brought into vogue by Beau Brummell. If, on reaching Osterley Park, he apologises to his hostess for being late, his excuse is that he has been occupied from an early hour in devising a particular sort of blacking which, he assures Lady Jersey, must eventually supersede every other. His very particular snuff mixture has long since made the fortune of tobacconists ; he is also the original author of the china mania that endured to our own day. No metal contrivances, however bejewelled and precious, for holding this splendid patrician's snuff ; nothing will do but a light blue Sèvres box. Another guest catching sight of it, expressed his admiration. " Yes," languidly drawls its owner, " nice enough for summer, but would never do for winter wear." He is, in fact, the reputed possessor of a snuff-box for every day in the 365. A motley company, indeed, of lords, ladies, wits, ambassadors, statesmen, buffoons, and butts had availed themselves of the Osterley invitations when George IV. called the dance and his parasites paid the piper. Every one laughs at a certain lawyer, poor old "Vice" Leach, attempting to play the fine gentleman. The hostess can scarcely control her amusement when she sees him on horseback, posing as a squire of dames, while suffering from an attack of lumbago which is, as the great lady pleasantly remarks, "a grievous enemy to gallantry and address." Here, too, are Erskine (a professional talker like Macintosh, but with a fatal habit of repeating his stories, his epigrams, his "wise saws," his "modern instances"), and a famous fox-hunting squire, known as "Cheek Chester," who gratifies Lord Byron at the close of the evening by admitting that, though a poet, he drinks like a man. Among the ladies the most noticeable, after the hostess, is Lady Melbourne, called by Byron "as fresh as if only sixteen summers had flown over her, instead of four times that number," and with her her daughter, Emily Mary Lamb (who, having first married in 1805 the fifth Earl Cowper, in 1839 found a second husband in the famous Lord Palmerston). It was Lady Melbourne, described by her second son William, afterwards Prime Minister, as not merely clever and engaging but sagacious beyond all other women, that struck Byron as a sort of modern Aspasia, uniting the energy of a man's mind with the tenderness and delicacy of a woman's. As seen this afternoon at Osterley, adjusting her feathers in the looking-glass above the mantelpiece, she wears on her still beautiful face the exact expression caught by Reynolds in the picture, "Maternal Affection," of herself and her eldest son. At one of Lady Jersey's Osterley parties, too, Lady Melbourne presents to Lord Byron the Miss Milbanke, her niece, who, after having refused him, as well as some half a dozen others once, eventually became the poet's wife. Other foreign notabilities of the time at Osterley were Count Sebastiani, the great Napoleon's ambassador at Naples and London, afterwards, "the Cupid of the Empire," and Napoleon's aide-de-camp, the graceful and accomplished Flahault, who eventually married an Englishwoman whom he first met at Osterley, Margaret Mercer Elphinstone, at one time looked upon by Society as likely to become Lady Byron, and always fondly remembered or regretted by the poet himself. The Osterley of those days was the most cosmopolitan of all the polite world's suburban haunts. The same year, 1814, witnessed among Lady Jersey's guests Hardenberg, Nesselrode, Metternich, the King of Prussia, and the Emperor of Russia. The last of these remained the lion of the whole season. Having been called to a University function at Oxford, he returns in time to go through two country-dances with Mrs. Arbuthnot at Lady Jersey's ball, and to waltz with the hostess herself, much to the disgust of the Regent, who happens to be at feud with Osterley.

Byron appreciated Osterley almost as much as he did Lord Oxford's Herefordshire house. The authentic Byron tradition rooted itself nowhere more deeply than at the Isleworth mansion. The foreigners and English residents abroad during the poet's later years and after his death, recalled at the Osterley dinner-table how, throughout continental Europe, the poet came to be regarded as a personification of Satan in sin and beauty. Some of these visitors had been shown

Goose, Poet and Emperor

by Madame Guiccioli at Ravenna a large box full of
letters from ladies of all ranks and nationalities, offering themselves to him on his own terms.   Others
had seen the play-bills or other odd scraps of paper
on which Byron, with glasses of gin-punch always by
his side, wrote the rough draft of the later cantos of
" Don Juan," or had beheld him rush out of the
room to revise what he had so put down, and perhaps
to read it aloud to Madame Guiccioli herself.   His
theatrical abuse of his native land and its customs
did not prevent his religious observance of English
customs abroad : whether at Rome, Ravenna, or
Athens, he always insisted upon plum-pudding on the
25th of December, hot-cross buns on Good Friday,
and roast goose on Michaelmas Day.   This last
fancy had enabled one at least of the Osterley guests
to witness a droll consequence.   Buying a live goose
at Pisa, that it might be fat enough for September 29th,
he fed it himself daily for more than a fortnight.   As
the fateful day arrived, he found himself so fond of
the creature, that he determined to spare its life and
buy another in its place.   The respited fowl now
began to travel with him, being swung in a cage
under his carriage.   At Osterley, too, some perhaps
even yet living saw with Queen Hortense her son,
then just come of age, the future Napoleon III.   No
remarkable talent, only a fixed idea that some day he
would rule over France ; a figure short but very
active and muscular, a perfect horseman, good at all
athletic games, a grave and dark face, lit by a bright
smile.   Such was the future Emperor as seen by the
Osterley guests in 1829.

From Osterley to Ascot

The last half of the nineteenth century still saw Osterley a fashionable institution, but brought to it some troubles. In 1845 Lady Adela Villiers' elopement with Captain Ibbotson was the scandal of the season. Eleven years later Lady Jersey received a second blow in the death of her other daughter, Lady Clementina. She was no longer the lady paramount of her party, as she had been when she suggested to Disraeli her portrait as the Zenobia of " Endymion." Among the Osterley guests in the spring of 1856 were Disraeli with his wife and Lord Malmesbury. The peer upset the social arrangements by flatly refusing to take Mrs. Disraeli in to dinner. Only the other day, he said, the Dizzies had cut him dead. Lady Jersey's social prerogative had begun to decline when the patronesses of Almack's ceased to be despots. Her place was gradually filled by Queen Victoria's deserved favourite, the Duchess of Sutherland. " That woman," said poor Lady Jersey to one of her Osterley guests, " is cutting me out in everything." The great country houses of England in whatever part have, however, as has been seen in so many instances, the gift of social permanence. With the inevitable changes, Osterley to-day holds its historic position as a parade and rendezvous of Anglo-Saxon fashion and distinction. In the early Victorian age the three most accomplished men of the world then living were Charles Greville, Henry Greville (both of them diarists, but in all other matters of taste, habit, and deportment complete contrasts), and George Payne. Payne, with the social manner of the old world combined the contemptuous dislike of mere aimless frivolity that, if sometimes concealed, has always been the well-bred Englishman's hall-mark. These were all *habitués* of Osterley. So, too, in more recent years, have been their most accomplished successors as experts in mundane wisdom, the three Frasers and Henry Calcraft. To-day, as befits a place owned by a former representative, under the Southern Cross, of the English Crown, Osterley is known throughout the Empire as a social centre free to all duly accredited citizens of Greater Britain. No member of the English governing class to-day realises more keenly than the present possessor of Osterley the differences between the component parts of the British Empire. Among his visitors in 1898 was the one survivor among the signatories of the address to Lord Palmerston at the time of the Don Pacifico affair. This was the third Earl Fortescue, who had been one of Lord Melbourne's private secretaries, and who only died quite recently. " I have been just reading once more," said Lord Jersey, as he pointed to the book on the table, " Ruskin's ' Seven Lamps of Architecture.' My own official experiences at the antipodes bring home to me, as it was never brought home before, his sagacity and truth when he contrasts a country with an immemorial past behind it, like India, through much of which I once travelled, with a land like that in which my own lot was cast, and in which everything is brand new."

Of other mansions in the Isleworth district for size, solidity, and the eventful associations of more than three centuries, none surpasses the southern seat of the Dukes of Northumberland. This historic home of the Percies, as it is conventionally called, was built by Protector Somerset, then came to the Dudleys, who supplied one Duke of Northumberland. After an interval, during which it was a religious house, it passed to the Percy Dukes of Northumberland. The chief creator, however, of the present Sion House was the famous Sir Hugh Smithson. He, having married the daughter of Algernon, Duke of Somerset, and assumed the Percy name, became the first of the modern Dukes of Northumberland. Like most ducal dwellings, Sion and Albury have never condescended so far as to be popular, smart, or even fashionable. The sixth Duke of Northumberland, when Lord Lovaine, marrying the daughter of Henry Drummond, Edward Irving's enthusiastic and important disciple, acquired a connection with Albury Park. This ancient and picturesque spot, not Sion House, is the link uniting a great religious movement in the first half of the nineteenth century with the ducal family which, having inherited Sion House by immemorial right, was indebted for its Surrey home to Henry Drummond's purchase from the Finches, to whom the place had come after its earlier Howard owners. Sion House was probably never visited by Edward Irving. As the scene of the 1826 conferences, Albury became the birthplace of the Catholic and Apostolic Church. So, twenty years later, the Deepdene in the Dorking district was to take rank among the creative forces of modern Conservatism. The genius for religion, once a Jewish possession, united itself in

The Drummond of Fiction and Fact

Edward Irving with perfectly astounding eloquence and a power of personal fascination which increasingly showed itself not more irresistible by others of the class to which Drummond belonged than to Drummond himself. In establishing and developing the new spiritual movement, the organisation of Albury was the indispensable accessory to the pulpit in Hatton Gardens. The shrewd, enthusiastic host of Albury at the date now referred to, remained a conspicuous personage in imperial, as well as local, politics, long after the conferences at his country house had receded into history. The well-known portrait of Henry Drummond in the Greville journals is too serious and at points life-like to be called altogether a caricature. Not till some twenty years after the Albury conferences did his blue coat, white waistcoat, and plaid cravat become objects almost as familiar at St. Stephen's as the Speaker's wig and mace. Seeing everything through Whig spectacles, Greville deliberately caricatures Drummond's spiritual enthusiasm, and, as he thought, fanatical devotion to Irving. He is silent on the Parliamentary shrewdness and political wisdom of the sagacious and broad-minded Conservative squire; Drummond, while member for West Surrey, was habitually consulted on vital points of policy by Disraeli, when Chancellor of the Exchequer in the Derby Administration that replaced (1852) Lord John Russell's Government, defeated by Palmerston's influence on the Militia Bill. On March 5, 1852, Drummond had written to Disraeli a characteristic letter of humorous advice. Patrick Boyle Smollett's robust outspokenness, Bernal Osborne's

From Osterley to Ascot

satiric humour, and W. E. Henley's Nestorian, sar-
castic wisdom, were united in this Surrey host.
Having received Disraeli as his guest at Albury,
Drummond recapitulated his counsel to his visitor in
a letter, first, I think, published in the *Quarterly
Review* (October, 1895),[1] enclosing a sketch of a
Conservative Reform Bill, to be held *in petto*, and to
be brought forward only in case of dire necessity,
Drummond advises the "buying of Bright, Gibson,
and a host of other revolutionary blackguards." As
for the Albury conferences, held during the first
quarter of the nineteenth century, these, if he had not
known them before, introduced Irving to Perceval,
son of the former Premier, shot in the Lobby of the
House of Commons, and to Dr. Joseph Wolff, who
also assisted at one at least of the meetings. All these
were outlived by a member of the group, an aged
lawyer, who, when he passed away some years since,
must have been quite the oldest of the Albury fathers ;
though to a period only ten years later than the
conferences belongs a still living member of the
Catholic Apostolic Church, Sir J. H. A. Macdonald,
formerly a Scotch University M.P. The communion
perpetuating Edward Irving's name is now equipped
with stately churches in many places. The Surrey
home of the ducal owners of Sion House remains,
however, the spiritual headquarters of the faithful.

At other centres of social interest that abound in
the region watered by the Thames we must be
satisfied now with flying calls rather than settled

---

[1] It will be found on page 363, incorporated in the article
"Rival Leaders and Party Legacies."

visits. In 1780, George III.'s favourite minister, Lord North, who then seemed almost a fixture in Downing Street, possessed a house of his own at the south-east corner of Grosvenor Square. Never disguising from himself his precarious tenure of Downing Street, he would not let his private abode for more than a year; generally occupied by newly married couples, it was known by the name of "Honeymoon Hall." To see the minister really at home, his friends went to him at Bushey Park, the rangership of which, held by his wife, gave him a country house rich in social charm. Surrounded by his daughters, with the high spirits of a boy, he lived simply, diffusing gaiety and good humour round his family and visitors. So, at least, thought his old opponent Barré. This former champion of the Whig opposition to North, paying a business call at the suburban villa, to his surprise found himself seated at the luncheon table. Both host and guest had been overtaken by nearly complete blindness. After some allusion to past passages of arms, North smilingly said, "But now, Colonel, there are not two men in England who could be more happy to see each other." The eighteenth-century Bushey, therefore, presented in its happiest aspect that type of animated geniality which set an enduring fashion of social deportment for English statesmen.

Within an easy drive of Bushey was the beloved rural retirement of the man who was alternately North's most truculent opponent and most important ally. From 1797 Charles Fox, having sulked out of the House of Commons, took to horticulture,

From Osterley to Ascot

scholarship, letters, and domesticity at St. Anne's Hill, Chertsey. Here, as he walked in the garden before breakfast, he wished aloud "good morning" to the mist-covered hills in the distance. They were not forgotten when, in July, 1802, he went with Rogers to Paris, in quest of materials for his work on James II. On a tropically hot day his companion, as they walked through the Louvre gallery, now talked to him about the surrounding objects of art, now amused him with some story as to the way in which the Paris exquisites were making it the fashion "to ape Mr. Fox." For the afternoon an interview with the great Napoleon had been arranged. In the hurry of his different movements, Fox hopelessly mislaid all the notes for his book, for whose making he had journeyed from the Surrey hills to the Seine. That did not trouble him. When coming out of the Louvre into the full glare of the summer day, his only fear was, "This hot sun will burn up my turnips at St. Anne's Hill." At St. Anne's Hill, when Secretary of State in 1782, he received Sir George, then Mr., Jackson for final instructions on an important foreign mission. On the visitor being announced, Mrs. Fox, *en déshabillé*, had slipped into a cupboard or closet opening out of the room. The interview was prolonged; the lady, becoming impatient, was heard to exclaim, "Mr. Fox, my dear, surely the young man's gone. Can't I come out, dear, I am so very cold?" Some five-and-twenty years later the scene had changed to Chiswick House; Fox lay sick unto death. The same lady, bending over him, received the dying man's last words, "I die happy, Liz." The news of all being over was too terrible to be formally announced at the not distant Holland House. There the only intimation of the end having come showed itself in Lady Holland, speechless and weeping, walking about with her apron over her head. For years Fox used to accomplish the journey between St. Anne's Hill and Holland House on foot. On one of these walks, having no money, he left his watch as security at a wayside tavern for a mug of porter. On reaching St. Anne's Hill, whither he was bound, he found the publican had already left the chronometer with the servant. At his Chertsey house in the evening of his life, Fox had received the call of Grey with an offer of a peerage from the King. "No, not yet," was the answer, "I have an oath in heaven against it ; nor will I end like others in that foolish way." From St. Anne's Hill, too, a visitor, Edward Gibbon, brought away the impression of his host's first-rate powers blended with the softness and simplicity of a child, without a taint of malevolence, vanity, or falsehood. Here another guest, Lavater, the phrenologist, made the scientific observations which caused him to record as the most marked features in Fox's physiognomy the "development of the imaginative and ideal organs, the imperial eyebrows, the sensual cheeks, and the magical genius of the eyes."

Between 1865 and 1878, not far from the entrance into Richmond Park, there might be seen, sitting under the verandah of the first house one reaches, a little, shrunken, old man, sometimes reading or talking, but more often, as it seemed, intently studying a scientific instrument that, standing at his side, indicated not only the quarter, but the exact force of any breeze which happened to be blowing. The student of this wind-gauge, then living at Pembroke Lodge, was the Earl Russell of that day, the famous Lord John of an earlier epoch. There he received many guests or callers ; the only ones personally recalled by the present writer were the then Mr. M. E. Grant-Duff and Mr. Henry Calcraft, of the Board of Trade. Sometimes there came to Pembroke Lodge Professor Owen from his neighbouring cottage, Charles Dickens the novelist, and his future biographer, John Forster. In the talk on these occasions Forster and Russell took the leading part, recalling more than once Napoleon III. in his early London days. The only sign of intellectual promise they both agreed in having ever recognised in him, was a clever description of his being had up before the magistrate at Bow Street. The venerable Whig sage slightly shook his head in gentle dissent, saying, " One of your brother novelists, Mr. Dickens, showed himself more far-seeing. Bulwer Lytton, who often met Louis Napoleon at Gore Lodge, received from him the present of a book, in whose fly-leaf, after the donor's signature, he pencilled the prediction that Louis Napoleon would one day be great in France. Lytton based the prophecy on Napoleon's devotion to one idea and the skill with which that devotion was masked." Other notable utterances by famous men were first heard at Pembroke Lodge. Brought there

Shaving at Shepperton

by G. S. Venables, Carlyle, remarking that he had many objections to the Church of England, said he nevertheless thought it the best thing of the kind in the world, and that he was therefore sorry to see it falling to pieces and going the way of all the earth. As for Napoleon III., Carlyle only lamented there was not a strong angel of the Lord with a great sword reaching from one end of France to the other, to sweep it across and to say to the endless talking "Peace!" Carlyle also expressed to Russell a high opinion of the then Bishop of Oxford, Wilberforce. "I met him," recalled the sage one day; "we were both of us on horseback. He was going, he said, to the dog show; I turned round and went with him. He stayed there two hours. I found him a delightful companion, a most active, ardent creature, bound to succeed better than every one else in anything he was set to do."

Another great social meeting ground of celebrities in the suburban district now visited was Sir Coutts Lindsay's roof at Shepperton. Here John Bright passed the Sunday before delivering his famous speech on the desolations wrought by the Crimean War. This oration he partly rehearsed to the Shepperton company upon the lawn on Sunday afternoon, but not the famous Angel of Death simile which immortalised it. "You did not," said Lindsay to Bright, after the speech had been reported, "give us that bit." "No," was the reply, "it came into my head while I was shaving at your house on Monday morning." The nineteenth-century table-talk of this suburban district would constitute the contemporary story of Parliament and policy, foreign or domestic, from behind the scenes. Bright would be heard disclaiming, as too much trouble, the reputation of writing out his speeches before delivery. " I make pretty full notes," he said, "but often do not use them. Cobden, like Disraeli, and like myself" (he added with a smile), " when I get the chance, used no writing preparation, but talked his speech over beforehand." Few dwellings in any part of England are more suggestive of the social continuity characteristic of England's rural homes than Strawberry Hill, Twickenham. The ideas and interests represented at this spot have differed in successive epochs. Under all dispensations the influence, social or intellectual, exercised has been equally far-reaching. What Holland House was not only up to, as Macaulay's well-known description of it might seem to imply, but through, a great portion of the Victorian age, Strawberry Hill remained without a break till the death of the most famous among its modern hostesses. Lady Carlingford, as she eventually became, was married first to Mr. Waldegrave. She took for her second husband his brother, Lord Waldegrave. She next married a cousin of the late Lord Granville, Mr. George Harcourt. Her last marriage was with Chichester Fortescue, Gladstone's Irish Secretary ; he thought out the details of the Gladstone Irish Land Bill at Strawberry Hill ; this most distinguished of her various lords was so fondly attached to her that his friends at first scarcely dared to hope he

"Labby" at Home

would survive her loss. Her power of attaching
all sorts and conditions of people and of never
losing a friend remained with her throughout life ;
it was curiously illustrated by the composition of her
house-parties. Whoever her husband for the time
might be, the relations of his predecessors were
always copiously represented beneath her roof. The
Fortescues of the last dispensation mingled on the
most happy and intimate of terms with the Walde-
graves and Harcourts of earlier *régimes*. An im-
partial and irresistible *bonhomie* always accompanied
the tact with which she issued her invitations and
the kindly cleverness with which she received her
guests, of all political or indeed religious creeds and
of almost all classes.

Near Strawberry Hill, during the Waldegrave
period, flourished other hosts who conspired to
justify for the river near which they lived the
cosmopolitan character to-day so eminently belonging to the Thames. At Pope's Villa, Mr. Henry
Labouchere gathered together smart diplomatists
like the then Lord St. Asaph or Mr. Percy French ;
Parliamentary experts in foreign affairs, such as the
surviving Sir Arthur Otway and the late Lord
Henry Lennox—a born orator if ever ducal house
produced one ; operatic prima-donnas like Patti ;
theatrical artists such as John Hare and Henry
Irving. About the same time, too, the intelligent
foreigner who had his nocturnal heaven at the
Cosmopolitan Club in Charles Street, found his
daylight paradise at York House, Twickenham,
then occupied by Sir Mountstuart E. Grant-Duff.

From Osterley to Ascot

There, week by week, constantly changing, but always interesting, assembled a company more representatively international than at any other point on the Thames littoral. Ernest Renan, when visiting England, was generally beneath the roof of his British proxenus. Here a future Prime Minister of Republican France, Monsieur Ribot, more Anglicised in the grave formality of his aspect than the French Ambassador Waddington himself, first became acquainted with English political notabilities — with Mr. Joseph Chamberlain, then giving his earliest promise of future greatness; with William Rathbone, who as member for Liverpool filled at St. Stephen's the same kind of place as before him had been held by Mr. Whitbread. To make Macaulay's omniscient "every schoolboy" a familiar phenomenon in actual life was the tendency of the York House hospitalities, ornamented as these were by the miscellaneously learned—in Parliamentry lore almost infallible—Thomas Erskine May, who became Lord Farnborough only a few days before his death; by Lord Arthur Russell, quietly overflowing with the intellectual quality that his fellow-guest, Renan, happily styled "*la grande curiosité*"; by Sir John Lubbock, the Lord Avebury of to-day, whose temperament and manner, ever freshened by an inbred courtesy and alertness of varied interest, suggested then as it suggests still, an adaptation of Bulwer's words about the fourteenth Lord Derby in " The New Timon "—" time still leaves all Eton in the boy." At Lord Avebury's High Elms, already visited, W. E. Gladstone and John Morley had met

What Happened at York House

some years before. The first set conference of the statesman with his future Cabinet colleague and biographer took place May 18, 1879, in an apartment that might have been transplanted from the Granada Alhambra to the banks of the Thames, the drawing-room of Sir M. E. Grant-Duff's York House. In other parts of the house or in the grounds bordering the river might, in that period if not on that particular day, have been seen, if not Benjamin Jowett, yet the most intellectually gifted of Jowett's Balliol contemporaries, Henry Smith, the pride and pillar of mathematical and scientific Oxford, but scarcely less great in classical scholarship also. There, too, was Lord Reay, who since then has passed from the Government of Bombay to the chairmanship of the London School Board. Wherever he may have been, in the country house as in the London club or drawing-room, by the breadth of his sympathies and the quick penetration of his insight, he still shows himself a true disciple of the York House school. One day he may be in office, the next in opposition. Neither the burden of the former lot nor the freedom of the other interferes with his wider and more delicate usefulness in brightening and sweetening as well as in instructing the refined cosmopolitanism whose most representative centre was found in the last century beneath the roof of Sir Mountstuart and Lady Grant-Duff. The creation of a better understanding between the leaders, political or literary, of English and foreign thought was the beneficent object of all their hospitalities. The death of this host was, therefore, an international loss. Nor could anything be more characteristic of his social function and aim than a letter from him shortly before his death, addressed to the present writer and containing these words : " The Governments and Chanceries of Europe would get on in perfect peace with each other but for a press always trying to excite jealousies and stir up bad feeling. It is a disgusting spectacle, and I thank God I am more than seventy years of age."

" I and my friends," one of Grant-Duff's most frequent guests, Matthew Arnold, used to say, " lived at the Oxford of our day as in a great country house." That gives no bad idea of the little, old, unreformed Oxford, occupied by the sons of the aristocracy, of untitled landowners, of well-to-do clergymen, and of the pick of the professional or commercial class. No interval of roads lined with villa residences, mutilated by tramcars, noisy and malodorous with automobiles, then separated the gates of the colleges from the green country lanes. It was not only the Oxford of the cloister but of the middle ages. Amid such surroundings as these grew, in the nineteenth century's first half, the scheme for rehabilitating the national Church, promoted by Newman, Pusey, and others. Whatever the view taken, the movement was an imposing one, full of humbling awe to some and of exultation to others. The idea animating the Oxford Anglicans of the thirties was the presence and operation of the Holy Spirit, not like the wind " blowing where it listeth," but communicating itself by ceremonial channels. A vast spiritual edifice consisted of a multitude of individuals ; all, however, could be identified as parts of the one structure. This unity involved the assumption of every bishop being directly descended from the Apostles, from whom they had in unbroken succession, at the moment of their consecration, received the special gift of the Spirit. The ecclesiastical policy of Whiggism had filled the Oriel divines with a disgust and dread of the Reform spirit, civil or ecclesiastical, then in the air. The Oriel common-room was the home of good breeding, of the grand manner, as well as of faith, learning, and virtue. The primitive High Churchism of the nineteenth century began by being intensely aristocratic and above all things anti-Liberal. Social privilege was an article of religious faith. The Hursley curates wept because Corn Law Abolition obliged their squire to put down one of his carriage horses. The early Anglicanism, therefore, found its natural home in the Tory country houses, within easy distance of the uniformly Tory colleges, and its chief leader in him whose connection with the territorial class caused J. H. Newman to speak of him emphatically as "the Great." This was E. B. Pusey, the descendant of an ancient stock of substantial Berkshire squires. His father, the first Lord Folkestone's son, and so born a Bouverie, had assumed the Pusey name on inheriting the Pusey estates. These had been in the family from the tenth century. Pusey House, near Farringdon, Berks, has always been a Tory centre, and when Philip Pusey, a Protectionist, sat for Berkshire, was Lord George

From Osterley to Ascot

Bentinck's recruiting ground. The value of such a social centre as this to the Oxford Anglicans was appreciated by no one more than by the future head of the Birmingham Oratory. It was his ancestral connection with this place rather than any other qualifications for the office which gave E. B. Pusey the leadership of the Oxford movement. Another country house nearer to Oxford than Pusey often opened its doors to the Anglican reformers, not as Church partisans but as guests. This was Nuneham, through whose park the friends often rode. Newman and Pusey were both fair horsemen and kept their own hacks. Archbishop Harcourt, to whom Nuneham then belonged, may not have had much in common with the Anglican ideal ; the sacerdotal and sacramental notions of the set did but very gradually, it must be remembered, declare and develop themselves. To their Nuneham host the visitors from Christ Church and Oriel would have seemed intellectual Tories of the most orthodox kind, exactly after his own heart ; with delight he would have heard R. Hurrell Froude satirising the strange creatures who had got into the new Parliament. " Fancy a gentleman, as one supposes an M. P. to be, not knowing Greek ! " That would have pleasantly recalled to Nuneham's archiepiscopal host a sentence in the University sermon of another guest, Dean Gaisford, often approvingly quoted at the Nuneham dinner-table : " The chief advantages of a classical education are that it opens up posts of emolument both in this world and that which is to come, and that it enables us to look down on our inferiors."

"Less than your Mother's Pin-money"

Newman, moreover, during his early days as fellow and tutor of Oriel, was not only not a Romaniser, but as low a Churchman as had been John Wesley himself when Methodism began to take shape within the walls of Lincoln College.

Another Berkshire country house in the Pusey neighbourhood at the close of the eighteenth century had connected itself with a movement, more or less intellectual, of a kind very different from that associated with Pusey or Nuneham. If one is in London one must play to be in the fashion ; if one is out of it, without cards one would die of *ennui*. Mrs. Montagu and her friends attempted to mend matters by parties at which no cards should dull the edge of intellect, and all the mental powers be perfectly fresh for conversation. The London dwelling that witnessed the beginnings of this experiment was in Hill Street, Berkeley Square. The rural home which saw its further elaboration was the Berkshire Sandilands. Mrs. Montagu, the most frugal of social and fashionable leaders, at the last house-party ever given at Sandilands, boasted to her guests of having built and furnished both her Mayfair and her Berkshire abode from the savings of an income of £6,000 a year. "You will soon," she whispered to her nephew and heir, Matthew Montagu, "find the advantage of having had an aunt who could organise and entertain the blue-stockings in country as well as town at a less cost than your own mother's pin-money." Certain visits of Mrs. Montagu to Nuneham were discovered by a great expert in her epoch, Sir William Harcourt,

445

during the short time of his possessing and inhabiting his family home. At Nuneham was he staying when he lost, in 1880, his seat for Oxford, conferring, before he drove back from the town, the final benediction on his erstwhile constituents. " And now, good people, go home quietly, and God bless you every one." The sentiment recalled to a ribald critic the captain in Marryat's novel who, cautioned by the Admiralty against inordinate swearing, from the point of command exclaimed to a seaman, " You've tied a granny's-knot instead of a slip-knot, God bless you ! You know what I mean ! "

To the country-house era of Oxford, as Matthew Arnold called it, as indeed the place remained for many a long day afterwards, the pleasant districts wherein lie the mansions now mentioned seemed but the outskirts of a wide-stretching college park. That description would have held at least periodically true throughout much of the nineteenth century. Charles Reade, the novelist, was then established during part of the Long Vacation at his rooms in Magdalen, and entertained Saturday-to-Monday guests from the Athenæum and the Garrick Clubs. At the adjacent Queen's were Robert Steward Falcon, of the fine presence and magnificent golden beard, the best scholar of his day, a former " Ireland," and his brother-fellow Dykes, the model of an old world country squire, the one shooting over and the other managing the College estates. The best part of the Victorian age had therefore gone by before at least one Oxford college parted with some among the most characteristic and robust features of a genially

Rusticating on the Isis

intellectual country house. Falcon's latest provost was a fine old English gentleman of the best squarson type, Dr. Jackson. His successor, Dr. Magrath, lacks no qualification for practically perpetuating the best social traditions of the old *régime* in the college that under his rule has produced its first " Ireland " scholar since Falcon, half a century ago. Long before Queen's second " Ireland " the typical Oxford college had resumed, if indeed it had ever entirely lost, those social aspects which bring it as much within the country - house category as any private mansion known to Society's Arcadia. Benjamin Jowett abounded in kindly and hospitable instincts. His roof and table were perpetually available for young and old to whom he thought it might be an object to avoid hotel bills. He was, however, by no means the original inventor and patentee of Society's modern Saturday-to-Monday sojourn on the Isis. H. G. Liddell's bi-terminal gatherings at the Deanery, Christ Church, had attracted Whig or Liberal states-men and other celebrities, before as well as after the conversion to Free Trade of another Christ Church man, at one time Liddell's particular friend, Sir Robert Peel. On the other side, the college of Archbishop Laud and of Dean Mansel had, under President Wynter, been at the head of Oxford's Tory houses. Jowett's parties, both in the rooms occupied by him as a tutor, looking out upon the Martyrs' Memorial, and at the Master's Lodge, were the adaptation to new social conditions of the some-what earlier hospitalities of Pattison at Lincoln and Wynter at St. John's. None of these reunions were

From Osterley to Ascot

less essentially country-house rites because they were presided over by the head of an Oxford house instead of by the lord of some rural manor. With Disraeli, Gathorne Hardy, and other party managers among the guests, the new academic Conservatism socially organised itself beneath the roof of the President of St. John's, while at Balliol or Lincoln was being evolved the comprehensively national Oxford which now exists. Loyalty to Tory leaders was the virtue that the St. John's hospitalities tended to evoke and strengthen. A representative diversity of *personnel* had been studied by Pattison at Lincoln, and was still more piquantly cultivated at Balliol.

All these academic entertainers said many good things. Their form, and the circumstances under which they were first uttered, have conspired to bestow the widest currency upon Jowett's. Such was his reply to the young lady's "Won't you marry me, Master?" "Certainly not; it would not be to my happiness or yours." Of course the girl had alluded to the priestly performance of the nuptial ceremony. Again, to some of his guests, who had shown a disposition to risky stories over the coffee, "Don't you think we had better finish that anecdote with the ladies upstairs?" Dean Stanley, Archbishop Tait, R. W. Dale, the Birmingham Congregationalist preacher, mingled with the chief High Churchmen, Talbot, head of Keble, and H. P. Liddon, in Jowett's academic country-house company. So, too, at one time did Lord Selborne's brother, William Palmer, the dream of whose life was a union between the Greek and the Anglican Churches. A lady of his

" As Thou Killedst the Egyptian "

acquaintance had been so misguided as to exchange subjection to the Pope for allegiance to the Patriarch. " I will," said Palmer, in a fever of righteous indignation, " devote all my energies, resources, and opportunities to making her regret what she has done." " Rather," chirruped Jowett, " a poor ambition for an entire lifetime." Talbot, a good scholar but a bad coachman, had upset into a ditch, from a carriage in which he was driving him, the then Khedive's son, Prince Hassan. Proposing, at Jowett's table, to drive Liddon home, he received the reply, " What, intendest thou to kill me, as thou killedst the Egyptian yesterday ? " It was at the Balliol Lodge that, soon after the event had happened in July, 1873, some people from Lord Granville, then a guest, heard for the first time the account of Bishop Wilberforce's fatal fall from his horse on Evershed Roughs. The Bishop and the Foreign Secretary, asked to meet the Gladstones at Mr. Leveson-Gower's Holmbury, were to do the last part of the journey thither on horseback, riding from Leatherhead fifteen miles over the Surrey downs. " The first I knew of the accident," said Lord Granville, " was the dull, dead sound of a falling body on the grass. Hoping against hope that life might not be extinct, I sent away the groom to get some conveyance, and was meanwhile left with the Bishop alone. It was an agonising ordeal. Before a carriage came, all was over." The nearest house was Lord Farrer's Abinger Hall. Thither the body was taken ; there it remained till the funeral in Lavington churchyard, already described in the Sussex section of this book.

From Osterley to Ascot

The temporary resting place of the dead prelate was one of a group of pleasant habitations in the district, the best known, perhaps, belonging to Sir Algernon West, Mr. Pandeli Ralli, the late Mr. Simpson, the Chancery lawyer, and the late Charles W. Earle. At Cranleigh, near Guildford, Mr. Ralli, then in the House, and his sister first introduced to Society here the greatest of modern Greek statesmen, then the Hellenic Premier, Tricoupis, and other Greek representatives at St. James's, Gennadius first, and afterwards M. Metaxas. Fellow-guests at the same time with these were Gladstone, Lord Fitzmaurice, and the present Lord Kitchener, who in those days had a delightful way of politely fencing off the personal questions as to the military school in which he had been trained for the greatness that seemed, with so little of preliminary advertisement, to have come to him. "'Specs," would blandly say the future Indian Commander-in-chief, "like Topsy, I growed." Other houses hereabout belonged generally to men moving in the same set as Sir Mountstuart Grant-Duff. Their most habitual guests were those who might also have been met at York House, Twickenham, in the Grant-Duff epoch. Such pre-eminently was Hatchlands, the home of Lord Rendel, one of the loyal Gladstonians whose amenities of person and of entertainment rendered Liberalism the same kind of social service which in an earlier generation it had received from Mrs. Milner Gibson's receptions at her house in Brook Street or beneath one of her rural roofs. At the Hatchlands dinner-table the host made one of those particularly neat remarks in which he excelled and which ought not to be forgotten. It was the supremely triumphant moment of the Jingo cult, of Lord Beaconsfield's and Lord Salisbury's bringing back of peace with honour from the Berlin Conference. "The truth is," quietly observed Lord Rendel, "Dizzy has taken John Bull to Cremorne and the old fellow rather likes it." Samuel Wilberforce, as Bishop of Oxford or of Winchester, pervaded most of the South of England houses now being visited. The agreeable prelate himself made Cuddesdon palace the model of a clerical country house. Two of his young friends from their colleges in the adjoining University, who had given the authorities some trouble, winning the nicknames of Hophni and Phinehas, were lounging about the hall singing the Lutheran refrain, " The Devil is dead." The Bishop walked very gently up to them, and in his most caressing manner, placing one hand on each head, said, in a consolatory tone, " Alas, poor orphans ! " The place where Bishop Wilberforce seemed at his best was Sarsden Rectory, then occupied by his old friend, Charles Barter. The other guest on the occasion now referred to was the then Earl of Shrewsbury, a famous critic of rare vintages. In his honour had been produced over night a super-excellent bottle of red wine. The peer, judiciously sipping a few drops, slowly gave his verdict. " This is the best second-class claret I ever tasted." The Sarsden Rectory garden was bounded by a little fence leading into what steeplechasers call a fair hunting country. The Bishop was late for a diocesan visitation for which he had made Sarsden his head-quarters. " By taking that cut," said our host, pointing

to the railing, "we shall be in good time after all."
At it accordingly they all went—first the rector giving
a friendly lead, then the bishop with a chaplain or
two, and the village curate bringing up the rear.
" Bishop," said a little girl, nestling up to him after
the day's labours in the drawing-room, " why do they
call you Soapy Sam ? " " Because, my dear, I am
always getting into hot water and coming out with my
hands clean." At the dinner-table of Wilberforce,
whose curate he had once been, Archbishop Trench
thought himself overtaken by his life-long terror,
paralysis. " At last," he murmured, " it has come.
Total insensibility of the right side." " It may
console you," said the lady next to whom he was
sitting, " to know it was *my* leg you were pinching."
About this time it was that Wilberforce, charged
by his most frequent lay-guest, Lord Houghton,
with having imputed to him an offensive expression,
indicating an emphatic dissent, explained, " What I
did say was, that had such and such an expression
been, as I was informed, actually used by the noble
lord, those who knew him less well than I did might
have thought it verging on the unsavoury."

To pass on to one or two more secularly sporting
hosts within easy distance of the country hunted by
the Bicester hounds. At the Durdans, just out of
Epsom, Lord Rosebery occasionally received guests
quite as noticeable and interesting as those who came
to him for Epsom week. When at Oxford he had
read the " Ethics " with the cleverest if least conventional Aristotelian scholar and teacher of his day. This
gifted man, Robert Williams, eventually exchanged

Uncle Sam Purrs

Oxford for the bar and for journalism. In these latter capacities he fell upon evil days; he was not forgotten by Lord Rosebery as he had been by so many others. With him at the Durdans might sometimes be seen both the then Sir Edward Lawson, now Lord Burnham, chief proprietor of the *Daily Telegraph*, and one of his most accomplished writers, the late Frank Lawley, who, in his younger days, had been everywhere, known every one, done everything, and run through a considerable fortune. "My dear Lawley," said one of the company in reference to his recent *Daily Telegraph* "Reminiscences of Limmer's," "how did you get such an inexhaustible knowledge of rapid life in every conceivable aspect?" "By," was the answer, "an expenditure on the learning of exactly £333,000." During Lord Rosebery's most hospitable years at the Durdans, the most frequent intellectual guest outside the fashionable sporting set was Mr. G. W. Smalley, then representing in London the *New York Tribune*. Occasional companions on his Epsom visits were Mr. F. Marion Crawford, Mr. Henry James, the novelist, and the late Samuel Ward, better known as " Uncle Sam," a well-groomed, sleek, silky little old gentleman who, as a compliment to a clerical fellow-guest, the Rev. " Hang-Theology " Rogers, of St. Botolph's, used to make a show of occasionally quoting Horace, and if petted enough by any ladies who might be present used audibly to purr. The Ascot houses would be a more prolific theme even than the Epsom roofs. The forerunner of the latter-day Ascot host who rents or own a villa near the heath and fills it with guests of all sorts and con-

453

ditions, was, I think, a Mr. Angerstein, whose drolly hospitable *ménage* is probably to-day remembered by Mr. John Delaval and the present writer. At a neighbouring small villa the luckless Marquis of Hastings spent the last summer he was ever destined to see on earth. It was the race week, and he wished to make a bet with a professional bookmaker whom he saw a few paces off. The fellow, huge, hulking, and insolent, lounged up to the pony-carriage in which the taker of odds was being driven by his beautiful wife. " Mind, my lord," said the man, with something between a scowl and a sneer on his face, " I shall expect this bet to be paid."

CHAPTER XVI

THE NEW HOSTS OF THE HOME COUNTIES

455

The New Hosts of the Home Counties

IT was the Berkshire and Oxfordshire country houses generally which, visited by Alexis Tocqueville and other nineteenth-century guests, received from them the name of the finishing schools for English conversationalists. Here, they said, dwelt the charming art of touching and setting in motion a thousand thoughts, without dwelling tiresomely on any one. Except that the long-imperfect avenue leading to the house has been completed, Mr. Albert Brassey's Heythrop is unchanged since the days when the irrepressible Mrs. Duncan Stewart exhausted the possibilities of small-talk in " History Hut." One story she never forgot, the interview of her daughter, a lady-in-waiting at the Court of Hanover, with George Sand, and the novelist's reply to some criticism on her writings, " Je ne suis pas moraliste ; je suis romancière." About the same time, at Kingston Lisle or at the home of the Barringtons, a large, luxurious Tudor house, Beckett, near Shrivenham, used to be the Berkshire worthy, Squire Aitkins, who figures as the hero's father in Hughes' " Tom Brown " (both the Rugby and the Oxford books). With him were old Lady Stanley of Alderley, from her beautiful Holmwood, Henley-on-Thames, furious in the thoroughness and tenacity of her opinions, but the brightest and easiest of guests, as well as, at her own pretty place with its wealth of flowerbeds and grandchildren, the most popular of hostesses. Oxfordshire, like the neighbouring county of Northampton, contains one of the comparatively few houses which, from being social strongholds of the seventeenth-century democratic movement, have ever since formed the neutral ground for Whig and Tory alike.

David Copperfield at Broughton

Broughton Castle, Lord Saye-and-Sele's, and the equally ancient home of the Knightleys, Fawsley, both lay on the great north road from London. Each possessed a private printing-press belonging to the Parliamentarians. A key of each was in John Pym's pocket during his political campaigns in the vacation before the Long Parliament. Thus he could, and sometimes did, enter the bedroom set apart for him, without his arrival being heard of till the next morning. Our grandparents knew Broughton Castle as the place to which George V. of Hanover, introduced by his private tutor, Canon Jelf, of Oxford, first became a personage in English society. Dr. Jelf, a stately ornament of the old world Oxford, married one of the Hanover Court ladies, the Countess Schlippenbach. In this way it may be that Broughton was so often in the mouths of fashionable and patrician Germans of the time. At Broughton possibly was first heard the story of the blindness which overtook Jelf's royal pupil in 1833, having been caused by the collision with the eye of a long silk purse whisked round too vigorously and too closely. Owned by the cricketing family of Fiennes, Broughton has more recently been known for its private theatricals. Here, in the days of Mr. Fiennes and Lady Augusta, the most ubiquitous country-house figure of his time, Mr. Augustus Hare, in a dramatic adaptation of some parts of the novel, played David Copperfield to Lord Saye-and-Sele's Steerforth. Only a few years earlier, in the same drawing-room where these theatricals took place, Lady Granville related the secret history of the Battle of the Nile as she had heard it from her first husband. Born a Dalberg, she had married into another international family as famous as her own, that of the Actons. Her husband's father, Sir John Acton, was the famous admiral, the English generalissimo on sea and land of the Neapolitan King, Ferdinand IV. During the year 1798, in which he had driven the French from the South of Italy, the enemy's fleet had seemed to escape into invisible space. Lady Acton's French maid had a brother a seaman on a French man-o'-war. Unable herself to read a letter received from him, she asked her mistress's help in deciphering it. Its address gave the clue to the whereabouts of Napoleon's warships. The information, passed on to Nelson enabled him to come up with and defeat the hostile squadrons in Aboukir Bay.

The Daylesford of Warren Hastings stands so near the point at which four counties converge, that it may almost rank as the common possession of Oxford, Gloucester, and Worcester. Not from Broughton but from Sarsden, whose squire was then J. H. Langston, M.P. for Oxford City, reputed in his time the best timber-jumper in the shires, frequent excursions to Daylesford were enlivened by the personal recollections of the place possessed both by Lady Granville and Lady Ducie. Daylesford itself, then owned and occupied by Mr. Grisewood, a City magnate, was hospitably open for the inspection of visitors. Having been repurchased by Warren Hastings in 1788, it remained for the rest of his life the home where he sometimes entertained Anglo-Indian or political acquaintances, but more frequently some of the few

Hatfield Archery

survivors among his contemporaries at Westminster School. Lady Ducie's memory did not go back to this, the greatest of the Daylesford squires. She had, however, been acquainted with Hastings' step-son. On his voyage to India, the great proconsul fell in love with the married lady who before land was reached had in all but name become his wife. This was the Countess Inhoff. To the son by her former marriage Hastings left Daylesford. The Countess herself, dressed in white satin and swansdown, like one of Romney's pictures, used to pay state visits to Lady Ducie at Tortworth in Gloucestershire. The one change in connection with Daylesford, as the present writer saw it in the sixties, since its great owner's time, was the modern building with which Mr. Grisewood had replaced the Saxon church, restored in the tenth century of its existence by Hastings, with the text, "A thousand years in Thy sight are but as yesterday."

Among the gifts accepted by Queen Victoria from the last of her Prime Ministers was a miniature reproduction in silver of certain objects at Hatfield, especially associated with Queen Elizabeth's stay beneath that Hertfordshire roof, itself too famous in its history and too universally familiar in its chief features to call for any specification of them now. Always a social citadel of Toryism, Hatfield politically stood apart from most of the other great houses in the county. The first Marchioness, Lord Downshire's daughter, was a skilful and enthusiastic archer. Her garden parties, from 1789 onwards, first associated Hatfield and the surrounding district with the revival of the bow and arrow as a pastime both fashionable and popular. This lady lived to November, 1835, when, at the age of eighty-four, she perished in the fire which destroyed the west wing of her home. Long after political differences had separated the two men, common sympathies on some matters of State and on many more of Church, brought Mr. Gladstone for an occasional week-end to the Hertfordshire home of the Cecils. What, however, will be chiefly recalled by those of Hatfield's nineteenth century still-surviving visitors is the imposing figure of the host himself, courteous and kindly, even when visibly preoccupied by public anxieties, or worn and haggard by concern he could not conceal for Lady Salisbury's health, always at work with his secretaries to the last moment before every meal, and then stalking slowly into the room, invariably accompanied by his great boarhound, Pharaoh, "so called because he will not let the people go." Among their fellow-guests they will remember Lady Lytton, still beautiful with all the charm of high-bred refinement, the Prince of Wales, now King Edward VII., the Grand-Duke of Baden, and the two most characteristically different talkers of their time, Maria, Marchioness of Ailesbury, and Count Herbert Bismarck, the latter flinging each of his sentences from him with an air of defiant self-assertion. A big man this, as well as a big eater and drinker, filling, upon principle, two glasses of wine at once, so as always to have one in reserve, in a chronic state of surprise at the hard-worked Salisbury ladies, ever going, as he complains, to found or open charities, patriotically denying that Anne of Cleves came after Anne Boleyn, seldom missing a chance, in season or out of season, of girding at the faculty. " In medicine," he growls out, "you will never be sure of effect following cause till the doctor's brougham precedes his patient's body to the grave." To Lord Selborne, his next-door neighbour, he confides a very ancient "chestnut" from Munchausen, who talks of keeping the College of Physicians up in a balloon a month, sending them down to find all the sick restored, but all the undertakers ruined.

On the occasion of the last visit paid by King Edward VII., when Prince of Wales, to Hatfield, some readers of these lines will, like their writer, recollect a patriotic vindication of the English climate as the best in the world made by the royal guest in particularly happy, epigrammatic French when talking to the then Ambassador from the Republic, at one of the garden-parties that, under the third Marchioness's dispensation, were the tolerably frequent incidents of the Hatfield summer. Lady Salisbury, as a hostess, was distinguished by her unaffected kindliness of manner towards, and air of personal interest in, the family belongings of those innumerable visitors, comparatively few of whom she might have been expected personally to remember. It was about the middle of her Hatfield reign that she met in the park a stranger, who, ignorant of whom he was addressing, said he had come down to see the Hatfield labourers' cottages, which he understood were none of the best. " Let me show them to you," said the lady, " and you shall judge for yourself." The visitor, it afterwards transpired, had been commissioned by a Radical newspaper, then very bitter against the Cecils, to investigate the unhealthy housing of the Hatfield dependants. In the way now described he ascertained the contrast between the facts as they were and as they had been reported to his editor. Returning to the office of his journal that night, he answered the editorial inquiry with the two words, " No case."

It was rather earlier than the date of the Hatfield incident just mentioned that Mr. Gladstone was announced to be paying a Saturday-to-Monday visit at another home-county house, near to, and not less famous than, Hatfield itself. " I suppose," said Lord Beaconsfield, then Prime Minister, of his rusticating rival, " he can say that he is where the wicked,—I,— cease from troubling, and the weary are at Wrest." Before the Disraelian pun had been made, late in the autumn of 1873, it was at Wrest that Mr. Gladstone decided on the stroke of policy which had the effect of keeping him out of power for six years. Confined to his bed by a severe cold, he discovered, when the expenses of the Ashantee War were paid, he would have a surplus of £5,000,000. This would render possible a new scheme of local taxation, coupled with the repeal of the Income Tax. Lord Granville and the chief Liberal Whip, Mr. Glyn, afterward the first Lord Wolverton, summoned to their chief's Wrest bedroom, strongly approved the idea. In the early January of 1874, the country was surprised by the announcement of an immediate Dissolution. Disraeli, then at Hughenden, received Lord Cairns with the words, " My adversary has delivered himself into my hands." A week or two later every Conservative country house in the kingdom had illuminated itself in joy for the first working majority the party had gained since the days of Peel. The scene of preparation for these events, Lady Cowper's country house, afterwards passing to her son, Earl Cowper, is to-day, like so many other ancient homes of Whig or Tory peers, the possession of a Transatlantic Crœsus, Lord Mount Stephen. Amid all social and political changes, there has been no break in the social history of Wrest. Among several symbols of this unity inside the house is that picture of a former hostess of the place which, in 1736, causing Horace Walpole's question whether it were a good likeness, constrained Mrs. House-keeper to answer, " Oh dear no, sir, it's much too handsome for my-lady duchess. Her Grace's chin is far longer than that." The Wrest hostess flattered by this portrait was the Earl of Portland's daughter, the second wife of Henry de Grey, Duke of Kent, who then owned Wrest, and died there in 1740. Hatfield, we have seen, is connected with the toxo-phile renaissance of an earlier century. The Wrest of the Victorian age did much to promote the once consuming popularity of croquet. That was chiefly due to Henry Greville, whom his brother Charles described as differing from himself in that Henry lived in "ceiled houses," whereas Charles dwelt only in tents. Having brought to Wrest his chief operatic intimates, Mario and Grisi, he surprised them by show-ing himself on that occasion more keen about croquet even than about music. Before the game was over it became dark. Henry Greville insisted upon lamps of all sorts being brought into the garden that the balls and hoops might be visible. These illuminants were artistically arranged by him after the French fashion of Mabille. "It was," said my kind old friend who had been present, Mr. Alfred Montgomery, "a sort of moral Cremorne." Montgomery, who survived till late in the nineteenth century, was the last of the professional dandies of the Regency to be seen at Wrest. At Wrest he used to relate how, not, I think, he himself, but one of his relatives, never went to Devonshire House without seeing the Duchess at her knitting in one corner of the room and Charles Fox snoring in another. Among his predecessors there had been George Brummell and "Poodle" Byng, so called from his curly hair, and so well known beneath all these Hertfordshire roofs as to be called "the tame cat of the Home Counties." Lady Hester Stanhope's appreciation of Brummell's concealed but genuine abilities had been first expressed to Mr. Montgomery. "Poodle" Byng married his mother's maid. Devoted to a little girl she had borne him, he could not, he said, do less than make the child's mother an honest woman. Not received in Society, Mrs. Byng had some friends who, in the district where we now are, sometimes included her in invitations to her husband. Lady Cowper belonged to the *grandes dames* of a former generation, who condescended in her conversation to entertain, as well as to impress, her guests. Apropos of a visit paid by Mrs. Byng to some country friends, she had heard about that lady's delight at her hospitable reception. "Only fancy!" exclaimed the Poodle's better half, "they had all our linen washed for nothing. So lucky, as Frederick's trunk was half-full of soiled shirts."

The next of the Hertfordshire political houses has an interest entirely its own and quite different from any of its neighbours. Brocket Hall, the home of Melbourne and Palmerston, is the monument of the social and political rise of a family now first incorporated into the governing class. In the eighteenth century Matthew Lamb, a solicitor of Southwell, had for his clients some of the most considerable Nottinghamshire families. Amongst these were the Cokes of Melbourne Hall. A daughter of this house, marrying his son, brought the Melbourne property into the Lamb family. She also became the mother of Sir Peniston Lamb, afterwards the first Lord Melbourne, the father of the Prime Minister. In 1746 the future Prime Minister's grandfather, then member for Stockbridge, acquired a territorial status in the South of England by the purchase of the Hertfordshire estates and residence of the Winnington family. Thereafter Brocket formed the headquarters of at least two famous Whig families. Brocket stands among the sheltering woods and soft pastures in the district through which the River Lea flows sleepily towards the Thames. To its most famous possessor, Queen Victoria's earliest Premier, the place was pathetically endeared by its having witnessed the illness and death of his only son, Augustus, nursed by the fond father with maternal tenderness on his Brocket sick-bed, and long mourned with maternal grief. These experiences in his Hertfordshire home no doubt helped to train Melbourne himself for the almost paternal part which, as her minister, he was afterwards to perform towards his young Sovereign, Queen Victoria. To Brocket he had, in the June of 1805, brought for the honeymoon his bride, the volatile Lady Caroline Ponsonby, whose eccentric story half grotesquely, half tragically, interlaced itself with the life of her womanhood's idol, Lord Byron. At Brocket, when her connection with him had come to a close, in a fit of mortification she burned Byron in effigy on the lawn before the house. At Brocket she remained for some time after the separation from her own husband, who had settled himself at Melbourne House, London. At Brocket died, in 1828, Lady Caroline, and, twenty years later, Lord Melbourne himself. The place figures almost as prominently in its connection with Palmerston as with Melbourne himself. Here, in the autumn of 1865, his future biographer, Mr. Evelyn Ashley, had seen his old chief coming out of the house bareheaded, walking straight up to some high railings immediately opposite the front door. Then, looking round to see that no spectator was near, the old man climbed deliberately over the top rail on to the ground on the other side ; next, turning round, he climbed back once more. It was his way of testing his strength, and discovering whether ground had been lost or gained. In this same park, during his last summer there, he had, in conversation with his doctor, said, " When a man's time is up, he must be content to go." His brother-in-law, Melbourne, had closed his eyes at Brocket some seventeen years before : at the same house, which his wife had made his own, on October 18, 1865, Palmerston passed away.

Meeting Richard Cromwell

After Hatfield, the most ancient of Conservative houses in this home-county is also the most interesting, less, however, for its political than its literary and diversely various social connections. To-day Knebworth owes a new kind of interest to the agrarian experiments of which the second Earl Lytton has made it the scene. His famous grandfather—still, perhaps, best known as Edward Bulwer Lytton—has given glimpses of the house and its surroundings in the best descriptive passages of his novels. It was in the lanes near Knebworth that one of his own ancestors had met a remarkable looking old gentleman who, entering into casual conversation with him, dwelt upon the vanity of mundane honours. He turned out to be Richard Cromwell, the Protector's son, passing his last years in complete retirement at a Hertfordshire cottage. The entire incident finds its record in "Devereux," one of the best, if also one of the less known, of the historical novels. During his Colonial Secretaryship (1858–9) Bulwer Lytton was seldom without visitors at his Hertfordshire home. It was there that he conceived the idea and worked out the plot of "The Caxtons." "I intended it," he used to say, "for a colonial parable. As for its hero, Pisistratus Caxton, who repairs the shattered family fortunes in the Australian bush, who and what is he but a type of the England which, having lost her empire beyond the Atlantic, more than compensated herself by a Greater Britain beneath the Southern Cross?" It was some years later than this that, as a very young man, the present writer occasionally found himself, with only one or

The New Hosts of the Home Counties

two more, a guest at Knebworth. On these visits
the host remained invisible in his private rooms till
a seven or eight o'clock dinner. If any glimpses of
him were caught before then, they were merely those
of a figure wrapped in a dressing-gown, walking with
a book under his arm through one of the corridors.
At the dinner-hour, glossily radiant with all the arts
and appliances of the toilet, he welcomed his visitors
in the saloon and led the way to the evening meal.
Throughout the evening he seldom changed his position from a circular divan in the drawing-room, where
he sat smoking, rather languidly, a Turkish pipe. It
was in this posture that, asked by the Lord Carnarvon
who had been his Colonial Under-Secretary, which
he considered the best of his novels, he, after
some deliberation, replied " I think, upon the whole,
'Zanoni.'" He never lost his interest in Colonial
matters or touch of Colonial acquaintances. These
latter were once, I recollect, represented by a young
Australian visitor to whom particular attention was
paid. Looking at some China ornaments especially
prized by their owner, the young man nervously let
one of them slip through his fingers—not, however, to
the ground, because, with the presence of mind of
which an instance at the Taunton ball has already
been given, Lord Lytton, at once putting out his
hand, arrested the fall of the ornament with the
words, "Fielded, by Jove! and saved my crockery."

The story, already told, of Brocket and its Lamb
possessors may serve for a specimen of that fusion
between the newer and older elements in the social
system, suggested by the Home Counties or East

Woburn and Whitbread

Anglian houses. The earliest of the famous Whig homes in this district was Houghton; its master, both as Sir Robert Walpole and Lord Orford, used his hospitalities for the organisation of politics as well as sport. During the interval between the destruction of the old monastic building and the very gradual raising of the present structure, the lords of Woburn lived much at Stratton, now Lord Northbrook's, in Hampshire. The fame of Woburn as a socio-political institution began with the sixth Duke of Bedford in 1802, and ended with the seventh Duke in 1861. Other mansions in the same county, on not so stately a scale, are associated with transactions not less important to the country than the negotiations between noble hosts and guests, of which for more than half a century Woburn remained the scene. The movement of prison reform, conducted by John Howard, originated at Cardington. Samuel Whitbread (1758–1815), married in 1789 Elizabeth, sister of the second Earl Grey, of Reform Bill fame. Inheriting a fortune from his father, the famous brewer, he became M.P. for Bedford in 1790; no keener Foxite ever adorned a Whig drawing-room. His house at South Hill soon became a more useful recruiting ground than the neighbouring Woburn itself for the new Liberalism. So did the country home of one of Whitbread's Parliamentary friends, Michael Angelo Taylor. These South Hill hospitalities were not only worth many votes in a division to the Whigs; they formed the starting point in a family career which has shown the Whitbreads of several generations to be equal powers in society and politics.

The New Hosts of the Home Counties

We pass to another Parliamentary connection. Without political co-operation and personal cordiality between Mr. Winston Churchill's father and the present Duke of Devonshire, Unionism could never have existed. Such an understanding was first shown to be practicable beneath the roof of Mr. and Mrs. Oppenheim in Bruton Street. The alliance cemented itself in the Rothschild palaces of Beds. and Bucks. The special scene of the personal negotiations between the future Duke of Devonshire and Lord Randolph Churchhill was Baron Ferdinand Rothschild's Waddesdon, near Aylesbury. More conspicuously than any of the Rothschild homes in this region, Waddesdon forms a monument of the creative power of wealth. What is now a wooded park or lawn was naturally a bare expanse of rather ungenial soil. Struck by the possibilities of the situation, Baron Ferdinand had no sooner acquired the spot than he began to secure for what was to be his park the woodland charms with which nature had not invested it. All the large chestnuts and limes to be found in the neighbourhood were bought. From the spots on which they grew they were bodily transported on tree-lifting machines specially built for the purpose. To those conveyances ten and twelve cart-horses were sometimes harnessed, bringing their load often a distance of sixteen miles. "The giant cedars brought from Lebanon" exist only in the pages of some local guide-books. As a fact the large beeches and oaks were failures; the trees of any size that have thriven best are the chestnuts and limes. Under

the shade of these it was that, in 1886, not only
the political conferences already mentioned, went
forward, but the late Sir William Gregory, one of
the best classical scholars among the officials of his
time, convinced the Lord James of Hereford of
to-day and the late Sir William Harcourt of the
accuracy in every detail shown by Virgil's description of agricultural processes, or demonstrated to
Baron Ferdinand himself and to Sir John Willoughby
that the same Roman poet could have had nothing
to learn about the breed and paces of a horse
from the collective wisdom of nineteenth-century
Newmarket. Meanwhile, some ladies had joined
the group ; Sir William Gregory turned to give
Lady Elizabeth Biddulph an account from a new
point of view of the National Gallery, or to recall
his reminiscences of the French stage for the benefit
of Lady Charles Beresford. In another corner of the
garden, that distinguished admiral was, in his own
breezy phrase, over a trial of skill at picquet
"serving up Lord Ribblesdale on toast." On
such a visit as that now described there would probably have been none of the then royalties who
delighted in Waddesdon, but very likely Mr.
Gladstone or his great rival, whichever happened
to be in power. Both appreciated the place
equally. Here the Liberal leader successfully tried
to interest in Homeric word-painting the most
beautiful and intellectual American lady of the time,
Mrs. Mahlon Sands. Here Disraeli, looking up at
a fashionable siren of quality, gazing upon him
from an upper window, turned round to his host

with a languid inquiry, " Who is that grinning little ape ? "

Many of these guests, especially Lord and Lady Feversham, with their two daughters, each a study in a different style of perfectly superb beauty, the two comeliest of *beaux sabreurs*—Keith Fraser and his brother Charles—the Sir E. W. Hamilton of to-day, most musical, most cheery, most *répandu* of men, and Sir Charles Dilke, might have been seen passing the next week-end beneath some other roof belonging to the same family in this district. Even Lord Roseberry's Mentmore, the traditional guest-house of monarchs, ministers, diplomatists, millionaires, and sportsmen, was brought to its present owner by his Rothschild marriage. The rural dominion of the Rothschilds begins with suburban Gunnersbury ; it stretches to the Chilterns. Their country houses within this area have brought fertilising capital into impoverished neighbourhoods, have studded them with model farms and with improved dwellings for a long neglected peasantry. In the nineteenth-century Bedfordshire, the most fashionable hostess of her time, Madame de Falbe, made the smartest of country houses a beneficent centre of good influences for her humbler neighbours within a wide circumference. The Rothschilds and their kinsfolk have done the same on a larger scale. Smart, indeed, or rather magnificent, all their dwellings are, but to-day, whether it be from Lord Rothschild's Tring, Mr. Alfred Rothschild's Halton, his brother's Ascott, or his cousin's Waddesdon, the Israelitish annexation of Buckinghamshire and its

The Buckinghamshire Kishon

modish hospitalities have given the toiling masses of the county no reason to regret the replacement of old landlords by new.

The spirit of the political genius, who, in his own phrase " educated " the Conservative party into household franchise, incarnated itself in the statesman, the greatest of whose personal delights was to be and to feel himself a Buckinghamshire squire. Where, John Bright had pessimistically asked, were John Hampden's three hundred Buckinghamshire yeomen? "Where," rejoined Disraeli, "should they be but in Buckinghamshire itself? And they still return a constitutional member to Parliament in the humble individual who now addresses you." One of Disraeli's most frequent Hughenden guests was a political opponent, the late Sir William Harcourt. Of two other visitors, both newspaper men, one happily survives to-day in Lord Glenesk, the Algernon Borthwick of the Hughenden visits. The other was Thomas Hamber, formerly editor of the *Standard* and its parent print, the *Morning Herald*. Each of these visited Hughenden without any fellow-guests ; each had heard the host speak of the gurgling stream that waters the park as " that ancient river, the River Kishon." Each, too, from the lips of his distinguished friend, might have offered an authentic comment on the twentieth-century association between the squire of Hughenden and the floral cult that visibly perpetuates his memory. " My wife," he said to Hamber, "was a child of nature, unversed in books, and ignorant whether the Greeks or Romans came first. She loved primroses, therefore I do so too." Pointing to peafowl nibbling on the

The New Hosts of the Home Counties

lawn, Lord Glenesk had made some remark about the destructiveness of the birds of Juno. " It may be so," replied the lord of the manor, " but I prefer the peacocks to the flowers." Disraeli's pleasantest talk at Hughenden related to the vicissitudes of the great families in the county : he could recall that particular wearer of the Buckingham strawberry-leaf described as being " Duke of very duke." In his youth he had been present at a dinner of the Stowe tenantry, felicitously addressed afterwards by the magnificent nobleman himself. " How well," the young Disraeli had said to a farmer, " the Duke suits his words to his audience." " Yes," replied the other, " a very good speech by a very bad man." This was the duke who, shortly before the crash, consulting a business-like peer as to possible retrenchments, was told that he might perhaps put down one or two Italian pastry-cooks. " What ! " pitifully exclaimed the splendid spendthrift, " mayn't a man have a biscuit with his glass of sherry ? "

" In an earlier generation, the Midland dukeries," said Lord Beaconsfield, " were real centres of gravity. There, perhaps, under the old patrician *régime*, a Prime Minister might have picked up such an ideal private secretary as the late Lord Rowton afterwards became." Mr. Montagu Corry's predecessor, his chief, had been Ralph Earle, already mentioned in these pages. Him, indeed, Disraeli had first seen at the British Embassy in Paris. The final details of the arrangement were made at Rayners, the Buckinghamshire home of the Mr. Putney Giles of " Lothair," whose son, the present master of Rayners, is the second Sir Philip Rose, and

" You Call Them Savages ! "

at Rayners the most illustrious of its owner's clients generally found time to pay a yearly visit. Disraeli, indeed, owed much of his earlier success to country-house patronage. A Jew dandy, not of the best type, was what he seemed to Society even long after he had given it a taste of his intellectual quality. "My dear John" (the Lord John Manners who, as Duke of Rutland, was the last survivor of the Young England group) had indeed been warned by his father, the Duke of Rutland, against "unbecoming intimacy with one who, notwithstanding all his cleverness, is still a mere soldier of fortune." By this time, however, the doors of Belvoir Castle had been opened to the adventurer. They could not henceforth be closed. Belvoir thus became the stepping-stone to recognition by a scion of Nottinghamshire dukeries first, Lord George Bentinck, and by the fourteenth Lord Derby afterwards. Of all the stately homes of rural England —many of them visited in these pages—between 1870 and the final failure of his health, Disraeli's special delight seemed to be the palace of the Shrewsbury earls, Alton Towers. The physical climate of the place suited him as well as the magnificent perfection of its arrangements within and without. "I find," he said at Alton on one occasion, "this air to be quite clinical." Every one was impressed and delighted, but could only guess what he meant. Here, too, a few years later, apropos of the Colenso heterodoxy and the Zulu military troubles, he uttered his "They convert our bishops, they outwit our generals, they defeat our troops, and you call them savages!"

CHAPTER XVII

FROM THE CHILTERNS TO THE CHEVIOTS

Westwood Park—Sir John Pakington, afterwards Lord Hampton—
C. N. Newdegate—Sir Stafford Northcote—Expressions that
originated at Westwood—The Anglican Deputation to Disraeli
Kinsham Court—Byron and his guests—The Countess
Guiccioli's visit to England—The Duke of Beaufort's Troy
House—Sir Richard Hill at Hawkstone—Lord Dartmouth,
"the psalm-singer"—Rowland Hill, the evangelist—Edmund
Burke's Butler's Hall—An asylum for religious refugees—
Famous visitors—Sir Joshua Reynolds and the "infant
Hercules"—Lord Nugent ("Squire Gawkey") at Gosfield—
Lord (Squire) Western of Rivenhall—His hatred of Canning—
Twentieth-century Essex hosts and guests—Mr. Chamberlain's
Highbury—Alnwick and Raby as social patterns for Gunners-
bury, Tring, Highbury, and West Dean.

SETTING our faces north-westward we enter
Worcestershire between Evesham and Stratford-
on-Avon. A journey of something less than twenty
miles into the· county brings one within sight of a
landmark in the story of Conservative Parliamentary
Reform. In 1831, the headquarters of the Whig
reformers had been the Northumbrian country houses,
notably Chillingham. Here took place the conferences between Lord Durham and "Bear" Ellice,
intended to secure the cooking of the schedules

and of the new franchise, in such a way as to dispose of local Tory interests. The lodges and other buildings of Westwood Park still display the monogram "J. P." These initials belonged to the Sir John Pakington who, dying in 1880, transmitted the title of Lord Hampton to his descendants. His compact, erect figure, hastening from St. Stephen's at the end of the week to catch the train for his country home, will be fresh in the memory of many who may read these lines. No invitation from premier or primate ever caused him to miss a Sunday at the immemorial home of his family. "There are not, there can nowhere be," he fondly says to any friend who accompanies him, "any avenues like those of Westwood Park." The Warwickshire neighbour, C. N. Newdegate, who was often his visitor, would truly add that the United Kingdom possessed nothing equal to the Westwood rose-gardens and lavender beds. "I do not know," another guest, Pakington's chief, Sir Stafford Northcote, might rejoin, "whether this reminds me most of Proserpine's flower-beds on the plains of Enna, of the Cids' Granada gardens, of Versailles in the old *régime*, or of the Crystal Palace in its happiest holiday dress." In the period from which these conversational scraps are recalled, Sir John Pakington, revisiting his constituents and Westwood, struck out two phrases now historical. Till he spoke of the "ten minutes Bill" no name had been given to the last of the Derby-Disraeli franchise schemes that made way for household franchise pure and simple. The host of Westwood was also the first to fasten the nickname of "the tea-room party"

From the Chilterns to the Cheviots

on the Liberal malcontents who refused in 1867 to follow the Gladstonian lead against the Conservative reformers. Nothing, indeed, in the Derby-Disraelian epoch did more than Westwood's social agencies to convert tepid Liberals into fervent Conservatives. The staunchness of Westwood's ecclesiastical orthodoxy did not prevent its owner, with his keen sense of humour and rare gift of mimicry, appreciating his leader's bantering way with clerically-minded laymen, even when he himself happened to be of their number. He had been one of the deputation to Disraeli, including every shade of Anglican opinion from Beresford Hope to Newdegate. The visitors, received at Downing Street with something like paternal tenderness, stated their case to the great man listening in respectful silence. The business concluded, Disraeli, in his impassively solemn tones, said, " And now, having, I think, heard their case, I will say farewell to the children of the Church." The voice in which the master of Westwood repeated the words might have been Disraeli's own.

On or near the Welsh and English border, within easy reach of Westwood, the houses of most interesting associations are those connected with Byron ; the poet, at the height of his fame, lived much in this neighbourhood. In 1812 a direct descendant of Queen Anne's Prime Minister, Bishop Harley, had not long since died at Kinsham Court. This was a dower-house belonging to the Harley family, whose Hereford headquarters were at Eywood. Kinsham was more than once rented by the poet. Here among his other guests were Vassal, Lord Holland, Samuel Whitbread,

Organising Evangelicalism

and George Combe, both brewers, and both like
Holland, associated with their host in arranging
details for the opening of the new Drury Lane
Theatre. At Kinsham were read the competitive
poems, which, sent in to celebrate the opening of the
new playhouse, formed a text for Horace and James
Smith's famous parodies, " Rejected Addresses." The
Countess Guiccioli, of Byronic memory, first visited
England in 1832 ; her British pilgrimage in her idol's
honour included not only his grave at Hucknall
Torkard, his school at Harrow, the house of his
sister, Mrs. Leigh, but several Herefordshire houses,
especially Kinsham. The Countess's first companion
was her brother, Pietro Gamba. She seems to have
been in Herefordshire a second time, several years
later, with that second husband, the Marquis de
Boissy, who saw so little to be ashamed of in the
Byron *liaison* that he introduced his wife to strangers
as " La Marquise de Boissy, ma femme, ancienne
maîtresse de Lord Byron." The only other roof in
this part of England beneath which there ever met
so strange a social medley as at Kinsham, is the Duke
of Beaufort's Troy House, near Monmouth, where
at one time or another stayed most of the lights of
both sexes of the nineteenth-century stage.

Other than political movements have issued from
the country houses in this part of England. Oxford
Anglicanism owed, we have seen, much of its socially
diffusive power to the Berkshire home of the Pusey
family and to other considerable houses in that region.
The Evangelicalism that preceded the Oxford Movement was socially organised at Hawkstone Park, the

seat of the Shropshire baronet, Sir Richard Hill. Appropriately enough he was descended from an Elizabethan ancestor who had been the first Protestant Lord Mayor of London. Resistance to Romanism in every form, and devotion to the Scriptures as the rule of life and faith, were the legacies bequeathed by this ancestor to his posterity. The eighteenth-century head of the Hills of Hawkstone was Sir Richard, described in the " Rolliad " as " friend to King George, but to King Jesus more." A personal intimate, as well as adherent, of Pitt, he amused his guests at the Hawkstone dinner-table by comparing Charles Fox's conduct towards the East India Company with the perfidy of Joab to Amasa, stabbed to the heart at the moment of a pretended embrace by his treacherous friend. Among Sir Richard Hill's most frequent visitors at his Shropshire place was Lord Dartmouth, his colleague in all good works, irreverently named, by the Whig Opposition to North, "the psalm-singer." Reminding all who knew him of Addison's Sir Roger de Coverley, Sir Richard Hill, by his letters to his younger brother, when an Eton boy, had first caused the future evangelist, Rowland, the youngest of six, to think seriously on religious subjects. A few years later, it was in the baronet's Hawkstone Park that Rowland Hill made his first attempts at open-air preaching. Hawkstone continued to be Rowland Hill's chief home in all those spiritual tours, involving not less locomotion than those of John Wesley. Wherever, indeed, they dwelt, most of the religious leaders of the period regularly met at Hawkstone to consult about the lines on which to make the advance against the powers of darkness and sin.

The Hawkstone propaganda had no more practical well-wisher than Edmund Burke. With him in his beautiful house and pretty grounds at Beaconsfield, the Hawkstone company often exchanged visits. After 1793, Burke's Buckinghamshire home had become the asylum, not only for refugees from France, but for homeless religionists from all parts of the world. Amongst those who were housed, now at Hawkstone, now at Beaconsfield, were two Brahmins ; they were accommodated with lodges in the park at both places for performing the rites of their religion. Burke's country house received many other guests than these needy foreigners. Beneath the roof of Lord Burnham's Hall Barn, he completed the arrangements for buying the Gregories. On that estate stood the dwelling improved by the buyer into Butler's Court, so magnificent within and without as to provoke Samuel Johnson's well-known "*non equidem invideo: miror magis*"; then came the words, " I wish you all the success which can be wished by an honest man." Fox, Sheridan, Garrick, Grattan, Mirabeau, and Sir Joshua Reynolds were frequent guests at Butler's Court. On one of these visits Reynolds, struck by "a monstrous fine child" he saw sprawling on the floor, painted it as the infant Hercules strangling the serpents. The muscular babe was the son of Burke's local man of business, Rolfe ; he lived to become the father of the Rolfe brothers who act in a similar capacity to-day for the master of Hall Barn. Another visitor, less distinguished at the time, but afterwards famous, the poet Crabbe, owed his first fair start to the Butler's Court hospitalities.

The international events that brought aliens of all kinds to Burke's rural home, also formed a connecting link between the county in which it lay and Lord Nugent's Gosfield, in Essex. Tall and powerfully built, Nugent was compelled by some infirmity to use a sort of crutch in walking ; this and the stoop of his back caused him to be locally known as "Squire Gawkey." Reluctantly, and with clear signs of personal aversion, George III. invested Nugent with the Garter. Returning home with the blue ribbon, he received a local ovation from others than his own tenantry. Such were the French exiles who, overflowing from Beaconsfield, were permanently domiciled beneath the Essex roof. The years between Canning's first rise to fame and Roman Catholic Emancipation in 1829 were anxious and eventful in the social centres of rural Essex, then the most Conservative district of England. The leader of the East Anglian Tories was a man who died in 1844, Lord Western of Rivenhall, but locally famous always as "Squire" Western. It was he who, apropos of his special aversion, George Canning, devoutly expressed gratitude at having always voted against "that d——d intellect." "The way in which that fellow talks," growled Western, when Canning happened to be amongst the dinner guests, "is enough to make one sick. As for the scoundrel's duel with Castlereagh, I know nothing of the facts, but I can take my oath Canning was the aggressor."

Worst Vices of the Country Gentleman

Can't you see the fellow is stark, staring mad?"
Except for its great vegetable-growing industry,
Essex, with its small, highly-cultivated farms, good
farmhouses, and the old-world mansions, remains
to-day less affected by the nearness of London than
any other part of the kingdom. Only the hosts and the
guests have changed. In the Georgian epoch, the
typical entertainer was the Charles Callis Western just
described. In the reign of Edward VII., Western's
successors are Colonel Lockwood, of Bishop's Hall,
near Romford, or Lord Howard de Walden at
Audley End. Chief among those asked to meet their
sovereign at Bishop's Hall are Sir William Walrond,
Sir Schomberg McDonnell, Lord Lansdowne, Mr.
and Mrs. Graham Stewart, Mr. and Mrs. Petre, Mr.
Henry Chaplin, and Mr. Howard Morley. At Audley
End, the house party on like occasions has generally
included the Duke and Duchess of Somerset, Lord
and Lady Ludlow, Sir Bache Cunard, Mr. and Mrs.
Van Raalte.

"Upon my word, Chamberlain, you are perpetuating in this pretty place the worst vices of the
country gentleman." So, on the lawn of Highbury,
near Birmingham, said Sir William Harcourt to the
master of the place, in those days when both host
and guest, as Liberals together, were co-operating
against Lord Salisbury. Mr. John Morley is to-day
the most famous survivor of the Highbury guests,
always a pleasant company, in the era preceding the
Home Rule split.

The houses still to be visited in the extreme North
all resemble each other in the continuity of their life

From the Chilterns to the Cheviots

preserved unbroken since the thirteenth century. As these lines are being written (July, 1906), King Edward VII. is on the eve of becoming the Duke of Northumberland's guest at Alnwick. A year ago he visited Raby, with its immense hall and front door of dimensions enabling a coach-and-four, were the experiment made, to be driven across the threshold. The social life of Raby, under its nineteenth century owners, and as ordered by the Duchess of Cleveland, was the same as that which we have already seen at Battle Abbey ; those who figured in the northern hospitalities were often identical with those whose acquaintance the reader has already made in Sussex. Alnwick, a monument of past baronial greatness, as seen by King Edward to-day is the greatest social stronghold of national ecclesiasticism *à la mode*. From one point of view both these places owe their interest rather to their august past than to their stately present. The authority exercised by the self-propagating force of their example upon the social system is still felt. Montalembert, visiting England in 1855, saw the best omen for the social and political future of the country in the *marchand enrichi*. A generation or two earlier, the owners of Alnwick, Raby, Hatfield, or any other of patrician splendour's ancient haunts, towered high and unapproachable above those who preceded the typical hosts of the twentieth century, such as we have recently visited at South Hill, in Bedfordshire, at Gunnersbury, at Mentmore, at Waddesdon, or at Tring. The modern passion for founding houses has received, in these pages, illustrations at Mr. Chamberlain's Highbury,

The New Men and the Old Life

at the home-county palaces which are the rural annexes of New Court, as at the West Dean of Mr. and Mrs. William James. The correlative, as it is also most frequently the cause, of the country house in the aspect specially distinctive of our time, is the office in the city. The system also implied a deeply rooted, historic idea of country-house life. The model for that was first given by and is still impressively embodied in the structures, themselves a part of our social and political annals, under whose shadow the goal proposed in the rounds of visits now paid is appropriately reached. There has been a change of scene, but not of spirit or method. Nowhere are the old traditions preserved more faithfully than beneath the new roofs.

INDEX

Index

Index

Index

Index

491

Index

Index

Index

Index

Index

Index

Index

Index

Index

Index

Index

Index

Index

Index

Index

Index

Index

Index

Index

Index

Index

UNWIN BROTHERS, LIMITED, THE GRESHAM PRESS, WOKING AND LONDON.

ImTheStory.com

Personalized Classic Books in many genre's

Unique gift for kids, partners, friends, colleagues

Customize:

- Character Names
- Upload your own front/back cover images (optional)
- Inscribe a personal message/dedication on the
  inside page (optional)

Customize many titles Including
- Alice in Wonderland
- Romeo and Juliet
- The Wizard of Oz
- A Christmas Carol
- Dracula
- Dr. Jekyll & Mr. Hyde
- And more...

Lightning Source UK Ltd.
Milton Keynes UK
UKHW021012010519
341924UK00013B/1571/P